ONLY GOOD

CAN JUDGE ME

JEFF PEARLMAN

The Many Lives of Tupac Shakur

MARINER BOOKS

NEW YORK • BOSTON

HarperCollins books may be purchased for educational, business, or sales promotional use. For information, please email the Special Markets Department at SPsales@harpercollins.com.

The Mariner flag design is a registered trademark of HarperCollins Publishers LLC.

hc.com

FIRST EDITION

Designed by Chloe Foster
Title page lettering by Joel Holland

Library of Congress Cataloging-in-Publication Data

Names: Pearlman, Jeff, author
Title: Only God can judge me : the many lives of Tupac Shakur / Jeff
   Pearlman.
Description: New York : Mariner Books, 2025. | Includes bibliographical
   references and index.
Identifiers: LCCN 2025026703 (print) | LCCN 2025026704 (ebook) | ISBN
   9780063304574 (hardcover) | ISBN 9780063304598 (ebook)
Subjects: LCSH: Shakur, Tupac, 1971–1996 | Rap musicians—United
   States—Biography | LCGFT: Biographies
Classification: LCC ML420.S529 P43 2025 (print) | LCC ML420.S529 (ebook)
   | DDC 782.421649092 [B]—dc23/eng/20250609
LC record available at https://lccn.loc.gov/2025026703
LC ebook record available at https://lccn.loc.gov/2025026704

ISBN 978-0-06-330457-4

Printed in the United States of America

25 26 27 28 29 LBC 5 4 3 2 1

ONLY GOD CAN JUDGE ME

Also by Jeff Pearlman

The Last Folk Hero • *Three-Ring Circus* • *Football for a Buck*

Gunslinger • *Showtime* • *Sweetness*

The Rocket That Fell to Earth • *Boys Will Be Boys*

Love Me, Hate Me • *The Bad Guys Won!*

For my dad, Stanley Pearlman. The Original G.

I can picture you in heaven.

With a blunt and a brew.

At the risk of sounding like a weirdo, I equate my brother to Jesus. Like, we're all God's children, but this one is special. This one makes a difference. This one rises above. There are people like Gandhi, like Muhammad, like Tupac.

And the thing is, the weight for people like that is unbearable. You think you know my brother? You think you understand him? Really? My brother didn't die happy. He died alone.

—Set Shakur, March 14, 2024, New Orleans

Contents

Introduction

We are sitting outside a Starbucks in Las Vegas. The sky is light blue, pocked by cloudy streaks of white. It is a Saturday morning in early April of 2023, and here, two miles off the Strip, the world feels tranquil and still.

Davonn Hodge is drinking a water.

I am sipping on a coffee.

He is a handsome thirty-three-year-old Black man with a faded goatee and brown eyes that peek out from beneath a Yankees cap. His voice is soft. Though this is our first time meeting, it feels familiar. We chat about LeBron, about Mahomes, about the weather and Wendy's and marijuana. The reason we are here looms, of course, hanging above us like an oversized umbrella. But we talk enough to push back the awkwardness until silence overtakes us and it can be pushed back no longer.

"So," I say. "Brenda."

Davonn nods.

"Yeah," he replies. "Brenda."

On the morning of April 21, 1991, a nineteen-year-old rapper-actor named Tupac Amaru Shakur was in New York City, working on his debut film, *Juice*. The project was low budget in every sense of the word—a mere $5 million to play with, a cast of inexpensive newcomers, a director (Ernest Dickerson) trying to break free from the shadows of his mentor, Spike Lee. Shakur, who captured one of the four starring roles with an out-of-the-blue audition that, decades later, Dickerson refers to as "at a different level," had been kicking back in his trailer, likely smoking one of that day's fifty (or so) Newports or twenty (or so) blunts, when a production assistant knocked on the door and handed him the latest edition of the New York *Daily News.* A voracious news junkie who grew up devouring *The New York Times,* Tupac sat down to read. The stories were mostly standard Big Apple fare—a Bronx National Guard unit being called up for active duty, an infant's arm torn off by a dog, Brian Quinnett starting at forward for the Knicks.

Then Shakur's eyes turned to the headline atop page 7, CRIES IN THE NIGHT.

The piece, penned by staff writer Linda Yglesias, told the story of a twelve-year-old Brooklyn girl who had been raped by a cousin, hid her pregnancy from her family, delivered a baby on the bathroom floor of an apartment in the Noble Drew Ali public housing project in Brownsville, wrapped the infant in a Job Lot bag, and threw it down the garbage chute.

A few hours later McArthur Williams, the building's maintenance man, pushed a button to activate the trash compactor when he heard a high-pitched cry—"Like somebody fighting for life," he said. The police were called, and a Sergeant Philip Insardi stepped to the compactor, flicked on his flashlight, and knelt down. "I saw two toes pointing at 2 o'clock, the bottom of its feet facing me, under a double-page newspaper," he told Yglesias. "The baby was dry and sticky. It felt dehydrated. The cord looked ripped. It was cold. There was a little dried blood on the left shoulder, in the armpit.

"Its hair was matted to its head. Little pieces of leaves were in its eyes. It didn't look like it had been washed. It didn't make a sound. I thought it was dead."

When Insardi touched the baby's stomach, he felt it squirm. He removed his jacket, wrapped the infant in a sleeve, and carried him to an ambulance.

Shakur couldn't believe what he was reading. Actually, scratch that—as the son of a crack addict, who knew what it was to be homeless with rats burrowing through his mattress, Shakur *could believe* what he was reading. He sought out pen and paper and returned to his trailer.

"I need a half hour," he said to a PA. "Alone."

Upon emerging, Shakur handed a piece of notebook paper to Omar

Epps, his seventeen-year-old costar. In blue ballpoint pen, with his trademark neat handwriting, the words soared from the page . . .

She didn't know what to throw away and what to keep
She wrapped the baby up and threw him in the trash heap
I guess she thought she'd get away, wouldn't hear the cries
She didn't realize
How much the little baby had her eyes

He named the song "Brenda's Got a Baby."

Seven months later, Tupac Shakur's debut album, *2Pacalypse Now*, hit stores and received a fairly muted reception from the hip-hop universe. There are thirteen tracks, twelve of which failed to resonate on a national level.

Yet something about "Brenda's Got a Baby" stuck. To this day, the opening line—"*I hear Brenda's got a baby. But Brenda's barely got a brain*"—is widely recognized. It is not merely a song, but Shakur screaming, "Fucking pay attention!"

With the exception of hip-hop diehards, however, few were ever made aware of the story behind the story. To most listeners, Brenda is a fictional character. And as the years passed, and Tupac Shakur rose from star to superstar to—in the aftermath of his 1996 murder—icon, curiosity about the song largely faded. With so much to discuss, why bother with a thirty-something-year-old tune?

And yet . . .

The mind of a biographer is overwhelmed by obsessiveness. In tackling a subject, one doesn't merely observe. He dives in. He chases. He craves. He crawls. He seeks. It is never enough to know that Martin Luther King smoked cigarettes. No. The biographer needs to know he smoked Kents and L&Ms, as Jonathan Eig wrote in *King: A Life*. When Mark Kriegel wrote *Namath: A Biography*, it wasn't sufficient to report that Broadway Joe enjoyed nights on the town. No—the clubs he hit were The Pussycat and Bachelors III.

So as I worked on this book, I found myself returning to "Brenda's Got a Baby." Via a lightly viewed Epps YouTube interview from nine years ago, I learned the skeletal basics of the song's origins, and then I tracked down Yglesias's article. What continued to gnaw at me, though, was the fate of the baby—and of Brenda. Over the three decades that have passed, the identity of neither child nor mother had ever been revealed.

Were they alive?

Were they dead?

Hell, had they ever actually existed?

Thanks to the good fortune of having attended Mahopac (New York) High School in the late 1980s, I knew Michele Soulli, a former classmate and one of America's outstanding researchers. I reached out to her, and we discussed the complications of trying to locate a nameless baby and a nameless mother.

"Lemme see what I can do," Michele told me.

A few weeks later, Michele texted me the phone number of someone named Davonn Hodge.

"Who the hell is Davonn Hodge?" I asked Michele.

"I can't guarantee," she replied. "But I think it's Brenda's baby."

I didn't believe it. Yet, according to Michele, the birthdays seemed to match, as did the geography. So on March 21, 2023, I fired off what must go down as some of the crudest out-of-the-blue texts in the history of modern telecommunication. First, I asked whether this was, in fact, the Davonn Hodge who had been born in New York City in 1991.

It was.

Then I asked (glub) whether he'd been thrown down a trash chute.

"I will call you tomorrow," he replied.

He called the next day.

That is how, less than two weeks later, I found myself at the Las Vegas Starbucks, sitting across from the ghost of "Brenda's Got a Baby."

"This is crazy," Hodge muttered.

A pause.

"This is *crazy.*"

Davonn had been raised in the Crown Heights section of Brooklyn until age thirteen, when his adoptive parents, Robert and Marsha Hodge, relocated to Las Vegas to retire in the desert. Davonn's mother told him he had been adopted out of a traumatic circumstance, but they never provided details. Then, within a short span of time, his mother and father died—Robert of cardiovascular pulmonary disease, Marsha of a heart attack.

That's why, on March 26, 2022, Davonn Hodge paid a hundred dollars to spit into an Ancestry.com tube and take a DNA test. "I was all alone," he said. "I wanted to find out who I really was."

When the results arrived via email, Hodge was confounded. There, before him, was a listing of names—all first cousins, all pinpointed in Brooklyn. He reached out to one, a woman named Lotitha Govan. "As soon as I told her my age, and being adopted, she knew exactly who I was," Davonn said. Within a few days, he was on video call with a handful of relatives. They laughed and sighed and bemoaned the weirdness of life. They told him about his old home.

Then one asked the question that changed everything.

"So, Davonn," he said, "how do you feel about Tupac?"

Davonn Hodge loved Tupac. He could run off all the songs, from "Hit 'Em Up" and "I Get Around" to "Dear Mama" and "Keep Ya Head Up." Had seen plenty of the movies. Knew of his relationship with Madonna, of his work with Snoop and Dr. Dre. Of Thug Life and Death Row and . . .

"Tupac," he said, "speaks to a lot of people."

So when his newfound cousin mentioned "Brenda's Got a Baby," Davonn nodded.

"Well," the cousin said, "supposedly that song is you."

Silence.

"What do you mean?" he asked.

"That song—'Brenda's Got a Baby,'" the cousin said. "We're pretty sure *you're* the baby."

With that, Davonn was filled in on the details of his infant odyssey. Seven months later, he took a trip to Brooklyn and the Noble Drew Ali public housing project in Brownsville, where many of his relatives still lived. He was greeted, Antwone Fisher–like, by scores of aunts and uncles, cousins and nieces and nephews. They hugged him, kissed him, and fed him. "Just the excitement on their faces," he said. "These are people who never thought I'd be back. They couldn't believe it. They looked at me as a miracle." At one point, a cousin's friend guided him into a hallway and pointed to a trash chute.

"That's where *she* put you," he said.

Davonn opened it and looked down.

"It was tiny and dark," he said. "To think I was thrown away like that . . ."

The mom went missing.

That's what Davonn's newly found relatives told him. She was a twelve-year-old mother who had nearly killed her baby, and she needed to escape.

So, one way or another, she vanished, never to be heard from again.

"No one has seen her in years and years," Davonn told me at Starbucks. "I'd obviously love to find her, because she *is* my mother. But I dunno if that's possible."

Reenter Michele Soulli.

Cobbling together bits of information from Davonn combined with bits of information from some old newspaper articles combined with a genealogist's intuition, Michele found what she thought might well be a phone number for the woman who birthed Davonn. This was a few weeks after the Starbucks meeting, and Michele was fairly certain she had the right person. But how do you approach someone who was raped as a child, then deposited *her* child into the garbage?

"I thought about it and I finally said, 'Screw it,' and called," Michele said. "I actually called twice, and then I just texted."

Without much of a plan, Michele wrote, "*Hey, Jeanette. How are you? It's Michele. How's it going? It's been so long.*"

Seconds later, her phone rang.

JEANETTE: "Who is this?"

MICHELE: "It's Michele."

JEANETTE: "Michele who?"

MICHELE: "I'm a researcher, and I was hired to find you."

JEANETTE: "Why?"

MICHELE: "You have a son named Davonn?"

This is where the screaming began.

Then, the tears. Lots of tears.

Some sobs, too.

JEANETTE: "You know where my son is?"

More screaming.

MICHELE: "Yes."

JEANETTE: "Oh my God! Oh my God! I have to get home to Newark. Oh my God! I need to get home! Oh my God!"

MICHELE: "Hold on. Please."

JEANETTE: "Oh my God!"

MICHELE: "Where are you?"

JEANETTE: "I live in New Jersey, but I'm away from home for a Red Hot Chili Peppers concert."

MICHELE: "Oh. Where are they playing?"

JEANETTE: "In Las Vegas."

They met that night in the lobby of Caesars Palace. For Davonn, the kisses felt like home. So did the hugs and the hours of conversation that went deep into the night. On her right forearm, Jeanette had a tattoo, in blue script, that read DAVONN, with a crown atop the D. It looked old and a bit faded, as if it had been inked long ago.

"After they found you in the garbage, they found me," she explained. "They took me to the hospital and let me hold you. I was able to name you, so I chose Davonn." Jeanette told her son she had spent decades searching for him, but with no luck. She had all but given up. So, way back when, she had his name affixed in ink.

That the reunion took place a mere eight-tenths of a mile from where, on September 7, 1996, Tupac Shakur was gunned down, on the corner of Flamingo and Koval, was lost on mother and son. They were basking in the moment.

A couple of days later, I called Yaasmyn Fula, Tupac's former business manager, longtime family friend, and the mother of Yaki Kadafi from the

Outlawz (Tupac's hip-hop group), to share the news. She listened quietly, and when I was done she told me the chills running up and down her arm were a sign from Tupac.

"He would have loved that one song brought those people together," she told me. "He would have *really* loved that."

Chapter 1

Panther

The hick from North Carolina sits in her cell.

Look at her. Unkempt. Nappy hair, knotted up into little beads. Shit-stained jail clothes hanging off her lanky arms. All elbows and knees.

Lord, the girl is unsightly. Yellowish teeth, brownish-gray grime gathering beneath her nails. Acne-blotted charcoal skin.

Even her name is confusing. Here in New York City's Greenwich Village, the Women's House of Detention forms list her as "Alice Faye Williams." The official log identifies her, simply, by an inmate number.

The visitor book says "Afeni Shakur."

The guards live for inmates like this. She's everything they love/hate in a prisoner. Love, because there's joy in witnessing an uppity bitch's day-by-day subjugation. Hate, because she personifies all that they abhor in modern society. Once, not all that long ago, we lived in a country where right was right and wrong was wrong, and law-abiding citizens could go about their days without having to worry about turning a street corner and seeing the neighborhood drugstore on fire. Sure, men like Bull Connor and George Wallace might have taken it a bit too far, but why do these uppity negroes have to make things so complicated? Was it so bad the way things used to be? When everyone knew their place?

This girl . . . this Afeni. It's 1971, and she's twenty-four and pregnant yet again. Seven miscarriages, she whispers to some of the other inmates. *I've had seven fucking miscarriages.* "I wanted a baby so bad," she'll later explain. This time it seems to have stuck, though she zips up when asked to identity the father. The guards are supposed to possess some level of sympathy for her. They're supposed to look at her belly, gauge her health, make certain she gets rest and nourishment. But here, in a cell block, she's merely another knocked-up whore sucking up New York City resources.

Rotting away in solitary confinement, her cell is a seven-by-six-foot concrete-walled pen with a moldy cot and a metal toilet. Twice a day she is fed Spam and white bread. At night, the rats crawl from their holes and scurry atop her body.

The guards know she's one of those Black Panthers, here for conspiring to bomb New York City landmarks. They saw the news footage of her arrest. Read about it in the *Post* and *Daily News*. BLACK EXTREMISTS ACCUSED OF PLANNING EXPLOSIONS. Boy, ol' Alice Faye sure thought highly of herself, didn't she? Walked the walk and talked the talk. Sunglasses and leather jackets and guns. Fist in the air. Power to the people. All that bullshit. Well, where's Bobby Seale now? Where's Eldridge Cleaver? Where are your boys, Afeni? Now that you need them, where are your boys?

To preserve sanity, all she can do is bury herself in thought. She replays her life, step by step. The tiniest of details. Colors. Smells. She tries to picture the shotgun house on Center Street in rural Lumberton, North Carolina, where she was born. "A midwife delivered me," she once recalled. "My mother almost died when I got here because the midwife didn't want to take the afterbirth out." She was raised unmistakably poor and Black in the Jim Crow South. Even in her cell, she can feel textures. The dirt in the front yard crumbling between her fingertips. The overgrown weeds tickling her ankles. With enough focus, she inhales the floral essence of her mother, Rosabelle McLellan, a homemaker whose rose-scented perfume filled a room. She cowers from her father, Walter Williams, a truck driver who beat his wife. Throughout her early childhood, during which Faye (she went by "Faye," never "Alice") and her older sister, Gloria Jean, were dragged from Lumberton to Norfolk, Virginia, then back to Lumberton, she was forced to sit and watch Walter—a smallish man with thick forearms—punch Rosa and mock Rosa. Bitch's food was terrible. Bitch was ugly. Bitch didn't walk fast enough. Bitch didn't take care of the girls properly. Bitch was useless.

And though Rosa ultimately worked up the courage to leave Walter (the last time he smacked her, Rosa threw a skillet of hot grease in his face), seeing her mother bloodied left a permanent welt on Faye's psyche. She would not let a man do that to her. No fucking way. She would be strong. She would be fierce. She would stand up and fight back. So when Rosa departed for New York City to work at a lampshade factory, she left ten-year-old Faye and Gloria Jean, twelve, with their grandmother, Lilianne Powell, in a dilapidated three-room home. The younger sister didn't flinch. And when, in 1958, the Ku Klux Klan held a march twenty-six miles away in Maxton, North Carolina, with the stated goals of putting the region's significant Native American population "in their place and to end race-mixing," eleven-year-old Faye paid close attention. Nearly seven hundred members of the Lumbee tribe greeted the robed KKK members with guns and spears—and kicked the living shit out of them. That confrontation, deemed the Battle of Hayes Pond, resonated. "Resistance is what I felt," she said. "Resist. A sense of 'don't let that happen to you.'"

Though Afeni had no Lumbee in her blood, she identified with the population. Like Blacks in Lumberton, they were treated as dogs. Unlike Lumberton's Blacks, however, they possessed a collective spirit of intransigence. In Lumberton, Blacks were relegated to the town's south side—the section with dumpier buildings and homes. They kept to themselves and, it seemed to Faye, accepted their fifth-class citizenry. She spent a good chunk of time with her cousins Barbara Jean and Charlotte Powers, and bristled at the way they bowed their heads in the presence of whites. "Afeni was loud from the start," Barbara Jean recalled decades later. "She wasn't one to just sit there and take it."

A few months after the Battle of Hayes Pond, Rosabelle summoned her daughters north; they caught a Greyhound bus up from Lumberton and moved into her one-room apartment at 1292 Third Avenue in the South Bronx. "[Mom] tried to warn us that up the road wasn't quite what we were led to believe it was, but how could we imagine something we had never seen?" Afeni said years later. "I got off the train at Penn Station and took a subway to 42nd Street. Oh, my God. Urine. Vomit. Steamed, porky hot dogs. Syrupy sodas. Dog doo. Underarms. Dirty feet. Morning breath.

"I couldn't see the stars, I couldn't run out at twelve o'clock at night and play hide and seek like I could down South—I was a tomboy first of all. In New York I had to be worried about somebody raping me and shit."

Despite the culture shock, Faye was made for the Big Apple. She was a girl who walked with confidence. She was in the first integrated class at Benjamin Franklin Junior High in the Bronx, and white kids ridiculed her pronounced Black features. They called her "Sambo," "Tar Baby." One boy, Myron Cohen (she never forgot the name), told Faye she looked like a creature from outer space. "I kicked his ass," she recalled. "All I wanted to do was fight—fight back . . . boys made me feel ugly and weak. So I'd go right to the source and beat the boys' ass. I had to have something else to offer besides being cute, other tools. I had a mind. I had a sharp tongue. And I could fight. I could fight through my fear. If a pack of motherfuckers attacked me, I'd pick the biggest and the strongest motherfucker and fight for my life."

With the exception of journalism class and dance, Faye hated school. Not because she lacked intelligence, but because she tired of the white teachers and children passing judgment. A kindly guidance counselor suggested she apply to the famed High School of Performing Arts,* so she took the entrance exam and was (to her great surprise) accepted. Yet the things she sought—companionship, togetherness, a sense of purpose— eluded her. The student body was largely white and affluent, and Faye was Black and broke. Her mother made about forty dollars per week piecing together lampshades, and she and her daughters survived on a diet of kosher bologna and fatty hamburger meat. Rosabelle begged neighbors for money to pay for the necessary bus fare to transport her daughter to the school's 120 West Forty-Sixth Street location, but they couldn't afford other necessities. Like, for example, lunch. "I'd get high off Thunderbird wine before school even started just to deal with my hatred [of wealthy classmates]," Faye would recall. "I was trapped. I couldn't tell my mother we needed even more money to go to this school. I wouldn't tell my teachers shit either. So I'd just leave at lunchtime."

Faye walked the hallways with a bottled-up rage, furious at the wealthy white kids, furious at the content Black kids, wondering why people were looking at her, pointing at her. One day she packed several knives and a zip gun in her backpack, and brought them to school with plans of attacking

---

* The school has produced too many performers to count, and is also known from the movie and TV show *Fame*.

a classmate who had showed her disrespect. "When somebody hit me or somebody hurt my feelings," she recalled, "all I wanted to do was kill them."

Following but half a year at the High School of Performing Arts, Faye dropped out and transferred her energies toward the Disciple Debs, the sister gang of the infamous Disciples. At the same time her mother assumed she was sitting inside a classroom, Faye was roaming the streets of New York, stealing, stabbing, shooting, snorting cocaine, dropping acid, and sleeping with a string of men—including (when she was eighteen) a thirty-three-year-old boyfriend. A rival Puerto Rican gang, La Cabeza, held turf that brushed up against Disciple territory, and the two entities fought furiously over rights to the three-hundred-foot swimming pool inside the Bronx's Crotona Park. "The water was blue but the pool would be red with blood," she recalled. "We were killing each other. I mean, every week there was a body in Crotona Pool. Every week."

In the spring of 1967, less than a decade after her arrival from Lumberton, a twenty-year-old Faye was strolling down 125th Street in Harlem when she reached the corner of Seventh Avenue. It was an early Saturday afternoon, and there was a crowd of people, all Black, encircling a man atop a wood platform. Through the years, she had witnessed a stream of aspiring leaders riling up crowds about fighting the power, but the spirit never moved her. It was all just words to young Faye. Blah, blah, blah. This, however, felt different. Like church. "The people listening were a mixture of people," she recalled. "It wasn't just the cultural nationalists, the people dressed in dashikis. But it was the niggers with processes, too, and hustlers. I mean, everybody was standing, listening."

The speaker was Bobby Seale, cofounder of the Black Panther Party for Self-Defense. Based out of Northern California, the Panthers initially existed to challenge the excessive force and misconduct of the Oakland Police Department. The Panthers were perceived by the mainstream media to be predisposed to violence by any means necessary, but it was far more complicated. Back in the late 1960s, an obscure California law allowed one to carry a loaded rifle or shotgun as long as the weapon was publicly displayed and not aimed at a fellow human. Having learned of this legal quirk, Seale and cofounder Huey P. Newton encouraged Panther members to arm themselves, then go out and monitor police behavior. So, as the organization's ranks grew, more and more Oakland police officers found themselves shadowed by Black men. On May 2, 1967, for example, a half dozen Panthers marched into the state capitol building in Sacramento, carrying weapons with fully loaded magazines. The outcries from lawmakers were intense ("They scared a lot of important people that day," wrote *The New York Times*), but there was little they could do. The law was the law.

The Panthers grew exponentially throughout Northern California. But while the guns and outfits garnered the attention, the group simultaneously devoted manpower and resources to education initiatives, free lunch programs, delivering books and school supplies, offering medical checkups. "When you talk about the civil rights struggle in America, you're talking about the Panthers," said Billy Jennings, a former Panther who identified as Billy X. "We were about community building, about fighting sickle cell, about helping with senior transportation, about eradicating hunger and homelessness. We wanted to make life better for people."

They also wanted to expand to New York.

Seale was thirty years old, small, with a tight Afro and neatly shaved goatee. He wore a dark blue shirt, black pants, black socks, and black shoes. His voice wasn't overly dynamic, but his message was: The Panthers didn't give a shit what you looked like, what your hair looked like, what your clothing looked like. They didn't care whether you were wealthy or broke. Whether you liked whites or hated whites. No, what they cared about was Blackness. Bold, beautiful, empowered Blackness. "And then Bobby Seale says the Ten Point Program of the Black Panther Party," Afeni would recall. "He says, 'Number one: We want freedom. We want power to determine the destiny of our Black and oppressed communities. Number two: We want full employment for our people. Number three: We want an end to the robbery by the capitalists of our Black and oppressed communities. Number four: We want decent housing, fit for the shelter of human beings. Number five: We want education that teaches our true history and our role in the present day society. Number six: We want completely free health care for all Black and oppressed people. Number seven: We want an immediate end to police brutality. Number eight: We want an immediate end to all wars of aggression. Number nine: Trials by juries of our peers. And ten—community control.'"

For Alice Faye Williams, ashamed of her Black skin and her Black features and furious with the whites who made her feel so small, it was a revelation.

Four months later, in August 1967, she attended a Black Panther rally in Harlem's Mount Morris Park. This time the featured speaker was Eldridge Cleaver, the Panthers' minister of information. Cleaver was bigger than Seale. More powerful in appearance and tone. With hundreds of Black New Yorkers standing at rapt attention, Cleaver dared those surrounding him to spend the next day at a Panther political education course. The dare felt like a command. Almost biblical.

Less than twenty-four hours later, Faye found herself at the Panthers' Harlem office at 2026 Seventh Avenue, where the class was being held. The first voice she heard was that of Joudon Ford, the Panthers' regional deputy minister of defense. "How many people here are Panthers," he asked, "or plan to become Panthers?"

Faye raised her hand.

In many ways, Alice Faye Williams was the perfect addition. First, the male-dominant organization needed female voices to help with recruiting. Second, in the years since dropping out of high school she had grown increasingly estranged from her mother. The Panthers provided a sense of family and belonging. Third, she was fearless. Faye knew how to wield a switchblade and fire a gun. She was familiar with the feeling of being punched in the jaw and stabbed in the gut. The police didn't scare her. White mobs didn't scare her.

Before long, Alice Faye was all in. She helped start the New York City Panthers' breakfast program to feed undernourished children. She worked in the Panthers' expanding string of free public health clinics. She found herself under the tutelage of two men: Sekou Odinga, her Bronx section leader. And Lumumba Shakur, the Harlem section leader.

And she changed her name.

It wasn't as dramatic as one might think. "Alice Faye" had never thrilled her. It was perfectly fine and normal. Most people called her "Faye" or "Faye-Faye." But over time she came to see it for what it was—a slave name.

Williams was "Williams" because her great-great-grandparents had been owned by a Virginian family with the last name Williams. Why would any self-loving Black person want to identify with such trauma? The Williams family had enslaved her people—*and now she was supposed to honor the moniker?* Around this time she had been studying the Yoruba belief system, a traditional West African religion that features a supreme creator and a slew of deities who serve as intermediaries between humanity and the celestial. One day her teacher and guru, an older man, announced that Alice Faye was now "Afeni"—which translates to "dear one" and "lover of people."

In the fall of 1968, a mere seven months after joining the Panthers, Afeni married Lumumba Shakur, the charismatic Malcolm X disciple who had helped transform Harlem into an early Panther stronghold. Lumumba served as the section leader of the Harlem Panthers, with a primary responsibility of adding new members. Remembering what it was to be a little girl, watching her father pummel her mother, Afeni found herself enchanted by Lumumba's core values and militancy. "My entire view of men and family was shaken up," she recalled. "I went from this dismal, dismissive attitude of men, from having no concept of a man's true role or job in a family structure, to this beautiful, strong, definitive and rigid role of a man's position in a family."

Because she was simultaneously savvy and naïve, Afeni was unbothered by Lumumba's main motive for the marriage: an urgency to have sex with her ("I wouldn't sleep with him without a commitment"). She also expressed little dismay that her new husband already had a wife of two years, Sayeeda, as well as two children.* It was, he explained, perfectly acceptable via the Qur'an. In fact, there was no need for a formal wedding—with his brother Zayd acting as witness, Lumumba stood before Afeni and uttered "This is my wife" three times. And that was that.†

Lumumba, Sayeeda, their two children, and Afeni cohabitated in a small two-bedroom apartment at 112 West 117th Street in Harlem. Yet two months after his wedding with Afeni, Lumumba was arrested in New

---

* In a diary from the 1990s, Afeni referred to Lumumba as "my co-husband."
† Only years later, while reading the Qur'an cover to cover, did Afeni realize she'd been somewhat hoodwinked. No such marital law existed.

Haven for failing to register his sawed-off shotgun and traveling with the weapon from New York to Connecticut. With her husband behind bars inside the Bridgeport Correctional Center, Afeni was placed in charge of the Panthers' Harlem and Bronx operations. She was barely twenty-one years old.

"She was so intelligent, so hardworking," said Cleo Silvers, a fellow Panther. "She had an artistic grace about her. She was this dark-skinned sister with a little Afro, and you could be mesmerized by her. But she was so damn smart. She memorized the demographics. She knew what the infant mortality rates were in the South Bronx and Harlem. She knew that one in four people in the South Bronx was addicted to heroin. She knew all the laws connected with housing. She had the trust of Blacks, sure. But she also had the trust of Puerto Ricans. You listened to her speak and you were like, this woman knows her stuff."

Although she had her suspicions, Afeni was ignorant of the lengths law enforcement agencies went to monitor the Panthers. In particular, the New York Police Department's surveillance squad, the Bureau of Special Services and Investigations (BOSSI), devoted hours of manpower toward undermining the organization and finding ways to tar it as a terrorist operation. Wrote the author Santi Elijah Holley: "Throughout the late 1960s and 1970s, BOSSI infiltrated political organizations in New York City, installing undercover detectives to spy on subversive groups and individuals . . . some of these agents had infiltrated the New York Panthers, became trusted members of the group." The goal wasn't to disturb the Black Panthers. It was to destroy them.

Which leads to the predawn hours of April 2, 1969.

No longer imprisoned, Lumumba was sleeping alongside Afeni in their Harlem apartment. At approximately 4:00 a.m., they were stirred awake by a pounding on the front door.

KNOCK! KNOCK!

"What the fuck is that?" Afeni said.

KNOCK!

KNOCK!

KNOCK!

On the other side of the front door stood four New York City police officers, led by Francis Dalton, a veteran detective. The men wore blue uniforms and bulletproof vests. In his right hand, Dalton gripped a rag that his men lit aflame. Smoke filled the hallway.

"Fire!" Dalton screamed. "Fire! Open the door and get out! Fire!"

Husband and wife groggily walked through their apartment. Lumumba looked through the peephole and saw smoke. He turned the stainless steel top lock, then the dead bolt beneath it. When he cracked open the door, the officers pushed it inward, sending Lumumba stumbling backward. One policeman pointed his shotgun at Lumumba's chest. Two others, who had been squatting on the fire escape, crashed through the window and held Afeni at gunpoint.

The couple was handcuffed, walked to the nearby police car, booked at the New York District Attorney's office inside the Elizabeth Street Station, and placed in separate holding cells. Inside the apartment, the officers said they found two shotgun shells, buckshot pellets, black explosive powder, and thirty-one feet of primer fuse. "When I was arrested it took a while before I fully realized the situation/trouble I was in," Afeni wrote in a diary. "At first I thought there was a misunderstanding and so it would all be sorted out and I would be charged with something not too serious and I'd take my medicine and move along."

Only after being booked did Lumumba and Afeni learn they were one piece of a massive NYPD assault upon the Panthers. Thirteen simultaneous raids took place that night, and the holding cells were filled with party leaders. All told, in New York City ten members of the Harlem Panthers were arrested and jailed. In the coming days, eleven other Black Panthers would be nabbed across the tristate region. The twenty-one total members of the organization—labeled the "Panther 21"—were accused of planning coordinated bombings and long-range rifle attacks on two police stations and a New York City education office. One by one they were walked from cell to courthouse and ordered to stand before a judge. Because Lumumba was deemed the ringleader, the case was documented as *The People of the State of New York v. Lumumba Abdul Shakur et al.* They were indicted on charges of conspiracy to shoot police officers and bomb police stations, railroad tracks, Manhattan department stores, and the New York Botanical Garden in the Bronx. An Associated Press piece noted that the Panthers were trying to disrupt "the white power structure." They were each charged with thirty counts of conspiracy, and faced 356-year prison sentences.

Every Panther pled not guilty.

Every Panther was held on one hundred thousand dollars' bail.

Later that night, the Panthers were placed inside a paddy wagon and taken to assorted New York City detention centers, including the Detention Center of Long Island City for Lumumba and—in Afeni's case—the dreaded Women's House of Detention.

For the next *ten* months, she sat inside her seven-by-six-foot cell, reading, meditating, dining on white bread, and wondering when there would be an actual trial. Sometimes, if she misbehaved or drew a guard's ire, she'd wind up in a "psychiatric cell"—a room with no bed, mattress, toilet, or hot water. So what if the police never found a single stick of dynamite, which the Panthers were allegedly planning to use to blow people up? So what if the evidence against the Panthers was paper thin and dependent on the lies and exaggerations of undercover officers? So what if police officers had physically assaulted members of the Panthers sans cause? The Panthers were Black and they were militant, therefore they were surely guilty.

Then, on January 30, 1970, Afeni was (to her shock and delight) set free when supporters (largely members of the Episcopal and Presbyterian churches) worked together to come up with the hundred-thousand-dollar bond. She was twenty-three years old and—as the first liberated member of the Panther 21—charged with the task of raising as much bail money as possible for her imprisoned cohorts. Over the next seven months she traveled extensively, explaining to Blacks and whites and all who would listen that the Panthers they were hearing about weren't the real Panthers. That, if anything, the actual terrorists were the police and the FBI. She was a dynamic speaker, blessed with a booming voice and a Baptist preacher's passion.

During her travels, Afeni encountered many handsome, dynamic Black men who lived the Panther ethos. Sure, she was married to Lumumba. But Lumumba had another wife. He also didn't believe that the husband needed to show true fidelity to his *women*. This offended Afeni. So, not long after being bailed out, Afeni started fooling around with a fleet of suitors, most notably a Jersey City–based Panther named Billy Garland.

The two had met months earlier, when Afeni briefly took cover in a New Jersey apartment, and at first blush had little in common. Unlike Afeni, Billy boasted (for a Black family in the 1960s, at least) a fairly picturesque American suburban upbringing. Just two years before joining the Panthers, he was a six-foot-three star of the Pioneers, Somerville (New Jersey) High School's varsity basketball team. He was popular and smart and an enormous fish in a small pond. On January 31, 1968, Jim Sermons of *The Daily Home News* in New Brunswick wrote: "Bill Garland, an agile basketball player who is loaded with talent, made Somerville High cage history yesterday when he became the first Pioneer courtman to reach the 1,000 point career plateau."

"He was not a kid who you'd look at and think, 'One day he'll be a Black Panther,'" recalled Chuck Schaub, a high school teammate. "He was like a Clyde Drexler for us—a gifted basketball player, a nice guy."

Yet one year after graduating, Garland was arrested for the first time when he refused to leave a local board of education meeting. He soon joined the Panthers and became a leader of the Jersey City operation. He was attracted to Afeni, and for months they had sexual relations—despite Garland's being married with three children and despite Afeni's viewing him as merely a pleasant life distraction. "It relieved tension," he later explained. "It was serious shit [we were going through]. We might get killed tonight. They was breaking in Panther offices and apartments on the regular. . . . So we had a relationship."

In the fall of 1970, Afeni became pregnant.

The news was not received well. Not only was she carrying Billy Garland's child, and not only was she dealing with Lumumba's wrath after delivering the news via prison phone call (she recalled: "Lumumba called me a slut and said three times, 'I divorce thee. I divorce thee. I divorce thee'"), she was also helping propel a movement *and* preparing for the Panther 21's inevitable trial date. At the direction of Lumumba, the Panthers hired three attorneys. Two were men, but Afeni's assigned representative was—in her words—"a [woman with a] tiny, squeaky voice." Facing 350 years in prison, Afeni opted to serve as her own lawyer. No one agreed with the decision. Literally *no one*. Afeni Shakur was not an attorney. She had never studied to be an attorney. She was a high school dropout with a hair-trigger temper and questionable impulse control. Lumumba mocked her as "too emotional" and predicted she would "fuck everything up."

The trial began on September 8, 1970. It was held in Manhattan, in state supreme court, on the thirteenth floor of 100 Centre Street. The Panther 21 had been whittled down to thirteen—three Panthers were on the run, two were in jail in Newark on burglary charges, one was ill and had his trial postponed, and two were granted youthful offender status. The presiding judge, John M. Murtagh, was a stern fifty-nine-year-old white man known to have strong empathy for police officers, general indignation toward Black Power movements, and, wrote Patrick Owens in *Newsday*, "no more business sitting in judgment on Afeni Shakur than they would sitting in judgement of him."

The majority of legal experts presumed the Panthers were doomed and the trial might span one month. It lasted *nine*. It was long and unruly, with fights and outbursts and fines and hostilities and Black Power salutes and dramatic entrances and endless rhetorical flourishes. "I was young," Afeni later recalled. "I was arrogant. And I was brilliant in court. It was because I thought this was the last time I could speak. The last time before they locked me up forever. I had to make a record there for later, because I would never be able to speak again. So this was my last chance, and I had to make the best of it. I thought I was writing my own obituary."

In early October, Afeni's bail was revoked for five days after she arrived forty minutes late to court. The prosecution, led by Assistant District Attorney Joseph Phillips, called the Black Panthers "terrorists" and "mass murderers" and "fanatics." It relied heavily on the testimony of Gene Roberts, a Black undercover officer who infiltrated the Panthers. But a lot of Roberts's material proved to be junk. Even less credible was Ralph White, another Black undercover officer who took the stand and admitted to having sex with three Black Panther women. White's value as a prosecution witness dissolved when he was cross-examined by Afeni, who tore into his honesty.

Wrote Edward Hershey in *Newsday*: "Had White ever seen her with a gun, Mrs. Shakur asked. No, the detective conceded. Had he seen her destroy anything? No. Hit anybody? No. On the other hand, had White seen her do volunteer work in schools? Yes, he answered. In hospitals? Yes. In community street programs? Yes. How then, Mrs. Shakur asked, could the undercover agent classify her as 'militant'?"

Afeni Shakur was a revelation. The jury was composed of five Blacks and seven whites, and Afeni was able to reach the entirety. She was sharp with her language. She listened intently. Even Murtagh—as white as bleach—seemed impressed. "She has emerged," wrote Hershey.

Yet the tide shifted on February 3, 1971, when Dhoruba Moore and Michael Cetewayo Tabor, two of the Panthers on trial, snuck off to Algeria, and Judge Murtagh punished the organization by revoking bail and ordering Afeni back to her cell.

It was one thing to be imprisoned. It was another altogether to be imprisoned *five months pregnant*. Afeni was apoplectic, especially when the House of Detention refused to make any concessions for her condition. She pleaded with the court to consider the well-being of her unborn child, telling Murtagh that "the boilers are broken there. There is no hot water. The conditions . . . are inhuman." The House of Detention lacked toilet paper and edible food. She said the prison doctors performed invasive exams that rendered the inmates cattle. Because of her pregnancy, Afeni was ultimately granted one daily glass of whole milk and a hard-boiled egg.

The return to the House of Detention was hell for Afeni. The guards welcomed her back with hatred and hostility. She was mocked, ridiculed, dehumanized. They knew her backstory—the North Carolina sticks, the single-parent home, the poverty. "She had so much on her shoulders," said Yaasmyn Fula, a New Jersey–based Panther and close friend. "She was tough, coupled with real vulnerability." Every weekday morning she was ferried via van from her cell to the courthouse, and every day she showed those in attendance that law school was no substitute for savvy.

Wrote Hershey in the April 29, 1971, edition of *Newsday*:

Afeni Shakur lugged two transcript volumes across the courtroom and dropped them on the table in front of the jury. "You've heard it all and seen it all," she said, and for the next 10 minutes everyone in the room sat transfixed.

The edge of the table indented her oversized belly as she spoke. Her voice was barely audible, in sharp contrast to the many times she had blurted shouts of protest at State Supreme Court Justice John Murtagh or the prosecutor, Joseph Phillips. She had taken on her own defense, she told the jury, "against the advice of my co-counsel, the court, friends, my own instincts. I do it now as I have in the past because I know I am innocent.

"I want you to do one thing: Judge me as you would want to be judged," she said. "I ask you to end this nightmare, because I am tired. I am tired and sick. I'm sick of all this. He's not proven any of the charges against me. He could not because they were not true. Lies have to be supported by more lies and more."

Five days later, in the midst of closing arguments, an uncharacteristically sympathetic Murtagh looked at Afeni's pronounced belly and reintroduced bail.

"Will you give me your word that you will appear in court as you are required and as you are able?" he asked.

"Yes, sir," she replied faintly.

On May 13, 1971, following just ninety minutes of deliberation, the jury reached its decision. James I. Fox, the fifty-eight-year-old foreman with a pronounced West Indian accent, stood and was asked by Murtagh for a verdict on the charges against the thirteen defendants.

He declared "Not guilty" 156 times, and the courtroom burst into applause and shrieks of "Power to the people!" Twelve of the thirteen exonerated Panthers—shocked by the turn of events and overcome by the sweetness of liberation—hugged and cried and praised God for the justice at hand.

One Panther sat alone in stunned silence.

No one thought she should have represented herself.

No one thought she possessed the wherewithal, the smarts, the courage to pull this off.

No one thought Afeni Shakur knew what in God's name she was doing.

Now, however, she was a free woman.

About to have a baby.

Chapter 2

Lesane

During her time imprisoned inside the House of Detention, what with the meager provisions and the racist guards and the vermin scurrying up and down her cot, Afeni Shakur had stumbled upon—of all the things in all the places—a friend.

Her name was Carol Crooks, and in 1969 she was eighteen years old and incarcerated for a drug deal gone wrong. Little was made of the Brooklyn teenager, who listlessly shuffled from cell to yard and yard back to cell. She was a stocky young woman—dark Black skin, pronounced forehead, the build of a couple of scoops of mashed potato. Crooks's face was affixed with a permanent scowl, a warning to others in the House of D, "Don't fuck with me."

Raised in public housing by a single mother, Crooks began running the streets at age nine. According to Hugh Ryan's outstanding book *The Women's House of Detention*, a prepubescent Crooks was "playing cards and shooting dice with men, and stealing food to support her mother and sister." By sixteen she was pulling down five figures working the corners in Harlem, slinging weed and cocaine. And while most inside the House of Detention could read the body language well enough to steer clear of Carol Crooks, Afeni Shakur was no ordinary inmate. She saw something in Crooksie.

That's what she called Carol Crooks—"Crooksie." How could someone *that* hardened warrant a nickname so cuddly? "Crooksie," said Yaasmyn Fula, "was a gangster, drug-dealing dyke. And I say that affectionately." During their time together inside the House of Detention, Afeni and Crooksie bonded over the struggle, over life as Black women, over the inevitable disappointment of men. They bonded, too, over physical and emotional attraction, and commenced a romantic relationship. They were jail girlfriends.

By the time the Panther 21 trial wrapped, in May 1971, Crooksie was out of the House of Detention and Afeni was looking to start anew. She was pregnant and—save the support of her sister, Gloria Jean—very much alone. Her marriage to Lumumba Shakur was over, and Billy Garland, father to her unborn child, was back in New Jersey with his wife and children.

Making matters worse, Afeni was broke. Most of her past four years had been spent either behind bars or clawing to devise a legal defense. She had zero money and nary a room to hang her hat. Which is why, with nowhere else to turn post-trial, she moved into the Brooklyn apartment of Karen Kadison, her favorite (and only) white Jewish friend and one of the few people who supported her lesbian relationship with Crooksie.

Afeni and Karen had met several years earlier at a Black Panther gathering in Manhattan, and the bond was immediate. That first night, Afeni brought her new friend to Glo's house for dinner, announcing, "You're about to meet the coolest white chick ever." And, indeed, Karen was cool. She had wavy dark brown hair and a notably laid-back strut, thought all cops were pigs and most older white people were assholes. The daughter of a World War II bombardier who flew over Normandy, Karen—born and raised in Brooklyn—came from a family of veterans and Holocaust survivors. She wound up going to Brooklyn College to study psychology, and was working as a professor at the school in the early 1970s. "It was always stressed that I need to live my life in a way where I contribute more to the world than I take," she recalled decades later. In her early twenties Karen lived in Peru and Cuba, Colombia and Mexico. She was drawn to subjugated people and the fight to lift them up.

Hence, she opened the doors of her third-floor apartment on Park Slope's Union Street to her pregnant friend. At the time, Afeni was overflowing with paranoia—both justified and irrational. She worried that members of the Panthers might be after her. That the police might be after her. So once she walked through Karen's entranceway, she rarely exited. And one of the few people who knew she was there was the out-of-her-head-in-love Crooksie. The Black Panthers were notoriously misogynistic, so much so that Afeni told almost no one she was bisexual. But, in the last month of her pregnancy, when she needed someone to rub her belly, it was Crooksie. And when she needed someone to make her a milkshake, it was Crooksie. And when she needed someone to stroke her hair, lotion her feet—it was Crooksie. One hour, Crooksie could be out on the streets, making drug deals and smacking fools who failed to pay up ("Feni told us she actually witnessed Crooksie killing someone," said Billy Lesane, Afeni's nephew. "I don't doubt it"). The next hour, she could be cooing in Afeni's ear. It was a sight to behold—two women known for striking fear in those around them, now cuddle bunnies. "Afeni and Crooksie," said Karen, "was a relationship of both friendship and love."*

On the morning of June 16, 1971, when Afeni finally went into labor, she was rushed to New York Flower-Fifth Avenue Hospital, on York Avenue between Sixty-Third and Sixty-Fourth Streets. She was accompanied by three strong, supportive women—Glo, Karen, and Crooksie. After roughly five hours in labor, Afeni—without the aid of painkillers—delivered a healthy six-pound, three-ounce boy. He arrived at 12:15 p.m., and wasn't merely the child of a proud Black woman, but of the Panthers, of prison, of fighting for survival, of doing whatever it took to pull through. "From the very beginning, Tupac's entire life was at war," Yaasmyn Fula wrote. "As a fetus, he felt the vibrations of his mother as she defended herself. He felt the frequent instances of injustice rage through the placenta."

As soon as the baby exited Afeni's body, he was handed to Crooksie, a one-foot-in Muslim who whispered a prayer, Al-Fatiha, softly into his right ear.

You alone do we worship, and You alone do we ask for help.
Guide us on the straight path,
the path of those who have received Your grace;
not the path of those who have brought down wrath, nor of those who
wander astray.
Amen.

---

* Since Tupac Shakur's 1996 death, the estate has retold Afeni's story numerous times. It has deliberately avoided her relationships with women.

When her baby was removed from the delivery room to be cleaned, Afeni found herself overcome by a terror only one who had been smoked out of her apartment would know. What if someone stole the infant? She ordered Glo to follow the doctor into the hallway and make certain nothing went wrong. He held the child out for Glo to see. "Okay, darling dear—there you are," she told the baby. "I know you now, ain't nothing going to happen to you because Auntie is here to make sure of that."

The newborn was returned to his mother, and Afeni directed the nurse toward the woman standing feet away. "Don't pass him to me," she said. "Pass him to Crooksie."

At that moment, big, bad Carol Crooks, infant in her arms, melted. Tears welled in her eyes. She started to sob.

After insisting to a hospital official that the space for a father's identity on the birth certificate would remain blank ("He ain't got a father," Afeni snapped), Afeni told her sister and lover to team up and name the child.

They decided upon Parish Lesane.

Parish was a nod to Leslie Parrish, a veteran character actress who had devoted much of her life to protesting the Vietnam War.

Lesane was Glo's married last name.

"OK," Afeni said. "Parish Lesane *Crooks*."

What?

Crooksie couldn't believe it.

For a woman who walked through life rarely knowing affection, this felt like the real thing. "My mom loved that child," Diamond Durant, Crooks's adopted daughter, said decades later. "As much as she would love her own."

In the immediate aftermath of Parish's birth, Afeni and Crooksie moved with Glo into her three-bedroom apartment at 1240 Woodycrest Avenue in the Bronx, a stone's throw from Yankee Stadium.

At the time, Glo was—like her sister—a single mother, raising four children, all under the age of eight. The pad was a fifth-floor walk-up on an urban street of cracked sidewalks and wayward trash. The building was a pasty beige, with a red fire escape snaking up the side facing the street. Space was tight—three bedrooms, a mini-kitchen, and a tiny bathroom. Sharing a room with Crooksie, Afeni rocked her baby to sleep most nights in a tiny wood cradle. With her drug money, Crooksie transformed half the room into a nursery, buying a crib, a mobile, a changing table. "I honestly thought Crooksie was the dad," said Billy Lesane, Glo's third child. It was during those early months here that Afeni decided her son required an identity shift.

Afeni later maintained she never intended to stick with "Lesane Parish Crooks" or "Parish Lesane Crooks" (the first and middle names had been swapped in the days after birth). Those were placeholders meant to conceal his identity from law enforcement. When she glanced downward toward her son, and perceived the potential greatness flowing inside of him, she didn't believe the flatness of the given name matched the moment. "He was always in my mind a soldier in exile from the beginning," she later said. "That's how I saw it." So she talked it over with the smartest person she knew—Karen Kadison. The white Jewish woman who taught at Brooklyn College.

A passionate historian, Karen offered Afeni a dissertation on the fourth son of Manco Capac, the first governor and founder of the Inca civilization in Cuzco. From 1533 to 1545, Capac is believed to have not merely ruled his people, but fought ferociously to resist Spanish colonialism. Though his land would fall to the Spaniards, Capac established Vilcabamba (aka the Lost City of Incas), which sat thirty miles outside of Cuzco and served as a safe haven for his people.

After Capac's death in 1545, his sons each took a turn serving as ruler. By the time his fourth and youngest child was handed the crown in 1571, Spain determined that it was time to conquer Vilcabamba.

Within a year, the son was captured, brought to Cuzco, tried, and sentenced to death. His name: Túpac Amaru.

On the morning of November 14, 1572, he was dragged into the central plaza of Cuzco, where thousands of residents gathered around. Four horses were walked into the square, each one tied to one of Túpac's limbs. "Horses tugged at the end of each rope in an effort to tear the rebel limb from limb—yet, they couldn't tear him apart," wrote the historian Miguel La Serna. "It would do wonders for the insurgent's mystique: Túpac Amaru, more powerful than four horses; Túpac Amaru, the Inca incarnate with supernatural strength; Túpac Amaru, the anti-colonial hero who refused to die."

The defiance didn't last. Túpac Amaru's head and limbs were chopped off his body, then displayed as threats to those still resisting Spanish rule.

One hundred and sixty-six years later, José Gabriel Condorcanqui was born in Cuzco to a father who served as kuraka (magistrate) of three towns. José Gabriel's parents died when he was sixteen, and in his early twenties he, too, became a kuraka, while repeatedly urging the ruling Spanish governors to lower taxes for locals. After being ignored, José Gabriel took two major steps:

1. He kick-started an uprising to fight for the freedoms of indigenous and enslaved people.
2. He changed his name.

The self-anointed Túpac Amaru II led a valiant rebellion that included the capturing of the town of Sangaraa. Yet early success faded, and on May 18, 1781, Túpac Amaru was captured, taken to Plaza de Armas in Cuzco, and forced to watch as his wife, son, uncle, and brother-in-law had their tongues removed, then their heads chopped off. Túpac Amaru's death was even more gruesome—first his tongue was removed. Then his arms and legs were, like his namesake's, tied to horses. Lastly, he was beheaded. At the same time his torso was burned in a bonfire, his head was placed atop a pike and displayed outside the city of Tinta.

Although Túpac Amaru and Túpac Amaru II both died, their legends persisted. They emerged as symbols of fighting for what's right—even when the odds seem impossible.

Once Karen Kadison finished with her story, Afeni knew what she would call her son.

He would be Tupac Amaru Shakur.

Before he was old enough to walk, Lesane Parish Crooks was being called "Tupac" and "Pac" and "Lil' Pac." But it was not officially his name, and even had Afeni felt compelled to change it, she wasn't about to hand the government the $13.50 to update the records. So while she introduced her son as "Tupac" and referred to her son as "Tupac," he wasn't legally Tupac.

Not that it mattered.

In the first year of motherhood, Afeni faced challenges that far exceeded the naming of a child. First, she had no money. Second, her ex-husband, Lumumba made it clear to the Black Panthers that Afeni—adulterous, knocked-up-while-he-was-behind-bars Afeni—was persona non grata. Third, she lived in a constant state of paranoia—aftershocks of prison and the lengthy trial. Fourth, she *really* liked cocaine. Fifth, her baby's father—former prep basketball star/married father of three Billy Garland—displayed zero interest in his new son.* Sixth, her on-again, off-again romance with Crooksie petered out, and while they remained acquaintances, the much-needed emotional support faded (in 1972, Crooks—who ran a heroin distribution ring—was charged with first-degree manslaughter in the murder of an associate, and sentenced with up to fifteen years in prison). "There's nothing romantic about Afeni's story," Fula said. "She became mythological because of the trial, but she was a very troubled and vulnerable woman.

"When the trial ended, everyone built her up to be this superhuman thing that defended herself against the Man. But she couldn't live up to that. No one could. Her heart belonged to the preservation of Black people, but she was this lost soul."

Roughly twelve months after giving birth, Afeni landed a job. She and Fula were hired by an attorney named Richard Fischbein to work as paralegals at Bronx Legal Services. With a South Bronx office located near Glo's apartment, it was an ideal merging of proximity and purpose. "There were a bunch of young, white Jewish lawyers like me," said Jim Braude, a Bronx Legal Services attorney, "and radical, smart, intense Black Panthers like Yaasmyn and Afeni. You might not think we'd all get along. But there was a kinship. We shared the goal of helping people."

---

* According to the author Dean Van Nguyen, when Tupac was an infant Afeni took him to see Louis Farrakhan speak at the 168th Street Armory in Upper Manhattan. She ran into Garland, placed the baby in his arms, and said, curtly, "I think you want to meet your son."

"Afeni Shakur came with a reputation," said Dwight Loines, a Legal Services staffer. "She would fight."

She worked on prisoner rights reform, on union creation, on community organizing. She gave speeches and headlined rallies. "She was our hero," said Fula. Perhaps the biggest perk of the job, which paid little above the $2.10 minimum wage, was that she could lug her child to the office. On most mornings, Afeni walked through the glass doors of 579 Courtlandt Avenue with a lit Newport smoldering between her lips, a backpack slung over her shoulders, and a young Tupac in her arms. If she had tasks to complete at her desk, she'd plop Tupac down by her side and let him entertain himself with various office supplies. If she had to attend an event, she'd scan the office, lock eyes with a friendly face, and ask, "Can you watch Tupac?"

A sucker for kids, Braude logged his time. "It would either be an hour or four hours and there's this engaging sweet little boy you'd hang out with," he recalled. "He was cute, so . . . I dunno. We were young guys without kids. It was fun.

"Little did I know who I was babysitting."

Along with her Bronx Legal Services work, Afeni threw herself into the national effort to disband COINTELPRO, the FBI's controversial and illegal program to infiltrate what it believed to be anti-American organizations (like the Black Panthers). Afeni served as the coordinator of the National Task Force for COINTELPRO Litigation and Research, which was right up her alley.

But, personally, Afeni's life was a disaster. She was often high, and when she wasn't high she was drunk. She was sent home from the office on multiple occasions. "Her financial inability to maintain a stable living home led to escapism with drugs," said Fula. "Cocaine, weed, emotional depletion." In an age where open bisexuality was shunned, she slept with men and women. She was the most intelligent person wherever she went, yet lacked basic common sense when it came to money (she refused to open a checking account) and the trustworthiness of others. Not long after the Panther 21 trial ended, Afeni was being invited to speak at places ranging from Harvard and Columbia to the United Nations. She naïvely presumed the opportunities (along with four-figure stipends) would continue. They did not.

"When Black radicalism stopped being chic among the white upper classes," the Tupac biographers Tayannah Lee McQuillar and Fred Johnson wrote, "Afeni's audiences vanished and so did her income." Though her mother also lived in the city, their relationship was strained. Rosa was a sweet woman who babysat Glo's children and fried fish for them every Friday night. But she failed to understand Afeni's path. She hadn't left North Carolina so Alice Faye would wind up changing her name and doing . . . what, exactly, was she even doing?

Save for rare moments where she rented a small studio or squatted in the empty apartment of a Panther sympathizer, Afeni depended on Glo for shelter. Her sister, who was divorced from a first husband and stayed home raising the children, wound up marrying a motorman for the New York City Transit Authority named Tom Cox. Even as a spouse and mother, she viewed her primary role as being Afeni's protector. "My mom loved her sister more than she loved her children," said Billy Lesane, Gloria's son. "That's not an insult, it's just the truth. Anything Feni needed, my mother was at her beck and call, even at the expense of us."

On the outside, people considered Afeni strong and heroic. On the inside, she felt useless. She talked confidently, but mooched off her sister. She preached self-empowerment, but relied heavily on others. When Tupac cried, she often handed him off to Glo, who knew better how to placate an ornery infant. Though never diagnosed with any mental illness, Afeni was prone to crippling bouts of depression, which oftentimes resulted in self-imposed isolation. Afeni could be coming home to Glo's for dinner. She could also go missing for five days. She could be a doting mother. She could also be an absentee mother. "She wasn't an enigma," said Fula. "She was traumatized. There's a difference."

In 1975, when Tupac was three going on four, Afeni paired off with Mutulu Shakur (formerly Jeral Williams). A Baltimore native who had moved to New York as a young child, Mutulu was known for his work with Lincoln Detox Center, the South Bronx–based program that revolutionized drug rehabilitation for heroin users by incorporating acupuncture. He was a proud, militant man who sought a partner who shared the values of the Black empowerment movement. Afeni volunteered a handful of times at Lincoln Detox, and Mutulu quickly learned to love her little son. Like Afeni's marriage to Lumumba, this union was . . . untraditional. When asked, Afeni referred to Mutulu as her husband. He was. Sort of. The author Santi Elijah Holley called the relationship "informal and largely ceremonial." The two sometimes cohabitated in a rented apartment on the sixteenth floor of 626 Riverside Drive and sometimes did not. They might have held hands once or twice, though nobody remembers it. The rhythms of Afeni confused Mutulu. She could be warm one minute, icy the next. Sane and reasonable at three o'clock, off the handle at 3:01. There was always music playing in the apartment, but the bubbly mood was largely illusionary. When she was sober, she was moody. When she was high, she was annoying. Her passion was off the charts. So was her unpredictability. On October 3, 1975, four years after Tupac arrived, Afeni gave birth to Mutulu's daughter, Sekyiwa Shakur, at Women's Hospital in Harlem. Everyone called her "Set."

Afeni mothered through the prism of paranoia. She always believed someone was watching, plotting, conniving. Maybe to kidnap her children. Maybe just to corrupt them. If she walked one path home on a Monday, she'd walk a different path on Tuesday. She glowered at strangers. Snapped with no regard for normal human conduct. *Why is that guy standing there for so long? Did that waiter put something in my drink? Why does that security guard look so familiar?*

"She wore many faces," said Fula, "to cover up her pathology."

"Go to prison and spend all those days and weeks and years in isolation," Fula added. "And you're pregnant. Now emerge unscathed and normal. I dare you. Afeni was motherfucking damaged goods. A great, *great* woman. But you don't get back all those emotions and feelings that were beaten out of you. You're forever scarred."

Afeni used a telephone, but presumed it was tapped. The FBI, maybe. Perhaps some rogue Panthers. Afeni liked whispering. Don't let people hear you. She trusted no one, yet simultaneously allowed a motley crew into her sphere. The company she kept formed a rainbow coalition of eccentrics. "She'd bring people home for dinner," recalled Billy Lesane. "Gangsters, drug dealers, revolutionaries, hippies. They'd slip us kids some money, tell us crazy stories about the streets."

Afeni spent time with Tupac and Set in Fula's second-floor apartment at

61 North Arlington Avenue in East Orange, New Jersey—in part because Fula (whose son, Yaki, was fathered by Sekou Odinga, Afeni's superior when she joined the Panthers) was unofficial aunt to the children; in part because the abode felt like a hideout. Inside the three-bedroom pad, Afeni and Yaasmyn had the children listen to music that chronicled the Black struggle—jams like the Main Ingredient's "Black Seeds Keep on Growing" and "Stagger Lee" by Lloyd Price. One could feel the bass thumping off Fula's walls. The women lectured on Malcolm X and Marcus Garvey. Back to Africa wasn't a concept, but a game plan. Afeni sat Tupac in a chair and read him articles from *The New York Times*. Other children his age were digesting Dr. Seuss. Tupac—not yet five—was asked to break down Gerald Ford's policies toward Black people. Because she had carried him through prison and a trial, Afeni considered Tupac a golden child. Everything she had survived, he had survived. In her eyes, he emerged from her womb with a glowing halo and cloak of invincibility.

If Afeni had any doubt about this, it vanished on June 16, 1976, Tupac's fifth birthday. That morning nearly twenty thousand Black students in the South African township of Soweto walked out of their schools to march in protest against the Afrikaans Medium Decree, which mandated all Black schools use Afrikaans and English as the languages of instruction. Police first unleashed dogs on the young protesters. Then they shot into crowds. The first to die, Hastings Ndlovu, was fifteen. The second, Hector Pieterson, was twelve. Over the course of the next two months, more than six hundred people were killed, and the images of young Black boys and girls being murdered by law enforcement spread around the world. What became known as the Soweto Uprising didn't end apartheid, but it served as a wake-up call to millions of people who had been blind to its scale. "That it took place on Tupac's birthday *really* impacted my mother," Set recalled years later. "It reinforced her belief that Tupac was born as a zeitgeist for our generation."

Though Woodycrest Avenue was merely the name of an obscure Bronx street, it felt, to the children of Glo and Afeni, like a magical playground. Back in the late 1970s, the area was patrolled by a pair of gangs, the Savage Skulls and the Ghetto Brothers, who brawled among themselves but looked out for kids sprinting sidewalk to sidewalk. To sit on a Woodycrest Avenue stoop in the hours after school let out was to hear the blissful squeals and bellows of youth. "It was Black kids, Puerto Rican kids, Irish kids, Jewish kids—all in the same neighborhood," recalled Billy Lesane. "It was so beautiful." They played everything—kickball and stickball, football and kick the can. "We made go-karts with our hands," Billy said. "We made bikes with our hands. You'd go out and never wanna come back in." There was a bodega on the corner, Four Brothers, run by a Puerto Rican family. When playtime ended, the kids stormed through the front door, armed with change for Coca-Colas and push-up pops.

Tupac was a spindly young child, with a shock of dark hair flowering from his head. He was talkative, but not particularly brash. He had large brown eyes and effeminate eyelashes. He was addicted to Saturday morning cartoons and *Star Wars*, and was as coordinated as a stump—he could neither throw a ball nor catch one. But he had quick hands and, beginning at age six, a propensity for fighting.

In the early months of 1978, Tom and Glo relocated with their children to a new apartment on Leland Avenue in the Bronx. Afeni and Yaasmyn Fula rented an apartment inside a building at 200 West 108th Street in Harlem, but Tupac was always tagging along behind his cousins. He was particularly enamored by the two older boys, Billy and Kenny Lesane. Unlike life on Woodycrest Avenue, there wasn't a ton to do on Leland Avenue. So on weekends the boys spent their time in one of the building's asbestos-laced basements, playing hide-and-seek in the expansive laundry room. One day a boy named Kuma smacked Tupac in the head before mocking his unusual name. "Pac comes to me and he's crying," recalled Kenny. "He wants me to step in and do something."

Kenny pushed his cousin toward the bigger, stronger boy and said, "Nah, you're fighting him right now."

Still sniffling, Tupac drew back his right fist and cocked Kuma in the teeth. Blood dripped from Kuma's upper lip. Tupac pounced, unleashing a dizzying barrage of punches. "He whooped that boy's ass," Kenny said. "I saw the lion in him. Six years old, and I saw the lion."

Billy and Kenny could be cruel to Tupac ("They bullied him relentlessly," recalled Set, his sister. "They don't like talking about that part of it all, do they?"), but their little cousin was a sponge in need of attention.

If they fought, he fought. If they ridiculed him, he shrugged it off. As a boy raised entirely by women, he often expressed sadness over the lack of men to guide his way. Mutulu was a presence, but other priorities trumped looking after Afeni's son. His uncle, Tom Cox (Glo's second husband), was a reliable provider, but stern and emotionally unavailable.

Though Afeni maintained Tupac didn't know the identity of his father until adulthood, this was not true. When he was still a young boy, Fula—not using the best judgment—informed Tupac that some guy named Billy Garland was his dad. "I was fed up with Afeni's bullshit about it," she said. "So I told him who his dad was and said, 'Any time you want me to take you to meet him, let me know.'" It was a moment of clarity: *Your pop wants nothing to do with you.*

The Lesanes, on the other hand, were always there. Only they weren't ideal role models. "We were welfare recipients, ghetto, drug dealers and drug abusers," recalled Jamala Lesane, another cousin. "We were the no-hot-water, no-heat, no-Christmas, doped-up, drugged-out kind of family. We were lazy. Sheets hanging up in the window." In 1980, when Tupac was nine, Billy was seventeen and working the streets surrounding Times Square, selling fake drugs to tourists and hustling them with sidewalk card games. The money he made supported a mounting addiction to crack cocaine. "Sometimes Billy would use me to help," Kenny recalled. "One day I was with him around Forty-Second Street, and we were going somewhere to rip someone off, and we got in the back of a cab. He turned to me and said, 'Yo, Black, you wanna try this shit? This is *the shit*, man.'"

"What is it?" Kenny asked.

It was crack.

"I knew better, but I hit that shit," Kenny said. "I hate to say this, but it was better than a hundred orgasms. That was it for me. I was hooked."

Both brothers wound up full-fledged addicts, in and out of prison for the next three decades.

"I was a mess," Kenny said years later. "Thank God Pac didn't follow my footsteps. Thank God he found his own path."

Drugs weren't a problem only for the Lesane brothers.

Try as she might to serve as a role model for her children, Afeni was, at her core, an addict. Be it cigarettes, weed, cocaine, or LSD, rare were the days her bloodstream ran clean. Sobriety wasn't an uncommon state for Afeni Shakur. It was a nonexistent one. "A lot of alcoholics and drug fiends came out of the [Black Power] movement," said Watani Tyehimba, a former Panther who years later worked as Tupac's manager. "People under stress will self-medicate. It's not that Afeni was weak. It's just how she dealt with the pressure."

Even though her marriage to Mutulu was far from traditional, he remained an important figure in her life and the lives of her children, and worked with Afeni on the National Task Force for COINTELPRO Litigation and Research. Then, on October 20, 1981, two police officers and a security guard were killed when a heavily armed gang of self-professed revolutionaries robbed a Brink's truck in Nyack, New York. The lead suspect, Mutulu Shakur, refused to turn himself in, instead disappearing into the underground and landing on the FBI's Ten Most Wanted List. He would spend the next four and a half years on the run, leaving Afeni alone to raise their daughter.

With that, life spiraled to a new low. Afeni dove hard into a relationship with yet another man, this one a noted New York City street hustler named Kenneth "Legs" Saunders. A dashing figure who stood six foot one and dressed in fur coats and pin-striped suits, Legs was—for a brief spell—the male role model Tupac craved. He owned an arcade called Games People Play on 125th Street in Harlem, and would let the Shakur kids and their cousins play free pinball and Skee-Ball. "It was the first time anyone handed me a pile of quarters," recalled Kenny Lesane. "For a kid, what's better?"

Because he worked under Nicky Barnes, the New York City crime boss who ran much of Harlem's heroin trade, Legs was perceived by many to be a high-level gangster pimp hustler who chilled with Hugh Hefner at the Playboy Mansion. "It wasn't entirely accurate," said Set. "Yes, he was a true gangster in every sense of the word. But he loved us, and when he was home with us he brought structure to the house. With Legs, we had a curfew. We had to go to sleep at a certain time. We had to take vitamins. You couldn't wear shoes in the house."* For a little less than a year, Legs lived

---

* He did, factually, hang with Hef.

with Afeni and her children in an apartment at 92 Morningside Avenue in Harlem. Tupac and Set shared a room. The Shakur children had been around some cool characters, but none *this* cool. Legs was confident, charismatic, smooth. So what that, like Lumumba before him, he had a wife and child living at a different address? What Afeni and her children didn't know didn't hurt them. "Pac would brag about Legs," said Kenny Lesane. "*Really* brag. 'Legs loves me!' He needed that. Real affection from a man. He craved it, because it was never available to him."

Legs Saunders also introduced Afeni to crack.

The year was 1981, and this new form of cocaine was treating New York City like its own petri dish. Initially, crack had to be explained to potential customers—it was cocaine mixed with baking powder, then cooked down to a pellet. Unlike the high from cocaine, which went from ingestion to blood to brain, with crack the span from inhalation to impact was seconds. "The drug," wrote Parren J. Mitchell of the *Baltimore Afro-American*, "provides users with reactions that range from exhilaration to a sense of power and superiority."

Crack was dirt cheap, and while Legs liked it ("When we first met him he looked like a star," said Billy. "But when he started using, he fell apart"), Afeni *loved* it. Loved it more than she loved her nephews and niece, her sister, *her children*. She was the ideal client: poor and in need of the highs life failed to provide. Wrote David Farber in his book *Crack: Rock Cocaine, Street Capitalism, and the Decade of Greed*: "Crack poisoned bodies, ravaged minds, ripped apart families and tore jagged holes in communities."

Afeni had been employed at Bronx Legal Services for almost a decade, but was fired in the early months of 1982 because of her crack addiction.* "Once you try it, everything else vanishes," said Billy. "You're not thinking about sex or food. Just the next high." Thanks in large part to her newfound drug abuse, she simply stopped showing up at the office. Her desk remained vacant, her chair unfilled. "It's not complicated," Fula said. "She was on the pipe. And even though she wasn't that bad yet, it wasn't gonna

---

* According to Set, Afeni lost her job when the FBI "threatened her boss to let her go." However, Fula, her coworker, insisted this was not the case. "She was an addict," Fula said. "She was no longer reliable. It's regrettable, but it's true."

get better for her. Drugs grabbed a hold of Afeni. And drugs don't let go easily."

For all her shortcomings and trauma, Afeni placed an emphasis on education. Even though she distrusted the public school system, what with its overwhelmingly white staffs and focus on (what she considered to be) base-level thinking, she wanted her children to be informed. They needed to read and problem-solve at the highest levels, be quick on their feet and able to outsmart the opposition.

No matter her own self-destruction, the betterment of her offspring remained important.

The first place to educate a young Tupac was the Little Red School House Community Center, a tiny K-through-sixth-grade education center located on Dyre Avenue in the Bronx. At age five, Tupac was believed by his mother to be uniquely gifted. What she wanted, the biographer Staci Robinson wrote, was a facility where he would "gain a sense of structure and discipline to augment his homeschooling." Yet on one of his first days at the school, Afeni arrived for pickup to find her son standing atop a table, imitating the gyrational dance moves of James Brown. "Education is what my son is here for," she screamed at Elsie Soderberg, the school's director, "not to entertain you all!" Afeni spanked her son in front of three staffers and dragged him out by his ear. He was homeschooled the remainder of the year.

Because Afeni rarely maintained a single address for long, Tupac and his sister were educational vagabonds, hopping from one classroom to another to another. In one particularly nomadic academic year, the two children attended *six* different schools. "Maybe seven," Set recalled. "I lost track."

The one that made the greatest impact was the Lower East Side International Community School, located at Rivington and Pitt Streets in Manhattan. Hailed by *The New York Times* as "innovative," the school served two thousand mostly underprivileged Black and Hispanic students and offered such unique classes as Arabic and Swahili. Based out of a converted department store building with towering red front doors, the school used the first two floors for classes; the top four floors were condemned. Parents were encouraged to sit in on courses. The school's founder, Wallie Simpson, told *The New York Times* she was "obsessed with freeing children from the limitations that confine them."

"I always like to tell people that the Lower East Side International School was where the Black revolutionaries in New York sent their kids after the civil rights movement," said Crystal Charles, Tupac's classmate. "It was a mindset of that place. Survivors of the struggle all united."

Afeni's children were living temporarily in Brooklyn when they attended the Lower East Side International School. One day, Tupac and a gaggle of classmates were riding the F train back to Flatbush when a white police officer approached.

"You kids need to lower your voices," the officer said.

"All we're doing is talking," replied Tupac—who was in *fourth grade.* "We're not bothering anybody."

"Son," the officer said, "you've got a real chip on your shoulder."

Tupac smirked. "Well," he replied, "why don't you knock it off?"

Dead silence.

"We thought we were all going to jail," said Kashi Johnson, a classmate. "But he stood his ground with no apprehension. The cop backed off."

Tupac attended fourth grade at the school, then a little bit of fifth. His time there ended when a teacher, Robert Lincoln, took all of his students on a field trip to a museum, then—sans permission—brought them to his apartment for a spaghetti lunch. Simpson fired Lincoln, only the move backfired. The teacher was twenty-five, with long dreadlocks and a dog-eared copy of *The Autobiography of Malcolm X* perched on the corner of his desk. Instead of returning Tupac and Set to the Lower East Side International School, Afeni enrolled them in a new homeschooling setting—Mr. Lincoln's apartment. "That's my mom," said Set. "She believed in that man more than she believed in the school. We were all different ages, and we all stuck with Mr. Lincoln. It sounds crazy, but it was integrity."

Tupac spent sixth grade at PS 28, an elementary school at 475 West 155th Street in the Bronx. For a brief spell, in between stays with Glo and various family friends, the three resided inside a homeless shelter. "There were days where my mother would drop us off at a movie theater, because you can sit in a movie theater all day," Set recalled. "We would sit there and watch one movie, and when it'd end we'd go watch another movie. It'd be *The Muppets Take Manhattan* followed by *Indiana Jones.*

"Another day, when Mom left us to try and find a job, Pac and I got a bucket, some sponges, some towels, and we literally washed windshields on the Harlem River Drive. Walked car to car, asking for change. We were just kids."

School served as an oasis for the children, especially Tupac. Classmates remember the young boy as exceedingly quiet ("He was nice, but he just didn't say very much," recalled Robin Gordon, a fellow PS 28 student) and notably inquisitive ("He was really smart," said Lisha Davis, also a PS 28 student. "The kind of smart you remember forty years later"). Because of circumstances beyond his control, Tupac missed plenty of days, but he was fortunate to have the understanding Joyce Greenleaf as his teacher. A white woman who had started at the school in 1966, Greenleaf wanted her students to see and feel and touch and grasp the world around them. That's why, for no extra pay, she created the school's drama and glee clubs. It's why she took her classes on trips to Lincoln Center. And it's why she headed *Junior Dimensions,* the PS 28 student newspaper. The December 1981 edition featured a front-page class photo of twenty-six students— including a boy, sitting crisscross applesauce, a broad smile plastered across his face. The caption identified him as "Tupak Shakir."

That image was taken in front of the New York Times Building in Manhattan. Greenleaf thought it important to show her students the magic of media, so she arranged a tour of the newsroom, the printing presses. The boys and girls were taught how to fold and unfold the paper, how headlines were written, and why certain articles wound up in certain places.

It was, for Tupak Shakir, a joyful escape from the dark realities of life.

It was also one of his final days at PS 28.

"He just stopped coming," said Sherrieff Davis, a classmate. "Sometimes I wonder if he was ever there at all."

Chapter 3

Rapture

As a teenager in the early 1980s, David Ash walked the earth with two primary wishes.

1. For summer to arrive.
2. For his airplane to take off.

For seven months of the year, David lived with his great-grandparents, Robert and Ida Ash, in Demopolis, Alabama, a town of sixty-five hundred residents with a medium-sized park and little else. It was located smack-dab in the middle of the Yellowhammer State, which—to a young boy with big dreams—could feel like Siberia.

That is why, come the end of school, David Ash was so damn giddy. The day after Demopolis High let out, he would catch a ride to Birmingham Municipal Airport, board a plane, and fly the two and a half hours to New York City, where he spent his summers inside a two-family house rented by his mother, Christine Ash, at 2265 Walton Avenue in the Bronx.

David didn't merely like coming to New York. He *loved* it. The sights. The smells. Black people next to white people next to Puerto Ricans next to Orthodox Jews. He loved the music blasting from car radios and boom boxes—Grandmaster Flash and Donna Summer, Stevie Wonder and the Sugarhill Gang. He loved street vendors and subway taggers, fat bagels dripping cream cheese and one-dollar pushcart hot dogs topped with mustard and relish.

"New York," David said years later, "was a dream."

This was the place where David Ash encountered a young Tupac Shakur.

And his gift for music.

He vividly recalled the halcyon days of 1982, when Ash was sixteen and Tupac was ten turning eleven and they were two young Black kids living innocently in a complicated world. By mere coincidence, Christine Ash's residence was located across the street from a six-story building at 2260 Walton Avenue. This is where Gloria Cox, her husband, Tom, and their (by now) six children lived in a fourth-floor apartment. And even though Afeni Shakur and her son and daughter were hopping from flat to shelter and back again, from June through August Tupac usually slept on his aunt Glo's couch.

"But it wasn't about the couch," Ash said. "It was about the stoop."

Hell, yes. The stoop. Positioned before the building was an eight-step stoop, painted charcoal gray and supported by a pair of black metal handrails. It was, by American stoop standards, subpar. Unevenly applied coating. Lopsided cement slabs.

Yet, for the block's Black and Puerto Rican kids, the stoop was the epicenter of magic. Within its proximity there would be games of stickball, breaks for Italian ices, scampers through abandoned buildings. "We would hang out around the stoop for hours," David said. "We'd debate, talk, joke, laugh, play. But best of all, we'd rap."

It was *the thing*, he recalled. This was when hip-hop was still a relatively new and niche New York–generated art form, just nine years old, crudely identified in the entertainment industry as "Black" or "Urban" music and relegated to a corner of the local record store. Slowly but surely, however, the sounds of Kurtis Blow and Whodini were working their way through the boroughs, enough so that they landed on the stoop.

At first, the kids tried their best to imitate the giants of the genre. But before long, they wanted their own sounds and identities. Which is how Ash became known as D-Money. And how Tupac became known as . . .

. . . MC New York.

In hindsight, the name is a bit corny. But in the age of MC Shy D and MC Shan and an ever-growing number of MC . . . *somethings*, there was method to the madness. Plus, Tupac/MC New York possessed legitimate base-level skills. His early efforts at poetry (a gateway to rap for the youngster) spoke to a mind that loved cobbling together words. He dabbled in haiku well before most of his peers knew what a haiku was, and touched on the themes of faith ("Faith is what we need") and dreams ("You drift to another land") that parroted the lessons of his mother.

When Tupac was ten, Kenny "Legs" Saunders, Afeni's boyfriend and New York drug kingpin, bought him his first-ever boom box. It was a silver two-cassette special, with an AM/FM radio dial and a black handle. For a boy who didn't always know the whereabouts of his next meal, this was akin to receiving a thousand gold bars. Tupac would pop in blank tapes and record R&B songs off WBLS, New York's home for soul music. He analyzed the lyrics, studied the flow, took note of pacing and delivery. As a wee lad, Wolfgang Amadeus Mozart had tapped out rhythms on his bedroom floor at Getreidegasse 9 in Salzburg. Such was Tupac in the Bronx. "He was a prodigy," said Billy Lesane, his cousin. "There's no arguing it."

Although it's difficult to pinpoint MC New York's exact debut as a songwriter, two originals—both penned around age twelve—are contenders for first-ever Tupac Shakur hip-hop creation. The Shakur estate identifies "First Step," a rap that pays homage to the TV show *Fame*, to be his initial try as a lyricist.

You're looking at a dream
You're starin' it in the eye

Yet according to Kenny Lesane, Tupac's older cousin (who went by "Kenny Black" in the neighborhood), his first creation was actually "MC Cop"—a song that was performed multiple times on the ol' stoop. "He was a baby," Kenny said, "and that song blew everybody out the park because it was so intelligent, so masterfully crafted the way he took a story and turned that shit into a rap song. I can't remember the lyrics, but the shit was dope."

It was on the stoop outside his aunt's apartment where Tupac first learned the lifelong coping skill of compartmentalization. In one compartment, his mom and cousins were drug addicts. In another compartment, he wasn't sure where he would sleep at night. In another compartment, his father was MIA. In another compartment, he hated wearing the same shirt to school two days in a row; hated his size-too-small Goodwill sneakers with the frayed fabric near the toes. In another compartment, his stomach was empty.

But on the stoop, all of it vanished. He wasn't Tupac, son of an addict. He was MC motherfuckin' New York, rapper and storyteller. And even though he was not yet entering puberty, something in his voice crackled with the intensity of hunger. "He loved the movie *Scarface*, and was really influenced by it," said Ash. "He and his cousin Scott [Lesane] performed monologues, word for word, on the stoop. Acted it out. If you're gonna have a movie influence you at that young age, *Scarface* is an interesting one."

Every Friday night during that summer of 1982, a handful of former Black Panthers congregated in Glo's apartment to smoke weed and drop acid and talk old times. The children were prohibited from attending, so they used the two-hour span to gather on the stoop and put on shows for one another. There'd be dancing, singing, jokes—and MC New York, spitting grenades. "He wasn't great yet," said Ash. "But he had promise."

While many of the participants later failed to remember his lyrics, they all recalled Tupac's cadence. Even back then, he seemed to grasp the spacing of syllables and words. When Ash rapped—well, it was fine. When Tupac rapped, it was elongated and punctuated and *Pop! Bam! Pow!* With no training, he knew ending a line with "damn" wasn't as potent as ending a line with "dah-*yaaaammmmm*." Somehow, the sound of gravel filled his throat. It felt raw. Years later, the rapper Shock G of Digital Underground would praise Tupac for rapping "from the pit of his stomach." That was birthed on the stoop.

Also, while there were exceptions to the rule (like Grandmaster Flash and the Furious Five's "The Message"), rap at the time was primarily a land of self-love and party anthems. The themes concerned being the baddest MC or scoring the most ladies or having the sweetest ride. But for all her shortcomings as a parent, Afeni instilled a potent sense of Black pride in her son. Even in a diminished state, she reminded her children that they were descendants of kings and queens. That Black was beautiful. So as he began to think about music, and as he started (infrequently, at first) jotting down ideas into a notebook, the etchings rarely boasted of riches (he had none) or bitches (also none), but freedom, liberation, forcefulness. Whereas other aspiring rappers were paying homage to Rolls-Royce and *Foxy Brown*, Tupac, not yet a teen, was thinking Malcolm X.

"Even at that age," said Ash, "he was ahead of the game."

On November 4, 1983, Rev. Jesse Jackson stood before an estimated four thousand people inside the Washington Convention Center in the nation's capital and announced he would be running for the presidency of the United States.

At age forty-two, Jackson was full of hope. "I offer myself and my service," he told the crowd, "as a vehicle to give a voice to the voiceless, representation to the unrepresented and hope to the downtrodden."

As the first mainstream Black presidential candidate, Jackson garnered a good deal of national attention. Did he have a realistic shot of earning the Democratic nomination and taking on the incumbent, Ronald Reagan, in the general election? Not really. But he put everything he had into the effort, and crisscrossed the United States trying to convince ordinary Americans that Jesse Jackson, man of the people, deserved their vote.

Which is how, in 1984, Jackson came to Harlem's famed Apollo Theater, where he would share the stage with Tupac Shakur.

Knowing her son's flair for the dramatic, as well as his love of attention and the spotlight, Afeni had recently enrolled her son in the 127th Street Repertory Ensemble, a fabled African American studio founded by Ernie McClintock, the award-winning director. His cousin Scott Lesane was already a member of the company, and Afeni thought it a secure (and free-of-charge) spot for both her children to spend their afternoons. "We needed a place to be in the daytime while my mother figured things out," Set Shakur recalled. "Him being involved would give us a safe spot. He was the actor. I was the tagalong running behind the stage and in the hallways."

The Ensemble served as a springboard for a slew of stage and film's Black performers. It also offered stability. The adult actors recognized Tupac for what he was—prematurely charismatic, but also impoverished, malnourished, and under the care of a drug-addicted mother. He often showed up in dirty clothing, with tired eyes. For his thirteenth birthday, the regulars pooled together to give Tupac money as a present.

"Afeni was going through her problems with substances at that time," recalled Levy Lee Simon, a member of the Ensemble. "So he took that money and went grocery shopping. He was selfless like that."*

Tupac loved the Ensemble just as he loved standing on the stoop and busting rhymes. Most of the members were older, but McClintock utilized children whenever possible. "Tupac would breakdance for us," recalled Bahni Turpin, an adult company member. "That stood out."

Added Simon, "Whatever that 'it factor' is that people talk about, the indescribable thing that certain performers or artists have, he already had it."

On the night of August 10, 1984, to help Jackson fundraise, members of McClintock's company trekked to the Apollo to perform *A Raisin in the Sun*, the acclaimed Lorraine Hansberry play. It starred Minnie Gentry, who had also acted as "Mama" in the Henry Street Settlement production. Tupac played Travis Younger, the son of the main characters. He was the only child in the cast, and the show opened with his character asleep on a couch. "I woke up and I was the only person on the stage," he recalled. "I can remember thinking this is the best shit in the world." All told, he had but a handful of lines, and appeared onstage for a grand total of, oh, ten minutes.† Whether the themes of the production resonated with the young actor, we will never know. But Tupac failed to forget the buzz of that night.

"When the curtain went up," he recalled, "I just caught that bug that everybody talks about. I was like, 'Wow! This is it!' It was better than sex and anything, money, everything. It was like, 'Wow! I want this!'"

Shortly before this time, Tupac's world had been ripped from its hinges when Glo, Tom, and seven of their children mimicked a portion of the *Raisin in the Sun* plot and relocated from their New York City apartment to a home in White Plains, New York, nineteen miles north in Westchester

---

* "You have to understand," said Set, Tupac's sister, "our mom loved us, but she wasn't maternal by nature. She would make decisions for the betterment of upward mobility. But she wasn't baking cookies."

† Never one to turn down the spotlight, Jackson spoke during the show's intermission—*for more than an hour.*

County. "That was us trying to expose our kids to better things," Glo said. "Better schools. Better this. Better that."

They settled upon a two-story, 1,885-square-foot rental at 2 Carrigan Avenue. It had three bedrooms, three bathrooms, and a .31-acre yard covered with grass and plants. The home was a far cry from the cramped apartments the family had lived in through the decades.

Because she felt responsible for her kin, Glo insisted Afeni, Tupac, and Set accompany them to the suburbs. Whether Tom was in favor of his sister-in-law and her children moving in was a nonissue. Glo said they were coming—they were coming.

New York's twenty-ninth largest municipality, White Plains is one of the state's most diverse cities. Carrigan Avenue and the surrounding streets, however, were primarily white. Which was eye-opening for Tupac, who had spent the majority of his life hanging with Blacks and Puerto Ricans. Furthermore, for the first time he possessed some of the things he'd only seen on TV shows like *Silver Spoons* and *Who's the Boss?* For example, the privacy of a bedroom (he shared it with his little cousin Katari). Space from his mother (Afeni slept in the basement). A bicycle.

Right after moving in, Tupac made his first White Plains friend, who also happened to be his first white (well, technically half Jewish, half Haitian—but white in appearance) friend. His name was Jesse Davis, and he and his family lived a couple of blocks over on Branchbrook Road. Jesse and Tupac were both seventh graders at Eastview Middle School, and upon initially meeting on the morning school bus Jesse noticed two things about his new neighbor:

1. He was Black.
2. His teeth were *awful*.

"They were so messed up," Davis recalled. "He smiled a lot, and he had this big bucktoothed grin with teeth at different angles. It wasn't pretty."

Despite that, Jesse took to Tupac. He was a fun, boisterous kid with a high-pitched laugh and a unique level of confidence. He introduced himself as Tupac—but insisted Jesse call him "Pop."

"Pac?"

"No, Pop."

It was weird.

"There was a girl he was really into," Davis recalled. "A Latino girl with curly hair who wore tight jeans. She had a boyfriend, but Tupac didn't care. He was the first guy I knew who talked to girls with no shyness. Even with those teeth." On the bus, Tupac busted out raps (whether classmates wanted to hear them or not), and after school he and Jesse sat by a radio inside the Davis household and listened to Chuck Chillout and DJ Red Alert on KISS FM. "Tupac really knew music," Jesse said. "He'd fill me in on what's new, what's hot." Sometimes they played catch in the street. Other times they hopped on their bicycles and rode to the Rosedale Deli, about a mile away. After a month or so in town, Tupac landed his first-ever job, making a solid twenty dollars per week delivering *The Reporter Dispatch*, the local newspaper, door-to-door on his bicycle. He gave a chunk of the cash to his out-of-work mother and kept the rest for ice cream, soda, and gum.

Though Tupac was an above-average reader and orator, school was never a comfort zone. In New York City, he felt self-conscious about his clothing, his cleanliness. In White Plains it was more of the same. "He was clearly poor," said Delphine Burton, who sat near Tupac in Mr. Glenn's art class. "That was obvious."

"Kids were not the nicest to him," recalled Lori Green, a classmate. "Most of the shirts he wore were Le Tigre, and that wasn't cool. He had bad teeth and his Afro wasn't well put together. Oh, and his name. They called him 'Two-Door Sedan' instead of Tupac. It wasn't nice."

Tupac laughed it off, because that's what you do as a young teenager—you laugh things off. But inside, he was hurting. Back on Carrigan Avenue, his mother spent much of her time in the basement, getting high. He could go to Jesse's house and listen to music, he could ride his Schwinn to the Rosedale Deli, he could mack on the curly-haired Latina honey. But come day's end, he was Afeni Shakur's son. And Afeni Shakur was a broken addict, channeling her pain and trauma into drugs.

Glo loved Afeni, and felt the need to serve as her protector. Yet the relationship was volatile, and Tom—working as an engineer—grew tired of having his deadbeat sister-in-law take up valuable basement space while contributing nothing but addiction and debt. Food cost money. Heat cost money. Rent cost money. Afeni had no money, and made little effort to generate income outside of her son's paperboy scraps.

On multiple occasions, fights between the sisters led to Afeni packing her bags and storming out with her children. She, Tupac, and Set spent several weeks in a run-down extended-stay motel, and Afeni's pride was tidal-waved by cruel reality. "There was a time when she didn't have the money to pay," said Set. "She had us go to the [motel] room by ourselves, because she knew the motel wouldn't kick kids out when they were alone. So she kind of hid."

During another two-week period, the three Shakurs holed up with the family of Otis Williams, a Black White Plains firefighter who, with his wife, Theresa, had eight children and charitable hearts. "They were just these really nice people," Set said. "But it couldn't last forever."

Ultimately, come winter Afeni, Tupac, and Set returned to Glo's house. They stayed for a while, until one night when the sisters engaged in a particularly heated dustup. Punches were thrown. Screams could be heard down Carrigan Avenue. Someone inside the house called 911, and within minutes officers from the White Plains Police Department knocked on the door. Glo explained the situation—her sister was a drug addict and she needed to leave.

One of the officers looked at Afeni. "Ma'am," he said. "It's time to go."

According to Set, the night was blisteringly cold, and it was too late for her, her mother, and her brother to head to the bus station. "That's the first time we were legitimately homeless, in that we had nowhere to go," Set recalled. "I think we spent the next few days riding a train, trying to figure out what to do. The one thing my mom would not do was beg for money. That was not allowed."

A decade earlier, Afeni Shakur had been a hero of the Black Panther movement. She stood up to the pigs, stood up to the Man, fought the power, represented herself in court, won in court, delivered a miracle baby boy. She was speaking at universities and making headlines and being held up as an example of powerful womanhood.

Now she was a homeless drug addict sitting next to her two children on a Metro North train to nowhere. At one point, White Plains had felt like an answer to the family's prayers. Now, after less than seven months in town, it seemed more nightmare. Afeni and her children returned to New York City, where they again bounced from place to place, seeking out elusive stability.

"She was very lonely," said Set. "The three of us were very lonely. Not too many people have seen what we saw or what we experienced. Our so-called loved ones left us in the street. My mom was a proud woman who didn't know what to do next. It's horribly sad."

Fortunately, Afeni Shakur had family.

In Baltimore.

Chapter 4

Coming to Baltimore

Although nearly forty years have passed since Afeni Shakur and her two children moved to 3955 Greenmount Avenue, in Baltimore's Pen Lucy neighborhood, on the city's northeast side, time remains frozen. A small patch of grass before her row house is overgrown and blended with the shattered glass of a broken beer bottle, a Hershey wrapper, two frayed lollipop sticks. The cement staircase appears as cracked now as it was in 1984. The air smells of rust and salt.

"This is Black Baltimore," Phyllis Cannady, a sixty-three-year-old woman on a nearby porch, tells a white reporter. "Welcome."

With little money to her name and no particular plan in place, in November 1984 Afeni and her children moved into the 1,798-square-foot row house, which was occupied by a cousin, Lisa, and her son, Jamal—both of whom moved out within a matter of weeks.

Were one to read the day's sparkly travel brochures, he would learn of a magical municipality featuring the splendor of Inner Harbor, the excitement of Cal Ripken Jr. and Baltimore Orioles baseball, the deliciousness of steamed crabs. Yet that was illusory. To be white and wealthy is to know an upper-crust Baltimore that never existed to the denizens of Greenmount Avenue. All one needs to do is scan through copies of the *Baltimore Afro-American*, the weekly Black newspaper of record at the time, to understand. With rare exception, the articles called for people to fight drug addiction, escape homelessness, embrace Jesus. The headlines bled trauma—SHOOTOUT AT SOCIAL SERVICES and NO SUSPECTS YET IN THE PIMLICO-5 EXECUTIONS and GROCERS IN CITY COUNTY CITED FOR FOOD STAMP VIOLATIONS. Beneath TWO BALTIMORES, the columnist

R. B. Jones once wrote, "There has [*sic*] always been two Baltimores. That is an irrefutable fact and people get upset when they hear it. But it's the truth."

The three Shakurs entered their new home for the first time sight unseen—and it was not a tableau to behold. The place was a dump, with paint chipping from the ceilings, floors slanted at strange angles, rodent droppings situated along the floorboards, and paper-thin walls that welcomed in bitter winter air. There was no phone. No heating unit. The pipes froze. Once Lisa and Jamal moved out, Tupac slept mattress to floor in a coffin-sized bedroom, while his mother and sister laid out their mattresses and box springs in the dining room.

"There was nothing good about that home," said Set Shakur. "It was disgusting from the start. Everything in our lives was traumatic. That move—trauma. All trauma." In particular, she recalled the rats—toaster-sized creatures who entered and exited the kitchen through gaping holes in the floor. Years later, Set could still hear the haunting nighttime sounds of monstrous vermin tiptoeing through the house. "Those rats ate our food," she recalled. "And once they got in it, we couldn't touch it."*

To his credit, Tupac made his little room work. Before leaving, Jamal had covered the cement floor with a greenish-blue Astroturf. The walls were paper-like plywood, and Tupac decorated them with images of his heroes—Bruce Lee, LL Cool J, New Edition, Sheila E. "In every corner," wrote Staci Robinson, "were cups half-filled with sunflower-seed shells, a habit he had developed shortly before they left New York." By near any measure, the quarters were condemnable. Yet for a kid who had never had a room to himself (or, really, anything to himself), there was magic to it. It was a dump. *His* dump.

The neighborhood matched the interior. Many of Greenmount Avenue's houses had fallen into disrepair, but attentive parents wisely kept their children from spending much time on the streets. "My one prayer back then was, 'Lord, just let me make it out of high school and survive,'" recalled Kobi Little, a Black Baltimorean. "You had drug dealers all over

---

* As an adult, Set agreed to attend therapy. "I've gone through so much in my life—sexual abuse, emotional abuse, poverty," she said. "But the first thing I said to the therapist was 'We had rats.'"

who had all these nice things—cars, gold, jewelry, leather. And everyone wanted it. So one way or another people got it. Usually either by selling heroin or sticking people up."

As Afeni set about finding a job, Tupac entered yet *another* school—he enrolled as an eighth grader at Roland Park Middle School three months after the academic year began. Located three miles away on Roland Avenue, the school was known as a "citywide magnet," which meant students from across Baltimore could attend. Approximately six hundred young teens composed Tupac's grade, and classes were capped at thirty per room. "It was a really good school," recalled Donyale Smith, Tupac's classmate. "We had Black kids, Asian kids, white kids, Hispanic kids. It was definitely more of a mix than most kids were probably used to."

That diversity, however, was limited. Homeroom placement was designated by test scores, and Smith rightly recalled that her homeroom class with Tupac was filled by twenty-eight Black students—and a gawky white kid named William Yates. "I hate to say it," she said, "but a lot of the kids I was with were always in trouble."

"It was a lot of wealthy white kids who had all the advantages," added Shawna McCoy, a classmate. "Every year they'd come to the poor neighborhoods and take the best and brightest of us Black kids. Then they'd put us all in a class together."

Tupac arrived in November, and—as was the case in White Plains—he immediately stood out. His name, to begin with, was unusual. What the heck was a Too Pack? But it was more than that. Though later in life he embodied a large persona, at Roland Park he was a runt. "Tiny," recalled Michelle Carter, a classmate. "With feet that pointed out. He literally walked like a duck." He also smelled bad—a kid in need of a deodorant stick. "A lot of the students used to look at him like being a bum," Carter said. "You could tell he didn't have much money. He didn't have stylish clothing." Tupac owned two pairs of thrift-store-purchased pants—Lee jeans and black suit pants. Both were too long. He styled his hair in a mangled high-top fade, but it was sloppy and slanted, with no true definition. "And his teeth were really bad," said Carter. "Kinda gross."

Tupac wore braces. But not normal, quality orthodontist-approved braces. These were more like bargain-basement metal plates that filled a portion of his mouth. His teeth were spread apart and stained, Carter recalled, almost as if someone had painted them to match a glass of iced coffee. At an age when boys start liking girls and girls start liking boys, nobody showed the slightest bit of interest in Tupac. He asked multiple classmates out, and was summarily rejected. "Girls laughed about him," Carter said. "I didn't. He was nice. But the smell, the teeth, no money, so small. Tupac was no catch, I can tell you that."

When he wasn't being ridiculed and ignored, Tupac was writing. Always writing. Classmates remember him walking through the hallways carrying a notepad, jotting down words and thoughts with a blue Bic pen. When asked, he told people he was creating a play for his future as an actor (according to an old Roland Park Middle School library record, in February 1985 Tupac twice took out *The Young Actors' Workbook*, by Judith Roberts Seto). There was no reason to believe him. Or not believe him. He was the quiet new smelly kid with the screwy name. He was marginalized.

Then, one day during Mrs. Gee's math class, Tupac Shakur emerged. Carter was sitting in her chair, listening to a lesson, when Octavius Johnson, a classmate who had a crush on her, started to fire off insults. It was adolescent jilted lover stuff—"Why are you being a bitch? Stop being such a bitch"—but the undersized, stained-gap-toothed kid heard enough.

"Yo, don't talk to her like that!" he barked. "Don't call her that!"

Johnson—bigger, presumably stronger—asked Tupac what he planned on doing about it.

"Well," Tupac said, "how about I fuck you up?"

Johnson opened his mouth to laugh, and Tupac shocked everyone in attendance by firing off a left fist into his teeth. Down went Johnson.

"Tupac beat him up," Carter said. "Beat him up good. I knew Tupac liked me, because he told me once. But . . . I dunno. I think he liked every girl at one time or another.

"But I can always say Tupac Shakur punched someone in my defense. That's pretty cool."

As he navigated his way through life, Tupac Shakur rarely spoke of his brief time at Roland Park. It was seven largely miserable months, and when his last day wrapped, he left and refused to look back.

And yet, through the brown teeth and the raggedy clothing and the indifference of the opposite sex, Tupac found someone within the long gray hallways whose presence would prove life-changing.

Like Tupac, Dana "Mouse" Smith was an eighth grader in Mrs. Gee's homeroom class. Also like Tupac, he was a creative soul, always writing in a notepad, always jotting down thoughts and observations. Decades later, Smith recalled Tupac's first day at Roland Park, when he entered Mrs. Gee's classroom and slid into a chair that already belonged to an obese student named William. When William returned from the bathroom, he demanded Tupac rise.

"I don't see your name on this seat," Tupac snapped back.

Years earlier, William had mangled his hand in a lawn mower accident. He was known, according to Smith, as "the dude with no nail." You did not fuck with the dude with no nail.

"Get out of my seat!" William said.

Tupac rose, but begrudgingly. It was an uncomfortable moment that stuck in Smith's brain. This new kid was no punk.

When he wasn't at school, Tupac could be found in his bedroom, on his mattress atop the blue Astroturf, listening to rap, studying rap, writing rap. The boom box he'd long ago received from Legs Saunders remained his prized possession, and the buttons were smoothed down from Tupac pressing play, then stop, then rewind, then play, then stop and rewind and play again. He didn't enjoy academics, but he loved studying music.

Although he thought of himself, rap-wise, as MC New York, with the move south came the adaptation of a second hip-hop name: Casanova Kid. It was unintentional irony—Tupac Shakur was anything but a Casanova. Yet, as a fan of LL Cool J, the ultimate hip-hop ladies' man, Tupac liked the idea of shape-shifting and becoming something he wasn't. If, in real life, he was the impoverished, gap-toothed son of a drug addict, on paper he could be anything he chose. Music, he learned, was the ultimate mental vacation.

At Roland Park, Tupac's English teacher was a stern woman named Thomasina Porter. He and Carter sat next to one another in the class, and bonded over their disdain for the instructor. "She was mean just to be mean," Carter recalled. "She liked embarrassing students." As an assignment, Porter had all students write a poem, with the knowledge that, come Monday, they'd be reading it aloud to the class. One by one, with sweaty palms and cracking adolescent voices, the pupils rose and read.

When it was his turn, Tupac stood. His poem was an ode to the joy of summer, only instead of reading it, he rapped it. Mouse, sitting a few rows up, was gobsmacked. "It was like a rap, but it was a poem," he recalled. "The poem was nothing like anybody had heard before. We looked at this guy, you know, with the flop-sided hairdo and half braces. And everybody just looked at him a little bit different after that."

Later that day, while riding the bus back home, Mouse and Tupac got to talking for the first time. Unlike the newcomer, whose approach to music was strictly lyrical, Mouse practiced the art of beatboxing, which in the moment was being perfected and mainstreamed by Darren "The Human Beat Box" Robinson of the hip-hop trio the Fat Boys. Tupac had absorbed endless hours of music, but never before had he been in the presence of a peer who could create so many beeps, blurps, and murmurs. The boys bonded quickly (Mouse wisely insisted Tupac stick with MC New York, not Casanova), and were soon spending much of their free time together. Though neither teen was even remotely wealthy, Mouse's life was blanketed with a security Tupac's lacked. He lived in a three-bedroom apartment with two uncles, a sister, his mother, his aunt, and two grandparents. And even though money was tight, Mouse's grandmother made sure he attended school in the latest fashions.

With no spare dough for musical development, Tupac and Mouse relied on ingenuity. In a small park near their homes in the Pen Lucy neighborhood sat a large plastic bubble-like structure. Initially designed as a play place for tots, it had been overtaken by the homeless and used as a bathroom. "It smelled like piss," Mouse recalled. "But the acoustics were crazy. You couldn't get acoustics like that nowhere." Armed with their boom boxes and cassette tapes, the boys braved the stench and recorded songs. Mouse knew his pal had talent. Classmates, however, weren't feeling it. "[Tupac's] offerings were always met with the same indignant and unpleasant looks from everyone around, who would almost cringe at the sound of unfamiliar lyrics," Darrin Bastfield, a friend of both boys, wrote in his memoir. "He hadn't the clothes and he hadn't the dancing ability.

And they saw nothing to be appreciated. They often asked Mouse why he hung out with this strange-looking reject."

Unlike so many of the other students at Roland Park, Mouse didn't sit in judgment of Tupac. He saw the holes in the kitchen and didn't care. He was well aware of Tupac's financial situation, and didn't care. Tupac's home life was a disaster—on the times people came across Afeni, she was often smoking a Newport and/or high from the latest hit. "Afeni was cracked out in Baltimore," said Yaasmyn Fula, her longtime friend. "Sometimes I'd come down from New York, get the kids for the weekend, then bring them back." Afeni wanted to get clean. Tried to get clean. Aspired to straighten out. "Afeni was a very complex person," said Watani Tyehimba, another longtime family friend. "She would give you the shirt off her back, but she'd also take your shirt." Afeni enrolled in a program to learn data entry on computers, then took a temporary, low-paying job entering information for a law firm. Despite pride and hubris begging her otherwise, for the first time she filed for welfare and food stamps. At one juncture she sent Tupac to a pawnshop to sell off some gold earrings, then used the money to buy meat and a few bags of potatoes. There was no other choice—her children needed to eat.

"Their lives," said Fula, "were without hope."

For Tupac, music was an escape from it all.

He needed it desperately.

They called themselves the East-Side Crew.

And while it was hardly original (Tupac and Mouse *were* from the northeast side of Baltimore), the name made perfect 1985 sense.

This was a year when rap music was heavily into crews. There was 2 Live Crew. Doug E. Fresh and the Get Fresh Crew. The Juice Crew. Tuff Crew. Find a multi-person hip-hip outfit, odds were you'd find yourself a crew.

So, yeah, long before Tupac Shakur emerged as an international icon, he was one-third (with Mouse and a boy named Kevin McLeary) of the East-Side Crew, preparing to make its professional (i.e., in front of people with actual ears) musical debut on a February night in 1985, at the Cherry Hill Recreation Center in South Baltimore.

All these decades later, the beforehand details are blurry, but the event itself is not. The headliner would be a Brooklyn-based Jamaican named Kurtis el Khaleel, whose song "Fresh Is the Word" was about to land itself on the *Billboard* Hot Dance Single Sales chart.* Up-and-comer status gifted el Khaleel's group, Mantronix, with the glory of a four-hundred-dollar gig at the rec center, home to youth basketball games, baton-twirling competitions, after-school child care, and—on occasion—community concerts.

For Tupac and Mouse, opportunity was opportunity. This wasn't about money (there was none) or record deals (there would be none). It was about the chance.

Mouse had been to the Cherry Hill Recreation Center before. Tupac had not. In his naïve mind, he was expecting . . . well, if not Madison Square Garden, at least a decent facility with seats and concessions. Instead, the Cherry Hill Recreation Center was dumpy and a bit grim. When Tupac and Mouse entered (along with their DJ for the night, a local man in his mid-twenties who identified as "Buddha"), they were surprised to see Mantronix on the stage, already performing before a small yet packed crowd of entirely Black and Brown faces. When Mantronix finished, a second act—the rapper Just-Ice—did a brief set. At that moment, it occurred to the two novices that the show was, sans explanation, going in reverse order.† The East-Side Crew would take the stage *after* the bigger acts.

It went well. They played five songs, and, Mouse recalled years later, "We really didn't get any boos or nothing." They sounded professional, moved stiffly, received enough applause to feel good about themselves. Afterward, they were approached by Virgil Simms, Mantronix's manager and a Jive Records A&R executive, who praised the teens for their poise. He expressed some light interest in signing them to a management deal, but— according to Bastfield—Afeni was resolute that her thirteen-year-old son would focus on school, not a music career.

"Tupac," Mouse recalled, "cried about that."

The summer of 1985 was not so wonderful for Tupac and his family.

Though the row house at 3955 Greenmount Avenue was an icebox in

---

* Yes, this was a thing.
† Odds are they were a late addition, and inserted into the lineup without much thought.

the winter, Baltimore's humid summer days transformed it into an oven. There were a couple of small fans that sometimes worked, but no central air-conditioning. To sit inside, roasting alongside the rat excrement and mold, was slow death.

Tupac and Set returned to New York City, via train, to visit family for a couple of weeks, and that, too, was something of a shitshow. On the one hand, Tupac desperately missed the Big Apple. Yet far removed from the joyful days of hanging out on the stoop with friends and cousins, he now faced the crushing reality that most of his relatives were hooked on either cocaine (best-case scenario) or crack. Four of his cousins were in prison, as were a handful of childhood friends he had grown up with. Having watched his mother's devolution through the years, Tupac hated to be in the presence of addiction. He likened drug addicts to walking zombies. Why couldn't these fuckers get themselves straight? Hell, why couldn't *his mother* get herself straight? What was more important to her—her children or the high?

Although her son was unaware at the time, even on welfare Afeni oftentimes failed to make rent, and would delay eviction from the row house by having sex with a man named Roy, the building's landlord. She was not proud of this, just as she was not proud of her dependence on drugs.

That September, Tupac enrolled for his freshman year of high school. He was now fourteen, but saddled with tragic dental work and an Olive Oyl physique. "Scrawny dude," said Laray Rose, a classmate. His new stomping ground was Paul Laurence Dunbar High, located a half-hour city bus ride away. In Baltimore's pre-desegregation days, Dunbar had been one of two Black high schools, and it maintained a sterling reputation well into the 1980s. Much like Roland Park, Dunbar drew students from myriad neighborhoods. It was fairly big (approximately 1,300 total students), Black (there were no whites in Tupac's freshman class of 239), and well regarded for its affiliation with the around-the-corner Johns Hopkins Medical Center (Dunbar had a top-shelf nursing apprenticeship program) and its nationally praised basketball program. Over the past decade, Dunbar had produced some of America's finest players, including Wake Forest point guard Muggsy Bogues and Georgetown forwards David Wingate and Reggie Williams. "It was known as one of the best academic institutions for the Black students of Baltimore," said Alejandro Danois, author of *The Boys of Dunbar*. "Dunbar served as a hub for the community."

As had been the case at the start of eighth grade, Tupac showed up at Dunbar knowing nobody. Mouse, his best (and only) close friend, attended Northern High School. Tupac was on his own.

On the first day of school, Dunbar's freshmen were told to wait outside in a single-file line, and enter the building one by one. "Tupac was standing behind me," recalled Devena Allen, a classmate. "I looked down and I was like, Why is he standing like that? He had these crazy feet that pointed in weird angles."

Allen was far from bashful.

"Boy, your feet are crooked," she said.

Tupac looked down. He was wearing pin-striped Lee jeans and brown thrift-store-purchased dress shoes.

"What's your name?" she asked.

"Tupac Shakur," he replied.

"Tupac Shakur?" she said. "What kind of name is that?"

"My mother was a Black Panther," he explained. "It means strong and powerful warrior."*

Tupac said his family had recently relocated from New York, and that he didn't want to be there.

"I don't care about this school," he said. "It doesn't mean shit to me."

Over the next several weeks, he made sure to let everyone know he had no desire to attend Dunbar. He also created a story explaining why the Shakurs came to Baltimore. According to young Tupac, the violence of New York ran them out of town—"He told me someone got shot in his house up in New York and died," recalled Steven Gregory, a classmate. "So they escaped to Baltimore."

It was not true. But if his classmates figured him to be a street-hardened kid out of the Big Apple, who did it hurt? It certainly wasn't the first time Tupac created a narrative for himself, and it wouldn't be the last. Strolling from class to class, he introduced himself as "MC New York," and bragged not merely of his work as part of the East-Side Crew, but as an inevitable

---

* That's not exactly what it means. But close enough.

future star. "He would say all the time that he was gonna be famous," said Gregory. "'I'm gonna be famous, bro! You're gonna remember me, bro!' It wasn't a guess to him. He was certain of it."

Tupac lived multiple rap existences. Outside of school, he could be found alongside Mouse, working on new rhymes, new beats, trying to uncover opportunities to perform. That October, he spotted a flyer that read, in bold black lettering, RAP CONTEST! Baltimore's Enoch Pratt Free Library was celebrating its one hundredth anniversary with a special competition—*write and perform the best library-themed rap song, win $100!*

As soon as he heard of the opportunity, Tupac hunkered down in his bedroom, lined notebook paper before him, black pen in hand. Beneath the title LIBRARY RAP, he wrote away:

> *Because reading and writing are important to me*
> *That's why I visit the Pratt Library*

It took the fourteen-year-old no more than thirty minutes. He submitted "Library Rap" a day later, survived the semifinals, and was invited to perform the song at the Pratt Library's Pennsylvania Avenue branch the following week. With a hundred or so onlookers seated in chairs positioned in a semicircle in the library lobby, the contestants took turns busting rhymes. Some were good. Most were bad. A few were awful. The East-Side Crew—Tupac, Mouse, and McLeary—reached the finals, where they squared off against a platoon of adorable preteen girls whose song was simple and unimaginative and . . .

"Library Rap" took second.

It was a gut punch. Mouse handled the setback well. His friend, however, did not.

"Tupac," he recalled, "wanted to stop rapping forever."

Back at Dunbar, Tupac told no one of the loss. He considered himself the baddest MC in all of Baltimore, and to lose to a bunch of girls didn't sit well. He brooded and pouted and replayed the event in his mind.

At school, Tupac didn't have a ton of friends, but life wasn't all bad. In geometry class, he sat directly behind a large-headed sophomore named

Sam Cassell, a rising basketball star who would go on to a fifteen-year NBA career. "He talked a lot—yap, yap, yap," said Cassell. "I also talked a lot, so we got along well. I didn't know much about the Black Panthers, but he was always talking about his mom, her history. He was a cool kid."*

Though Tupac played no sports (again, he was as athletic as a fig), he had a crush on a classmate named Woodena Ferguson, and liked accompanying her to the basketball games (in his mind, it was a date; in hers, it was not). He went out of his way to offer Cassell energetic pep talks ("Y'all gonna win today, right! You better represent us, Sam! Represent us!"), then cheered and pumped his fists. "He was trying to impress me," recalled Ferguson. "He was a nice guy. Really fun. But I didn't like him like that. He was too small and he wore tight pants."

As a student, Tupac was forgettable. His grades were in the Cs and high Ds, and he missed a good number of classes. During first-period homeroom, he picked out a chair in the back row, right next to Brian Gault, a fellow freshman. Within days, the two figured out that if they left campus for lunch (students were granted this luxury), school officials never updated attendance rolls to mark their return. "That created a monster as far as Tupac and some of the stuff we did," said Gault. "We left and just never came back." Because Tupac lived closer to Dunbar than Gault, the two would ditch campus, take the bus to Greenmount Avenue, sit on the front porch, and smoke weed. One frigid day, Gault requested to use the bathroom.

"Fuck," Tupac replied. "Why didn't you go when we passed a store?"

"It didn't dawn on me then," he said. "But I have to go now."

Tupac scowled at his friend. "Fuck," he said. "Come on."

Tupac unlocked the front door and poked his head inside. Nobody was home. "Go on," he said to Gault. "Bathroom is in the corner."

He entered—and what hit him wasn't the mess (it was messy) or the stench (it smelled terrible). No, it was the temperature. If it was thirty

---

* In 1993, when Cassell was a rookie with the Houston Rockets, he was eating at George's, a Los Angeles soul food restaurant, when Tupac entered. "I called out his name," Cassell recalled. "He had a big smile on his face. 'Yo, Sam! We made it, Sam! We made it!' He said he'd holler at me. I never saw him again."

degrees outside, it had to be ten degrees inside. "It was way colder in there than it was in the fresh air," Gault said. "Fucking unbearable. Humans shouldn't have lived there. And, at that moment, I felt terrible, because I realized he was embarrassed of his life."

Oftentimes, Tupac and Gault wound up whiling away lunch (and beyond) at the Old Town Mall, a run-down shopping center two hops and a skip from Dunbar. They spent hours inside the arcade, working their way up from Glass Joe and Piston Hurricane in *Punch-Out!!* Tupac loved the arcade—the smells, the sounds, the lights. It felt life-affirming. One day, in between games, he nudged Gault and said: "I've got two goals. Just two. I wanna put some damn heat in my house, and I wanna be able to afford studio time."

Gault was surprised. "Studio time?" he asked.

"Man, I would *live* in the studio," Tupac said. "I don't care if it's a fucking shed out back. I would never, ever leave."

Though he was only fourteen, Gault's heart broke for his friend. Like Mouse, he didn't come from wealth. But Gault always knew there'd be food on the table and heat making winter nights tolerable. "Tupac's life was awful," he said. "There were no comforts." Sometimes, Tupac stared longingly at the mall's store windows, knowing he could afford none of it. Warm winter jackets taunted him. Sleek parachute pants laughed at him. A six-pack of socks, a satchel of clean Fruit of the Loom underwear, cozy pajamas—nothing was within reach. Even shoppers nibbling on, say, a slice of pizza seemed to be mocking him. He couldn't afford it.

Gault was an intermediary for a bunch of neighborhood guys who sold drugs, and he asked Tupac if he'd like to make some extra money slinging product. "I didn't love the idea," Gault said. "But he was *so* poor."

"Oh, fuck, yeah!" Tupac said. "Let's go!"

Gault told Tupac he would hook him up with the lightest drug possible (marijuana), but that he could not, under any circumstances, deal from the corners of Greenmount.

"Why not?" Tupac asked.

"Bro," Gault replied, "you're not from around here and you're not very street-smart. Those dudes on your block will never let you get away with it. They'll fuck you up and leave you dead."

"I ain't afraid of them," Tupac fired back.

Gault wasn't having it. Tupac talked tough. But it wasn't real machismo. It was pretend. Less than a year earlier, Tupac and Mouse had been in line to see the movie *Beat Street* at the Boulevard Theater. A fight broke out, and a teenager was killed. Tupac witnessed the boy being shoved through the cinema's glass front door—and it haunted him. Many of his peers had already witnessed death. For Tupac, a sensitive soul trying to wear a rough exterior, it was too much. "I'm not hooking you up to see you get killed," Gault said. "Seriously, you're not *that guy*."

Over the next couple of weeks, Gault connected Tupac with the bare minimum amount of weed—roughly twenty-five dollars' worth per week. He was inarguably the worst drug dealer in the history of Maryland—a state founded in 1632. He didn't know how to approach people, or when. He wasn't sure how to charge customers, or collect. In two months as a dealer, he made less than a hundred dollars. "He also got some extra work sweeping the ground out front of a convenience store," Gault recalled. "Cigarette butts and stuff. Which was a good thing, because his future wasn't on the street corner."

Gault was not musically inclined, but he felt he knew talent when he saw it. And what he saw in his new friend was brilliance. During his time at Dunbar, Tupac arrived most mornings with three thick binders jammed with loose-leaf paper. He'd caress them as one does a newborn. One day Gault asked, "Pac, what is all this shit?"

"Poetry," he replied. "I have a poem for everything."

"Bullshit," Gault said.

"Try me," Tupac replied.

"And it was crazy, because I'd say 'Valentine's Day,' and Tupac would go through his binders and pull out a beautiful Valentine's Day poem," said Gault. "I'd say, 'Death,' and there'd be a poem about dying. And it wasn't rap. It was poetry. But I don't think Tupac necessarily saw rap and poetry as different entities. He was a poet, therefore he was a rapper. He was a rapper, therefore he was a poet."

When he was hanging with Mouse, Tupac was part of the East-Side Crew. At Dunbar, he found different guys to perform with. Though rap had yet to fully break through to mainstream America, inside his urban high school it was the music of youth. From Public Enemy and Salt-N-Pepa to Run-DMC and Kool Moe Dee, hip-hop reigned.

Tupac formed a particular kinship with James Moore, a fellow freshman whom everyone at Dunbar knew as "Chico." Born into poverty in the shadow of old Memorial Stadium, Chico had light mocha skin, greenish-brown eyes, and a tail that dangled from the back of his head. "He looked just like J. T. Taylor from Kool and the Gang," Laray Rose, a classmate, said. "Just smaller." On those days when he didn't cut out for lunch, Tupac would find a chair inside the cafeteria alongside Rose and Moore. "I had this really nervous habit of making beats on the table," Rose recalled. "Just with my hands—*Bop! Bop! Pa-bop! Bop!* We'd be laughing about it, and then Tupac would start rapping over it. Then Chico would start rapping over it, too. Everything came together."

The trio would stroll the hallways, rapping as one. Then arrive to class and keep rapping. Then pull up at lunch, still rapping. After school, they'd sit on the Dunbar steps and rap. Then head over to Chico's basement and rap some more. Initially, Chico was sort of the front man. He sounded like an unpolished Darryl "DMC" McDaniels—hardened edges, good flow. Tupac mainly wrote the lyrics, and Rose was the DJ/beatbox. "We knew each other's lines by heart," said Rose. "We were dope."

Rose, Chico, and Tupac made their official debut at the annual Dunbar talent show, a staple event held in the school auditorium that brought out singers and rappers, dancers and actors, jugglers and ventriloquists. "It was *the* thing," said Timothy Simon, a classmate. "If you wanted to express yourself, this was the place." As freshmen, Rose, Chico, and Tupac were relative unknowns. Newcomers tended to watch the show, not participate. "Ninth grade, you're supposed to keep quiet," said Gault. "Not Pac." Most of the other acts featured students dressed up in costumes or snazzy duds. Tupac wore the same outfit he'd had on at school during the day—Lee jeans, black shirt. Though classmates don't remember the precise song, many recall Tupac grabbing the microphone, stepping forward, "and owning it," said Yolando Moody, a freshman. "I knew he liked rap and I knew he wanted to rap. But I didn't know he *could* rap. It shocked me."

The trio won ("No money," said Rose. "Just glory"), and proceeded to perform three or four more times at small house parties.

Mostly, Tupac and his friends kicked back, smoked weed, talked shit, and dreamed of bigger things. One day, he and Simon were sitting on the porch, sharing a spliff. They could spend hours ruminating on all topics from MCs to movie stars to Dunbar's coed hotness.

"We're talking, and Tupac gets real serious," recalled Simon. "He told me he had a dream the night before that he was doing a show and fifty thousand people were watching. He said it was the greatest dream ever. The kind you don't want to end."

Tupac, Simon said, took a long drag. "You think it can happen?" he asked his friend.

Simon was no expert on the process of making it big. He was, like Tupac, a poor Black teenager in Baltimore just trying to navigate high school. But he lived for rap, and listening to Tupac bust rhymes felt bigger than Greenmount, bigger than Dunbar, bigger than Baltimore.

"Bro," he said, "if anyone around here can do it, it's you."

Chapter 5

School for the Arts

Toward the end of her son's freshman year at Dunbar High, Afeni Shakur was standing outside her home when a car screeched across Greenmount Avenue and slammed into a dog. The noise was loud enough to draw the attention of Tupac and Set, who bolted out the front door and toward the scene of the accident.

Alas, by the time they arrived, the vehicle had sped off. The mutt, however, had not. It lay there, mid-street, sprawled out in its own blood. "I was crying," recalled Set. "Screaming, 'Save the dog! We need to save the dog!'"

Although the Shakur pad was located in a rough part of Baltimore, across Greenmount Avenue were more-expensive homes with lawns and driveways and (gasp!) white people. As the three Shakurs lingered over the prone canine, two white women—Gail and Karen—emerged from their abode. This was their pet.

After digesting the hellscape before them, one rushed to get the car as the other cradled the animal in her arms. Tupac, not yet fifteen, watched in silence, tears streaming down his cheeks. When the victim was placed into the vehicle, Tupac asked if he could come along to the animal hospital. The women nodded, and he hopped in.

A few hours later, atop a gurney, the dog died.

Through their heartbreak, Gail and Karen felt genuine appreciation for the young Black boy with the oddball name and big heart. The following day, they invited him over for some cookies. It was, at first blush, an unusual setting for Tupac Shakur. Though the two lived but two hundred yards away, it could have been another solar system. He had known white people throughout his life, but, except for a handful of teachers, he didn't *know* white people. They were a foreign species, to be acknowledged and simultaneously kept at arm's length. White people, Afeni had told her children, weren't all bad. She had befriended and worked alongside some good ones. Why, Tupac was named *by* a white person. But . . . you never knew what they were thinking, or plotting, or inferring. White people, according to Afeni Shakur, had ulterior motives. They saw Blacks not as fellow humans, but as a lesser species. They reduced Blacks to clichés—drunk, high, dribbling a basketball, illiterate and incurious. She did not hate white people. She also did not trust them.

But Gail and Karen were kind. They had a home decorated with colorful paintings and photographs (the Shakur walls were mostly bare), and when Tupac's eyes gravitated toward Marc Edo Tralbaut's coffee-table book on Vincent van Gogh, they pushed the thick volume the teenager's way and encouraged him to leaf through the photographs. Though Tupac's musical tastes leaned toward R&B and rap, he had been exposed to a wide range of songs—classical, opera, even the occasional Johnny Cash and Charley Pride. One of his favorites was the Don McLean tune "Vincent (Starry Starry Night)," which he learned of from a one-dollar record Afeni had bought at a thrift store. An ode to van Gogh's pain and suffering, the song spoke to Tupac. He played it repeatedly and memorized the lyrics (*Now I understand / What you tried to say to me / And how you suffered for your sanity / And how you tried to set them free*).

So when he saw the book, Tupac felt a jolt. These two white women—not from the other side of the tracks, per se, but from the other side of the street—understood a language that he, too, felt.

A few days later, Tupac was stirred by a knock on the front door. He answered and saw Gail and Karen—holding in their hands a brand-new copy of Tralbaut's *Vincent van Gogh*. The Shakurs never felt comfortable having guests (especially white guests) step into their dilapidated home, but . . . what were they to do? The women entered and chatted for a few moments. Before leaving, one asked about Tupac's studies. He was a freshman at Dunbar, the boy explained, but he hated it. He really loved music and art and . . .

"Have you heard of the Baltimore School for the Arts?" Gail asked.

He had not.

"I used to teach there," she said. "It's something special."

On December 19, 1927, the Alcazar Hotel opened in downtown Baltimore.

This was no small thing. Located at Madison and Cathedral Streets, the hotel was grand and lavish and emblematic of what the city aspired to become. Namely, a destination for the wealthy, a place worth traveling to, a hot spot.

No expenses were spared. The hotel held 124 guest rooms, each one meticulously carpeted and wallpapered. There was a basement swimming pool and a projecting marquee over the sidewalk to keep the rain off visiting dignitaries. Bellhops scurried forward to grab your luggage. The manager—decked out in a three-piece suit—greeted VIPs in the lobby. The Jimmy Dorsey Orchestra played many a date at the Alcazar.

But as the decades passed, the city's mojo faded, and the Alcazar's glow dimmed. By the mid-1970s, it was, according to the *Sun*, "an esteemed relic." Before long, the Alcazar Hotel was empty and rat infested.

Then, a savior arrived.

In 1977, the building was sold for $850,000 to the City of Baltimore, which committed to turning the enormous structure into a school. But not merely any school—the city's first-ever school for the arts.

On April 10, 1979, the new entity—officially named the Baltimore School for the Arts—announced it would audition prospective students in music, dance, theater, and visual arts. There would be up to three hundred attendees, occupying grades 9 through 12. Tuition was waived for city residents, and ran fifteen hundred dollars if you came from outside the metropolis. Unlike Baltimore's other specialty high schools, this one would not consider academic records in its selection process. If you were a D student who tap-danced like Gregory Hines, you had a shot. If you were a mathematical dunce with Jane Fonda's acting chops, your odds were strong. The goal wasn't to bring forth the next Einstein. It was to bring forth the next Baryshnikov.

The Baltimore School for the Arts officially opened on September 15,

1980, and it was magical. Enter through the front doors and one was greeted by the sounds of stringed instruments, of operatic sopranos. The dean, David Simon, was a former Manhattan School of Music head whose lone goal was to foster creativity and inspire greatness. And it worked. Within a few years of its debut, School for the Arts grads were appearing in commercials, on TV shows, in off-Broadway and Broadway productions.

So when the white women from across the street told a young Tupac about this mythical land filled with fellow artistic souls, he didn't require convincing. In the spring of 1986, Tupac submitted the four-page application for the School for the Arts; a few months later he took the 3 bus to Howard Street, trotted two blocks, and entered the building for an in-the-flesh audition. Although he would later gain most acclaim for his musical work, in this moment he considered himself an actor. Really, a *thespian.* So he walked through the lobby, up the marble staircase, and into the grand auditorium, where a dozen or so other aspiring theater program attendees were told to take a seat in the shop room adjacent to the stage. He was joined by a handful of potential classmates, including Yvette Ebb, who had also attended Roland Park Middle School. They ran in different circles, but for both it was reassuring to spot a familiar face.

Tupac was not dressed for the occasion. Lee jeans. Ratty black T-shirt that read INTO NEW YORK in white block letters. A thin windbreaker. Boots. The room's inhabitants were nervous and quiet. A lot of pacing. Nail biting. "It's terrifying," said Teresa Altoz, among those waiting to audition. "All you're thinking about is not screwing up."

The silence did not last.

"Hey! You guys wanna hear my monologue?"

Um . . .

It was the skinny Black kid with a bad haircut.

"He whips out a hat," said Altoz. "And he says, really loud and excited, 'I came in costume!'"

With that, Tupac went to town.

"I'm like, Who the hell has the confidence to do this while they're waiting for the audition that can change their life?" said Altoz. "I mean, who the hell *is* this guy?"

When his name was called, he headed ("really, swaggered," said Altoz) toward the center of a large wood stage. To audition for the School for the Arts was no joke. The auditorium was Carnegie Hall–like, with dangling decorative lights and booming acoustics that could gobble up a meek voice. Before him, occupying four seats, were the designated judges, four BSA teachers: Richard Pilcher, Nancy Krebs, Donald Hicken, and Denise Diggs.

"*Whenever you're ready . . .*"

Two years earlier, Tupac had stepped on the stage of the Apollo to play Travis in *A Raisin in the Sun* for a Jesse Jackson fundraiser. Now, channeling that experience, he took a deep breath, cleared his throat, and dove into a speech delivered by Travis's father, Walter Lee.

Was he good? Great? Otherworldly? Memories are blurry. But years later, Altoz recalled a sound that wasn't all that common during the audition process: applause.

"He comes back into the room with a huge grin," Altoz said. "They *loved* him."

"He was a natural," said Pilcher. "That was obvious."

When he received the letter officially offering him a slot in the BSA Class of 1989, Tupac neither cried nor screamed. He digested the news as one would the arrival of mail. It was expected.

"I can tell you one thing," said Hicken. "Tupac Shakur always believed in himself. More than any student I knew, he owned self-belief.

"It was his superpower."

Imagine, for a moment, you are Tupac Shakur, and it is the Lord's year of 1986.

Over the past half decade, you have attended a dizzying number of schools. You have watched multiple relatives—including your mother— battle addiction. You were temporarily homeless. You have no money, crooked teeth, duck feet, a Salvation Army wardrobe, and zero game with the opposite sex. You're also short—maybe five foot five in Payless boat shoes. You view yourself as a future star, but the evidence doesn't exist. You're a nothing. A speck of lint. A poor Black kid sleeping alongside the rats. "Had to be the head of the household at nine, ten," said Set Shakur. "Raised on the streets, hungry, exhausted."

And now, this.

The School for the Arts.

The big time.

You belong here. And you are certain of this because you always knew you belonged here. You are special. Even if not everyone sees it, you do. You have an aura exuding from your body. A halo atop your head.

You just fucking know it.

"Tupac was here for one reason," said Hicken. "To blossom."

Six years before his arrival at BSA, the movie *Fame* hit theaters and caused audiences to reconsider the societal role of the insufferable artsy kid with purple hair, a booming voice, and a need to be seen. The film, based on Manhattan's High School of Performing Arts, was a phenomenon, and for a rare moment in time placed the teen who wanted to play cello and dance ballet on a higher plateau than the meathead quarterback.

His sophomore year of high school began on September 2, 1986, and as soon as he entered the School for the Arts, Tupac sensed it *immediately*. Unlike Dunbar, a sports school known for pumping out NBA prospects, BSA was a land of misfit toys.

"Baltimore," said Jeremy Kasten, a classmate, "is the only place other than New Orleans where you can get beat up for not being weird enough."

There was brown hair painted blue, blue hair painted red. Students sang as they walked through the hallways—sang *really* well. Danced, too. And the wardrobes—whoa. Pick a style (any style) and BSA attendees would sport it. Some wore suits and ties. Others broke out baggy jeans and Meat Loaf T-shirts. If you wanted to wear a top hat—wear a top hat. If you wanted to show up in shorts and a muscle T—do it. *Please*, do it. "And all those people with different styles were hanging out," recalled Yvette Ebb. "So you had the kids in dress clothing laughing with the kids with spiked hair. You found your people." The air reeked of pimple cream, creativity, and ambition. Most of the students came from the city and were of modest means. Roughly 20 percent, however, shuttled in from the wealthy suburbs. It was a rare blend of race, class, status, and world outlooks.

His entire life, Tupac had been surrounded by Black faces and Black voices, and that felt familiar. He was a by-product of American Blackness. But the BSA magic struck him like a smack to the forehead. At home, on Greenmount Avenue, he wondered whether his mom would be sober or strung out, whether bills would be paid and lights *might* be on. He loved Afeni, but he hated Afeni. She was unreliable and irrational. She could go off on cruel rants that reduced him to tears. At her most volatile moments, she wouldn't hesitate to beat her children with the nearest inanimate object. Or punch them with a closed fist. Set, his sister, was only ten, but was oftentimes left alone to fend for herself, no more nurtured or cared for than one of the rats under the floorboards. "Mom was there a lot," Set recalled. "But also gone a lot." Tupac was old enough to understand that Afeni's anger was the manifestation of trauma, but it didn't make things easier. He longed for the stability some of his friends enjoyed, but knew it was unattainable.

The Baltimore School for the Arts, however, was an immediate oasis. Wearing the same T-shirt on back-to-back days wasn't scorn-worthy. It was . . . inventive. Having thrift-store pants wasn't cheap. It was . . . trendy. His lopsided haircut and gapped teeth and ratty jeans with MC NEW YORK spray-painted up a leg made him stand out. And at BSA, everyone *aspired* to stand out. "I used to call him 'Toothpick' because he was so scrawny," said Sheareen Redlener, a classmate. "And he had this kick-fucking-ass style. He would dress like an old Black man. Like, he dressed like an old jazz musician or something. And he could wear whatever the fuck he wanted and pull it off. There's an old photo of Tupac wearing some sort of ridiculous pimp leather jacket, like a motorcycle jacket. And he looks fucking badass."

"For students like me and Tupac—Black, poor, from the projects— you'd stay at school for as long as you could," said Craig Scott, a classmate. "I needed an escape from Presstman and Baker, where I lived. Pac needed an escape from East Baltimore. School did that for us."

At Dunbar, an inability to shoot a basket was borderline treasonous. At BSA, no one could shoot a basket. Or swing a Louisville Slugger. Or throw a spiral. "I don't think anyone wanted to do those things," said Marisa Cohen, a classmate. "We were artsy kids. Sports had no place."

As part of the school's theater program, Tupac was assigned to an ensemble, which meant a dozen or so young actors in a room along with an instructor. School began every morning at 8:45, and for the first four hours you would be with your ensemble, working on the craft. The teachers rotated and the focus always changed. One day the theme could be, oh, the utilization of silence. The next day it could be a lesson on how to cry. Then, at one o'clock, you'd leave for different locations within the building to tackle academic courses—math, English, and science. There was a basement cafeteria adjacent to the school's smoking section (yes, *smoking section*), and teachers and students gathered over muffins, chocolate milk, and Marlboros. Instructors were referred to by first names. If students wanted to leave campus and grab lunch at the nearby Albert's Deli, they could. Hell, if they wanted to take a flight to Nairobi, they could. As long as they were back in time for the next period. "Think of the most free, liberated school ever invented," said Kittrell Decator, a classmate. "We were there."

Tupac was accustomed to a world where he had to conceal his vulnerabilities while projecting an air of resilient toughness. It was textbook machismo, reinforced for decades among Black men. You didn't cry. *Ever.* And if you did cry, more often than not an adult would hit you with a switch to the backside for doing so. Sensitivities were to be hidden. Yet here, within the safety of his ensemble, Tupac was being asked to sob and scream and giggle and guffaw and prance and sing and leap and crawl. He was being asked to grab hold of his pain and use it to summon creativity. "We spent weeks working on the Alexander Technique and just dropping our bodies [to the floor] over and over," recalled Redlener. "Being physically present and nothing else." It was unlike anything he'd ever experienced. The raps he'd been writing . . . the poems he'd been composing—they were, in hindsight, pulp. Words connected to words, but minus the depth of a true artist.

On one of Tupac's early BSA days, Donald Hicken, the head of the theater program and a veteran stage actor, told the class they were to form groups of three, and select a painting and a song that related to one another. Then they had to create a three-dimensional expressive dance routine to perform to the music. Tupac was placed with Redlener and Coretta

Washburn, both returning BSA students. There were assumptions made—Tupac was a Black kid from the bad side of Baltimore. He was the son of a Black Panther. "He would pick a rap song," Redlener recalled. "Of course."

Nope.

Tupac convinced his peers to roll with Don McLean's "Vincent," a soft, poetic ode to Vincent van Gogh's *The Starry Night*. It was a peculiar choice, made even more peculiar by the sight of a young Tupac prancing, doe-like, across the room as it blared from a pair of crude speakers. "It was the last thing I expected from him," said Hicken. Far from a competent dancer, a barefooted Tupac closed his eyes and slid to and fro. The song consumed him, just as Hicken had wanted from his pupils. "I didn't get it at first," said Redlener, "but if you listen to that song and you hear the lyrics, he completely identified with being Vincent van Gogh—a tortured artist with a lot to say and no one listening."

"Tupac grew up in neighborhoods where he was expected to be this thing," Hicken said. "But he wasn't. And he felt misunderstood."

Around this time, the BSA administration invited members of Tmu-na, an Israeli theater-movement group, to come to Baltimore and conduct workshops. Nava Zuckerman, the Tmu-na founder, was a performer's performer who said of acting: "Our creative energy comes from the tension of living on the edge. Everything comes from frustration, otherwise you are dull." She and her colleagues aspired to teach the youngsters how to act, but—more important—how to conjure the agony required *to* act. So they would sit in silence, sometimes for hours, and try to ensnare the invisible forces swirling around their heads. Or they would stand, eyes closed, like totem poles, attempting to breathe in the universe's textures. You are a horse. You are a fence. You are the wall. *Be the wall.*

In the company of rap friends like Mouse and Chico, Tupac sang the merits of LL Cool J and Public Enemy and Salt-N-Pepa. And he was being sincere. Hip-hop moved him. But his true love was a recently released duet from a pair of English singers, Peter Gabriel and Kate Bush, called "Don't Give Up." Tupac didn't merely like "Don't Give Up." He felt *possessed* by it. In particular, a verse from Bush ("Rest your head / You worry too much / It's going to be all right / When times get rough you can fall back on us / Don't give up") conjured all sorts of feelings. During one of the Tmu-na sessions, Tupac and two female classmates, Avra Warsovsky and Juliet Brown, did a freestyle dance routine as "Don't Give Up" played in the background. They lost themselves in the music. It felt as if they had somehow physically transformed into giant feathers drifting through the air. When it ended the three returned to their bodies and squealed with delight. "I remember us running down to the cafeteria right afterward," said Warsovsky, "agreeing we had experienced this mind-blowing moment together."

"Tupac," recalled Cameron Francis, a classmate, "was sort of like Puck from *A Midsummer Night's Dream*. He had that little wink and that sly smile, and he joked around, but never in a mean way. He just . . ."

A pause.

"He just wanted to be loved."

Classmates like the comparison. Tupac *was* Puck, the mischievous fairy who delighted in hijinks. He fluttered. He floated. He seemed to levitate. He sometimes walked the hallway sans shirt, wearing nail polish. Other times he arrived at BSA gripping a pink baby bottle, from which he would suck water via the nipple. He liked making up personas and occupying their skins. His favorite, "Red Bone," was a dirty older Black man who reveled in inappropriate comments. "He'd walk around, being Red Bone," said John Cole, a friend and classmate. "He'd keep it up forever and never break character." During those early ensemble days, Hicken emphasized trust as a cornerstone of the theater, so he had his students, one by one, stand on a riser and fall backward into the arms of their peers. When it was Tupac's turn, he leapt, flew . . . and plunged toward the ground, slipping through arms and fingers before—POW!—slamming onto the wood floor. "Oh my God!" Hicken said. "Are you OK?"

Tupac leapt to his feet. "All good!" he said. "Like new!"

"It's sort of like a metaphor," said Altoz. "We weren't ready for him—and neither was the world."

Of the twelve people in his ensemble, the one Tupac bonded with most was a kid named Seth Bloom—the perfect encapsulation of BSA. Short, Jewish, theatrical, and a product of the leafy Baltimore suburb of Baldwin, Bloom suffered from a congenital back condition that kept him from playing sports. Around age six, he realized he liked boys. "So I was a gay theater kid," he said. "Without any athleticism. That school was made for me."

Tupac and Seth made for an odd pairing, but they shared a willingness to try anything. Having long wanted to be a professional actor, Bloom wore his emotions on his sleeve, and hid nothing. And Tupac—well, he just went for it. Wherever Bloom went, Tupac went. Wherever Tupac went, Bloom went. One day Hicken took the ensemble on a field trip to Baltimore Center Stage, a nearby theater, to watch a matinee performance. Midway through the half-mile walk, Bloom turned to Tupac and said, "Wanna get a drink instead?"

They separated from the group and headed to the Owl Bar, known as a place where IDs need not be displayed. They ordered two beers, found a corner table, and smoked one cigarette after another. "Then we had a joint," Bloom said. "We were young and empowered and living our best lives."

Unlike Dunbar, where there was a strict divide between school and out-of-school universes, the BSA experience was a melding of lives. It wasn't merely the cliché Kumbaya of Blacks hanging with whites or gays hanging with straights. No, to be a Baltimore School for the Arts student was to party with classmates, drop acid with classmates, sleep over with classmates, sleep *with* classmates, sleep *with* teachers (it happened, according to several alums interviewed for this book). It was immersive. Not cultlike, but a cocoon of artsy kids who felt misunderstood by the outside world. If you were wealthy and white, it exposed you to poor and Black. If you were poor and Black, it exposed you to wealthy and white. Numerous were the days that, before classes began, Tupac split a six-pack of beer with a classmate. Numerous were also the days when, after school let out, Tupac and various ensemble members headed down to the Inner Harbor to just stroll and talk. "You're young and free and with your people," said Ebb. "It was special."

On the afternoon *Evil Dead II* dropped in theaters, Tupac, Kasten, and a small handful of classmates cut school, took the bus to a shady movie theater (recalled Kasten, "like a bump-and-grind burlesque house in a scummy downtown building"), got their hands on some industrial-grade hash, and watched in slouched glee-horror. "We're putting our heads under our coats and blowing smoke," Kasten said. "It was awesome." Within the week, Tupac invested in an *Evil Dead II* T-shirt that he wore every third day for the rest of the year. "He loved that movie," Kasten said.

Halloween fell on a Friday in 1986, and Tupac and a slew of classmates came to (of all the places) Greenmount Avenue to trick-or-treat up and down the dilapidated block. Before heading out, Tupac invited his friends into the row house to meet his mother. This was Tupac stepping far outside his comfort zone, as the school had taught him to do. He was trying to be less ashamed of who he was and where he came from. Plus, he had called beforehand to tell Afeni they were coming.

"We walked in," one classmate recalled, "and she was smoking crack."

It was awful. Afeni sat, alone and ghostlike in the dark, crack pipe aglow against her lips. The BSA students stared dumbfounded. None had ever seen crack up close. "Mom!" a humiliated Tupac screamed. "What the fuck are you doing?"

Afeni mumbled something, shooed her son and his friends away, and continued with the task at hand. She was in another mental dimension, and unaware of Halloween. Maybe unaware it was even October. As the students shuffled out the front door, Tupac pretended to be unfazed. "But you could see it," the classmate said. "He was crushed."

For Tupac, the biggest perk of Baltimore School for the Arts may well have been the girls, who actually seemed to notice him.

Although he would later become a hip-hop sex symbol, Tupac's earliest sexual experiences were dark ones. According to conversations he had with a close classmate, and confirmed by his sister, Tupac's first sexual dalliance had come at age fourteen, when he had intercourse with a cousin. The girl was also a teenager, and it only happened one time. As the years passed, Tupac—an open book on most subjects—never discussed the situation, save to note it was an offshoot of limited parental supervision. "Would *you* talk about it?" asked Set. "Would *you* be bragging?" His second time came with a friend of Afeni's. Like his first try, Tupac rarely discussed it. But he later confided in a girlfriend, Simi Cruise, "The next day I thought I was in love with my mom's friend. And she ignored me.

She was a woman, I was a boy. That changed my way of thinking about sex. It wasn't love. It was just sex."

How did this impact Tupac's psyche? It's hard to say. At Dunbar, Tupac had faced a steady string of rejections. Girls simply didn't take an interest in him. He was short, poor, funny looking, and shabbily attired. A nice guy, *but*. And it ate him up. For all the outer-leaning swagger, with the opposite sex Tupac felt like a loser. He knew he had game, only nobody wanted to play it.

At BSA, that changed. He was hooking up on the regular. Not sex, but drunk and/or high party make-outs. One girl one weekend. Another a different weekend. "It was a pretty fucking horny school," said Bloom. "We were artistic and experimental." Although mainstream American society was decades away from embracing homosexuality, the arts school doubled as a petri dish. One night, while at a class party, Tupac and Seth were downing shots of tequila and playing truth or dare. A classmate dared Tupac to kiss his gay friend. "So he did," Bloom said. "He kissed me. We kind of vamped it up, our lips touched. I know I wasn't the only boy Tupac kissed. When we were alone I always felt a thing. You know that sexual tension where you hold a glare a second or two too long, or you touch someone longer than normal? That was Tupac. My belief is he was somewhere between heterosexual and bisexual."

Melanie Hood was a classmate who didn't know Tupac well. She had a well-known crush on one of his ensemble cohorts, and the school was abuzz. "We were not friends, but Tupac pulled me aside and told me that he and the boy had engaged in a three-way with a girl who was also in the ensemble," Hood recalled. "He said, 'You're a nice young lady and I want you to know the truth before you start something with him.'" In telling the story decades after the fact, emotion overtook Hood's voice. "It was so loving and protective," she said. "What I always felt about Tupac was he was somebody who definitely liked girls, but he also seemed respectful toward women. Teen boys can be very predatory. He didn't have that."

In hindsight, some classmates chalk at least part of Tupac's sexual appeal to the curiosity factor—Black kid from "the wrong side of the tracks" meets white girl from money (who views it all as some grand societal experiment). It's an age-old trope, both ugly and common. Yet, in regard to Tupac, there was more. He had a swagger that caught the fancy of many a coed student. A confidence that exceeded his age. "He had the longest eyelashes," said Nancy Krebs, a voice teacher. "I remember telling him it wasn't fair that a young man should have longer lashes than any of the girls." Tupac was also slowly starting to fill out. Still skinny, but a bit more proportioned. "And he hit on *every* girl in school," said Sheareen Redlener.

For Warsovsky, a white Jewish junior, initial interest in the new classmate pertained to geography. "My mother's from Brooklyn," she said. "And I remember hearing that Tupac was from the Bronx. And, yeah, he was goofy. And tiny and adorable. But I had this thing for New York, and he exuded it." Avra and Tupac attended a school dance together, and she was simultaneously amused and mortified when, without warning, he broke into the Wop, the gyrational hip-hop dance. "It looked ridiculous," she said. "I was like, 'I'm not dancing with someone doing the Wop.' But he was really comfortable in his own skin. That was attractive."

Before long, Avra and Tupac were a couple. Not in any serious way, merely the hold-hands-in-the-hallway, make-out-in-the-stairwell high school sense. They attended weekend parties together, and Tupac impressed her with top-of-the-head raps and poems. "I laughed so much with him," she recalled. "He was special."

Avra was dating Tupac after ending a relationship with a hotheaded boy named Chuck who attended Northwestern High, located nine miles to the north. When Chuck caught wind of his ex's new relationship, he threatened to come down to BSA and wreak havoc. "I was freaking out," Avra said. "I was like, 'We're not even together anymore. This is ridiculous.'" Despite multiple pleas to her ex, Chuck promised that, come the following Monday, he would arrive on the front steps of the Baltimore School for the Arts and smack his replacement in the nose.

Avra warned Tupac. He was smaller than her ex, and far from the most coordinated kid in town

"Fuck that," he said. "I'm not gonna hide like some pussy."

That Monday, as promised, Chuck and two of his friends came to the school, seeking out Tupac. Although Avra begged him to stay inside, Tupac exited through the front doors, walked down the four steps, and approached Chuck, Clubber Lang–like. "The truth is, he was a nervous mess," said Becky Schnydman, a classmate. "He was terrified. It's the only time I ever saw a hint of anxiety in Tupac."

Tupac cleared his throat and clenched his fists.

"You here to see me?" he said.

To Chuck, it had to be a joke. This funny-looking alien was with *his* girl?

"Are you fucking her?" Chuck snapped back, nodding toward Avra.

"*What if I*—"

Whoosh. The three boys leapt toward Tupac, pummeling him with a series of punches to the face and body. By the time a couple of BSA classmates and security guards came to his rescue, Tupac was a bloodied bowl of oatmeal, lumped up on the steps and trying to save face.

He watched as Chuck and his friends departed.

"Keep walking!" he screamed. "'Cause I'll get you next time."

Chapter 6

Mary, Mary

The coffee is watery.

Mary Baldridge doesn't seem to care, perhaps because here, inside the understated Side Street Deli and Catering in Central City, Nebraska, one should not have particularly high standards for quality caffeinated beverages.

She takes a sip. Another.

"Not great," she says, "but it's the Midwest."

The date is September 22, 2022, and resting before Baldridge—on a table, peeking from a yellow envelope—are roughly 150 pieces of white paper. She sets down the ceramic coffee cup, raises her left hand, and shuffles through them, indifferent to the reality that the documents before her could fetch a small fortune on the open market.

"These are the letters," she tells a reporter. "This is what you came thousands of miles to see."

Baldridge is fifty years old and white, with long brown hair, a warm smile, an understated *Who, me?* way about her. She works as an office manager at a local accounting firm, has five grandchildren, and is married to a man named Tony who hunts ducks. When pressed, she acknowledges the weirdness of it all. How she wound up living in a Nebraska town with 3,078 people (Mary's great-aunt Margie died and she bought her house). How she married a guy who voted for Donald Trump ("He's evolving," she said, laughing). How, nearly four decades ago, she was the recipient of hundreds of love letters from a very horny Tupac Shakur. How the correspondence was sitting beneath her mother's bed in a cardboard box, forgotten about, until a few years ago.

"That all feels like another lifetime," she says.

A pause.

"Really, it *was* another lifetime."

And, with that, she is no longer in rural Nebraska, but back in Maryland. It's the fall of 1987, and Mary Baldridge is a fifteen-year-old sophomore at the Baltimore School for the Arts. A product of the theater program at nearby Chinquapin Middle School, she first walked the BSA hallways as a sixth grader, when a school production of *The Nutcracker* required a younger child to dance as Clara. Ballet, to Mary Jean (as she was called by family and friends), was an escape. She loved the feeling of losing herself in motion; of being one with the music. "I was hooked," she says. "Dancing became my reason to be."

She was admitted to BSA's dance program, and one day Sylvester Campbell, the program head, announced they would be performing *Firefly* at the Lyric, a Baltimore opera house. It was a ballet with a modern edge, and Campbell sought out someone from the acting corner of the school—a male student, preferably someone with some spunk—to handle a theatrical role. "Tupac got that job," says Baldridge. "And that's when we became connected and started spending time together."

Mary found Tupac . . . intriguing. He was mostly arms and legs. Skinny and goofy and all over the place. But he was also fun. Funny. Electric bolts seemed to shoot from his body. He asked lots of questions and talked a hundred thousand miles per minute. His laugh—a deep-throated cackle—filled a theater. And when he spoke to you, he had this way of locking in. "He was infectious," she said. "And his eyes were these twinkling twin flames that had a mischievous joy."

From the moment he spotted Mary, Tupac was hooked. Most of the BSA dancers were stick figures—giraffes with tiny breasts and booties. Mary Baldridge, by comparison, was a woman. She had developed early, and—especially in her dance leotard—the boys noticed. "My God, Mary was sexy," said Kittrell Decator, a classmate. "A body before the other girls had bodies. If you were a straight boy and you didn't have a thing for Mary, you weren't paying attention."

Because Tupac was a junior in the theater program, and Mary was a sophomore in the dance program, they shared no class time. That's why, once *Firefly* wrapped, the notes commenced. Tupac would write something and pass it to a friend of a friend, who then slyly made sure it wound up in Mary's hands. Then Mary would reply, and the letter would get back to Tupac.

They officially became a couple on November 2, 1987, and the notes that followed were, to quote Mary all those years later, "incredibly special. They tell the story of a really unique young man."

December 2, 1987
Dear Mary
Last night U hurt me so much. U R putting me through emotions that I have yet to experience. Last night, I realized that U can do 2 men what no one else can. . . .

December 9, 1987
My Dearest Marie, Beauty, lumberjack and angry ballerina!
I love you so much. I look at your picture and get lost in your face, your hair and your eyes . . .

On Christmas Eve, he handed her a six-stanza poem, written in block letters, titled "Always." It began . . .

NO JAIL COULD CONTAIN ME
NO ONE COULD RESTRAIN ME
FROM LOVING U ALWAYS

"He was sweet," says Mary. "Very sweet."
The letters arrived daily. Sometimes twice daily. Sometimes three times daily. Some were in script. Some were not. Most were on notebook paper. A few were on copy paper. He expressed concern for her family and her dancing. He wanted to know what movies she was watching. What television programs she enjoyed. He asked about her goals and dreams. He was listening to Randy Travis's "Forever and Ever, Amen" on repeat. He made her a tape featuring songs by everyone from Frank Sinatra and Stevie Wonder to Bob Marley and Everything but the Girl. He needed new pants.

He smoked too many cigarettes. He lamented having so few male friends. He very much liked the hickey she gave him. He was tired of his cousin Scott (visiting from New York) staying at the house. He dreamed of marrying her. Literally jotted down, "Will U marry me?" and "I will die if U don't marry me." He nicknamed her "Marie" and "Lumberjack." He wrote her a song called "4 yrs. 2 Come"—"*4 three months we've been together / more than just average friends / 2gether we discovered there's more 2 / being lovers and our love will never end.*" On Valentine's Day, he ordered Mary roses from Janda Florist and presented her a two-page love letter ("I can no longer look at the gentle waves of the ocean without being reminded of the grace u so modestly exhibit") that made her swoon.

Mostly (and age appropriately), he *really* wanted some action.

February 1, 1988: *When I go to the bathroom and I feel the soreness of my 'Ding-Ning', I think of u! I love u! I am so sore!*

Also February 1, 1988: *I want to be inside of u . . . I want to feel the warm moisture of your mouth around my erection while u're teeth gently nibble the sensitive portion of my erect member.*

February 18, 1988: *I'm so preoccupied with thoughts of making love. I'm so scared because I know that the only way to do it will be with some pain. I don't think we should do it yet! I changed my mind, we should do it!*

February 23, 1988: *I need u in the worst ways. I need 2 be with you very soon or I'll die.*

Mary was raised in an über-liberal household, and her parents, Jim and Margaret, liked Tupac from the start. They were active members of the local Communist Party, and his mother's Black Panther roots spoke to their sensibilities. Tupac spent much time inside their home, talking civil rights and economic inequalities. The passion in his voice stirred her folks. "My mom would launch into what was happening at the moment in Nicaragua, or how the policing in Baltimore's Black neighborhoods was abusive," Mary recalled. "She dove into the lion's den and never backed down. That was also Tupac. He was the exact same." Tupac signed up for a Young Communists League membership, and attended multiple meetings with Mary's family. He visited museums with the Baldridges. Enjoyed meals at their dining room table. At home, on Greenmount Avenue, chaos was the norm. He once called Mary from a pay phone near his row house, only to have the conversation punctuated by the sound of gunfire. "Shit—there's a shoot-out!" he yelled. "I've gotta go!" By contrast, inside Mary's house everything felt cozy.

The Baldridges owned a red Volkswagen van, and one day, while returning from a family trip, Margaret positioned herself alongside Mary in the back row.

"Is it time for a talk?" she asked her daughter.

"About what?" Mary replied.

"You and Tupac," Margaret said. "I think we need to talk about you getting birth control."

Mary turned bright red.

"Listen, he's a good kid," Margaret said. "We just want you to be careful."

Mary and Tupac spoke at length about sex. She was a virgin, but unopposed to sleeping together. He told her, via letter, that he had asked a female classmate for sexual guidance—but "her hyman [*sic*] broke before sex. So she couldn't give me advice about our situation. Hope you don't mind me discussing this with her." Mary had no idea about Tupac's traumatic previous sexual experiences.

At long last, roughly two and a half months into their relationship, it happened. A Baldridge family friend was leaving town for the night, and she offered Mary the use of her apartment.

"That," Mary said, "is where I lost my virginity. I was sixteen."

Was it good?

"Oh, Lord, no," she said. "We were on the floor. I was on my back. And it hurt everywhere. Rug burns all over. Very awkward. Age appropriate, but I did not enjoy it."

Tupac, on the other hand, left on cloud nine. He told Mary she was his sexual fantasy come to life, and that every moment felt like a merging of heaven and euphoria. "I can't wait to make love 2 U again!" he wrote in a follow-up letter. "I just wanted to tell you how much I love you!"

The relationship did not last. They broke up a few weeks later ("To The Girl I'm Not Talking To!" he wrote in a despondent note). Mary later learned Tupac had been cheating on her much of the time.

"But the memories," Mary said decades later, "are still special."

The letters a young Tupac Shakur sent to a younger Mary Baldridge during their time together tell the story of a high school kid in love, in lust, overflowing with passion, and longing for sensual pleasure.

They also, however, tell the story of a high school kid living in a state of upheaval. Inside the Baltimore School for the Arts, Tupac the junior was very similar to Tupac the sophomore—bouncy, loopy, excitable, itching for expressive moments. "His face shined," said his classmate Sheareen Redlener. "He exuded this beauty. Like his whole being was happy." Life on Greenmount Avenue, by comparison, was pure darkness.

"I don't know what to do," he wrote in one letter to Mary. "It's like everything leads up to money and I don't have it." He added that his mother was broke and his sister was broke and he felt like "everyone is demanding a lot. . . . I can't afford the prom or a car or driving school or jewelry that I yearn 2 buy 4 U."

Tupac twice brought Mary to his house to meet Afeni, and it went poorly. His mother was well-versed in Black men dating white women ("Fucking trophies," she would sneer). This girl—this ballet dancer, with her white features and her white upbringing and her white privilege and her white name—was all wrong. "She was not friendly to me in any way," Mary recalled. "You didn't have to be super perceptive to sense it."

In his notes to Mary, Tupac didn't hold back about home life. On February 10, 1988, he told her that Afeni was adamant he ditch the Young Communists League and focus more on his grades. He said that he dreamed of his mother suffering a deep, intense pain, and that the previous night he punched his bedroom wall until his hands were numb. "I intend to give her the coldest shoulder she's ever seen and make her life as miserable as she's made mine."

He offered similar sentiments in a follow-up letter the next afternoon, writing that while he felt like crying himself to sleep, he promised himself to never allow Afeni or poverty to evoke tears. "I feel like such a failure."

A month later, he told Mary that his mother was "truly pissing me off . . . [she] won't let me do anything. I'm going to have to start telling lies again."

In Afeni, Tupac saw nonstop contradictions. She could be loving and compassionate, then turn around and be cruel and abusive and emotionally vacant. She was a hard worker who landed a job as a data processor in nearby Columbia, Maryland. She was a drug addict who, on multiple occasions, turned to crack to ease the pain. She was prideful, strong, self-sufficient. She was also collecting $375-per-month welfare checks and food stamps—concessions to the poverty that drowned her. She was a Black Panther, something Tupac bragged about until everyone at BSA knew of her legacy. But she was a *former* Black Panther whose pride had withered.

"The last thing she wanted was to be dependent on the system," said Set Shakur. "But she also thought that somebody else . . . something else . . . somewhere else . . . would have showed up and supported us, or supported her, or protected us. She was always disappointed by the things that never came to be."

More than anything, Afeni Shakur walked with a palpable sadness. Her last husband, Mutulu, was now in prison. Her family was all back in New York and had little to do with her. Friends? *What friends?* She knew what people thought of her. She knew they considered her to be a has-been. A failure.

On April 4, 1988, Afeni—fed up with her son's unwillingness to listen, buried beneath a mountain of addiction, debt, and darkness, and in a toxic relationship with a new boyfriend who was both abusive and hooked on heroin—told Tupac he had to get the fuck out. Those were her words: *"Get the fuck out of my house."* They were stated on a Saturday morning, and she expected him gone within a few days.

"I saw him at school [on Monday] and he looked depressed and sad, and I'd never really seen him look down like that before," said Gerard Young, his friend and classmate. "He told me what happened. It was heartbreaking shit."

Later that day, Tupac wrote the darkest letter in his correspondence with Mary. He was departing home and striking out on his own. He could no longer stomach his mother, and would be stashing his clothing in a school locker and taking showers there before classes. "Starting Tuesday night I'll be on the streets. . . . Tomorrow I begin the life of the homeless. I love you very much. Please stand by me. Pray 4 me."

"It was so sad," Baldridge recalled. "He was in such pain."

Then a friend stepped in.

Two friends, actually.

Their names were John and Jada.

Despite his plans to plop down on a park bench, Tupac Shakur spent nary a night on the streets of Baltimore. That's because he had a pal who fully understood what it was to face hardship without the necessary support.

Not that John Cole and Tupac Shakur were particularly similar. Unlike Tupac, Cole—a recent Baltimore School for the Arts graduate who was two years Tupac's senior—was both white and fairly well-off. He came from a seemingly stable household and, from afar, looked to have it all. With striking blond hair and high cheekbones, and dating a beautiful BSA theater student named Jada Pinkett, he was your prototypical big man on campus, and many aspired to bask in the glow of his presence.

And yet . . .

Upon closer inspection, the kinship of Tupac and John made *some* sense. They first met during Tupac's sophomore year at BSA, when John was a senior whose base of operations was the basement smoking section. Even at a young age, Tupac loved Newports, and often spent his free school time lighting up alongside John and Jada.

Similar to Tupac, Pinkett was a product of inner-city Baltimore—"the blessed daughter of two addicts," she later wrote, whose mother, Adrienne, gave birth to her at age seventeen. In Tupac, Jada felt a kindred spirit, both Black and understanding of the complexities that came with the designation. Together, they walked the BSA hallways and waved and smiled and laughed and performed, but together they knew what it was to put on an act. Even in the liberal, hippie-dippie BSA universe, there were judgments. The teacher who called you "Hood." The classmate who asked you about your lips and nose. The small mannerism shifts. "There were no airs between us," Jada recalled. "We could be raw and authentic without the constraints of having to impress each other. You got what you got. There were no butterflies, no tingles in the body, no hot desire to be in each other's embrace. Rather, there was something far more important unfolding between us—a friendship of a powerful strength." Tupac and Jada were in the same ensemble, and they portrayed slaves in a production the school put on at the 1840s House, a Baltimore museum devoted to telling stories of the past. "Jada played a housemaid, and Tupac was a slave sneaking over to see her," recalled their classmate Kittrell Decator. "It was poignant."

If Tupac had passionate feelings toward Jada, he never let on. He said he loved her as one loves a cousin (said Jada: "When you have somebody that has your back when you feel like you're nothing, that's everything"), but also saw her flaws and shortcomings. Around Baltimore School for the Arts, Jada was not thought of warmly. She had that thing people deem annoying in actors: a heightened self-awareness of her own importance, beauty, and future stardom. Teachers thought her pretentious. Other students thought her arrogant and smug. In the BSA solar system, Jada deemed herself the sun. "If you weren't an ass kisser for her, she showed you no interest," said Teresa Altoz, a classmate. "At best, she was tolerated."

"She was very opportunistic," added Jeremy Kasten, also a classmate. "Inauthentic isn't the right word for someone from Baltimore. She was authentically herself, but that person was very self-interested and dismissive of others."

But Jada and Tupac were tight, and John and Tupac were tight, and Jada had Tupac check John out (said John, "Pac vouched for me, and after that Jada and I started talking"). Soon enough John and Jada were boyfriend and girlfriend—which meant they were all part of the same cohesive unit.

So when Tupac was on the outs with his mother, and had his bags packed and ready to leave 3955 Greenmount Avenue, he wound up at the Coles' three-story town house at 1827 Bolton Street, where John lived with his mother, Jackie, stepfather, Harry, and two siblings. Much like Mary Baldridge's parents, the Coles were charmed by Tupac. He would arrive every now and then, sleep on a couch, catch rides, rap silly songs in the back seat. The large white refrigerator, overflowing with fresh fruits and vegetables and snacks and drinks, was his nirvana. He helped with the dishes and took out the garbage. He was a "Please" and "Thank you" kid. If he were at all uneasy with the fish-out-of-water surroundings, he never let on. Plus, the Cole kids had righteous weed. "Having come up his entire life with little more than absolutely nothing, and badly maligned for it," recalled Darrin Bastfield, a classmate, "Tupac was very much a kid ready to receive when he came across someone willing and able to give."

However, life inside the Cole household was turbulent. Two years earlier, on March 28, 1986, Jackie had been lounging around her den when she was overcome by a thunderous headache. "I'm having a stroke!" she cried as the pain shot down her left arm. Jackie was taken to Maryland General Hospital, where she spent six weeks in a coma and endured cardiac arrest, double pneumonia, a collapsed lung, and a blood system infection. When all hope was extinguished and the doctors conceded there was nothing more to be done, the decision was made to remove life support systems and let her die. "She was not living a meaningful life for anyone," Harry later recalled. "She was imprisoned in a coma."

However, a Baltimore City Circuit Court judge named John Carroll Byrnes intervened. He argued the brain wave recording displayed a slight flicker of electrical activity, and that Jackie deserved a final shot.

Six days later, she opened her eyes and smiled.

It was a miracle! It *had* to be a miracle! That's certainly what Harry Cole, John's stepfather and the pastor at the Lochearn United Presbyterian Church, told everyone about his wife. She was evidence that Jesus Christ died for our sins. *The Baltimore Sun* did multiple pieces about its city's own redemptive saga. *People* magazine was all over it. *Time* magazine trumpeted, in a headline, BACK FROM THE DEAD. Connie Chung and the *NBC News at Sunrise* crew stopped by for interviews. A couple of years later, Little, Brown & Company published *One in a Million*, Harry Cole's retelling of the supernatural phenomenon. "I believe God answered my prayers during the course of Jackie's illness," he wrote. "I learned that relief from our suffering could come only on God's terms and in God's time."

It was nonsense.

Not the stroke—that was real. As was Jackie's recovery; though never completely the same, she lived a full life before dying in 2024. But for John and his older brother Tom, Harry was using their mother to milk Baltimore and America for every ounce of sympathy (and money) he could squeeze. "To be blunt," said Tom Cole, "our stepfather was an awful human being with no redeeming qualities to speak of. He was an asshole."

Jackie's fight to recover was long and arduous, and her children found Harry Cole to be unbearable. By 1988, Tom—twenty-one years old and working as a restaurant manager—relocated to an apartment on the 700 block of Reservoir Street in Baltimore's leafy Reservoir Hill neighborhood. He found the place via a "roommate needed" advertisement in *The Baltimore Sun*, paid for by a young man, Richard Day, who had recently broken up with a girlfriend. Tom moved in, and John soon joined him. Only, he came with baggage. Tupac did not consider it realistic to return to the row house with Afeni and Set, so he asked (*begged*, really) John and Tom and Richard if he could somehow move in with them.

"It wasn't my first choice," Tom recalled. "But I also wasn't going to say no to a kid like that. He needed a place to stay."

"I guess it was OK," Richard added.

Located on the second floor of a three-level brick town house, the apartment featured two bedrooms, two bathrooms, a front den, and a long hallway leading to a small kitchen. Richard and Tom snagged their own bedrooms, and Tupac and John shared the den—one slept on a couch, the other on a hammock with a base bolted into the wall. Neither paid a dime of rent. "I didn't make 'em," Tom said. "They were poor." At the time, Richard was a workingman, eight years Tupac's senior and plotting the next steps of life. He had enough patience to endure the untraditional living situation, but only to a certain degree. Tupac was, all inhabitants recall, gross. He tossed his stuff everywhere. He oftentimes forgot to flush the toilet, then found himself amused by the lingering floating discharge. He was terrible at turning off lights, locking doors, shutting windows, wrapping perishable food. A clogged sink was left for others. A stuffed wastepaper basket could be unstuffed by the next man up. Having been raised with few boundaries, he failed to realize one man's box of Froot Loops was not another man's box of Froot Loops, too. Richard, in particular, struggled with the youngster's absent-mindedness, and plastered Post-it notes throughout the apartment.

DON'T TOUCH THIS!

WASH THESE AFTER USING!

PLEASE RETURN TO HAMPER!

The reminders bothered John, but they *irked* Tupac to the point where he deliberately misplaced Richard's possessions. Afeni may not have been America's best mother, but she had always been direct with her son. Richard was a fly in Tupac's soup. "It was not easy for him," said Tom. "He did his best."

In his time living at the Reservoir Street pad, Tupac split his hours between attending Baltimore School for the Arts and holding down his first-ever (non-drug-dealing or newspaper-delivering) job. Located downtown on Water Street was an eatery, the Market Restaurant, where the Cole brothers worked (Tom as a bartender and kitchen manager, John as a bar-back). Tupac was hired as a busboy making $2.25 per hour plus tips—and, as a bonus, a good amount of end-of-the-night uneaten scraps. The Market was owned by an entrepreneur named Lou Battistone, and his son Greg served as the maître d'.

Greg was ten years older than Tupac, and decades later he vividly recalled a spindly, somewhat yappy Black teenager going table to table picking up glasses and flatware. "Nice kid, but he definitely came across as cocky," Greg said. "Especially with the girls." In particular, Tupac had his eye on a pretty back-office worker named Cecilia Young. She was in her early twenties and barely noticed the busboy. But he noticed her. Every day, Tupac made as many efforts as possible to walk past Cecilia, to say hello to Cecilia, to compliment Cecilia's dress, her shoes, her hair. "*Hey, Cecilia! You look beautiful, Cecilia! What's that perfume, Cecilia?*"

Cecilia was Greg's girlfriend.

"He was relentless," Tom said. "And it was Tupac personified. He didn't respect the guy. He thought he was this privileged white guy with a wealthy daddy who was just flaunting his superiority." (Four decades later, Cecilia Young—in her early sixties, working in administration at Johns Hopkins School of Medicine—had only a flickering memory of Tupac Shakur. "I didn't pay a whole lot of attention to him," she said. "He was a kid.")

Back at the town house, the living arrangement with Tupac, John, Tom, and Richard was doomed to fail. They were four guys, all at different junctures in their lives, two paying full rent, two paying no rent, and one averaging fifteen Post-its per day.

So, five months after moving in, Tupac was pulled aside by John, who told him he and his brother would be relocating—without him. It was nothing personal; Tom had landed a job that came with lodging, but he could only have a single roommate.

Tupac flipped. It was another gut punch. On the bright side, he could remain at the Reservoir Street apartment with Richard Day. On the downside, he had no interest in residing with Richard Day. Or returning home. "I'm not sure he had any real options," said Tom.

He and Richard lived together for a couple more months. It did not go well. "Tupac was a nice kid," Richard recalled. "We didn't engage that much, but he was nice. And the thing is—I only had one rule, which was, 'Stay out of my bedroom.' That was it. And there wasn't anything fancy in there. I was a broke waiter trying to get into the mortgage business. But I valued my privacy.

"Well, Tupac had an orgy on my futon."

Um.

"There were visible stains on it," he recalled. "Sex stains. And as soon as I saw it, I was like, 'You motherfucker! You fucking motherfucker!' And I stripped the bed and went to the laundromat and washed all the sheets."

Within a few days, Tupac returned home to Afeni.

As a high school junior, most everything about Tupac's life was turbulent and uncomfortable. His friendship with John (temporarily) fell apart, his home life was terrible, he was back to a certain nomadic uncertainty. Far too many of his meals were either leftovers from the Market or inexpensive packs of Oodles of Noodles.

The one constant, however, was music. He *forever* had music.

As was the case at Dunbar, Tupac cruised through BSA with at least one notebook always in hand, and a blue pen tucked either behind his ear or in his front pants pocket. He wrote at the most random of times—in class, on the toilet, mid-bite of a hamburger. "When the spirit moved him," said Jojo Bransby, a classmate. And it wasn't just rap. Tupac penned love songs, ballads, pop tunes. The words were what counted, not the genre.

For many of his BSA peers, the first inkling that Tupac Shakur could rap dated back to his sophomore year, when a recent graduate named Zorian returned to campus, only now as a wannabe rapper going by the hip-hop moniker "Zori Z." In a scene that exemplified arts school life, Zori Z walked the hallways, seeking out a student to battle-rap. Because 99 percent of BSA's enrollees didn't actually participate in the medium, his offer was met with silence.

Until . . .

"I'll battle you!"

It was Tupac.

They retreated downstairs to the cafeteria. A circle formed around the two combatants.

"Go first," Zori Z commanded.

Tupac stepped forward, grinned, cleared his throat.

Your girl is crazy
Your girl is hot . . .

He went on to fire off a workmanlike takedown of a fictional love interest. The onlookers hooted and hollered and pointed at Zori Z, who shrank by the second. Tupac called the song "I Saw Your Girl." "One year earlier Zorian was everybody's hero," said John Cole. "And now Zori is almost in tears. I think he tried to rap, but stopped quickly. It was like, 'Fuck this,' and he left. Pac demolished him psychologically."

Not long after the Zori Z beatdown, BSA held its annual Beaux Arts Ball. Thrown in conjunction with Halloween, the ball was a costume-themed dance that took place in the school's ballroom each fall. Students came dressed in elaborate outfits and performed skits. Unable to spring for an inventive getup, Tupac wore black suit pants, a black button-down oxford, and a cardigan sweater. He brought along Dana "Mouse" Smith, his neighborhood pal/beatbox, and the two entered the school to a carnival-like atmosphere. At one point Gerard Young and Darrin Bastfield, a pair of visual arts students with hip-hop ambitions, took the stage dressed as Rev. Run and Darryl "DMC" McDaniels from Run-DMC. With another student playing drums, Young and Bastfield rapped two of the group's bigger hits, "My Adidas" and "Walk This Way."

"So we finished, and afterward everyone was like, 'Yo, let's go downstairs because there's a cafeteria and the acoustics are great,'" said Young.

When they walked the steps to the BSA basement, Young and Bastfield were met by Tupac and Mouse. History suggests the mood was tense—Jesse James and Billy the Kid facing off against Butch Cassidy and the Sundance Kid. But . . . not really. This was an arts school with a bunch of arts kids, and the next time someone pulled out a switchblade would be the first. "We were not a tough crowd," said Baldridge. "We were kids with pink hair and holes in our jeans."

The, oh, twenty people in attendance gathered around, and Bastfield stepped up. He was a workmanlike rapper, full of pep and spice but paint-by-number in execution. "Darrin was good for what he was," recalled Young. "But Tupac . . . man . . ."

There was no microphone. Just reverberation against the cement walls. But as soon as Mouse began beatboxing ("*Sooooo* much bass," said Young. "We was like, Oh, shit!") and Tupac joined in with his lyrics, it was clear to everyone—Gerard, Darrin, *everyone*—that this was a different type of creature.

"I never seen anything like it," Bastfield recalled.

"Tupac murdered everybody," Young said. "And instead of taking it as a tough loss in a rap battle, I think we were all like, You know, this is a brother we can get with."

Within a week's time, Tupac and Mouse dropped their old, cornball name (East-Side Crew), teamed up with Bastfield and Young, and debuted a new cornball name (Born Busy). Several months earlier, Tupac had been sitting in math class when he handed a sheet of paper to Teresa Altoz, the girl one desk over.

"What's this?" she whispered.

"I wrote a rap," Tupac said. "What do you think about it?"

Atop the page, in neat block letters, was BABIES HAVING BABIES. If anyone wondered what thoughts entered his mind during long lectures on equations—here they were. The plights of young, Black, inner-city mothers. The way America paid them little mind and showed zero compassion. Altoz read the lyrics.

Babies having babies
Oh boy, it's a shame
Society blames the mother
But she's not to blame

"Our city slogan used to be 'the city that reads,' and people changed it to 'the city that breeds' because we had such a high teen-pregnancy rate," Altoz said. "So that's what the song was. And it was breathtaking. Because Tupac—even at a young age—had an insight into what people were going through, and he expressed it better than anyone in our universe. I'm not sure at that age people are overly empathetic. But Tupac felt it. The agony."

Decades later, Altoz kicked herself for losing the sheet of paper. But Tupac and Mouse recorded "Babies Having Babies," then played it at a handful of gigs. It was an early taste of Tupac's passion for social commentary, a nod to his increased appreciation for the work of Public Enemy's Chuck D, a lyricist committed to Black empowerment.

The plan was to use what the East-Side Crew had started and grow it out. Young, who went by DJ Plain Terror, took a liking to Tupac, whose mother's home was only a mile walk from his place on Tantallion Court. Tupac would come over (Young lived in a stable household with two parents and an emphasis on education), have a bite to eat, beg his friend for a beat.

The rise and reign of Born Busy was more soft breeze than hurricane. The foursome would get together and lay down tracks, but mostly they walked the streets of Baltimore, smoking joints, cracking jokes, seeking rap battles with other crews. It was a uniquely 1980s modus for young, Black, inner-city residents with lyrical talents. "Obviously, we wanted to get a record deal," said Young. "But that's not so easy. In the meantime, you'd battle. Or at least try to."

One Friday night, Tupac and Darrin were walking along Baltimore

Street through the city's downtown when they came upon a small open market adjacent to an empty stage. It was late, and both teens hopped atop the platform to bust lyrics. Before long, a large group of kids from two area projects, the Murphy Homes and Lexington Terrace, surrounded them. "They used to roll thirty, forty deep through the city, just robbing people, taking shit," said Young. "And it was just Darrin and Pac."

At his best, Tupac was a subpar fighter. But the boys steeled themselves and clinched for the inevitable ass kicking . . .

"Hey," one of the rival teens said, "do you guys rap?"

Why, yes, they did.

With that, a rap battle commenced.

"But that's not the memorable part," Young said. "Not even close."

A few weeks later, Gerard lucked into four tickets to a hip-hop show featuring Salt-N-Pepa, Kid 'n Play, Queen Latifah, and Heavy D & the Boyz. The Born Busy crew filed into Gerard Sr.'s car, and he dropped them off on the lip of the parking lot at the old Baltimore Arena. This was the biggest event any of them had ever attended, and they were hyped. "So we walk up to the building, we get our tickets, and all of a sudden there are all these dudes," Young recalled. "They're big fellas with big gold chains on, like big truck jewelry style. Drug dealer chains and gold teeth and shit. And I'm a little uncomfortable. I don't know these guys. But then Pac and Darrin are like, 'Heeeeey! Yoooo! What up?' Giving pounds. It's the people from the night on the street."

It was, Young said, quintessential Tupac Shakur. Things worked out for the kid. He made you smile and forced your guard down. In the company of white artistic academics, he somehow shape-shifted into a white artistic academic. Surrounded by a bunch of gold-toothed gangbangers, he felt a part of the crew. Grandmothers loved him. Teachers loved him. *Everyone* loved him. You felt protected in his company, even though he was neither big nor strong nor tough. He had, Young said, "that thing."

Tupac and the Born Busy crew didn't approach the concert as mere entertainment. It was business. Midway through the show, they decided to make an effort to meet Hurby "Luv Bug" Azor, Salt-N-Pepa's discoverer, manager, and producer, and force him to watch them perform. Luv Bug certainly would be dazzled by their talent, sign them to a fat record deal, and whisk them off to fame and fortune and women and bubbly. *Hollywood, here comes Born Busy . . .*

The Comfort Inn was located less than a mile from the arena, and as soon as the show wrapped the four teens rushed out the exit and straight for the motel lobby. This, they heard, was where the acts were staying.

"Well, Hurby Luv Bug walks in," said Young. "Just as Pac predicted."

There are levels of extroversion—some high, some really high, some *really, really* high. Then there was Tupac. He spotted Luv Bug entering the front door, sprinted toward him, engulfed him in a hug, and said, "Hurby! Hurby! Can we perform for you? Just real quick? Can we? Please? Can we? We're Born Busy, and . . ."

"Sure, kid," Hurby said. "I'll be back in a few minutes."

Luv Bug headed for the elevator.

Pressed the button.

Boarded the elevator.

One Mississippi . . .

Two Mississippi . . .

Three Mississippi . . .

Seventy Mississippi . . .

He returned an hour later, drink in hand, and acted as if the four aspirants did not exist.

"Yo! Hurby!" Tupac shouted. "Hurby!"

The Luv Bug swatted his hand in the air. "Kid," he said, "I ain't got time for this bullshit."

Tupac was crestfallen. But he was also incensed. Nine out of ten high school juniors exit the hotel in shame. Not Tupac. "Fuck that nigga," he said to Young. "Let's go to the rooms."

"Seriously?" Young said.

"Fuck, yeah," Tupac replied.

With that, Tupac, Gerard, Darrin, and Mouse boarded the elevator and went floor by floor until they wound up outside a suite with loud music and marijuana smoke wafting through the door slit. Within seconds, they were chatting with Heavy D, talking shop with Queen Latifah, pinching themselves for their good fortune. "No audition with Luv Bug," said Young. "But an amazing night."

Toward the end of his junior year at Baltimore School for the Arts, Tupac was made aware that, talent be damned, he was failing too many classes and would be placed on academic probation.

Read the progress report sent home to Afeni: "*Tupac has very good potential. His energy and enthusiasm is very strong and can be an asset to the class, but he needs to control his energy and not be disruptive to the work process of others.*"

Said another report, "*Tupac's behavior is extremely disruptive in class. He hasn't done any homework assignments. He's also been absent a lot.*"

Tupac was a lousy student enrolled in a handful of remedial courses who struggled to pay attention. Looking back, classmates say he exhibited many of the characteristics of attention deficit disorder—which wasn't a widespread diagnosis at the time. "He couldn't sit still," said Mary Baldridge. "Ever. And he wasn't a book-smart person. He had an open and broad mind. But he wasn't a student's student."

Of course, it was more complicated than that. When Tupac lived with the Cole brothers, no adult enforced discipline. No one insisted he do his homework, wake up on time, sleep the proper number of hours, have an apple or banana. He was an uncaged robin, free to fly as he chose. Then, when he went back to the home at Greenmount Avenue, back to the mattress and the rats, Afeni remained a mess. Sometimes she was available. Sometimes she was high. Sometimes she would offer heartfelt lectures on Black independence. Sometimes she would shuffle around, glassy-eyed. Sometimes there was food in the refrigerator. Sometimes that food was moldy. Sometimes they would sit on the couch (alongside twelve-year-old Set) and smoke joints and Newports together. "I remember he gave me his phone number," Altoz said. "He wrote it on a scrap of paper. I lost it, but I knew it didn't matter because in two weeks his phone would probably be shut off again. His lights were always out. It was no way to live. He had so many reasons to put a bullet to his head. His life sucked away from school."

"One time at the start of class I asked how he was doing," said Nancy

Krebs, his voice teacher. "And Tupac looked at me and said, 'You have no idea what I go through to get here.'"

Krebs acknowledged he was correct.

"This morning I ran into some crazy guy with a knife," Tupac said. "I had to fend him off just to get to the bus. And then the bus broke down. And I have a dollar in my pocket. That's it."

Classmates recall Tupac arriving at BSA Monday mornings with all sorts of wild adventure stories. Drink! Smoke! Women! Fights! He spent a good number of weekend nights sneaking into Godfrey's Ballroom, a club on North Charles Street that closed at 4:00 a.m. "He'd have these tall tales that were probably true," said Altoz. "'*And then someone pulled out a gun and started shooting and I had to run, and . . . and . . .*'—I remember wondering whether he had any supervision to speak of."

During Tupac's junior year, Seth Bloom threw a house party as his parents vacationed in Europe. The Blooms lived in a spacious home in the posh Mount Washington neighborhood on the city's outskirts, and the property featured an adjacent pool house with a gym, an office, and a hot tub. "Beer, liquor, cigarettes, weed—the whole thing," Bloom recalled. "Everyone came. And there was *lots* of sex." That night, according to lore and eyewitnesses, a female classmate performed fellatio on Tupac in Bloom's bathroom ("True," said Bloom) and he dropped acid for the first time ("Also true," said Bloom). "Later he was rapping for everyone in the hot tub while strung out on acid," said Bloom. "Having the time of his life."

Late in the school year, when classes were wrapping up and thoughts turned toward summer, the theater students of the Baltimore School for the Arts were required to present juries. These were miniature productions performed before a panel of teachers. "If you flunked your jury," said Donald Hicken, head of the theater program, "you'd probably get kicked out and not be able to attend the following year."

For his outgoing-junior-year jury, Tupac teamed up with Bloom to do a two-man scene from *Fool for Love*, the Sam Shepard play. The only required props were a table, two chairs, a bottle of tequila, and a toy gun. "We agreed to split the props," Bloom said. "I'd get the tequila, Tupac would get the gun."

They arrived at school and were greeted by Krebs and Hicken, the teachers who would sit in judgment. Bloom excused himself, entered the bathroom, and took a few swigs from his bottle. "I'm a Method actor," he said years later with a chuckle. The two students were called to the stage, where they completed their five-minute scene. It was sub-mediocre, and Krebs and Hicken lit into them. *What was with Seth's cornball accent? Why did Tupac look so wooden? Had they even rehearsed this thing?*

Wait.

Hold on.

Wait.

Hicken stopped talking to stare in dumbfounded silence. That bottle? Was it . . . *actual* tequila? He rose, walked to the stage, unscrewed the cap, and sniffed.

"Boys," he said, "I shouldn't have to say this, but you *cannot* bring liquor into a school. Do you not know that? You have to take this out of the sc—"

He paused. The gun on the table. The one Tupac brought. That was one realistic-looking prop.

"Tupac," Hicken said, "is that a real gun or a prop gun?"

Nobody said a word.

"Tupac," he said. "Is that a real gun?"

Tupac cackled. The gun was, indeed, a revolver snatched from Afeni's dresser.

"Oh my God!" Hicken said. "Right now, you both need to take the liquor, take the gun, and get out of here. We're all going to pretend this never happened. You're gonna come back tomorrow with a prop gun and some water in a bottle, and you'll do it all again."

They returned the following afternoon and passed.

"I was happy, Tupac was happy," Seth said. "We'd be back for another year.

"I couldn't wait."

Chapter 7

The Transition Happened in Marin City

T hrough the depths of her troubles, from poverty to addiction to all levels of family drama, Afeni Shakur felt deeply connected to her Black Panther roots.

Had the group's members been sympathetic to her post–Panther 21 plight? Hardly. The same men who once preached the beauty of Blackness and the strength of togetherness largely kicked her to the curb, a relic of a bygone era. Many old Panthers knew of Afeni's dark days in Baltimore, yet most never bothered to lift a finger—be it assisting her financially or emotionally. She was expired product.

When she was of sound mind, however, Afeni continued to preach the old manifestos. She wanted Tupac and Set to know what it meant to be Black and strong; to gaze into the mirror and see beauty, intelligence, wisdom, and independence.

Of the Panthers she most admired, one who stood out was Elmer "Geronimo" Pratt, a decorated Vietnam veteran and former UCLA political science major who had served as the organization's deputy minister of defense. Afeni first encountered Geronimo when she flew to California to meet with West Coast party leaders and discuss Panther 21 options. At the time, Geronimo served as head of the Los Angeles chapter, and he impressed Afeni with his earnestness. He also was the rare male Panther who considered women equals. To Afeni, Geronimo symbolized everything a Black man should be—principled, well-read, honest, insightful. "As soon as I met him, I realized I was with the smartest person I'd ever come across," said Gaidi Faraj, the dean of academics at the American Institute of Applied Sciences in Switzerland and a former Pratt protégé. "The first time we played Scrabble he beat me by three hundred points."

On July 28, 1972, a jury found Pratt guilty in the shooting death of Caroline Olsen, a twenty-seven-year-old white teacher he had allegedly robbed, then murdered, four years earlier on a tennis court in Santa Monica. During the trial, Afeni returned to California (with an infant Tupac in tow) to confer with Geronimo's attorney, a young up-and-comer named Johnnie Cochran. She never doubted Pratt's innocence, but questioned whether an all-white jury would see past the Panthers' reputation for violence.

As the Los Angeles Superior Court clerk read the verdict, Pratt screamed, "I didn't kill that woman, you racist dogs!"—and he wasn't lying. The case against Pratt was based upon testimony from a corrupt FBI informant. Pratt had been 350 miles away on the night of the crime, and therefore could not have pulled the trigger. Despite that, he was sentenced to twenty-five years to life inside San Quentin State Prison, the maximum security facility located north of San Francisco. With her husband locked up in Marin County, Ashaki Pratt—who married Geronimo in 1976 during his incarceration, then birthed their two children—rented an apartment in nearby Sausalito.

None of this seemed to directly impact Afeni and the kids, who lived twenty-eight hundred miles away in Maryland's largest city. Yet in the late spring of 1988, with her life in turmoil and her judgment clouded by a new abusive boyfriend, Afeni reached out to Ashaki and asked if, just maybe, she had some spare room for her twelve-year-old daughter.

The idea, Afeni told Set, was to give her a fun month of escape in California. Only it was a lie. The reality was much more problematic. Afeni considered her daughter to be difficult and headstrong and more trouble than she was worth. "I had just got beat up in the neighborhood," Set recalled, "and Mom thought I needed to get away. From where we lived, of course. But also from *her*." Afeni offered Ashaki a bit of money to help pay off some of the inevitable hardship. "A mother needs to pass a sense of self-worth and self-identity and power and love to her daughter," said Yaasmyn Fula. "At that time Feni didn't have any of that shit."

Set relocated across the continent, and decades later her voice still trembled with the pain. "It was terrible and traumatic," she said. "I heard how the Pratts were *our* family, but I hadn't seen them since I was three or four. It's not like I had any memories of them, or talked with them on the phone. They didn't know me like that. They were strangers."

A few months later, toward the end of Tupac's junior year at the Baltimore School for the Arts, Afeni decided it was time for her and her son to make a break from the East Coast and join Set in Northern California. Baltimore had been nothing but poverty and hardship. The row house apartment was terrible, the weather was grim, the economic opportunities were rare. The theater arts school had served as a bright light for Tupac, but that shine rarely entered Afeni's orbit.

When told of the pending relocation, Tupac sobbed and screamed and cursed his mother out. The rage was palpable and justified. For the first time in his young life, Tupac was feeling not merely accepted, but valued. He had plenty of friends, love interests, teachers who recognized his talent. The halls of BSA cocooned him from a dangerous outside world. And now, his mother—his fucking drug-addict mother—was ruining everything.

Tupac told Afeni he would never leave Baltimore. It was home, and he was staying. Fuck Set, fuck the Pratts. Deep down, however, he knew the truth. At seventeen, he had neither the means nor support system to stick around.

Before departing, Tupac needed to take care of business. One day, while sitting in his office, Donald Hicken, head of the BSA theater program, heard a knock on his door. It was Tupac, eyes moist with tears. Less than a week earlier, Tupac had brought the gun and booze into the auditorium. Now he looked as if he wanted to leap from a window. "My mom is moving me to California," he told Hicken. "I don't have a choice."

The teacher was disconsolate. This wasn't merely another forgettable student leaving the premises. No, this was a kid with dynamite in his step. "His future was limitless," Hicken said. "And, as a teacher, the opportunity to work with students like that is gold."

The following day, Sean Stinnett, a friend and classmate, was sitting in the cafeteria, waiting for Tupac to arrive. "We always had lunch together," Stinnett said. "Well, he didn't show up. I asked another guy, 'Where's Tu? Have you seen Tu?'"

Alas, Tupac Shakur had left the building.

For good.

When an East Coaster is offered relocation to California, it's a standard ritual for them to envision palm trees and a bright sun shining down upon the Pacific. That's the cliché, and from *CHiPs* and *The Partridge Family* to *Adam-12* and *Beverly Hills Cop*, we have been conditioned by modern media to believe a state measuring 163,696 square miles and 104,765 million acres is one enormous Frankie and Annette beach party.

Is this what Tupac Shakur was anticipating in the spring of 1988, when Afeni placed him on a Greyhound bus (armed with a suitcase, a backpack, five dollars, and four chicken wings in a paper bag) and sent him off to Sausalito to lodge with his sister? Decades later, it's impossible to say. However, any delusions of grandeur vanished as soon as Tupac arrived at the Pratts' small apartment, located in a beige-and-brown public housing unit at 201 Drake Avenue. Although Ashaki and her children, Hiroji and Shona, lived in a nicer setup than the rat-infested pad on Greenmount Avenue, it was nothing to crow about. The apartment was two bedrooms, with one bathroom to be shared by six people. It was surrounded by patches of greenish-brown grass and a rusted playground. Ashaki quickly made clear that the freedoms Tupac enjoyed in Baltimore were no longer the norm. Wrote Staci Robinson, a Tupac biographer, "Everyone was to be in the house by eight o'clock every night. But Tupac, by then nearly a legal adult, had grown independent during his time living with John [Cole] in Baltimore and felt he was being treated as a child. He ignored the curfew and ventured out to see what his new community had to offer."

If Tupac thought Baltimore had prepared him for rough living, he was in for a shock. According to the authors Tayannah Lee McQuillar and Fred Johnson, Ashaki "didn't cook regular meals and never lost an opportunity to let [Tupac and Set] know that their presence was a burden. [She] . . . habitually cursed them out. She saved most of her venom for Tupac, who represented every Black male who'd ever hurt her or let her down."

Though the Pratt apartment was, technically, located in the tony city of Sausalito, it was actually positioned one-tenth of a mile from Marin City—a spot that, in 1988, was best avoided. "Think of an awful place," said Set Shakur. "Like, the worst place a person can live. Then double it. That's Marin City."*

Four decades earlier, Marin City had been considered a beacon of American opportunity. In 1942, one year after the United States entered World War II, the 365 acres were transformed from a land of dairy farms and grassy plains to a mecca of shipbuilding. Almost overnight, more than six thousand workers—mostly Black, mostly from Louisiana, Arkansas, and Mississippi—flocked to Marin City for jobs at Marinship, the Sausalito waterfront shipyard. "Money grew on trees in California," recalled Levi Bradley, who arrived from Mineola, Texas, in the early 1940s. "So I came." When the war ended, whites—as they have done throughout modern American history—abandoned town.

In the years that followed, the Marin Housing Authority constructed, according to the writer Mark Anthony Wilson, "grim, soulless, mass-produced concrete buildings that resemble military bunkers" to house low-income families. By the 1980s, Marin City—nicknamed "The Jungle" by its denizens—was a cesspool of crime, neglect, and, worst of all, crack cocaine. The average household income was approximately eight thousand dollars. The unemployment rate hovered around 30 percent. The primary housing development—825 one- and two-story town houses on mostly level sections and five-story high-rises on upslope portions—was named Golden Gate Village. Locals, however, referred to it as the heart of "The Jungle."

This is where, in his early West Coast days, Tupac Shakur found himself. From the very beginning, he stood out, and not positively. For Black teenage boys in Northern California, the hairstyles of the time were either

---

* When asked by the author of this book about "moving" to California, Set Shakur turned noticeably agitated. "It wasn't a move," she said. "You're thinking of it through a white privileged voice. We were relocated without a choice. A move sounds nice. This was traumatic."

the Jheri curl, cornrows, or a standard flattop. Tupac, however, arrived with a Gumby-like box cut, slanted to one side and split down the middle by a bleached strip of yellow. He wore a denim jacket that read FREE MANDELA! in white paint on the back, and his blue jeans were pocked with holes and more homemade paint, this time reading MC on one leg, NEW YORK on the other. His shirt rotation featured two black Ts and a white one. As was the case in Baltimore, he still waddled like a duck, and his teeth continued to have directional signals of their own. He was short and scraggly and decidedly not handsome. "His eyebrows were just butchered," said Demetrius Striplin, a Marin City peer. "He was a mess."

Tupac had little interest in spending the summer rolling with the Pratts and their irksome rules. Even when Afeni later came out, the last thing seventeen-year-old Tupac wanted was family time. Though not a particularly moody teenager, he was moody about this—about being here, with these fucking people, in this strange fucking land. One night, when he was particularly despondent, Tupac tiptoed to the telephone in the Pratt kitchen and made a long-distance call to Becky Schnydman, a former BSA classmate who was a freshman at New York University. It was two o'clock in the morning when Schnydman picked up. "He didn't sound like himself," she said. "He sounded frantic and upset."

Though half asleep, Schnydman asked whether Tupac was OK.

"I'm fine," he said. "I just miss you. I really miss you."

Click.

He hung up.

What Afeni quickly realized, to both her astonishment and horror, was that, in two years at BSA, Tupac had lost much of the edge she had tried to instill in him. The son of a Black Panther had dated white girls named Mary and Avra. He was citing Shakespeare and weeping (weeping!) to Kate Bush songs and writing letters that included sentiments like "Everything is so beautiful since I fell in love!"

"My son," Afeni confided to friends, "is sort of a pussy."

Golden Gate Village was no place for pussies. And yet that's ultimately where the Shakur trio found themselves, when Afeni locked down a two-bedroom apartment in building 89, unit 1. It wasn't fancy, but it included a functioning refrigerator, a tiled floor, clean white walls, and no vermin.

The problem with the Jungle was that, for a crack addict with some hope of a new beginning, it acted as quicksand. Back in the early 1980s, when the drug started slithering its way across the continent and poisoning American inner cities, Marin City felt like a natural breeding ground. "If you look at places where Blacks migrated to, they're spots where people left everything they had for spots where they expected better lives," said Donovan Ramsey, author of *When Crack Was King*. "And what they often wind up with are ghettos and sad lives. So what did many of them do? They smoked crack. To escape."

Marin City was crawling with peddlers, and Afeni succumbed. When she was clean and clearheaded, Tupac—even in his anger over the move—had no greater role model. But cracked-out Afeni was a sad, pathetic creature with bloodshot eyes, a ghost, wandering around but rarely present. She slept a lot, ate little, never changed outfits, and begged dealers for product. "She was at her lowest," said Yaasmyn Fula. Her kids existed, but only when she was aware enough to notice them. She loved them, but she loved the high more. "It was *really* bad," said Demetrius Striplin. "She was a sweet person. A good person. My biological father once told me, 'If Jesus did drugs and dope, he wouldn't have done what he did.'"

At seventeen, Tupac was old enough to stand up to Afeni. Within a month of her arrival in Marin City, Tupac demanded she get help and cease using. Afeni, however, was too far gone. She not only refused, but once again kicked her son out of the apartment. "*If you don't wanna live here . . .*"

Tupac didn't want to live *here*. He collected his belongings in a black trash bag, opened the door, and exited. This was close to midnight, when Golden Gate Village's silence was punctured by high halogen lights emitting a hypnotic buzz. He had nowhere to go, certainly no place to sleep. There were benches and patches of grass and slabs of concrete. Gun violence wasn't overly common in the Jungle, but with a high crime rate and an army of crack addicts, the community wasn't a place to wander aimlessly.

"He didn't know what to do," said Striplin. "Luckily, I saw him."

Perched on the balcony on the top floor of building 79, Striplin was standing outside his apartment—no. 20—peering out into the night. The son and nephew of crack addicts, he had much on his mind, especially for a young man of just nineteen who had dropped out of high school and recently fathered his first child. Striplin's biological father, Willie Elwood Cage, was a pimp and drug dealer who had little to do with his son. Demetrius was raised by his adoptive parent, Ronnie Striplin, a local drug kingpin who had recently been arrested and sentenced to a decade in prison.

Instead of finding another place to live, Demetrius decided to stay in unit no. 20. It was his home. And besides, where else was he going to go? Most of his close relatives were either dead, behind bars, or addicted to something. "We had a no-run rule in my family," Demetrius said. "If you run from a fight, you get dragged back to the fight and you better fucking win. Like, when I was twelve I got chased home by a gang of six motherfuckers with weapons. And my mom had already locked the gate. She's standing there in the window and she yells, 'You gotta pick up a brick or something. You sure as hell aren't running to my house from the fight.'"

Gazing down upon the kid with the Gumby haircut and black plastic bag, Demetrius knew what it was to be alone. He called to Tupac—"*Yo!*"—and motioned for him to take the stairs up to the second floor. When they finally came face-to-face, Tupac had tears welling in the corners of his eyes. Demetrius wasn't accustomed to this. Striplins never cried. But this Tupac was a stranger in a strange land. He was *in* the Jungle, but he most certainly wasn't *of* the Jungle.

"You can stay here," Demetrius told him. "Don't even sweat it."

Tupac entered the apartment. The two bedrooms were clean, as was the kitchen. The refrigerator was stocked, a fresh bar of soap sat atop the porcelain bathroom sink, and Demetrius didn't lack for weed. Though friends were always coming and going, there was plenty of space for Tupac to make himself at home, no rent required. "I saw he was hurting," Demetrius said. "I mean, I knew that type of pain."

Best of all, Tupac's new landlord wasn't just another son of addicts. No, Demetrius Striplin was DJ Shaboo—arguably the best and most inventive creator of music in Marin City. Demetrius first thought about DJing when he was eleven, and a neighbor named Paul Johnson worked as a drummer for the 1980s funk-metal band Psychefunkapus. "I was tearing up my mom's stereo, learning how to scratch and mix," Demetrius said. "Paul would be drumming four apartments down, and when his window was open I'd try scratching to his drumming." Within a few years Demetrius was DJing local school dances. Then bars and clubs. Instead of peddling drugs, he walked the Jungle blasting his music from a boom box in order to sell mixtapes to dealers, who would (ideally) spread word of his work to buyers across Northern California.

One night, while DJing a house party in building 59 of Golden Gate Village, Shaboo had Tupac tag along. Everything was going well—the music was flowing, the attendees were dancing. Anthony Marshall, Shaboo's cousin, grabbed the mic and busted a few rhymes. He was good. "*Very* good," said Demetrius. "He had skills."

Shaboo took the microphone and handed it to his new friend in the denim jacket. He didn't know whether Tupac Shakur knew how to rap, only that he bragged incessantly about his talents.

"So he started spitting," said Demetrius. "And . . ."

And?

"And I couldn't believe what I was witnessing."

The song was called "Girls Be Tryn' to Work a Nigga." Tupac had written the lyrics in Baltimore. What Striplin heard was the merging of a hurricane and a typhoon. Tupac wasn't just reciting lyrics. He was bringing them to life, gut to tongue to eardrums. He worked the room like an Otis Redding or Rod Stewart—strutting, bouncing, arms in the air, legs kicking left and right. "It sounded like a song that deserved to be on the radio," Striplin said. "Like, This song is a hit. Why don't we know about it?"

The next day, the two artists sat in the apartment, smoked weed, and combed through Tupac's five spiral notebooks, stuffed with finished and unfinished songs. "I was like, *Damn*," Striplin said. At the time, Bay Area hip-hop was most identifiable with the Oakland rapper Too Short, whose upcoming album, *Life Is . . . Too Short*, was bursting with sexual innuendo and P-Funk-tinged beats. "It was low rent," said Joel Selvin, who covered music for the *San Francisco Chronicle*. "People obviously found it amusing. But there was room for Bay Area hip-hop to grow." Too Short–esque material was what people anticipated from the region's rappers, and many fell in line with the expectations. Tupac's lyrics, on the other hand, read to Demetrius as lesson plans on Black achievement, community development, fighting for women, and protecting children. It was Malcolm X meets Martin Luther King meets Stokely Carmichael meets Peter, Paul and Mary meets Chuck D meets Neil Young meets Mozart meets Kate Bush. "Deep, deep, deep shit," he recalled.

Striplin's bedroom held crates of records, and he had Tupac flip through the albums, seeking out sounds that moved him. Most of the rappers Striplin had worked with were relatively narrow in their musical tastes—it was either rap, R&B, or funk. But Tupac's knowledge was astounding. He was as down with Barry Manilow and Air Supply as he was George Clinton and Earth, Wind & Fire. Striplin's drum machine was connected to his mixer, and he relished taking records, finding just the right hook, and creating beats. Tupac, the kid who simply wanted studio time in Baltimore, was over the moon. This was a dream come true. "He started rapping over the beats," Striplin said. "I'd never seen anyone on his level as a freestylist. It took me years to find a rapper that talented. And there he was, in my bedroom."

That summer, Demetrius and Tupac were inseparable. Marin City was not an exciting place to live (the big draw was a weekly flea market), and the friends passed time by strolling to Hayden's Market, the nearby convenience store. As they walked, Demetrius relished pulling out random subjects and daring Tupac to create rap songs.

"OK," Striplin would say, "bust a rhyme about applesauce."

Tupac rapped about applesauce.

"All right," Striplin would say, "give me one about mustaches."

Tupac's mustache rap would soar.

"Here's a hard one," Striplin might bellow. "Lemon trees and Chicago . . ."

"Nobody ever had the ability he had," said Striplin. "It blew my mind. His raps about what we were doing in the moment were just as good as the raps you'd hear on the radio."

A few days after Tupac moved in, Demetrius had a gig DJing an hour away at the Stargaze Club in Guerneville. He liked bringing rapper cohorts to help spice things up, and this time Tupac came along. Early into the evening, Demetrius passed his friend the microphone. The room was dark, the dance floor half empty. The air was overwhelmed by cigarette and marijuana smoke. Nobody was much paying attention, but in that moment Striplin felt like Gottlob Neefe, and Tupac was Ludwig van Bee-thoven. "He was seventeen and so fucking good," Demetrius said. "I told him he was gonna be more famous than LL Cool J. I said, 'In ten years, you'll be the world's most famous rapper.' He thought I was fucking with him. I wasn't." Decades later, the titles of Tupac's early songs rolled off Demetrius's tongue.

"Fantasy."

"Can't No One Stop Us."

"I'll Never Be Beat."

"Gimme Yo Butt."

"Song after song after song," he said. "Not all of them were great. But enough were."

Around this time, a Bay Area native named Ryan Rollins was living in Port St. Lucie, Florida, with his grandma Clara after having been kicked out by his mother for smoking marijuana. A former Santa Rosa Junior College football recruit, Rollins fancied himself more rapper (he went by Ryan D) than free safety, and was miserable flipping burgers at a Hardee's three thousand miles from home. "So I'm in Florida, hating my life," he recalled. "And everyone starts calling me about this new kid in the Jungle named Tupac. They're telling me I need to come home and see him to believe it. I'm like, How good can this nigga be?"

Ryan returned to California, and on one of his first days back caught the Golden Gate Transit bus from Novato to the Marin City stop and bumped into his old pal Demetrius. "Yo, Ryan!" Striplin said. "You're here!"

He turned to the person next to him. The kid with the haircut. "Ry," he said, "do you know Tupac?"

"*Yoooooo!*" Ryan D said. "I've heard about you!"

And in that moment, on that sidewalk, Tupac and Ryan D started to rap. Tupac went first, dropping some lines from "Girls Be Tryn' to Work a Nigga." Ryan D countered—"I don't remember what I did," he said, "just that I freestyled and I was dope."

When it ended, the two embraced. "He had on a leather biker jacket," Ryan said. "And nobody out here was wearing leather biker jackets. He was the total opposite of anything like us. But he rapped so good, you're like, This dude is dope. Man, let's hang out."

Like Tupac, Ryan D had nowhere to live. Like Tupac, Demetrius invited him to move into building 79, unit 20. Then, shortly thereafter, a third roommate—also a rapper, also a vagabond—entered the picture. Born and raised in Kenner, Louisiana, August Terry was a thirteen-year-old sixth grader in 1982 when a kid down the block removed a pedal from his bicycle and rammed it into August's rear end. Fed up with a lifetime of beatings and ridicule, August walked inside, found a box cutter, wrapped it in newspaper, and returned to the scene.

"Oh, you're back," the culprit said. "What are you gonna do, baby?"

August sliced the box cutter into the bully's thumb, nearly severing the appendage. Blood shot everywhere.

Before long, August was banished to a nearby reform school. He stayed for six months, and after being released he, his mother, and his stepfather sought a fresh start in Northern California. They moved to Novato, and it was here where August discovered breakdancing and beatboxing. "Whodini, LL Cool J, Run-DMC, Kurtis Blow, Salt-N-Pepa—those were the artists who spoke to me," he said. "I wanted to be in the world they occupied." One night, as a student at Novato High, August was challenged to a breakdancing battle by a crew from nearby Marin City. The star of the group was a kid in a Puma sweatsuit and white Adidas. "I looked at him and knew, Shit, I'm in trouble," said August.

That was August Terry's introduction to Demetrius Striplin. "From that moment on, he was my guy," said August. "Everything I was into, he was into."

When, in the summer of 1988, August's parents decided to return to Kenner, their nineteen-year-old son refused.

"Where are you planning on living?" his mother asked.

"Marin City," he replied.

"With who?" she said.

"Demetrius." His stepfather handed over five hundred dollars in cash, the keys to an olive-green Ford Pinto, and the haunting words, "I hope you know what the fuck you're doing." They drove off.

August loaded his belongings into the car and made the journey to Marin City. He might have told Demetrius he was coming—"But I probably didn't," he recalled.

He entered building 79, walked up to apartment 20, and knocked on the door.

A lanky kid with a bad haircut answered.

"Is Demetrius here?" August asked.

"Nah," the youngster replied. "He's downstairs with his girl."

"All right," August said. "Well, I've got all my stuff and I'm moving in."

"OK, cool," the kid replied. "I'm Tupac."

August entered. The apartment, clean when Tupac first arrived, was a bit of a mess. Open bags of potato chips were scattered across a table. Piles of clothing mounted in the corners. It smelled of foot. August brought up his bags and Tupac directed him toward his room, which had two beds, one unoccupied. Resting atop a small table was a cigar smoldering in an ashtray alongside a dog-eared copy of Shakespeare's *Macbeth*.

"I'd dropped out in tenth grade," August said. "I didn't know nothing about *Macbeth*."

He also knew nothing of the cigar. Which wasn't technically a cigar at all, but a cigar that had been hollowed out and filled with weed. Tupac referred to it as a blunt, and explained that he'd learned how to roll one from his friends in Baltimore. None of his new roommates knew whereof he spoke.

"Y'all really don't know what a blunt is?" Tupac asked, incredulously.

They did not.

"Shit," Tupac said. "Y'all have a lot to learn."

Years later, Striplin insisted Tupac was the man responsible for bringing the blunt—with origins in Philadelphia—to the West Coast. And while this is impossible to prove, he *at least* introduced it to Marin City.

When August finished unpacking his belongings, he plopped down on a couch in front of the television in the main room. Tupac flipped to Nickelodeon, which was showing a children's production of *A Raisin in the Sun*.

"Yo! I was in this play!" he squealed.

"Bullshit," August said.

"No! Seriously! Watch what's about to happen . . ."

August Terry had never met anyone like this. The two spent the next six hours smoking weed, eating chips, talking politics and religion and the plight of the Black man in modern America. "He was breaking down poetry to me," August said. "I'd never spent a minute thinking about poetry. This was the smartest brother I'd ever met."

When Demetrius returned to the apartment, he hugged August and nodded toward Tupac. "I see you've met the new rapper in our group," he said.

Our group was a bit of a stretch. Demetrius and August frequently discussed the idea of one day starting a hip-hop outfit and calling it One Nation Emcees.

"You can rap?" August asked Tupac.

Tupac shrugged.

"Man, let me hear something right now!" he said. "Let me hear what you can do!"

Demetrius led the two into his bedroom, which was where he kept his equipment and records. The walls were soundproofed with foam and plastered with photos of hip-hop's greatest artists. Demetrius flipped on some switches and played the instrumentals of Eric B. & Rakim's *Paid in Full*.

Tupac grabbed the microphone.

"I got chills," August said. "When we were talking, he sounded like a kid. But when he started rapping, his voice changed. And what got me was everything he rapped came from the heart. He freestyled for the rest of the night. About everything. Video games. *A Raisin in the Sun*. Nickelodeon. He said my name a bunch of times, and I just fell in love with him. He made it clear he didn't wanna be in Marin City. He was a Baltimore kid, and he hated it here. But that hate and anger—it fueled his talent. To hear him rap, man . . . it was just spiritual."

One Nation Emcees was born. Demetrius was a fantastic DJ. August was a quality beatboxer. Tupac and Ryan D could rap. Anthony "Ant Dog" Marshall was another rapper friend of Striplin's with flow, and Darren "Klark Gable" Page was an on-the-rise music producer. Jamal Page, Darren's cousin, was important because, Ryan D recalled, "he had a car." Much of One Nation Emcees' work was funded by drug money earned by some of the members—a reality of Jungle life. As Tupac's mom was chasing the high, some of the men supplying it to her were simultaneously funding his music. "That's just a twist of the hood," said Ryan D. "Drugs were the engine."

The members of One Nation Emcees viewed themselves as hip-hop blood brothers. They ordered matching o.n.e. medallions attached to red, green, and yellow Afrocentric ropes. The group's ambition trumped reality—they spent an inordinate number of hours practicing inside Striplin's pad and played a handful of gigs, but mainly showed up at parties and festivals to square off against other crews. "We always won," Ryan D said. "Always."

In a moment that shifted the course of music history, one day Ryan D and Tupac were sitting around, playing Nintendo, when Ryan pleaded with Tupac to stop referring to himself as MC New York. It was corny.

"That shit needs to stop," Ryan D said.

"What shit?" said Tupac.

"'MC New York,'" Ryan D said. "Your name is Tupac. That's a fucking dope-ass name. Use it."

One Nation Emcees had a song with a line, delivered via Ryan D, that went: "*Nobody could fuck with the O.N.E. / New York is like my homie / He could take you out quickly . . .*"—and Ryan D was tired of spitting it. "Think how dope that sounds if I say your name, not 'New York,'" he told Tupac. "It's so much better."

"OK," Tupac said. "I'll drop the New York."

Praise Jesus.

"I was so happy," said Ryan D. "It was a no-brainer."

More than anything, what One Nation Emcees gave Tupac was a sense of belonging. He would check in on his mother and sister one building away, but couldn't bear to see Afeni strung out and empty. She wasn't just using crack—she was buying from the very people he hung with. His sister, meanwhile, was largely raising herself. "Marin was a cancerous place," said Set Shakur. "I will never have anything fond to say about it. It's a bitter, dirty, vile part of my life."

When he wasn't making music, Striplin worked a job caring for autistic children. His salary paid for food, though Tupac didn't mind sneaking into the local 7-Eleven and pocketing candy bars and Fritos. There was also a local supermarket, Safeway, which featured a tantalizing selection of meats. "We'd all go there, pretend to be shopping, and come out with a bunch of [stolen] steaks," said Ryan D. "Then we'd grill and play Nintendo all night."

As far as roommates go, Tupac was less than ideal. On the one hand, he was a self-taught cook who excelled at making barbecue chicken and seasoned steaks. On those rare occasions he took over the kitchen, the crew ate well.* But he was, as John Cole could have attested to back in Baltimore, a slob. "He only had one pair of shoes, and they stunk," Ryan D said. "We'd be like, 'Tupac, leave your shoes outside!' He was the poorest person I knew. They were his only shoes."

There is a moment from the summer of 1988 that Tupac's friends insist goes tragically overlooked.

It involves a rap beatdown.

His rap beatdown.

From the time he began dropping bombs as a youngster in New York, Tupac believed he was the best of the best. He was prematurely confident, to the point where he would not only have battled a Chuck D or Big Daddy Kane—he would have entered the ring convinced of an inevitable Holyfield-style knockout.

"From jump," said Demetrius, "Pac knew he was special."

So it was that one day, atop the Marin City cement slab of nothingness referred to as "The Blade," a rap cypher broke out. Brian Times, a local drug dealer, parked his brown Chevy Blazer nearby and blasted music from his Alpine stereo. The bass thumped off walls. The ground trembled. The beats were created by Darren "Klark Gable" Page, the aspiring producer who was always on the lookout for new talent and in the process of forming the group that would be known as 51.50. One by one, those assembled stepped up to rap.

Ryan D went.

---

* "At that point, Tupac was a better cook than rapper," said his friend Kendrick Wells. "He'd stay with me sometimes, and we'd go to Safeway. I was used to eating stuffing for dinner. He'd be making gumbo, stews. He could really bring it in the kitchen."

A local MC named Carlos went.

Then Tupac cleared his throat.

And he was, as always, good. Really good. He rapped about Blacks returning to Africa and Marcus Garvey and Bobby Hutton, and those assembled nodded and clapped. "He did what Tupac always did," said August. "He's talking about the moon and stars aligning and being righteous."

Standing alongside Tupac was Gable's latest find, a local thirteen-year-old named Halbert Lofton. He went by "Tac." A tall, meaty Black teen with a high flattop and sleepy eyes, nobody knew much about the kid. Tac? What type of goofy-ass name was Tac?

When Tupac finished his verses, Tac unleashed. His first line—"Waking up in the morning in my hood"—connected like a sledgehammer to rotting wood. "Jesus, it was powerful," said August. "He's talking about the neighborhood, the streets, the drug dealers, pimps, hos. And he starts naming certain dudes, and everyone's like, 'Ohhhhhh . . .' The hood is going nuts because everything Tac is saying is real and relatable."

That night, back at the apartment, Tupac was inconsolable. He didn't want to smoke weed, or play Nintendo, or kidnap burritos from 7-Eleven. He asked August for a beat.

"My mouth is tired," he replied. "I'm tired of beatboxing."

Tupac scowled.

"Why," August said, "do you need a beat?"

"Because that nigga Tac got me," he said. "He fucking got me."

Not all that long ago, Tupac was watching ballet and attending parties at the swank homes of his wealthy white BSA classmates. To think he could come to the projects of Marin City and take command was naïve. "He was clueless on how the real-life game goes," said Marku Reynolds, a local rapper and dealer. "He was completely absent-minded to street values. He watched movies and pretended to have swagger. But it wasn't real. The man could talk a hungry dog off a meat wagon, but he couldn't fight, couldn't drive, couldn't play basketball, couldn't sell drugs. He was pretending."

Over the next week, Tupac went MIA. He didn't come home for dinner, for smoking, for sleep. At the time August worked part time making omelets at a restaurant in Sausalito. Finally, on Friday, he returned from the job to find Tupac on the couch, notepad in lap.

"Pac, where've you been?" he asked. "You getting some pussy or something?"

"Nah," he replied. "I've been hanging out around the Jungle."

Specifically, Tupac had attached himself to Bobby Burton, a local drug kingpin who supplied much of Marin City with its cocaine and crack. Though just twenty-one, Burton was a feared figure ("He wouldn't hesitate to fuck you up," a fellow dealer said) who most knew to avoid. Within the past year, Burton had been kidnapped at gunpoint and thrown into the trunk of a car. He escaped, and made clear to the community that, should the culprits be identified, they would cease to exist.

Tupac, however, was too naïve or dumb to know fear. Like an eager puppy, he bounded toward Burton, seeking tutelage. "I was sorta charmed by the kid," Burton said decades later. "You had to like him." So he let Tupac follow him and jot down observations. Now, back in the apartment, Tupac required August's assistance. "I've got a rap I want you to hear," he said, "but I need a beat."

August was tired. He smelled of bacon and wanted to flop into bed. But Tupac's expression screamed desperation.

August started to beatbox.

Tupac started to rap . . .

Born in the days of a criminal
Runnin' from the cops and can't let 'em see me
So I'm hopin' out the Benz
It's time to let the valet step, gotta make my ends

Holy shit. *Holy, holy, holy* shit. August was flabbergasted. How, in such a short span, had this kid captured the world he saw around him—without actually being a gangbanger or drug dealer? The tune, "Dayz of a Criminal," wasn't merely good. It was one of the best songs August had ever heard.

"Maybe *the* best," he said.

It turns out Tupac hadn't merely hung out in the Jungle. He'd spent his days and nights probing drug dealers. Burning scenes into his mind. Even though he was not an actual criminal, Tupac felt compelled to speak the part. The sagas of the streets mattered to him. It was a calling—the plight of the poor Black man in the projects wasn't being portrayed via radio or television. He *needed* to be the one to explain it. "The transition," said Kendrick Wells, Tupac's friend, "happened in Marin City."

It was undeniable.

"I had to stop rapping about what I was seeing," Tupac told August, "and rap about what I knew to be true.

"That," he said, "is what makes greatness. And I wanna be fucking great."

Chapter 8

Tam

Were it up to Tupac Shakur, he would have never returned to high school, instead devoting his time to hanging with the members of One Nation Emcees, smoking weed, eating crap food, playing Nintendo, talking shit, and honing his musical craft. To him, a diploma was nothing more than a sliver of fancy paper, deemed important and necessary by America's white power structure.

And (dammit) by his mother.

Alas, even as she failed to stay clean, Afeni enrolled her son at Tamalpais High School for his senior year, with expectations that he graduate. Despite her mistrust of white America and the inner workings of its culturally biased educational system, Afeni believed a diploma mattered. It carried weight, held significance, showed one could set a goal and complete the task.

As was the case with the Baltimore School for the Arts, "Tam" (as it was known) was a strange, fish-out-of-water spot for Tupac. Although but 2.7 miles from Marin City, the campus—beatific, grassy, and resembling a small college—was of a different universe. The school was located in the heart of blissful Mill Valley, a San Francisco suburb known for its über-liberal politics and community of artists, poets, and musicians. Among others, Mill Valley had been home to Janis Joplin, Jerry Garcia, Pete Sears, Huey Lewis, and Bonnie Raitt. It was a place where the lettuce was organic and milk came in seven different varieties. The town of approximately ten thousand people was 85 percent white, 8 percent Asian, and—if standing on its tippy-toes—*perhaps* 2 percent Black. Tam was one of the first American high schools to provide students with condoms. "Mill Valley is beautiful," said Joel Selvin, the *San Francisco Chronicle* writer. "It's also home to the most privileged fuckers on the planet."

Tupac knew almost nothing of Tam, and when his senior year commenced, on September 7, 1988, and he exited the Golden Gate Transit bus from Marin City, walked beneath the beige archway, up the steps, and through the front door, he could see this was a distant cry from the Jungle. Like BSA, the school was spectacular and grand and overflowing with money and creativity. But unlike BSA, it had little to no grit. Being based in downtown Baltimore gave Tupac's old haunt a certain edginess his new one failed to match. Also, Tupac certainly noticed the ocean of whiteness. Of the 227 students in the senior class at Tam, a mere nine were Black. "There was a divide," said Thor Thomas, a Black student who took the bus with Tupac. "The Black kids were Marin City people. Most of us went to the [majority Black] Martin Luther King Middle School and came from a world far away."

In a school overflowing with hippie chicks and skater dudes, the cliché Black kid was carrying a ball beneath his arm. Though it's a lazy and ugly trope, the Marin City imports were thought to be here to make certain Tam High won more games than they lost.

So when Tupac arrived, and he sported the Gumby haircut ("with layers of peroxide in steps!" said Olathunji Dean, a Black classmate), and his jeans were baggy and ripped, and the gold chain around his neck was a two-dollar street-corner knockoff, and he dressed more like Kris Kristofferson than E-40, students and faculty noticed. And when he could neither catch nor throw a ball, or name a single member of the San Francisco 49ers, students and faculty also noticed. "He always had a pencil tucked behind his ear," said Dean. "And I never remember him with a backpack."

"He was so different than most of the kids from Marin City," said Chava Bramwell, a white classmate. "Honestly, it was strange for us to see a Black kid like him. He was in touch with his feelings. He was feminine and soft and sweet and gentle. Really, he was effeminate. *Very* effeminate."

That word—"effeminate"—is affixed to Tamalpais High Tupac Shakur. Which is not to suggest classmates thought he might be gay. Or might *not* be gay. It wasn't discussed. But he was unlike anyone previously seen in these parts. Tupac arrived most mornings reeking of coffee, weed, cigarettes (the official scent of Demetrius Striplin's pad), and/or hyacinth and vanilla. "He smelled so good you wanted to follow him around," recalled Tatiana Bliss, a classmate. He was one of the few boys anyone knew with pink eye shadow, fingernails painted black, and both ears pierced (done with a classmate, Liza Monjauze, at the nearby Northgate Mall), and the strip of bleach running through his hair was, Monjauze recalled, "really confusing." His wardrobe was defined by his poverty (not too many Tam kids were spray-painting their own clothes), but La Donna Bonner, a Marin City resident and classmate, never forgot Spirit Week '88, when Tupac strolled through the cafeteria wearing a full blue, red, and white Indians cheerleader outfit—including skirt, shoes, and pom-poms. "I asked around—'Excuse me, who *is* this crazy boy?'" recalled Bonner. "'And what has he been smoking?'"

Tupac's ability to code-shift and adjust to his environs, which had taken flight in Baltimore, reached new heights in Northern California. At the apartment, surrounded by Striplin and Terry August and Ryan D, Tupac radiated the hardened air of the projects. He was rap battles and shit talk and "Fuck you, motherfucker." Sometimes he and his friends would head out to the mall to shoplift and antagonize the security guards with taunts of "Go to hell, pigs!" But once he entered the hallways of Tamalpais High, his demeanor changed. He was a drama geek—artsy, flamboyant, needing to be the center of attention. Was the role-playing intentional? Certainly. Was it duplicitous? Not at all. "He was the type of guy," said Bramwell, "who would pick up a ladybug and put it to the side." From the time he was a tyke in New York, Tupac adapted to his surroundings. He didn't "talk white" around white teachers because he was trying to ingratiate himself. He "talked white" around white teachers because that *was* survival. "He was a born people pleaser," Seth Bloom, his former BSA classmate, said. "Most people don't have that gift, but Tupac could be whatever his present status required."

Having arrived from a renowned performing arts school with a transcript pocked by Cs, Ds, and incompletes, at Tam Tupac was placed in largely remedial classes. He took math, science, social studies, as well as a physical education course that allowed him to sit on the bleachers and watch life (and runners) pass him by. His favorite class was humanities, a junior/senior elective taught by Barbara Owens, a beloved instructor who first came to Tam in 1978. Owens had the class study *Othello*, the William Shakespeare tragedy. Her students read the play aloud, with flair and brio. Through the years, Owens occasionally found herself moved by a certain pupil's rendition, to the point where she might brag to fellow faculty members about the performance.

She had seen some students do exceptional work.

None of them approached Tupac Shakur.

Decades later, Owens could still picture the teen, barely seventeen, embodying the voice and spirit of Othello. They were not on a stage, but inside a classroom. They were not thespians, but awkward teens trying to shuffle their way through high school. But when Tupac read from act V, scene ii, it felt as if everyone else in the room vanished and a spotlight lit his silhouette.

It is the cause, it is the cause, my soul.
Let me not name it to you, you chaste stars!
It is the cause. Yet I'll not shed her blood,
Nor scar that whiter skin of hers than snow
And smooth as monumental alabaster.

When Tupac finished, Owens paused class. "Students," she said, "you're never going to hear *Othello* performed as brilliantly as you just heard it right now."

Although it lacked the Baltimore School for the Arts' reputation and pedigree, Tam boasted one of the state's elite acting programs. It was called the Ensemble Theatre Company (ETC), and was headed by Dan Caldwell. A veteran character actor who had appeared in films directed by Woody Allen and Richard Lester, Caldwell came to Tam as a drama instructor in 1962, and fourteen years later started ETC. "Dan was a big believer in the arts, which was great," said Barbara Galyen, Tam's principal. "But there would be many times we'd be sitting in the office and I'd say, 'Dan, is this *really* appropriate?' One time we had a talent show and a kid came out wearing a trench coat. When he opened it something that looked like a penis in a nylon stocking came out."

ETC was unique, in that instead of students trotting out tired productions of *Oliver!* and *Funny Girl*, they wrote, directed, produced, and performed one-act plays at the local theater. "Usually they'd each be about fifteen to twenty minutes long," said Cael Kendall, an ETC participant. "You did everything, so you learned everything."

When Tupac arrived, he knew he would dive into the drama program. And even though ETC featured multiple returnees, he stood out. A small factor was the uniqueness of a Marin City kid with a flair for theater ("Black dudes, we didn't take drama," recalled K. C. Graham, a Black classmate). But the bigger thing was talent. Tupac Shakur could fucking act. Name something a performer was required to do—*anything* a performer was required to do—and Tupac mastered it. He could cry on demand. He could speak in a British accent. He could learn lines on the quick. He could turn his body into Jell-O. He could scream like a girl being stabbed by Jason Voorhees and howl like a boy holding his beloved dead cockapoo. "This kid shows up for drama—weird name, same shirt every day," said Christian Mills, a classmate. "And within, like, a month, he was in directing class with me, in a play with me, in advanced acting with me. He was everywhere."

On the afternoon of November 28, 1988, Tupac reported to rehearsals for his first Tam play, a one-act production called *April 5th*. Written and directed by a senior named Jessica Strauss, the show told the story of the day after Dr. Martin Luther King Jr.'s 1968 assassination in Memphis. As the lone Black ensemble member, Tupac was cast as MLK. Monjauze, a fellow castmate, kept a diary of the rehearsals leading up to the opening night at the Ruby Scott Auditorium on the school campus. In one entry, she wrote: "It's really wonderful acting with Tupac. It's incredible, actually. Every moment he was right there. Every time I looked at him he was right there." The sentiment, however, belied the difficulties. If there were forty rehearsals, Tupac showed up for, oh, ten and was late for another fifteen.

"Tupac just came when he wanted to," said Cael Kendall. "And the rest of the cast was always like, 'What the fuck, man? Where is he?'" It wasn't that Tupac didn't care so much as that, compared to the stuff he did at BSA, this was child's play. When he did show, Tupac was often accompanied by his own posse—Demetrius, Ryan D, Terry August, and a crack dealer/

rapper named Marku Reynolds, who would stand in the rear of the room, watch, and heckle. It was a scene out of a movie—the imposing Black figures, tatted up and (sometimes) packing heat, harmless yet terrifying to the theatrical nerds. "We were the whitest school ever," said Kendall. "So he's talking trash with his boys, and we're awkwardly pretending it's not happening." It was two-worlds-at-once Tupac, and Tam classmates saw his body language and voice change as soon as the Jungle guys arrived. He went from feathery and soft to hard and street.

April 5th opened on January 12, 1989, at the Marin Theater, one of several short plays performed that night. Tupac was the star, and, technically, it was awful. He was unprepared and unpracticed, didn't know his marks or the movements of his fellow actors. For Strauss, the writer and director, Tupac was everything you didn't want in a leading man.

But . . .

"There were probably 200, maybe 250 people in the auditorium," said Kendall. "And Tupac rolls in right before our one-act is about to begin. I mean, we're all there two hours early, and he comes in with fifteen minutes to spare. He's got his posse, only now it's ten to fifteen people. All Black. And they squeeze into the front row, because those are the only seats left. Next to all the yuppie white parents. And Tupac went out there, with us all holding our breaths, and just nailed it. He knew his lines, and whenever he didn't know a line he ad-libbed his way through. And when classmates were confused, he'd feed them lines. He probably stuck to 60 percent of the script. And he played the performance to the max. He had so much confidence and chutzpah. Like, one member of the posse was throwing out heckling comments during the show, and in drama you're not supposed to break the barrier between you and the audience. But Tupac—he would totally throw back one-liners at his posse. And it brought the house down. It wasn't like, Why is this asshole ruining the show? It was more 'a star is born.'"

Tupac and the cast received a standing ovation. Afterward, Christian Mills invited Tupac to grab some food. It was raining outside, and they folded into Mills's old BMW. As they pulled out of the lot, Tupac reached into his pocket and unfurled one of the fattest cigars his friend had ever seen. It was a homemade blunt, stuffed to the gills.

"Dude!" Mills said. "I can probably have a couple of beers and be all right. But if I smoke that type of stuff, it'll really work me over."

"Fuck that!" Tupac said. "Smoke this with me!"

They waited until reaching the Denny's parking lot, alternated a half dozen hits, then entered the twenty-four-hour eatery and ordered burgers, fries, and milkshakes. When they finished, Mills reached for the check.

"Fuck that," Tupac said. "We're gonna dine and dash."

Christian Mills was a white Mill Valley kid from a wealthy home. He did *not* dine and dash.

"We're gonna dine and dash," Tupac emphasized, "because I wanna see a fucking white boy run from the police."

And so, on that night, Tupac Shakur and Christian Mills rose from their table, casually walked toward the exit—and bolted.

"Tupac," Mills said, "was testing me."

There was another performance. Or, to be more accurate, another *scheduled* performance. Only, out of politeness mixed with confusion, those who acted alongside Tupac at Tamalpais High School tend not to mention it.

Because while the majority of Tam students lived with certain comforts and securities, Tupac's life was one of chaos, disruption, pain, uncertainty. The vast majority of his days were spent sleeping in Demetrius Striplin's pad, which was perfectly fine. But he also knew, one building to the right, his mother was rotting away. He would visit her on occasion, stop by to check in on Set and tell Afeni to—*please, Mom*—get her fucking shit together. It tore him up. The apartment smelled like feces, with little food in the refrigerator and clothes piled up. Through it all, Afeni Shakur remained his hero. Always. But what type of hero allows herself to reach such depths? "He'd go there and give her a few dollars—then get far away," said Kendrick Wells, a friend whose parents and siblings became crack addicts. "When your mom's a crackhead, you do what you can to avoid her."

During this period, Afeni visited a male friend in a nearby prison, and he impregnated her. She immediately decided to undergo an abortion, but complications with her uterus made it difficult to find a clinic willing to perform the surgery. Wrote the author Dean Van Nguyen: "Desperate to terminate the pregnancy, Afeni drastically increased her use of crack, expecting that the drug would eventually kill the fetus." Five months in, Afeni finally found a clinic willing to end the pregnancy. "The procedure went off without complications," wrote Van Nguyen, "but the scars left on Afeni's soul were devastating."

On occasion, Afeni, Tupac, and Set made a family trip to San Quentin, where Geronimo Pratt greeted the children with open arms while staring down Afeni with disgust. She felt it. *Hated* it. She could live poor, live in pain, even live without much love. But to be a disappointment? The humiliation was unspeakable. And yet—where was she when Tupac needed her? Afeni's oldest child was on his own. And Afeni was MIA.

In a sense, that explains why, on the early afternoon of January 26, 1989, Tupac was skipping school to hang out with Ryan D, Klark Gable, and another friend, Ryan Anderson, near Hamilton Air Force Base in Novato. It was a lazy day that commenced with weed and advanced to a shared bottle of Jack Daniel's. With little to hold their interest, they took a walk down Nave Drive and threw rocks at passing vehicles. "The drunk shit kids do," Ryan D said years later.

Around four o'clock, Tupac looked at his watch and panicked. He was required to be at the Ruby Scott Auditorium for that night's showing of *April 5th*. "Shit," he said. "I need to catch the bus." As if on cue, Anderson picked up a bowling-ball-sized rock and hurled it toward the street.

The sound—BOOM!—stopped the boys in their tracks.

When they looked up a car swerved toward the bank of the road, the front window shattered. A tall, muscular figure stumbled out. He was dressed in a green United States Army uniform, and was not smiling. The man stomped toward the teens, looked at Anderson, drew back his fist, and hammered him in the jaw. "Knocked him out cold," said Ryan D. As their friend languished on the sidewalk, Ryan D, Gable, and Tupac rushed the attacker ("Well, me and Gable rushed him," said Ryan D. "Tupac kinda hung back"). The man grabbed Ryan D, shoved him into a fence, and cocked his right arm to throw a punch . . . when Gable lifted a piece of scrap wood from the ground and walloped the man over the head. "I'll never forget the sound of the wood and his skull," said Ryan D. "You only hear that once if you're lucky." Gable, Ryan D, and Tupac pounced, kicking the fallen soldier up and down his torso.

"Then we took off running," Ryan D said. "But because of the fight, Tupac missed his bus."

On page A6 of the following week's *Novato Advance*, a small article ran beneath the headline MAN ASSAULTED.

Police are looking for two teenage boys who allegedly attacked a man after breaking one of his vehicle's windows as he drove on Nave Drive near the main entrance to Hamilton Field last Thursday night.

Police said the man stopped his car after it was hit by an unknown object and became involved in an altercation with two teenagers.

Police said the man was punched and hit in the back of the head with a wooden club.

Tupac arrived at the theater well after the performance had ended. Asked for an explanation, he lied his ass off. *There was this guy, and he started using the n-word. So he and his friends had to fight. And . . .*

It was nonsense.

His castmates were furious, and let him know the following day at school.

"He had a gift," said Kendall, "that couldn't be duplicated by an understudy."

Everything about Tupac felt surprising and different. He was a Black kid who loved theater. He was an artistic kid who couldn't sing. He was a shit talker who couldn't fight. He was a rapper who listened to Don McLean and Kate Bush. He was a mama's boy sleeping on a friend's couch. He took the bus from the Jungle, only to roll with the hippies and gays. He was rough and effeminate, upbeat and depressed.

During the first half of the school year, a documentary filmmaker named Jamie Cavanaugh interviewed various students for a project concerning urban life. The plan was to probe the minds of twenty high school students. One of the participants was Tupac. On an otherwise forgettable morning in high school Americana, Tupac—wearing an old black tank top, his hair crudely split by the bleached line, bushy eyebrows and narrow shoulders—sat against a white paneled wall.

He was instructed to introduce himself.

TUPAC: "Okay. My name is Tupac Shakur and I attend Tamalpais High School and I'm seventeen years old."

CAVANAUGH: "Do you like being seventeen?"

TUPAC: "Eh, seventeen is such a weird age, it's such a in-the-middle age. You're not eighteen yet and you're older than sixteen, but I like it. It's nice. It's like a learning stage for me."

CAVANAUGH: "Do you wish you could be eighteen then, when you can get some more rights?"

TUPAC: "Well, eighteen will bring lots of responsibilities that I don't want, but it'll bring respect that I feel like that's the only way I can get it. You know, I try to be as mature as I can be and demand it wherever I can get it."

As the decades passed, this thirty-six-minute video would (unfairly) be used to question Tupac's sexuality. His voice is butterfly soft, and the words leave his mouth as they might a cast-for-Hollywood interior decorator. His eyelashes, always preternaturally long, seem to flutter. He looks . . . pretty. Which is an adjective many apply to Tupac Shakur as a high school senior—neither handsome nor macho, but plenty pretty.

Tupac may have fooled his friends in Marin City into thinking his primary focuses were weed, rap, and Nintendo, and he may have fooled his Tam classmates into believing acting was his sole passion. But he was always reading, always paying attention, always observing, always studying the mannerisms of those around him. "The thing that strikes me," said Thor Thomas, a Black Tam classmate, "is he spoke proper English. A lot of people raised like we were are all slang. Not Tupac." It's a hackneyed cliché to discuss artists "taking mental photographs" of those around them, but Tupac took mental photographs of those around him.

CAVANAUGH: "Do you think if parents or adults had happier childhoods they would be better off when they grow up? I mean, like a lot of people say, if you have a troubled childhood you lack self-esteem when you grow up."

TUPAC: "No, actually I think it's, well, okay. From my mother's point, well, if you grew up happy, too happy, you know, like in fairy tale land, not fairy tale. I mean if you grew up where you know, every Christmas you got your present and every birthday you got a present and every holiday was a holiday and everything was peachy and your parents took care of everything and you just grew up.

"I don't think that prepares you for the world. You know? My mother had a really bad childhood and my father had a bad childhood and I had a bad childhood, but I loved my childhood, even though it was bad. I love it.

"I feel like it's taught me so much and I feel like nothing can faze me, you know, nothing in this world, nothing can surprise me. It might set me back, but only momentarily, only to spring back.

"And I think it's helped me to learn. It really did help me learn. And since my mother had a bad childhood, she knows the importance of being honest and the importance of facing each situation as it comes and not dealing with fairy tale land.

"Being realistic about the problem and analyzing it and solving it. See what you can do to solve it. So if you have a happy childhood, you tend to want your child to have a happy childhood. So you tend to want to keep the bad things out. And I don't think that's good, because you don't prepare them for the world."

Over the span of the sit-down, Tupac jumped from his mother's strictness to the plight of urban poverty ("If there was no money and everything depended on your moral standards and the way that you behaved and the way that you treated people, we'd be millionaires") to politics ("How did Bush win? I keep wondering and then that just makes me rebel more against society") to public school mediocrity ("It's just the place you go during the day to keep you busy") to homelessness ("How can Reagan live in a White House which has a lot of rooms and there be homelessness and he's talking about helping homelessness?"). It was the type of societal deconstruction a clearheaded Afeni Shakur would have once offered—informed, pointed, way beyond the years of its speaker.

Now it belonged to her son.

In many ways, the interview was Tupac's finest moment at Tam. His grades were not good, and his attendance record was spotty. He loved theater and tolerated English. He took chorus as an elective, donning an ill-fitting tablecloth-like robe and singing Christmas classics in a holiday concert at a nearby middle school ("We were the two brothers in chorus," said Thor Thomas). Everything else tied to school felt like drudgery. The vast majority of his class time involved Tupac pretending to pay attention while surreptitiously writing rhymes in the spiral notebook positioned on his lap.

As was the case in Baltimore, Tupac had a long list of crushes, accompanied by minimal success. "No girls would go out with him," said Dinah Leffert, a classmate and friend. "He actually came up to me and was like, 'Dinah, why won't girls date me?' And I was like, 'Well, you can't wear the same shirt two days in a row and think girls will find that attractive.'" Leffert was the rare Tam coed able to see past Tupac's fabricated exteriors. During the school year, a fire destroyed her family's home. She was a white Jewish girl from neighboring Bolinas, and nary a classmate reached out. "Except," she recalled, "for Tupac." When he learned of the inferno, Tupac called Afeni to see if his friend could relocate to her apartment, then told Leffert she was welcome to stay as long as necessary. "The only kid in the whole school who gave a shit about me was Tupac," Leffert said. "Think about that."

Marku Reynolds, the drug dealer/rapper, knew Tupac lacked money. So he hired the kid to sell weed in the Jungle. It wasn't out of necessity—Reynolds didn't need a new employee. "But you're supposed to look out for a young brother," Reynolds said. "That's how I was taught." Reynolds handed Tupac a couple of ounces of marijuana and sent him to a busy Marin City spot. It could not have been easier, and Reynolds's instructions were basic enough: "Sell it."

Tupac was enthusiastic. Here was a shot at genuine street cred. Ever since arriving in the Jungle, he'd been viewed warmly, but with a bit of a chuckle. The kid could rap, but did he walk the walk?

Answer: No.

"He was the worst drug dealer I've ever met," said Reynolds. "I mean, just terrible. One time the cops stopped us and Tupac fucking panicked and stuffed the drugs in the back seat of the cop car. So the police actually drove off with it. I was like, 'Pac, man, this isn't for you. I'd rather just give you money.'"

When Reynolds's charity ran dry, Tupac landed a job spinning pizzas at Round Table, a chain in Mill Valley. The gig came with a major perk—although it only paid $4.25 per hour, the always-hungry Tupac freely plundered from the ingredient bins. An indiscriminate eater, he was happy with a palm full of pepperoni, a fist stuffed with cherry tomatoes, fingers scooping into mushrooms. Plus, at shift's end there was always a leftover pizza or two that he could drop off for his mother and sister. "As far as I know, the number-one reason he got that job was so he could afford some new clothing and look good for girls," said Leffert. "I remember him coming to school in a new shirt and some pants. He felt good about himself, because you have to realize—there were poor people, there were really poor people, there were *really, really* poor people. And there was Tupac."*

Tam held a winter formal, and Tupac asked Ona LeSassier, a white senior involved with drama, to be his date. She was, in her words, "a back parking lot hippie girl"—neither popular nor part of an in crowd. So when the newcomer called her at home to engage in late-night flirty chats, she was smitten. Then, when he invited her to the dance, she was giddy. Leading up to the big event, Ona purchased a skin-tight black polka-dotted Betsey Johnson dress.

On the night of the dance, as Ona waited inside her living room, the LeSassier home phone rang. It was Tupac.

"He told me he wouldn't be coming," she said. "I was really upset. I went as the third wheel with some friends and felt like a loser. But, in hindsight, his real life was all sorts of difficulties and trials I couldn't have understood. Maybe he was being a jerk. But more than likely, he had some real shit hanging over him."

---

* Tupac tried his hand at a side hustle—throwing house parties with his friend Kendrick Wells. They called their operation SYNDO (Sexy Young Niggas Doing Orgies), with the dual plan of charging a cover fee and using the operation to have lots of sex. "We didn't make a ton of money," Wells said. "But there was a lot of fucking."

Chapter 9

A Chicken Named Red

When Leila Steinberg was a third grader at Crescent Heights Elementary School in Los Angeles, she had a pet chicken.

This was not the idea of her parents, Herb and Corina, who craved live poultry for the household as one craves a tapeworm. No, the Museum of Science and Industry gifted the school with its very own incubator, and Leila volunteered to take the first birthed fowl home and raise it as her own.

She named it Red.

Red was the love of Leila's life. She fed it by hand, tucked it in at night, macraméd a red-and-yellow leash and guided it on walks up and down La Cienega north of Venice Beach. If you happened upon a brown-haired nine-year-old girl yanking a bird in Southern California in 1971, it was almost certainly Leila Steinberg.

And, truly, Red was but the start of it. Leila became a collector of strays. Stray dogs, stray cats, stray rodents, stray people. "I brought home everything," she said. "My dad thought that my legal name should have been 'Volunteers of America,' because I always volunteered to help someone. When I see people who need help, I want to do something."

Throughout her youth, Leila was exposed to all sorts of eccentricities. Before their divorce, her folks used to take her to a nudist colony. Her best friend's parents hobnobbed with Charles Manson disciples. Her grandpa Marcos won the lottery in Mexico. Her father, a public defender, often invited clients to dinner. "I would ask my dad, 'How come all the kids you have are Black and Mexican?'" she recalled. "And he would say, 'The white kids get private attorneys.' His life cause was fighting for the people who no one else would fight for. It rubbed off on me."

Leila graduated from Santa Monica High in 1979, and the ensuing decade was a whirlwind of even greater eccentricities. She hosted house parties on the beach. She became the lead singer of the band Bomber. She moved to Panama. She took courses at Sonoma State. She was certified as a massage therapist. She reconnected with an old high school boyfriend, Bruce Crawford, and helped raise his baby. She married Bruce and had two biracial children of her own. She joined multiple dance companies and another band, O. J. Ekemode and the Nigerian Allstars (Yes—*O. J. Ekemode and the Nigerian Allstars*).

By 1988, Leila and Bruce were living in the Bay Area—he worked as a DJ, she for a nonprofit multicultural arts-based organization that brought musical artists into schools. "The idea was to talk to young people about life skills and racial identity and all the things they don't address," she recalled. "And we could find a creative way to do it by involving young, local musical talent." Soon, Leila hosted weekly workshops in her Rohnert Park apartment, inviting area high school kids (primarily from disadvantaged backgrounds) to stop by, have a bite to eat, and express themselves via poetry and spoken word. A core group of youngsters were regular attendees. There was Jacinta and Pookie and LeSean and Byron and . . .

Lawanda Hunter.

She was seventeen in the early months of 1988, a kid out of nearby Petaluma who spent the majority of her time attending Casa Grande High School and teaching African-style dance. One day, while out at a local club, Lawanda was approached by a short, white, twenty-seven-year-old Jewish woman. "It's Leila," recalled Lawanda. "I'm like, 'Um, who are you?' She complimented my dancing and said she wanted to talk about working together."

Before long, Lawanda was attending the weekly confabs. She looked at Leila as an older sister, and viewed things via new and creative perspectives. Dance wasn't just movement. It was a manner of thinking about space, about your body, about connectivity. "It was so eye-opening," she said. "Plus, there was always food."

On an afternoon in the spring of 1989, Lawanda received a phone call from her younger cousin, Diema Adams. There was this boy from Marin City she had started messing around with. "I want you to meet him," she told Lawanda. "He's so cute."

A couple of days later, Lawanda drove her blue Ford Escort to the Jungle, where she picked up Diema and her new love interest. He was funny looking. Not ugly, but memorably scrawny. Neck and knees. The three had been chatting for a few minutes when Tupac mentioned that he rapped.

"Oh, *do you*?" Lawanda asked.

He grinned.

"Well," she said, "show me what you've got."

Tupac's eyes widened. "Can you wait here a minute?" he asked.

Lawanda nodded, and Tupac sprinted to building 79, dashed up the stairs, came back down, and returned to the Escort armed with a tattered three-ring binder overflowing with torn-out pages and little Post-it notes.

"Well," Lawanda said, "let's hear something."

Tupac opened to a page, stared down, and rapped.

"In that instant, at that moment, I knew it was too big for me," she said. "The skill, the passion—there was no hesitation or reservation. The flow was unlike anything I'd ever heard. I almost wanted to cry, from the passion alone. *God,* the passion . . ."

In 1989, there were a mere one million cell phones in the United States of America, meaning only a third of a percent of citizens owned a mobile telecommunication device. One of these fortunate souls was Lawanda Hunter, who quickly dialed her mentor.

"Leila," she said, "you have to meet this kid. His name is Tupac. He's a rapper and he's really good."

"OK," Leila said.

"No," Lawanda replied. "What are you doing *now*?"

Leila had recently complained to Lawanda about seeking the unattainable—someone to serve as a social justice voice for high-school-aged students. Lawanda believed she had found him. The call was made on a Sunday. On Tuesday, Leila picked up Lawanda in her white Volkswagen and headed to the Jungle. They drove around the community until they spotted the kid walking near his building.

"Tupac!" Lawanda yelled. "Tupac!"

He approached.

"This is Leila," she said. "She knows people. You've gotta spit for her."

Tupac looked the white woman up and down.

He didn't have to be asked twice.

The song he performed was "Panther Power"—a highly personal and emotionally charged Black anthem that tied to Afeni's past and *his* present. Tupac was a keen and constant observer. All around him was hopelessness. The words "American dream" were tossed around ad nauseam in mainstream society—but whose dream was it? Certainly not the folks he surrounded himself with.

It begins thusly:

As real as it seems the American Dream
Ain't nothing but another calculated scheme
To get us locked up shot up back in chains
To deny us of the future rob our names

By now, Leila had heard dozens of aspiring rappers, and they had largely been predictable, mind-numbing, and generally juvenile. With rap's surge in popularity, the planet was suddenly overflowing with wannabes. "This," she recalled, "was unlike anything I'd ever heard. It had fire to it, and it had a message. It wasn't just words. It was passion." The kid was small, but his lines felt as if they were delivered by a snare drum. *Boom! Boom! Boom! Boom!* He was neither Kurtis Blow nor Public Enemy nor Heavy D. He certainly wasn't Too Short or Ant Banks or Mac Dre, Bay Area artists with Bay Area sounds. He was a hybrid.

"We left, and Leila said to me, 'This kid is special,'" recalled Lawanda. "And I was like, 'Yeah, *I know*.' Because it was actually obvious. He had that thing about him. That sparkle."

Leila invited Tupac to the next poetry circle at her home. There were seven or eight attendees—all Black or Hispanic, save Leila. By now, she had been embraced as someone who gave her all for diversity. Leila's husband was Black, her children biracial. Seven years before James McBride published *The Color of Water: A Black Man's Tribute to His White Mother,*

the youngsters surrounding Leila considered her to be the color of water. "She's the most open-minded person I've ever known," said Lawanda.
"You don't meet people without prejudice. Leila might be the one."

Yet as Leila kicked off the meeting, Tupac interrupted her to make a
point.

"You're white!" he said.

That would be correct.

"We're all Black!" he said.

Also correct.

"Well," he asked, "why are *you* in charge?"

Leila loved it. It was the precise question someone needed to ask. She
had yet to learn details of his mother, her history, her addictions, but
Tupac seemed like a hot piece of metal pulled straight from the fire. His
intensity vibrated. Third-rail energy. "He didn't view me as an authority,"
Leila said. "To him, I had no moral standing, no anything. It was, 'Who
the fuck are you?'"

Beneath his prickly exterior, however, Tupac dug the vibe. He returned
for the next meeting, then the next. The bond, stated most frequently
through performed poetry, was that everyone in the apartment was damaged. "We were all fucked up and dealing with abandonment issues," said
Leila, who had been raised alone by her father beginning at age twelve.
"We had the struggle of parents who brought us up in times of activism,
but also substance abuse. Tupac's mother was a crack addict. He arrived
with the feelings of a mother who lets you down.

"I'd never met a person like Tupac. He was so unique and outside the
box. I initially assumed he was gay, because he was extremely feminine.
Everything from his mannerisms to doing ballet in my living room. I do
believe, nowadays, he would have defined himself as fluid. He was comfortable with his femininity. But he was also hard and tough. He was an
addict's son. He felt the heartache of abandonment and poverty. He wore
that like a jacket. Like a jacket you can't take off no matter how hard you
try."

Tupac referred to Leila as "my nigga." Repeatedly. Always. With and
without humor. It initially rubbed her wrongly. She was white, the hue
of vanilla ice cream. Upon entering the apartment, Tupac would nod

quietly at Bruce, who actually *was* Black, then scream, "My nigga, what up?" toward Leila. One day, she told him it bothered her. He didn't care. "You're raising Black kids, and you need to understand the world sees them as niggas," he said. "You can walk around white and never think about race. But your children can't. So I'm calling you nigga because the world's gonna call *them* niggas."

Leila had plans for the newcomer. When Tupac first showed up at meetings, he was committed to completing his senior year at Tam High. However, his attendance began to lag, as did his interest in a diploma. By the spring of 1989, he was all but dropped out and focused on music. "I understood his position," Steinberg said. "He had a real opportunity to pursue his dream. And he took it."

Leila's day job involved creating assemblies and shows at local schools and local venues. Though Tupac technically belonged to One Nation Emcees, the group was a train moving nowhere particularly fast. Most of the members were more focused on drug deals than music, and even Demetrius Striplin, a gifted DJ, was limited in his connections. Marin City money was crack money, and though dealers funded studio time and paid for snazzy outfits and high-level equipment, they didn't have ties in the business.

Leila Steinberg did.

Granted, they weren't A-list ties. She didn't have Russell Simmons or Rick Rubin in her Rolodex. But she knew people who knew people, as well as regional promoters who—as hip-hop was blooming—were on the lookout for young acts capable of filling an auditorium.

Although the poetry groups were small, Leila felt as if she had been gifted with not one, but potentially two rap supernovas. Roughly a year before Tupac arrived on the scene, Leila was standing outside Santa Rosa High, passing out flyers for an Egyptian Lover concert she was promoting. She was seeking young artists to possibly serve as opening acts, and a tenth grader named Raymond Tyson stopped her. "I'm the biggest, baddest motherfucker here," he said. "I *have to* be in this."

Tyson told Leila he'd been preparing his whole life for this moment. Not only did he play classical piano, but he arranged his own hip-hop shows at local junior highs under the name MC Rock T. "I'd literally charge the schools a quarter," he said. "'Let me come to your school and rap. It'll cost you twenty-five cents.' It wasn't about money. It was exposure." Tyson's grandfather was Cab Calloway, the legendary jazz singer and bandleader, and his great-aunt was Blanche Calloway, the jazz singer and composer. His mother, Lael, scored her first gold record at age nineteen. "I grew up knowing that music was probably my destiny," he said.

Leila enlisted Tyson to perform at the Egyptian Lover gig, then he returned for another show a few weeks later. Yet despite his microphone skills and famous family, life wasn't going well. Around the same time he connected with Leila, Tyson left home after a falling-out with his mother and slept most nights inside the local twenty-four-hour laundromat. She thought, maybe, he needed a teammate. "So one day she introduces me to Pac," Tyson recalled. "I've got my belt buckle with my hip-hop name hanging to the side. I've got a Kangol on. Some Chuck Taylors. I'm B-boyed out. And Leila brings Tupac over. He's wearing blue jeans with cow print patches on them. He has angles shaved into his eyebrows. This is the weirdest motherfucker I've seen."

Tyson looked over Tupac suspiciously.

Tupac looked over Tyson suspiciously.

"I hear you can rap," Tupac said.

"A little," Tyson replied.

Tyson busted a few lyrics from a song he'd recently written.

"*Ohhhhh*, shit!" Tupac said. "I know you! I've heard your house tapes. You're dope."

Tyson was the Man. He'd always been the Man. There were good rappers, great rappers—and there was Rock motherfucking T, the best of the best.

Then Tupac offered up "Panther Power."

Oh, fuck.

"I'm stunned," Tyson recalled. "I'm rapping about tennis shoes, rims for a car, chicks. And here's this philosopher. It was the most humbling moment of my young life. And the most important."

It was creative love at first sight.

Tyson was already half of a local hip-hop outfit with a Latino kid named

Mark "DJ Dize" Dorado. The two had met as youngsters during break-dancing battles on the streets of Santa Rosa, and formed a tight bond while attending Cook Junior High. "Ray was a talent," Dorado recalled. "Older kids were coming from other schools to battle him, but he was pretty un-beatable." They went by DJ Dize and Rock T, printed up flyers, and took gigs wherever they could. Usually, they were accompanied by a three-person breakdance troop that went by T.M.S.—short for "Talking Maximum Shit." Steinberg was an early supporter of the duo, and she was convinced they would click with Tupac. "She was right," said Dorado. Tupac loved Dize's ability to create funkified loops and hooks from out-of-left-field records. But it was Tyson who served as McCartney to Tupac's young Lennon. One Nation Emcees were good, but no member approached Tupac's skill set. In Tyson, he felt challenged. "They loved each other," said Dorado. "But it was a rivalry. They were competitors." Within weeks, DJ Dize and Rock T absorbed Tupac and underwent a metamorphosis. They were now the trio "Strictly Dope"—the second word a corny acronym for "Down on Pushers Entirely." Early on, Tyson, Tupac, and Dize sat down and wrote four songs—a revamped "Panther Power," "Words of Wisdom," "Day in the Life," and "The Case of the Misplaced Mic." Having been around mu-sic his entire life, Tyson knew what it was to have a gift. Tupac *had a gift*. Most songwriters came up with a topic, then devoted hours to developing imagery. Tupac did it in seconds. It wasn't the stuff of Kid 'n Play—"It was Mozart and Beethoven," said Dize.

Although Marin City and Santa Rosa were rival towns, the members of Strictly Dope committed to defending one another at all costs. They were a Northern California group, unaffiliated with any particular turf. "The first day I met Tupac, he told me, 'You're coming to my neighborhood. If they get you, they're gonna have to get me, too,'" said Tyson. "There was a guy Pac knew who would shoot a motherfucker in 2.2 seconds. Pac made it clear I was off limits.

"The thing about Pac was his belief in self. It was unrivaled. We were on food stamps. All of us. And being on food stamps is embarrassing, be-cause back then they had these bright pink and green cards that screamed, 'I'm poor!' And Pac and I were going to the store, and they used to have to process them through a separate machine. So everyone knew you were the food stamp kids. We didn't have any money, we had tattered clothes. People were judging us. I could feel it. And I said to Pac, 'I fucking hate it here.' And you'll hear people tell stories like this and it sounds corny and it sounds like it can't be true. But it is. He told me, 'We're gonna be in the books. We're gonna make history. We're living history.' Think about that. I was, what, fifteen? And he said, 'I'm telling you—all over the world they're gonna be writing about us.'"

Strictly Dope bonds were oatmeal thick. Tupac urged Tyson to change his hip-hop name; that MC Rock T, eh, it could be better. "Pac thought it'd be cool to have these two guys taking opposite personas," said Byrone Dedrick, one of the T.M.S. dancers. "So he told Ray, 'You should go by Ray Luv, because that's passionate. The cool lover. And I'm a bit harder. I'm Tupac.'"

Tired of life in Marin City, Tupac left Demetrius Striplin's apartment and commenced upon a game of couch hopping. He spent time sleeping at Leila's pad in Rohnert Park, time with Tyson in Santa Rosa, time living with Dedrick. "One night we went to his mom's place to pick up some of his stuff," said Sonji Huerta-Moreland, a close friend of Dize. "It was dark and smelly and dirty. I remember thinking, I wouldn't want to be here, either."

New opportunities presented Tupac with an escape route from the Jungle. Afeni spent an inordinate amount of time dwelling with a boyfriend who, like her, was hooked on crack. This left Set, Tupac's thirteen-year-old sister, to fend largely for herself inside the first-floor apartment in building 89. Night after night she was there on her own, unsure what she would eat, how she would survive, who would take care of her. Eviction notices were slipped beneath the front door. Social workers made several visits, forcing Afeni to clean up for a few hours and playact loving sober mother.

Around this time, a classmate attacked and raped Set as she walked to school. Overcome by raw hopelessness, she never reported the crime. She also had two significantly older boyfriends—one was nineteen, the other was twenty-three—with whom she was sexually active. "I didn't think about it being inappropriate," she said. "I was just trying to live." At fifteen, she was impregnated by a resident of the Jungle who was four years her senior. She recalled him as a "nice guy"—but, looking back, recognized that the age gap was disconcerting. "I had a miscarriage alone in the apartment," she recalled. "My mom hadn't been home for months. It was just me. Even when she knew I was pregnant, no one ever took me to the hospital.

"You would think I'd have been frozen. But I wasn't. I think my fourteen-, fifteen-year-old body was so used to the trauma. It was systemic. From being homeless in New York, from my father being incarcerated, from the arguments with my mother and her sister, living in Baltimore amongst the rats and the poverty. I was in a complete state of traumatic shock. I was always afraid. I was always lonely. I was always scared. I wanted my daddy the whole time. I wanted my brother the whole time. But nobody looked out for me."*

Years later, Tupac spoke of his sister's fortitude. He also described their relationship as close. But he was incapable of attentiveness. In Baltimore, Set remembered Tupac browbeating her in front of friends, failing to offer the encouragement she desperately needed. "If he saw me outside," she recalled, "instead of, 'Oh, that's my little sister. I'm gonna hug her and walk her safely home to get her away from the bad element,' he would curse me out and scream at me and embarrass me. Maybe he felt if he did that, other people would back off. I don't know. But I needed someone to stand up for me. And he wasn't there."

In Maryland, at least he had often been present. Once he stopped attending Tam, and once people like Leila and Ray Luv and Dize consumed his attention, Set rarely saw her brother. "He was my hero," she said. "But from afar."

Around his new friends and colleagues, Set as a topic did not exist. Some didn't even know he had a sister. He was in his own world. "I have a lot of regret over that whole situation," Leila said. "I thought of myself as a person who wanted to help those in need. But Tupac's sister was all alone. She was a child. And in helping him achieve his goals, I inadvertently left her alone."

---

* At age sixteen, Set returned to New York to live with her aunt Glo. She graduated from Manhattan's West Side High School, but she said, "I never fully recovered from the trauma of California."

For Set, one of the low points came when, as an eighth grader at Martin Luther King Jr. Middle School, she entered a poetry contest. The student who could recite the most poems via memory would be crowned champion. Instead of turning toward the work of Maya Angelou or Robert Frost, Set pored through a notebook of her brother's writings and committed them to memory. One of the poems concerned Huey P. Newton, the Black Panther cofounder, and Set's teacher, Ms. Witten, just happened to live near Newton's wife, Fredrika. "She was so excited, and she asked if she could share the poem with the Newton family," Set recalled. "I thought Pac would love that." The next time she saw her brother, Set giddily broke the news. "I was looking to connect with him," she said.

Tupac responded angrily. Who was she to grab his work without asking? What right did she have? "He took the book from the house and gave it to Leila to keep safe," Set recalled. "It was devastating."

Having been brought up by an absentee addict ("People try and paint a sympathetic portrait of Afeni," said Eric Acker, a T.M.S. dancer. "They shouldn't. She was a crackhead. Seventy-five percent of the time I saw her she was fucked up"), Tupac never mustered the empathy Set required. One of his biggest strengths as a rapper was his single-minded focus. It was, however, his biggest weakness as a person. Tupac was entirely about Tupac. Years later he defended his behavior by insisting it was necessary to lift his family from poverty. But that wasn't the driving factor. Tupac wanted to be a legendary artist—period. His sister was crying out for help, but he lacked the wherewithal to receive the message. Like Set, he had been raised in a train-wreck home without sufficient love or compassion. He fended for himself—but that was the key to survival. You look out for you. *Only* you.*

Leila's goal wasn't to manage a rap group. She was an educator who liked organizing events and enlightening students. But Tupac, Ray Luv, and Dize begged her to help Strictly Dope become more than a local entity. "We wanted her as a manager," said Dize. "It wasn't like we knew too many

---

* In a 2024 interview with the author of this book, Set—who had her children when she was eighteen and nineteen years old—said she went on welfare as an adult to "spite" her brother. "My message was, 'I don't need your money. I'll handle it myself,'" she recalled. "I wasn't in a good place."

people." So Leila made calls and put out feelers. As a manager, Steinberg's primary concern was placing Strictly Dope on the map, and she largely succeeded. Within a brief period she booked the group a steady string of gigs, including opening for Rodney O and J. J. Fad at the Santa Rosa Fairgrounds and a series of fish-out-of-water slots at local reggae venues. They played the 100 Black Men of Santa Rosa convention—where fewer than one hundred Black men heard their music. A job was a job. "Strictly Dope wasn't huge, but we had an audience," said Acker. "We had a crew of girls who followed us. Some guys, too."

One of the most memorable nights came around Christmas in 1989, when Strictly Dope played at Zapps, a club in Cotati. Acker's ex-girlfriend Janine—apparently drunk and unrecovered from the breakup—heckled Strictly Dope throughout their set. As Acker (who is white) was leaving the building, Janine (also white) charged toward him and hollered, "Fuck you, Eric! You only think you're cool because you hang around with all these niggers!"

Standing inches away, Tupac lunged toward Janine and smacked her across the face.

"Bitch," he screamed, "don't you ever say that word! Ever!"

"It's obviously not right to hit a woman," Acker said. "But Pac had lines you didn't cross."

Tupac Shakur was blessed with many strengths.

Patience was not one of them.

Even as Strictly Dope was making progress and securing gigs, he was itching for bigger things. Toward the end of 1989, hip-hop was starting to take off throughout the Bay Area, what with the emergence of MC Hammer and Too Short and E-40 as local artists with mounting national appeal. They were providing templates for how to break into a universe largely controlled by East Coast entities. Their songs were on the radio. They toured and sold T-shirts and hats. From an (oft-exasperated) Leila, Tupac would receive daily lectures extolling patience. *Slow and steady. Walk before you can run. Baby steps. Inch by inch.*

"Tupac," she said, "didn't want to hear any of it."

He had recently purchased a book, *All You Need to Know About the*

Music Business, by the entertainment lawyer Donald S. Passman, and the dog-eared pages and underlined words told the story of a young man itching to climb mountains that were not yet scalable. He knew he was destined for greatness, knew he was being held back by circumstance, knew his talents exceeded those of the artists surrounding him. Opening for Rodney O and J.J. Fad was cool. But . . . shouldn't Rodney O and J.J. Fad have been opening for Tupac?

Although Leila believed in the kid, she cringed at his nonstop carping. Here she was, providing lodging, food, management—and nothing was *ever* good enough. He was a whiny, ungrateful young man who often left her apartment in ruins and habitually emptied the fridge of all its edible contents. He could be warm and endearing, or cutting and cruel. He alternated fits of affection with fits of rage. Leila was, he said, beautiful and compassionate. But Leila was also, he said, a wannabe white savior who needed to know her place. The two engaged in a never-ending string of heated conversations about "making it" in music. Tupac didn't want to hear stories about the bands who took years to break through. No, he needed it *now*. "He wanted success as badly as anyone I've ever known," Leila said. "He always said to me, 'You know people. I *need* a record deal.'"

She did not disagree. Which is why, on behalf of both Tupac and the other members of Strictly Dope, six months after becoming their manager Leila Steinberg finally made *the* phone call. "The one," she said, "that really changed Tupac's life trajectory."

Although he had yet to establish a national name, Atron Gregory was a mover and shaker when it came to West Coast music. His run had begun a decade earlier, when, as a junior arts administration major at San Francisco State, he was asked by a boyhood friend, the jazz musician Rodney Franklin, to serve as his tour manager.

"What would I do?" Gregory asked.

"Honestly," Franklin said, "I don't know."

He assumed the gig, and the first show he arranged for his old pal was a five-thousand-dollar performance in Los Angeles. "Well, we drove the van down from Northern California, did the show, then we looked for the promoter," Gregory recalled. "I never found him, and we never got the five thousand dollars. It was a lesson—always get paid before the show."

Gregory spent the next half decade establishing himself. He caught a break in 1986, when Franklin hired Jerry Heller to be his new full-time manager. At the time, Heller's major client was World Class Wreckin' Cru, an electro group out of Los Angeles that featured a young DJ by the name of Andre "Dr. Dre" Young. Gregory wound up managing the Cru, and stuck with Heller when, a year later, he created a label, Ruthless Records, that launched the Dr. Dre–Eazy-E–Ice Cube–powered gangsta rap behemoth N.W.A. Gregory served as tour manager for all of the Ruthless acts, from J. J. Fad and Michel'le to the D.O.C. and N.W.A. "I learned a ton," Gregory recalled. "You don't experience the Straight Outta Compton tour without picking up some things. But I finally decided I wanted to start my own thing, and I wanted to focus on hip-hop."

Among Franklin's close friends was Jimi Dright Jr., a classically trained pianist and the son of a heroin kingpin–saxophonist–haberdasher out of North Oakland. Franklin told Gregory that Jimi, aka Chopmaster J, was somebody he should meet, "if you like talent and you like ambition." So they arranged to dine at a Thai restaurant in Southern California, and when Dright arrived he was accompanied by a scraggly-looking Black man with arching eyebrows, high cheekbones, an exuberant laugh, and a thrift-store wardrobe. His name was Gregory Jacobs. He went by Shock G.

Over chicken satay and steamed sticky rice, Gregory, Chopmaster J, and Shock G talked music and dreams. In 1987 the musicians had teamed up with a third artist, Kenny "Kenny K" Waters, to start what they called Digital Underground—"an eccentric brand of hip-hop, backed by their love and respect for Parliament-Funkadelic," wrote the author Jonathan Abrams. And while they enjoyed regional success with a cassette single called "Underwater Rimes," few outside the Bay Area knew of their existence.

Atron Gregory, however, dug everything about Digital Underground and, in particular, *everything* about the twenty-four-year-old Shock G. Greg Jacobs had been raised in Far Rockaway, New York, until, at age fourteen, his parents' divorce resulted in a family relocation to Tampa, Florida. Set back by their new slow-moving rural lives, he and his younger brother Kent passed the time catching snakes in the canals, then selling them to a pet store for three dollars a pop. Gifted with an ear for music, an adolescent Greg taught himself jazz piano without knowing how to read a note. At sixteen, he learned to play Thelonious Monk's "Evidence." Greg enrolled as a part-time music student at Hillsborough Community College, but was ultimately expelled when a dean insisted he was incapable of learning. Come nighttime Greg snuck back into the music department and, in the darkness, played piano for hours. His fingers throbbed. His knuckles tightened. But he stayed through exhaustion.

In 1985, Greg relocated to Los Angeles and joined an R&B cover band that played reheated classics inside a Holiday Inn lounge. In his spare time, however, he dabbled in writing rap tunes. It played to his strengths of alliteration and verbal gymnastics. Greg loved hearing syllables hop and jump and slide. Rhyming did it for him. As did goofiness. He liked the newness of rap as a medium. Somewhere between classical piano and Dr. Seuss, he saw hip-hop.

Back in his New York days, Greg had a friend named Sean Trone, who rapped under the moniker "Shah T" in the hip-hop duo No Face. However, for years Greg mistook "Shah" as "Shock." Itching to rebrand, Greg dubbed himself "Shock G."

"By the time he figured out the mistake, he was like, 'Shit, it's too late,'" said Ronald "Money-B" Brooks, his future collaborator. "He didn't wanna change again."

Shock G it was.

Frustrated by what he considered to be a stagnant Southern California hip-hop scene, Greg uprooted to Oakland in late 1986. It was there where he bumped into Dright while shopping at a music store. "We connected," Dright said. "At that point Shock was happy making a tape and sending it home to his friends. He was a musician who loved creating and he was filled with potential. But he needed inspiration."

They named themselves Digital Underground.

The outfit was less trio than Grateful Dead–esque—on any given day, a random drummer or accordionist might jump in. Thanks to funding from Jimi's father, Digital Underground was able to afford studio time and write, record, and produce the goofy yet borderline-brilliant "Underwater Rimes," which takes place in the ocean and features Shock G rapping over his own beats. "Shock G was the creative genius behind the shit," said

Randy Brooks, an early Digital Underground collaborator, "and Jimi was the motivator, the engine, the Berry Gordy type who made shit happen."

Yet for all the musical splendor, they knew little about the business. So when Atron Gregory came along with an offer to make them clients of his new enterprise, TNT Records, the men jumped at the opportunity. Thanks in large part to Gregory's savvy, "Underwater Rimes" received regular spins on local hip-hop radio.

In late 1989, Digital Underground was wrapping up its first studio album, *Sex Packets*. The album featured "The Humpty Dance," a song that would later hit number 1 on the *Billboard* Rap Singles chart, highlighting Shock G as two characters—himself and a goofy hip-hop artist named Humpty, who wore a fake Groucho Marx big nose and glasses. "It was about to happen very quickly," said Gregory. "In a blink, everyone would know Shock G and Digital Underground."

When Leila Steinberg called Atron Gregory in the fall of 1989, she wasn't a stranger. He knew her as a scrappy local promoter, and had once told her to give him a heads-up should she stumble upon any special artists. At this moment, with Digital Underground preparing to soar, she felt compelled. "Atron," she said, "you said you'd help me if I had someone worthwhile. Well, I have a kid—actually two kids. They're both talents, and they're pressuring me. Can you help?"

Arrangements were made for Leila to bring Tupac and Ray Luv to Richmond, California, for a meeting with Shock G at Starlight Sound, a recording studio. The plan, at least in Leila's mind, was for Shock G to hear the two young rappers perform and send them on their way toward greatness. At the last minute, however, Ray Luv's father refused to allow his son to attend. The Tyson family had learned from experience not to trust the music business. Their Ray would be going to college, dammit. "So I sort of lied [to Shock G] and said Ray couldn't come because he was in school," said Leila. "I mean, he *was* in school. So . . ."

Leila drove Tupac to the studio. Though Richmond was only forty minutes south of her Rohnert Park home, it felt like another side of the world. Richmond was Black, poor, run-down, crack infested, and depressed. As a Marin City kid, Tupac had been warned to stay as far away from Richmond as possible. The two towns had beef. "Our folks knew not to go there," said Brian Times, the Marin City drug dealer. "There were a lot of places it was cool to visit. Not Richmond."

Tupac and Leila arrived, then waited more than an hour for Shock G. Tupac, a man of no patience, was irked. It showed.

"Sorry about that, bro," Shock G said upon finally emerging. "Come on in."

Tupac entered the studio's piano room, put down a backpack, removed his jacket, lit up a Newport, and asked, "You ready? You want me to do it right now?"

"Sure," said Shock G. "Let it rip."

"He had that whole Scarface, 'Is we doing this drug deal or not, nigga?'" recalled Shock G, who was eight years Tupac's senior. "It had that urgency to it."

Tupac launched into an a cappella rendition of "The Case of the Misplaced Mic," an upbeat song he'd written for Strictly Dope.

"It was street," Shock G later said. "It was educated. It was articulate . . . like hip-hop fantasy type stuff, a spy looking for his mic." Afterward, Shock G called Atron and raved. "He's good," he said. "He's really good."

An unofficial follow-up was held a week later outside Shock's apartment at Thirty-Eighth and Market in Oakland. This time the attendees included the three Strictly Dope guys and all of Digital Underground— including three new additions to the crew: Ronald "Money-B" Brooks, Neil "Sleuth" Johnson, and David "DJ Fuze" Elliott. Dright recalled Tupac looking "like a stick of beef jerky with teeth." Dize began beatboxing on the street corner, and Tupac and Ray Luv jumped in. "They both sounded all right to me," said Money-B. "But afterward, when we all hung out— that's when Tupac's personality popped. He commanded attention." Ray Luv had talent. There was no doubt about it. But Tupac was a July 4th fireworks show.*

To Shock G, Tupac wasn't another come-along rapper. He was Mick Jagger. He was Jimi Hendrix. He was the type of performer who consumed

---

* According to Kendrick Wells, Tupac's friend from Marin City, Ray Luv was largely discarded by Tupac. "Once it was clear he was the guy they were interested in," Wells said before his death in 2024, "he didn't really think much about bringing Ray Luv along for the ride."

you, and rendered those surrounding him invisible. When the afternoon wrapped, Gregory pulled Leila aside and said the words she both dreaded and expected. "We want *him*," he said, pointing toward Tupac. "Not *them*."

It was the age-old story of the front man leaving behind the band. Only, Tupac wasn't that guy. On August 2, 1989, Tupac signed a management contract with TNT Records, with the stipulation that he be allowed to record a demo with Ray Luv and Dize under the Strictly Dope banner. That work, recorded and produced by Dright largely inside a studio in Hayward, California, was sloppy and scattered, and Dright devoted far too much effort to preventing Tupac from hitting on the sound engineer's wife. But while most of the project vanished into the musical abyss, the experience proved invaluable. Tupac loved standing in a small booth, alone with a microphone, spitting lyrics and feeling his voice reverberate off the walls. So much of his life had involved trauma and stress and pain and fighting to be heard.

Here, creating music, he felt heard.

"He felt," recalled Dright, "motherfucking alive."

Chapter 10

Digital

Because he died, in 2021, at the fairly young age of fifty-seven, and because the later years of his life were spent as an unrecognizable motel-hopping drug addict with a couple of dollars to his name, Gregory "Shock G" Jacobs doesn't receive his proper due as a music visionary.

Sure, within the realms of hip-hop he's regarded as an innovator. And most fans of the genre can still rap along to "The Humpty Dance" and laugh at the beautiful audacity of his Humpty Hump creation.

But, for far too many, the legacy of Shock G sits on a dusty shelf, a fake plastic nose and some glasses, somewhere in the rear of the late-1980s/early-1990s discount rap bin alongside Young MC and Tone Lōc. "People don't understand," said Atron Gregory. "Greg is Beethoven."

"*Prince*," added Money-B. "He was on a Prince level."

Though he was best known as a rapper, Shock G's gifts came in production. Like a sparrow or Doberman, he picked up sounds others missed. Beats. Hooks. Riffs. It all slowed down for Shock G, to the point where he sometimes asked others for reassurance that they heard what he had just heard. "It was uncanny," said Jimi Dright. "Different-level stuff."

In the fall of 1989, Tupac Shakur was attuned to Shock G's talents as much as anyone. He had been signed to Atron Gregory's TNT management company, and worked with Dright in the studio, but Tupac looked at Shock G and felt musical kinship. Here was another person who shared the love, the passion, the drive, the sense of purpose. But Tupac also experienced pangs of envy.

Even though he was under the TNT umbrella, Tupac felt left out. He liked the Digital Underground guys, and smoked copious amounts of weed in their Oakland hangout pad. They talked rap and women and all sorts of topics. "It was definitely a family-like environment," said Money-B. "When you're together that often, and your bond is music, it's strong."

Yet, at the same time Tupac was acclimating himself to this new world, Digital Underground was taking off. The group was signed to Tommy Boy Records, and in August 1989, it released the single "Doowutchyalike." The song received extensive airplay on KMEL, the Bay Area's primary urban contemporary radio station, and was praised by Barry Walters of the *San Francisco Examiner* as evoking "P-Funk at its funky peak." Within a month's time, the members of Digital Underground were preparing for their first-ever European tour. "Tupac saw me and the DU crew constantly doing phone interviews for radio and national magazines," Dright recalled. "He could see and feel the buzz of all the shit going on and he had to be in on it. Once Pac felt that buzz, there was nothing else like it. He wanted to be down with us."

Only, he wasn't down with Digital Underground. Not really. Watching his musical cohorts rehearse and pack for their international adventure was torture. And when the seven members of the group jetted off for Berlin's International Audio and Video Fair, then continued on to England for the European tour, he was left behind. In London, the *Evening Standard* labeled Digital Underground "hip-hop's newest golden boys." At home, Tupac felt discarded. He had no record deal, Strictly Dope was falling apart, his pockets were largely empty, and his mother—still addicted to crack—remained largely MIA.

To earn extra money, Tupac walked the streets of Santa Rosa and Oakland, selling copies of *By Any Means Necessary*, the monthly newspaper of the New Afrikan Panthers. A new youth foundation affiliated with the New Afrikan People's Organization, the group's stated goal was to spearhead the creation of a New Afrikan nation-state. It borrowed many ideas from the old Black Panthers, and Afeni was happy her son was spreading the good word. Only Tupac's motives weren't entirely altruistic. Hungry, poor, and desperate, he peddled the one-dollar publication for double the cover price—and never turned in the profits. "It was amazing, because these newspapers weren't very kind to white people, and he probably sold most of the copies to whites," said Leila. "They would buy them because he was just so charming." To make even more dough, Tupac created crude faux-leather African medallions and hawked them alongside the publication.

Before long word reached Chokwe Lumumba, the Atlanta-based head of the New Afrikan People's Organization, that the oldest child of the legendary Afeni Shakur was as charismatic as his mother—and a worthy new figure to lead the fight for Black independence. Dating back to his childhood in New York City, Tupac was unusually preoccupied with the fleeting nature of time and the Black man's short life span. Thanks to his mother, who rarely hid truth from her children, Tupac could recite the statistics: That the average Black man in America lived just sixty-five years. That the homicide rate for Black men was 54 per 100,000 people (for whites, it was 8.4 per 100,000), and Black men were incarcerated at 9.6 times the rate of white men. He obsessed over the details. Death, for Tupac, wasn't something that would happen eighty years down the line, in a hospice facility surrounded by loved ones as Frank Sinatra's "My Way" played softly. No, death was a stray bullet fired from a stranger's gun. It was uncompromising and unpredictable and inglorious, and it would—he was certain—end his existence by age twenty. Find a Black Panther cub and you'll find a person well-versed in the grim reaper waiting by your bed. Death loomed. It was inescapable. "My mother talked about Black men rarely living past a certain age," said Set Shakur. "That became his understanding in life."

As a result, Tupac was perpetually in a rush to get here, get there, do this, do that. "He was always obsessed with time and that he wouldn't be here long," said Leila. "It was the most infuriating thing, because it impacted his ability to make reasonable decisions. A normal thinker would have watched Digital Underground tour and wait his turn. He was eighteen and on the verge of some great stuff. But Tupac didn't think like that. Everything was urgent."

That's why, when Lumumba called and asked Tupac whether he might consider relocating to Atlanta and taking over as national chairman of the New Afrikan Panthers, he didn't say no. Instead, he asked Leila what she thought.

"Tupac," she said, "you'd be making a mistake."

He didn't listen.

"Tupac was dead serious," she recalled. "So I called Atron and said, 'You *have* to get him going. You have to get him a deal.'"

Gregory was nonplussed.

"Atron," Leila said, "he's the most impatient person you'll ever meet."

Gregory needed time to figure things out. Tupac didn't want to hear it. He told Lumumba that, yes, he would come to Atlanta and get to work. The New Afrikan People's Organization asked Tupac for his mailing address, and sent him an envelope containing three hundred dollars in cash with which to book his flight from San Francisco to Atlanta.

Afeni stole it.

The money was there, on the table in the old Marin City apartment. Then it wasn't there.

Tupac knew what had happened. He just *knew*. Afeni lied at first, then admitted, begrudgingly, that she had used the money to buy crack. It was both the angriest and saddest Tupac had ever been. The three hundred dollars symbolized a fresh start in a new part of the country. The thievery symbolized the woebegone creature his idol had become. Tupac explained what had transpired, and Lumumba—a gracious man and the future mayor of Jackson, Mississippi—booked the flight for Tupac himself.

Informed of the decision, Gregory couldn't believe it. Alas, it was too late.

Tupac Shakur was heading to the Deep South.

Tupac arrived in Atlanta in the winter of 1989, and he moved in with Watani Tyehimba, a longtime Black Panther associate and a man who had recently relocated from Los Angeles to help establish the New Afrikan independence movement. Back in the late 1960s and early 1970s, Watani had taught members of the Black Panthers martial arts and self-defense. He also served as a paralegal and investigator helping to prepare the various appeals filed in California Supreme Court on behalf of Geronimo Pratt. Which brought him exposure to Afeni, a woman he remembered as "very articulate, very smart, sometimes manipulative. She could organize other people to do things, but she didn't always carry them out herself."

In Tupac, Watani saw a figure with the potential to accomplish things his mother had not. He had hope that the New Afrikan Panthers might emerge as a mouthpiece for young Black men and women tired of the status quo. The goal was for Tupac to create a membership database, to hold regular meetings, to spread word that the spirit of the Black Panthers was alive and well and percolating in Atlanta.

One problem: Tupac Shakur, just eighteen, had no clue how to get any of this done.

Within days of his arrival, Tupac appeared as the featured guest on a show, *Round Midnight*, that ran weekly on Georgia's public radio station WRFG. The host's name was Bomani Bakari, a forty-two-year-old Atlanta Legal Aid Society employee who wanted the new brother in town to share the word.

After five minutes of banter and Tupac letting listeners know there would be a meeting the following evening in room 302 of the Woodrow Library, Bakari opened up the phone lines. And it was a buffet of weirdness. Some of the questions were logical ("What does it take to be a Black Panther?"). Some were rambling ("I also was looking at the news where they showed how the Black students were being treated in Virginia. This one sister from Howard said she wanted to go back . . ."). One caller went on a circuitous diatribe about a Catholic priest with feminine features who molested choirboys ("So what do you brothers think about that?").

Mostly what emerged was that Tupac understood little of why he was in Atlanta or what he was supposed to say. He struggled to explain what the New Afrikan Panthers represented, or the purpose of their existence. His passion was off the charts. His knowledge? Not so much. The next day's meeting at the Woodrow Library was a disaster. Tupac stood before a fleet of empty chairs.

That being said, life with the New Afrikan Panthers wasn't all bad. Tupac was hanging up flyers one day when he met Thomas Dease, a student studying copyright law at the Art Institute of Atlanta. Dease and four roommates lived in unit H10 of the Lennox Woods apartment complex. All the occupants were amateur MCs, and they soon roped in several more friends to start a ten-person hip-hop group called (wait for it) H10.

As Tupac's interest in the New Afrikan Panthers waned, he found himself spending hours inside apartment H10. Another young man who frequented the pad was Steve Gibson, later known as half of Tag Team, the duo that brought the world "Whoomp! (There It Is)." Gibson had never heard of Tupac before Atlanta, and while he thought the kid had talent, he wanted him to stop blathering. "He was *so* hyped on himself," said Gibson. "Telling people over and over, 'I'm gonna make it big!' I got sick of hearing about it."

Inside H10, Tupac talked and talked and talked. But he also impressed. One of the other members of the group was Derrick Joiner, an MC out of Pittsburgh who had come to the Art Institute after going AWOL from the United States Navy. Widely considered H10's best pure rapper, Joiner boasted a herky-jerky style that mixed elongated syllables with quick-punch wording. Tupac didn't merely gravitate toward Joiner, he imitated him. Others who lived in H10 insist Tupac's style changed during his time in Atlanta. "We all knew he was copying Derrick," said Dease. "It wasn't a bad thing, because Derrick was talented. But it was obvious."

"Oh, he totally flipped his approach," added Joiner. "For years I'd have people tell me, 'Wow, you sound like a young Tupac.' And I'd be like, 'Try again. Tupac sounds like a young me.'"

Overall, Tupac only spent a handful of months in Atlanta. The young men of H10 liked his spunk, his passion. They liked the way he cared about Black people; how he was willing to fight for what was right.

They also were left with one lasting memory.

"So the apartment wasn't in a great area," Joiner recalled. "And there used to be a lot of crackheads. We'd stand at the front door, pretending we had drugs to sell them. They'd give us money, then we'd go out the back door and go get some pizza or something.

"Tupac thought that was really funny."

During his client's time in Georgia, Atron Gregory tried shopping a demo Tupac had recorded as a way of landing him a deal. Because Digital Underground was now on a roll, touring Europe and, on January 20, 1990, releasing "The Humpty Dance," the song that would become its definitive hit, Gregory assumed record company executives would return his calls.

And they did—with a standard response to this Tupac Shakur character: *Nah.*

"I literally got that demo to everybody," Gregory said. "No one wanted him." The reactions varied. One (quizzically) was that he sounded too much like Ice Cube. Some people just found it sort of dull. It was a so-so assortment of disjointed tracks that failed to showcase Tupac's talents.

Even as the group he fronted rolled through Europe, Shock G couldn't stop thinking about Tupac. He hated the idea of his throwing away his musical gifts to hang flyers on Atlanta light poles. He, too, knew what it was to be hungry and impatient. When he asked Atron what the youngster was up to, he was dismayed by the response. "He doesn't want to wait anymore," Gregory explained. "He gave the music business a year. If we don't do something, we're going to lose him."

This was in the early months of 1990, and the last thing Digital Underground needed was another member in its already large troupe. The group was on the verge of something big. They were in the process of preparing a domestic leg of the tour before jetting off for Japan. The hype was real. In New York's *Newsday*, John Leland wrote beneath the headline THE SOUNDS TO WATCH IN THE '90S, "Digital Underground looks like the new face of hip-hop." Added Jonathan Gold of the *Los Angeles Times*, "Digital Underground is the new sound, a shot of funky Adrenalin into the hip-hop scene."

One day, Atron Gregory called Shock G with a blunt request.

"Can you take Tupac on tour with you?" he asked.

"We're full," Shock G replied.

And it was true. Digital Underground was full. Touring was expensive. There was simply no space for another mouth to feed.

But . . .

Money-B had a younger brother, Cullen, who had been booked to serve as Digital Underground's domestic tour roadie. That meant lugging equipment, unpacking, packing. It was tough work, and while Cullen was down to handle the task, there were other things in life he aspired to do. So Shock G reached out to Tupac and asked whether he might like to occupy the least-glorious job in human history.

"What does that mean?" Tupac asked.

Shock G broke down the responsibilities. Dragging. Carrying. Schlepping. Busting ass for mediocre pay. "We might be able to use you onstage, too," he said. "But there are no guarantees."

"Stage"?

Did Shock G say "stage"?

Tupac was in.

Digital Underground was slated to hop onto the Big Daddy Kane: Chocolate City tour in early April. At the time, Kane—a New York City artist and gifted wordsmith whose hits included "Ain't No Half-Steppin'" and "I Get the Job Done"—was one of the huge draws in rap, and the tour featured DU, Queen Latifah, MC Lyte, and 3rd Bass. Tupac formally joined Digital Underground on March 17, 1990, when they were scheduled to perform at the annual Bay Area Music Awards (the Bammies) alongside a disparate lineup that included Todd Rundgren, Carlos Santana, Primus, and Tesla. The event was held at San Francisco's Civic Auditorium, and Tupac—who later earned a reputation for tardiness—arrived hours early. He wore blue jeans, a T-shirt, and a vest, as well as a homemade black-and-red Afrocentric necklace. And he was *excited*. Less than a year earlier he was trying to survive high school and the Jungle. Less than two months earlier he was an aspiring civil rights leader speaking to six people on late-night AM radio. Now he found himself in the midst of musical nirvana.

The United States tour officially launched on April 6 in Lafayette, Louisiana, inside a 13,500-seat Astrodome knockoff named the Cajundome. An estimated crowd of 2,500 showed up, leaving the artists to perform to an ocean of empty plastic chairs. Such was the state of hip-hop in the early 1990s—on the rise, about to explode, but not quite there yet (by comparison, the country singer Clint Black would sell out the building two weeks later). To Tupac, however, it wasn't about attendance or cheers. "It was about being there," said Richard "Daddy Rich" Lawson, 3rd Bass's DJ. "When you have that type of fire under you, and you want it so badly, and your family is struggling like his was . . . he needed this as his break."

The tour began as a southern swing, with the artists traveling via buses from Lafayette to Memphis to Louisville to Macon to Mobile to Atlanta to Roanoke. Tupac usually plopped down near the back of Digital Underground's leased Greyhound, but he rarely stayed put. Unlike the twenty-six-year-old Shock G, who enjoyed kicking back, smoking some weed, and watching the country pass, Tupac bounced from seat to seat and person to person, a whirlwind of oft-incoherent adolescent jabbering about music, politics, Black Panthers, bitches, blunts, brews, superheroes, cartoons, pizza toppings, Kate Bush songs.

"He was all over the map," said Pete "Prime Minister Pete Nice" Nash, the 3rd Bass MC. "He wasn't making much money, and the thirty-dollar-per-day per diem gets tight quick. So I found myself buying Tupac a bunch of Whoppers, a bunch of Pizza Hut. Keeping the kid fed." Tupac lived on junk food (including a bottomless thirst for Coca-Cola) and had Daddy Rich cut his hair ("He needed a makeover," Daddy Rich recalled) and slept, on average, three hours a night. Why snooze when there was life to live? "He was kind of just like one of your fun cousins at the barbecue," said Ramon "Pee-Wee" Gooden, a DU rapper. "Always on."

The members of Digital Underground could tell when Tupac had been drinking, and they dreaded the experience. An inebriated Tupac was unhinged and predisposed to brawling. "Annoying as fuck," said Dright. "I loved the kid. But . . . Jesus. Calm down." Weed, on the other hand, soothed Tupac, so the marijuana was plentifully supplied. Tupac smoked all hours of the day and night. Though not yet Digital Underground's best rapper, he was—without question—the group's biggest bud fiend. "Weed served as his sedative," said Money-B. "If you told me Pac had ADHD I'd believe it. But once the weed arrived, you could talk to him and he was cool."

Technically, Tupac's title (not that he really had one) was "roadie." The designation was imprecise. Yes, Tupac hauled equipment and plugged in cables. But Digital Underground was no diva collective. All the musicians toted their own gear. "It trips me how the media has created this story of Tupac carrying all our shit," said Gooden. "Shock didn't take him on tour because he needed an equipment guy. Pac was tight. He had the goods. Shock saw it and said, 'Kid, come with us. You'll dance. You'll rap. We'll figure it out.'"

Show after show, Tupac had several tasks.

First, he *did* carry stuff.

Second, he served as the hype man between the fifteen-or-so-minute gap when the prior act (usually 3rd Bass) wrapped and Digital Underground hit the stage. But this was a far cry from the famed histrionics of Public Enemy's Flavor Flav. Instead of hollering into a mic and encouraging audience members to rise, Tupac walked onto the stage wearing leopard-print underwear and carrying a blow-up sex doll.

His job: Dry-hump the toy.

"The guy is in his underwear, fucking a doll, rapping a few verses, and getting the crowd going," said Pete Nice. "Pac pulled it off."

Third, he served as one of two Digital Underground background dancers. Which was remarkable, considering he couldn't dance. "He was terrible," said Money-B. "I'd be dancing next to him and he'd do his arms all stupid. I'm still confused by it. 'Pac, what the hell are you doing?'"

The shows were wild, and the Digital Underground segments were the wildest. There was a Kiss-like mystique to their very existence. *Was Shock G also Humpty Hump? Were they different people?* No one would say for sure. "I hate to admit this, but it took me eight shows into the tour to realize Humpty and Shock were one dude," said Pete Nice.* Because they were promoting the new *Sex Packets* album, the group invested in "sex packets." One of Tupac's tasks was to fill small Ziploc baggies with "everything you need for a good little hookup evening," said Shock G—a condom, a shot of liquor, bubblegum, some popcorn, party favors, and a Humpty Hump sticker. "We ended up making these lozenges that were going to give you an orgasm," said Steve Knutson, the head of sales at Tommy Boy. "They were just candy, but we had a male one and a female one."

Tupac loved arriving at the arena, dressing backstage, strolling among the stars. It wasn't merely the fulfilment of a dream. It was escapism. The scrawny impoverished kid felt light-years removed from the hellscape of Marin City. However, his impatience and immaturity resulted in some uncomfortable situations. Tupac had no filter. He always believed he was right, and never apologized. His temper went from zero to a hundred in a split second, and it took him hours to cool off. "One thing Tupac hated is when I used to tell him to calm down," said Money-B. "'Don't tell me to

---

* To fully dive into the Humpty Hump mythology, Digital Underground used Kent Racker, Shock G's younger brother, to appear as either Shock G or Humpty Hump both onstage and in promotional materials. The two looked enough alike that it worked.

fucking calm down!' It was like a trigger word." During the Roanoke show (billed as the "Easter Rap-a-Thon"), on April 14 at the city's Civic Center Coliseum, Tupac flew into a rage when the mics went fuzzy and the feedback rose. Because Digital Underground was a new group with limited funds, Big Daddy Kane had allowed them to use his sound engineer. It was a charitable act that left Tupac unmoved. He charged the engineer and screamed, "I am going to fuck you up when we're done! You're a fucking dead man!"

"Yo, Pac!" Shock G lectured. "You *cannot* talk to him that way. You need to apologize."

He never did.

The next two shows took place in Detroit and New York City, and Tupac was shadowed backstage by security. "To prevent him," Dright recalled, "from beating down the tour's only sound engineer."

"If you hear someone tell you he was really tight with Tupac and never had a problem with him, he's lying or exaggerating the friendship," said Money-B. "Tupac was born combative. He was raised to question everything, and he never bit his tongue. He would challenge *every . . . little . . . thing*, and you were bound to get into it with him."

While he lived for music, Tupac *loved* the after-parties. All the performers on the Chocolate City tour stayed in the same motels and hotels, and often met up in the lobby to decompress. If there was a piano handy, Shock G inevitably slid onto the bench and played everything from Elton John and Billy Joel to Chopin and Rachmaninoff to Jerry Lee Lewis and Little Richard. It was here, inside your Macon Marriott, your Roanoke Hyatt, your Detroit Hilton, that many first learned Tupac could bring it. Standing alongside Shock G, Tupac and MC Serch of 3rd Bass regularly freestyle-rapped over the sound of the ivories. "Tupac was a different level," said Daddy Rich. "Just these amazing verbal onslaughts. Top-of-the-head brilliance. And it was like, Hmm, this is an all-star collection of rappers. Is Tupac the best one here?"

Although well regarded for his prowess with the women, Shock G was usually the first to call it a night. "I was starting to choose to chill," he said. "I was just discovering white chicks and ecstasy and staying inside." Tupac was without fail out the latest. His road roommate was Dright, a mild (by comparison) partier who was eleven years Tupac's senior. Dright initially believed he would be able to serve as a road mentor for the youngster. He was incorrect. "It became obvious really quickly that the whole backstage scene, the hotel scene, and the celebrity of the other rappers on tour fascinated Tupac," Dright recalled. "I never balked at being his roommate on the road. But it was bad. There I was thinking, What the fuck have I done?"

According to Dright, away-from-home Tupac Shakur was a horny tiger seeking out prey. This was the golden age of musical groupies, and young, scantily clad women inevitably learned the rappers' whereabouts. The vast majority sought out Big Daddy Kane, a noted lothario. Females lined up at Kane's hotel room door, but groupies traveled in packs, and Big Daddy Kane could only have so much sex. "We were getting the friends that were waiting," said Money-B.

Not all that long ago, Tupac had been desperate for female attention inside the Baltimore School for the Arts and Tamalpais High. Now, thanks to having opened for Big Daddy Kane and standing on the stage alongside Shock G and Money-B, he was a magnet. Tupac loved scanning the hotel lobbies for women, spitting his Digital Underground credentials, inviting them back to the room, having sex (recalled Dright, "Pac would choose five or six women and fuck all of them over the course of the night"), and, as a final touch, practicing the art of Urolagnia—i.e., urinating atop their bodies in a kink that filled him with perverse pleasure.

"That shit," recalled Dright, "was wild."

The members of Digital Underground spent the duration of the Chocolate City tour saving their used condoms. Each night, they placed their soiled prophylactics inside a jar in the road manager's hotel room—and if one member didn't have a used rubber, he was required to instead plunk down a hundred-dollar bill. At tour's end, the man responsible for the most sheaths took home the dough. "It was a nasty jar," Shock G said. "Money-B won it. But Pac should have won it because, man . . . he would bed two at the soundcheck. And then sometimes right then, that initial venue meeting. Just those 50 people, of staff running around, friends of friends, secretaries and grips and whoever. And Pac would bed two then. So those condoms didn't make it. Those times along the way on the road sometimes, the bus stops at Hooters or something and Tupac would bed one. He had it, man. He had that allure that girls just couldn't say no to."

On May 3, 1990, Tupac Shakur made his national television debut.

It was not what he had hoped for.

With "The Humpty Dance" a phenomenon, Digital Underground was invited to perform the song on *The Arsenio Hall Show*, at the time late-night television's coolest destination.

The entire segment lasted barely three minutes, and Tupac's voice can be heard twice—first, when Money-B announces, "The Underground is in the house!" and Tupac joins in to clumsily shout, "*House!*" Second, when he bellows, "Go Humpty! Go Humpty! Go!" before flipping the mic to Shock G, who—dressed in a black-and-white Zubaz top hat, gold medallion, and fake nose and glasses—steals the show. The remainder of the gig involves Tupac flopping around like an intoxicated llama.

For a young man who wanted to be heard, not merely seen, it was somewhat humiliating. He was tired of "The Humpty Dance" ("Shit gets old," he complained to Chopmaster J) and tired of being the sixth pitcher in the rotation. Shock G had thrown Tupac a couple of bars here and there during the shows, but it felt like charity.

Then, however, the calls came in.

From family in New York.

From friends in Baltimore and Marin.

"*Tupac, was that you on* Arsenio?"

"*Dude, I saw you on TV . . .*"

"*Bro, that was amazing . . .*"

"My friend called me and was like, 'Yo! Did you see Tupac dancing with Digital Underground?'" recalled Sean Stinnett, a Baltimore School for the Arts classmate. "I was like, Wow, well, he's definitely not coming back now."

"I remember looking up at my TV," said Dameene Dedrick, a classmate from Tam. "And I was like, Wait! Is that . . . Tupac? From high school?"

For Tupac, being this *widely* seen served as a necessary buzz. Although he had always been brash, he was also the fatherless son of an addict. He talked a good game, but, in rare quiet and sober moments, wondered aloud whether he was worthy of *anything*. Afeni had been a Black Panther. What was he? "Sometimes the people screaming the most are hiding the greatest insecurities," Money-B said. "That's pretty standard."

"Deep down he had that same gap foster kids have," Shock G said. "That whole shit from relative to relative. Never feeling loved, like he didn't fit in, didn't have a foundation. He didn't feel like anybody loved him unless he was Tupac the character."

So the notoriety mattered. And what came next for Digital Underground *really* mattered. Now that they were one of the hottest groups in America, Shock G was offered *a lot* of money to have DU leap from Chocolate City to a summer tour headlined by MC Hammer, whose *Please Hammer Don't Hurt 'Em* album had crossed the threshold from hot musical release to generational time stamp. A Bay Area native who cut his teeth as a mid-1970s Oakland A's batboy, Hammer was gobbling up every conceivable musical award, and his hit song, the Rick James–sampling "U Can't Touch This," was inescapable. For Tupac and his Digital Underground cohorts, spending the summer with Hammer would be dreamy.

But then, at the last minute, representatives of Public Enemy, the groundbreaking hip-hop group, called. They weren't forking over Hammer-level dough, but Chuck D, the PE front man, loved the DU sound, and had also been warned by promoters that his summer lineup needed levity. Hence, he requested that Digital Underground join a road show also featuring Heavy D & the Boyz, Kid 'n Play, En Vogue, and—for certain dates—Poor Righteous Teachers, Chill Rob G, Queen Latifah, Silk Tymes Leather, and the Afros. "When we found out Public Enemy wanted us," said Shock G, "we *had* to get on that."

Throughout his childhood, Tupac worshiped at the altar of Public Enemy, whose music struck the same themes Afeni Shakur had stressed. The titles of their biggest hits—"Fight the Power," "Black Steel in the Hour of Chaos," "911 Is a Joke"—spoke of a group taking no shit and a lead rapper unafraid of ruffling feathers. So when the news became official, and Digital Underground joined the tour with a June 27 gig in Richmond, Virginia, the giddiness was palpable. Less than one year earlier, Tupac had cut a day of school at Tamalpais High because he heard that Flavor Flav, Public Enemy's bombastic hype man, would be appearing at the KMEL studio in San Francisco. He took several photographs with Flav—images he considered sacred.

Now, they were all on the "Sizzlin' Summer Tour '90"—hailed as the "big hip-hop tour of the summer" by the *Los Angeles Times*.

Like the Chocolate City tour, this one had Digital Underground bounding across the country via bus. Unlike the Chocolate City tour, there was a pronounced edginess. Public Enemy had recently found itself in hot water when one of its members, Professor Griff, told *The Washington Times* that Jews were responsible "for the majority of wickedness that goes on across the globe." That, along with the group's emphasis on Black resiliency, had music's white-dominant power structure and media judges on edge. Wrote Larry Nager in *The Cincinnati Post*: "That most dreadful of all concert beats, the rap show, came to town Wednesday night." In a review of the Richmond show, Tracy Wimmer of *The Roanoke Times* referred to PE as performers who "champion themselves as the great black hope dramatically fighting racial oppression, rejection and alienation with music." Two paragraphs later, she explained to readers what, exactly, rap is—"a basic sound propelled by a slamming polyrhythmic beat. And its chanted lyrics are a mix of comedic boosterism and racial promotion—salted by some rap artists with profanity or demeaning remarks about whites, women and gays."

And this perfectly explained the strange place hip-hop occupied in American culture in 1990: beloved by a growing legion of fans, yet interpreted *and* translated by unqualified white people who could not get past the braggadocious imagery (yet seemed more than willing to overlook the violent and misogynistic lyrics of, say, Guns N' Roses). That's why a growing handful of radio stations stopped airing Digital Underground music—in Hawaii, KQMQ Vice President Kimo Akane pulled "The Humpty Dance" when a woman complained about her nine-year-old son asking about the song's use of the number sixty-nine. In Macon, Georgia, John Lynn, the station manager of Magic 101, yanked rap music in its entirety, noting that "it's not a matter of censorship. It's a matter of taste." It's why, in advance of the tour's second date, in Norfolk, the director of the arena—a sixty-three-year-old World War II veteran named William Luther—asked that Public Enemy not perform "Fight the Power."

Chuck D and co. agreed, then played it. Twice.

It's also why, during a show in Augusta, Georgia, Christopher "Kid" Reid and Christopher "Play" Martin were arrested and charged with simulating sexual intercourse for the horror of lying face down and pumping their pelvises. "It's a common rock 'n' roll gimmick," wrote Kathy Haight of *The Charlotte Observer*, "that never got singers such as Rod Stewart and Prince arrested." When, a few nights later, a nineteen-year-old named Leo L. Whitebear was shot and killed in the Kemper Arena parking lot following the show, *The Kansas City Star*'s primary culprit wasn't the shooter, but the musical genre.

Tupac found all of this to be disturbing yet unsurprising. As the tour went from Harrisburg to Rochester to Philadelphia to Pittsburgh, he earned his stripes barking at police officers, snarling at parking lot concessionaires, ignoring security guards. "He just couldn't resist a fight," said Kid. "Someone needed to be like, 'Tupac, what the fuck are you doing? Why are you yelling at that vendor? Why are you mad at the cop who's just standing there drinking water?'"

After a show at the Myriad Convention Center in Oklahoma City, the acts retreated to the hotel. A bunch of the performers were unwinding at the lobby bar when a young man sprinted past, with a mob of people from the tour following him. "I saw the whole thing," Kid said. "The guy tried leaping over the registration desk, and all these people piled on top of him." It was, Kid recalled, a swarm of beefy security guards—and Tupac.

"It turns out this guy was bootlegging Public Enemy gear in the parking lot," said Kid. "Not Digital Underground gear—Public Enemy gear. But Tupac was just down for the fight. In his mind, your beef was his beef."

"Pac had this dude yoked up," recalled Chuck D. "'I'll kill you! I'll kill you!' I'm like, 'Pac, it's not that serious. Calm down.'"

At nineteen, Tupac was one of the younger members of the traveling circus known as "Sizzlin' Summer Tour '90." Chuck D, for example, was eleven years his senior, earning him the title of "Uncle Chuck." Flavor Flav had twelve years on Tupac, Shock G had eight, Kid seven.

So while he certainly felt a kinship with his elders, they weren't people he was rolling with until the morning's wee hours.

No, Tupac's closest bonds came with two up-and-coming artists who were both of his generation. One was an aspiring nineteen-year-old rapper out of East Orange, New Jersey, named Anthony Criss. Hired to work as a roadie for Queen Latifah, Criss was presented with slivers of opportunities to rap. When doing so, he identified as "Treacherous." Or, if shortened, "Treach." Like Tupac, Treach was hungry. They shared passions for music and weed, and the dream of becoming hip-hop supernovas. "Every city we went in, we just started building relationships," Treach recalled. "Because while everybody else was sound-checking, we in the hood."

The second road blood brother was a twenty-two-year-old dancer and backup singer with Heavy D & the Boyz named Troy "Trouble T-Roy" Dixon.

Growing up in Mount Vernon, New York, Dixon had been a fairly shy kid who found self-assurance via movement. "I was the first one on the floor at parties," he once told a reporter. "And the people would say, 'Hey, you dance good.' That made me feel good and confident in myself, makes me try harder and harder." In 1986, Dixon was working in the mail room of the local newspaper (*The Reporter Dispatch*, which Tupac had delivered during his brief time in White Plains) when he connected the rapper Dwight "Heavy D" Myers with two other Mount Vernon pals—Glen "G-Whiz" Parrish and a DJ named Eddie Ferrell. Together, the four formed Heavy D & the Boyz, and emerged on the strength of fun, bouncy, fast-paced hits and slick, synchronized dance moves.

Though raised in a devout Jehovah's Witnesses household, Dixon was no holy roller. The father of a nine-month-old daughter, he liked his weed and his drink, and rarely turned down the opportunity to cruise alongside Tupac in the endless pursuit of pussy. "Troy was the coolest guy in Heavy's crew," said Kid. "He was down to go out, he was down to jump on bitches with you, he was down to fight, he was a great dancer, he was a charming motherfucker. Him and Tupac were tight."

Tupac loved Dixon, and Dixon loved Tupac. And on the evening of July 14, both were inside Indianapolis's Market Square Arena for a tour stop at the Indiana Black Expo's twentieth-anniversary show. The concert kicked off at 7:00 p.m., with Silk Tymes Leather (a three-woman hip-hop group out of Atlanta), then Kid 'n Play, Digital Underground, Heavy D & the Boyz, and last, Public Enemy. Because life on the road can get dull, members of the tour entertained themselves with varied backstage activities. Water blasters were a popular vocation for the rappers. So were water balloons, dominoes, and checkers. On this night, as the show was wrapping and the crowd of ninety-five hundred began to disperse, several performers (including Tupac) and entourage members sprinted up and down a raised indoor/outdoor ramp near the New Jersey Street side of the arena. "The rest of us were doing what we always do," said Kid. "Kicking it, chasing bitches. This and that. But those guys were fooling around."

Without warning, someone rolled a large wheelbarrow-like plastic trash bin down the ramp toward Dixon. The dancer leapt atop a four-foot retaining wall to avoid the object. However, Dixon's legs were clipped and he tumbled backward. "The ramp gave a false illusion of not being that high," recalled Ferrell. "I think we all thought it was just a few feet off the ground."

The Heavy D dancer plummeted more than twenty feet headfirst onto the street below. Tupac and the others rushed to the scene, gazed down, and screamed for help. Dixon's body was splayed out and motionless. Blood pooled beside his head. "We thought we'd look over and see Troy in the dirt brushing himself off," said Ferrell. "But then we saw how high it was."

Paramedics arrived and rushed Dixon to nearby Wishart Hospital. The artists followed the ambulance and filled the waiting room. Tupac paced back and forth, inconsolable and chanting, *"Oh my God . . . oh my God . . . oh my God."*

"There's like forty, fifty people in the lobby," recalled Kid. "Just waiting for any bit of good news." Early the following morning, Dixon's parents were told they should come if they wanted to be present for their son— showing no signs of brain function—to be removed from life support. By the time Dixon was pronounced dead that night, the members of Digital Underground were preparing to take the stage at New York City's Palladium. When the call came, and word spread from rapper to rapper, Tupac crumpled into a ball. "He went batshit and just lost it," Kid said. "You have to understand, it's one thing to be young and talk a good game about all the shit you've seen. But Tupac wasn't tough. He was a sensitive kid. This was his friend, and he was dead."

Decades later, Kid could still envision staring down and seeing Dixon on the ground. He could envision the hospital, the sadness, the quiet stillness, the news being delivered in Manhattan. Most vividly, he could envision Tupac Shakur. Destroyed.

Although he had lived through poverty and homelessness and drug addiction, this was the first time Tupac ever experienced the loss of a loved one. He talked and rapped about the pain of death, but until Indianapolis he knew not whereof he spoke.

Two weeks after the accident, Dixon was put to rest at the Camelot Funeral Home in Mount Vernon.* Approximately 250 people packed the chapel, and 200 more stood outside. Sitting alongside Kid, Tupac let out deep sobs. "He just broke," Kid recalled. "Just completely broke." Midway through Brother Elmo Street's eulogy, Tupac stormed out. Kid followed. "There was some kind of glass door at a nearby building," Kid said, "and Pac kicked the shit out of it until it shattered. And I was like, 'Yo, chill, chill, chill.' But looking back, I was wrong. Tupac needed to let it out.

"In hindsight, I can't blame him. It was probably the worst pain he'd ever experienced."

---

* In 1992, Pete Rock & CL Smooth released "They Reminisce Over You (T.R.O.Y.)" in honor of Dixon, their fellow Mount Vernon native. It remains one of hip-hop's most iconic songs.

Chapter 11

Juiced

Becasue the show must always go on, Public Enemy, Digital Underground, and the other artists continued with the remainder of the summer tour. Even Heavy D & the Boyz rejoined the circuit after a few days away, though nothing ever felt the same. The death of Troy Dixon cast a pall over what was supposed to be a joyful run for a slew of young musical artists living their best lives. "You don't just recover," said Eddie Ferrell, the Heavy D & the Boyz DJ. "You fake it best you can. You smile and play your songs. But the wounds don't heal."

By the time the tour arrived in California in late August 1990 for its final leg, everyone—and everything—felt tired. During a show at the Shoreline Amphitheatre, outside of San Jose, approximately forty suspected gang members ("Knuckleheads out for sadistic kicks," wrote Barry Walters in the *San Francisco Examiner*) scaled the facility's fencing and attacked random spectators. One night later, inside San Diego's Sports Arena, a brawl broke out by the base of the stage that involved members of the musical entourages. The show itself was flat, and the *Los Angeles Times* said it lacked steam and energy. A growing number of media outlets seemed to enjoy taking shots at rap as a genre and the Public Enemy tour as an emblematic example of all that plagued the medium. Too violent, too unpredictable, too horny, too Black. "The music wasn't for the faint of heart," wrote Kevan Goff in a review for *The Daily Oklahoman*. "Much of it was anti-establishment, sexist and sexually explicit."

When the tour finally wrapped after a quick jaunt through Japan, Tupac had an opportunity to relax and revel in his accomplishments. He used some of the coin he made with Digital Underground to rent his own one-bedroom, one-bathroom apartment—unit H in a beige building at 275 MacArthur Boulevard, in Oakland's Adams Point neighborhood. Schmoovy-Schmoov, a Digital Underground member, doubled as the building's property manager, and he gave the youngster a sweet deal. "Pac was really proud of that place," said Roniece Levias, a local singer and friend. "There were always guys around, and it wasn't clean. But it was his, and that meant something."

Yet the very idea of relaxation was anathema to Tupac, whose philosophy entailed experiencing as much life as possible between now and his inevitably young death. Sleep? Who had time to sleep? A nice sit-down meal? Nah. A couple of nights vacationing in Hawaii? No, no, no. Tupac needed to fulfill his destiny before it was too late.

Over the course of the two tours, Tupac regularly bugged Shock G about hooking him up with some verses on the next Digital Underground track. It was irksome. Most people in the music industry are familiar enough with rejection that, after a while, they take the hint. Tupac, however, continued to badger. Ultimately, Shock G relented.

The tune was a little ditty titled "Same Song." Its origin traces back to May 29, 1990, when Digital Underground came to Los Angeles for a gig at the Palace Theatre. The artists were in their cramped dressing room after the show wrapped. DU had built a celebrity following, and on this night Eazy-E of the rap group N.W.A was hanging with Money-B. "We're all laughing and having fun and getting undressed," said Shock G. "And the person to my left said, 'You want to spark a doobie?'"

The word itself caught Shock G off guard. "Doobie"? "And I look over and the first thing I see is the little white twisted-up old-school blunt," Shock G said. "I looked further to my left and see the face holding it. And it was fucking Dan Aykroyd!"

An unabashed cinephile, Shock G was well-versed in the canon of Aykroyd, the former *Saturday Night Live* star who had transitioned to hit movies. Shock G loved *Ghostbusters* and *Trading Places*, *The Blues Brothers* and *Spies Like Us*. So when the famed actor passed him the sad, droopy joint, Shock G hit it.

"We got this movie thing . . ." Aykroyd said.

That was all the rapper needed to hear. "Are you kidding me?" he said. "Anything you want. I'm such a huge fan."

A few weeks later, Aykroyd followed up with an offer: He invited the members of Digital Underground to appear in a film he was directing called *Valkenvania*, based on a screenplay he wrote with his brother, Peter. He followed by asking whether DU might create a song to be used in the movie. "There's an organ bit [in the movie]," Aykroyd said. "Could there be an organ in it?"

"No problem," Shock G replied. "What are we rapping about?"

"Nothing special, man," Aykroyd said. "Just keep that same song, that same song you got."

Lightbulb.

"I took it literally," Shock G said.

An upbeat and bouncy jam, "Same Song" wound up a Digital Underground hallmark. It is also the first tune to feature a solo from Tupac Shakur, who was asked by a worn-down-by-the-begging Shock G to both rap and write his own lyrics. His breakout lyrical moment follows verses from Shock G, Shock G as "Humpty Hump," and Money-B—and it's a *where-were-you-when-you-first-heard-it?* introduction to a hip-hop natural crying for a shot. As the biographer Staci Robinson noted, "Where the other rappers focused mostly on party flexes, Tupac's verse reads almost like a memoir, telling listeners about how his life had changed and, despite that, how committed he was to keeping it real."

Now I clown around when I hang around with the Underground
Girls who used to frown, say I'm down, when I come around
Gas me and when they pass me, they used to diss me (same song)
Harass me, but now they ask me if they can kiss me

"It's the first time I heard Tupac Shakur as a rapper," said Rob Marriott, the renowned music writer. "I'm not saying it was the greatest song, but he jumped out."

For Tupac, finally getting a verse was the frosting. The chocolate cake was the accompanying cinematic opportunity. As promised, Aykroyd invited the members of Digital Underground to appear in *Valkenvania*, a flick about two couples who make a trip detour and wind up in a middle-of-nowhere traffic court.

Filming took place inside the historic Greystone Mansion in Beverly Hills. Over a five-day period, Shock G, Money-B, Chopmaster J, DJ Fuze, and Tupac hobnobbed alongside the stars—Aykroyd, Chevy Chase, John Candy, and Demi Moore. It was a dream come true, as well as excruciatingly dull.

Anyone who has ever spent time on a Hollywood set knows the phrase "hurry up and wait." The Digital Underground members ate. They napped. They watched other scenes. They smoked weed and drank beer. They chatted with Aykroyd (lovely), Candy (delightful), Moore (forgettable), and Chase (an egomaniacal douche). Most of the rappers were simply happy to be there—they were getting paid decent money to be part of a major motion picture. Tupac, however, was Tupac—fidgety, loud, impatient. "Tupac pestered Aykroyd every chance he got," Chopmaster J recalled. "There were only so many speaking parts and there were five of us in the group. Tupac wanted a speaking part, and we were like, 'Man, you ain't no actor.'"

"At first, Dan Aykroyd thought Tupac was cool and amusing," said Chopmaster J. "But Tupac quickly became overbearing and annoying. What was even more annoying was when you shoot a film, everybody knows you have to maintain continuity in your appearance. But every morning when he would show up to the set, Tupac had gotten another tattoo or body piercing or nose ring or some shit like that. Pac never looked the same in the next shoot, and that got to be very annoying to the film crew."

Thanks to Aykroyd's optimism, Digital Underground members believed they had a chance at landing speaking parts in *Nothing but Trouble* (the studio changed the movie's title). Alas, it was not to be. For all their time on set, the group appears on-screen for a grand total of two minutes and forty-five seconds. They play "Same Song," and Tupac—wearing a New York Yankees pin-striped home jersey—bobs and dances and lip-syncs a chorus he didn't actually sing. The movie is dumber than dumb, and grossed a mere $8.5 million domestically.

When Candice Russell of the *South Florida Sun-Sentinel* tagged *Nothing but Trouble* a "perfectly dreadful film," she was being polite.

Two weeks after *Nothing but Trouble* opened in theaters, Tupac Shakur's career truly began.

That might sound odd, considering he had recently toured with Digital Underground, received his first verse in a song, and appeared (albeit briefly) in a major(ly bad) motion picture. But Tupac Shakur really became Tupac Shakur because of the events of February 27, 1991, when he signed to star in a low-budget movie that seemed certain to come and go without five people noticing.

It was called *Juice*.

In the months leading up to Tupac's affixing his signature to a Paramount Pictures contract, this thing—cinema as a possible career—felt eight million miles away. Tupac Shakur was a rapper. One with a theater background, sure. But a rapper nonetheless. So it was quite unexpected when, out of the blue, Cara Lewis, Digital Underground's booking agent, called Sleuth, the group's road manager, about a film that was being cast. Lewis knew almost nothing about the project, save the pulpy name and that the director, Ernest Dickerson, had worked with Spike Lee as a director of photography. Was *Juice* about orange juice? Papaya juice? She could not say for sure. But Jaki Brown, the casting director, was under the directive that Dickerson wanted to stock the movie with rappers ("Look, I love Malcolm-Jamal Warner," Dickerson said. "But this wasn't a Malcolm-Jamal Warner vibe"). So she asked if the DU guys might aspire to audition.

Though he lacked an acting background, Money-B landed a copy of the script and was smitten from the first word. Written by Dickerson and Gerard Brown, former Howard University classmates, *Juice* was the story of four Black teens in Harlem who struggle with police harassment, neighborhood gangs, peer pressure, violence, and respect. "Ernest called me [in 1988] at one o'clock in the morning with the idea," said Gerard Brown. "He woke me up—I was living in Harlem, he was living in Brooklyn. And I got out of bed and I got my yellow pad and I started to write stuff down. He just had a thumbnail sketch—just four scenes in his head and the character names of Raheem, Steel, Q, and Bishop. So my job was to do what writers do—flesh them out. I gave them backstories, I wrote a first draft in about five weeks, we worked on it, rewrote it. And then . . ."

Nothing.

For years, the script collected dust. Then, in 1990, Gerard Brown hired a new agent, Sara Margoshes, who was working with a trio of white writers on an inner-city drama. They wanted a Black scribe to handle rewrites, so Margoshes sent them *Juice* as a sample of her client's capabilities. "They called Sara back," said Gerard Brown, "and they said they no longer wanted to do the other project. They wanted *Juice*."

And now, at long last, Dickerson, Gerard Brown, and Jaki Brown were making things happen. "I told Jaki to go out to neighborhood theater groups, to church theater groups, to performing arts high schools—let's go to all these places to find the four main characters," said Dickerson. "I was daunted by the idea of finding four guys who could bond in such a way. They had to be real and authentic. This was a Harlem movie. It couldn't be a bunch of phonies." Money-B was among dozens of hip-hop artists given the opportunity to audition, and he practiced for the role of Steel. Knowing Tupac's performing arts background, Money-B requested his help running lines. "He didn't bitch about it or complain and say, 'I'm a real actor,'" Money-B recalled. "He was like, 'Oh, that's dope. This is how you do it.'"

Auditions were held at the film production office inside the Brill Building, at 1619 Broadway in New York City. Multiple auditioners came and went throughout the day, including Treach, the Naughty by Nature rapper and Tupac's old pal. Money-B was called in to read and, years later, offered this blunt assessment of his theatrical talents: "I sucked. I can't act." Tupac was sitting outside when a dejected Money-B emerged wearing a hangdog expression. Jaki Brown followed him out and spotted Tupac, an unfamiliar face but—by virtue of being young and Black and inside her office—as much a candidate as anyone else walking the planet.

"Who are you?" she asked.

"Tupac," he said. "Tupac Shakur."

"Can I help you with something?" she said.

"Yeah," he said. "I want to audition for Bishop."

In the minds of Dickerson and Gerard Brown, Bishop was a hyper-specific type: a big, muscular, brash, intimidating street hustler. So, staring at this scrawny kid in a white tank top and baggy jeans, Jaki Brown didn't see it. But, in a way, she also *did* see it. Throughout her ten-year career casting everything from *The New Odd Couple* to *Stand and Deliver*, she had found that creators often thought one way about a character, only to go a different route. "A lot of young guys came in and auditioned for Bishop by just going ballistic," said Dickerson. "All anger, no substance. It was all two-dimensional nonsense. They were trying to match exactly what we'd described." Jaki Brown had run through a small handful of more established young thespians, including Donald Faison and Daryl Mitchell. She handed Tupac a script and asked whether he had any money.

"Why?" he wondered.

"So you can take the scenes to the restaurant across the street and practice."

Tupac told Brown he had enough for food.

"OK," she said. "Come back to me in an hour and a half when you're ready."

An hour passed. Tupac stuck his head into her office and said, softly, "I'm ready."

Omar Epps, a seventeen-year-old Brooklynite and student at the prestigious Fiorello H. LaGuardia High School of Music & Art and Performing Arts, had recently been cast as Q, and Jaki Brown read his parts with Tupac as Bishop. "[Tupac] did an amazing cold read," she recalled. As soon as they finished, Jaki Brown tracked down Gerard Brown, who was also in the building. "I think I've found our Bishop," she said. "I really think I've got him!"

They walked back toward Jaki's office, and before entering Gerard spotted the auditioner. "Jaki," he whispered, "that skinny little kid is who you want me to see read Bishop?"

"Yeah," she said. "Trust me."

Tupac again ran lines. "He nailed it," said Gerard Brown. "He had a lightning-in-a-bottle quality." Two of the film's producers, Neal Moritz and David Heyman, were due back in the office in an hour or so, as was

Dickerson, and Jaki Brown asked Tupac if he'd be willing to return and perform for the biggest decision-makers.

"Of course," he said.

Jaki Brown remembered what followed: "They, too, saw this 'small person' waiting. Again, they, too, did some chuckling with a 'he's so wrong' comment. I went out and got Gerard and Tupac. Tupac had the three of them almost mesmerized. Smiling after the audition, I took Tupac out of the room and asked the men, 'So?' Neal Moritz asked, 'Can we hire him now?' 'Yes,' I said. He asked Ernest and David if they were in agreement and they said, 'Yes!'

"When I brought Tupac in they told him. He thanked them, then turned and hugged me and started to cry."

Less than three weeks later, on March 14, 1991, production began. Tupac bragged to friends that he was in a cast featuring (in a very small role) one of the founding members of the R&B group En Vogue. "I'm gonna get to fuck with Cindy Herron!" he raved to Kendrick Wells, a Marin friend. "How sweet is that shit?" The film would be shot over twenty-four days in Harlem on a paltry three-million-dollar budget. Of the four young stars—Tupac, Epps, Jermaine Hopkins (who played Steel), and Khalil Kain (who played Raheem)—Tupac was the lone out-of-towner. Paramount rented him a one-bedroom apartment on the ninth floor of a building on the corner of Fifty-First Street and Seventh Avenue. For an actor making a grand total of sixteen thousand dollars for the role, the housing was a sweet perk. Along with Tupac, a handful of other rappers secured spots on the film, including EPMD, Yo-Yo, Queen Latifah, and Treach. It was as if, overnight, life had immersed him in a dream. He had his own pad and, on set, his own trailer ("It was a beat-up trailer," recalled Kendrick Wells. "But Pac didn't care. A woman would knock on the door, bringing him coffee. That shit didn't happen to guys like us"). Food was provided. The three other protagonists were, if not people he felt any particular kinship with, likable and professional.

Best of all—*the character!* Bishop is simultaneously edgy and menacing while also savvy and manipulative. His goal is to reclaim the "juice" his friends lost at the hands of a local gang—and he'll do anything to achieve it. In one stretch, he kills Raheem, then feigns sorrow and grief while attending the funeral. He is also responsible for delivering the script's single best line . . .

Q: "Bishop, you're crazy!"

BISHOP: "You know what? When you said that last time, I was kinda trippin', right? But now, you right. I am crazy. But you know what else? I don't give a fuck. I don't give a fuck. I don't give a fuck about you. I don't give a fuck about Steel. And I don't give a fuck about Raheem, either. I don't give a fuck about myself. Look, I ain't shit. I ain't never gonna be shit. And you less of a man than me, so as soon as I decide that you ain't gonna be shit . . . POW! So be it. You remember that, motherfucker. 'Cause I'm the one y'all need to be worried about . . . *partner!*"

The role had Tupac conjuring the crack dealers and gangbangers from the Jungle. He wasn't of their ilk, but he had long aspired to be. They had what he lacked, which was respect and money and (best of all) fear. Folks *feared* them in a way that *no one* feared Tupac. Even if you didn't know the big guns of the Jungle, you knew who they were and did your best to steer clear. Tupac envied that level of terrified admiration. So he took all that he coveted, and he baked it inside of Bishop. "He was the Black James Dean," said Eric Payne, who played a police officer in the film. "He carried that whole rebel vibe right into *Juice*. You can see it in every scene."

The process of creating a film tested Tupac. With a shoestring budget and tight schedule, Dickerson needed the actors to be punctual. Tupac was habitually late ("It's one of the reasons we hired Treach," said Moritz. "To make sure Tupac would be on time"). More than that, Dickerson wanted actors to take direction. Tupac hated direction. He was stubborn and opinionated and convinced he knew best. He liked the way Dickerson and Gerard Brown had written Bishop's dialogue, but couldn't resist adding flourishes, sparks, punctuations. That his acting résumé was a blank page mattered not. He *was* Bishop.

And, even though they were often disturbed by Tupac's behavior, Dickerson and Brown couldn't argue with the results. Epps, for example, was a fine actor. But his portrayal of Q was unremarkable. Jaki Brown had auditioned more than a dozen young Black men for the role, and the reality set in that most any of them could have played the character as Epps had. The same went for Hopkins and Kain. They were good. Quite good. But they weren't exceptional.

"Tupac," said Dickerson, "was exceptional."

His trailer was nothing fancy—white, small, rented from a local outfit. But, as his scenes approached, Tupac used it as Mike Tyson would use his dressing room before a showdown with Bonecrusher Smith. He paced back and forth, psyched himself up, spoke in Bishop's voice. If one stood close enough to the door, he could hear him. *"I'll fuck you up!"* and *"Bitch don't talk to me that way!"* Tupac didn't think of himself as a Method actor, but the tools he'd learned under Donald Hicken at BSA proved useful. Let the material absorb you. Find oneness with the character. Forget self. That's why Tupac was always at his best on the first take, when he melted fully into Bishop. Payne remembered a scene where the character Radames (played by Vincent Laresca) holds a knife to Bishop's nose. "When they yelled 'cut' I went up to him and said, 'Wow, man, that looked *so* real!'" said Payne. "And I'll never forget what he said—'It *felt* real.' You could feel the heat coming off of him."

Yet with every "Cut! Let's do that again," Tupac's attention waned. He knew when he'd nailed something, and he couldn't stomach a Hopkins or Kain failing to meet his level of excellence. For Tupac, this shit wasn't funny. It was a ticket to a better life. On occasion he stormed off to his trailer, sparked a blunt, cooled down, returned, stormed off to his trailer, sparked a joint, cooled down again. He was an unusual mixture of inexperienced and high maintenance. His peers were just happy to have the job. Tupac expected more. "There's a scene where Tupac is supposed to jump from one building to another," said Bruklin Harris, the twenty-three-year-old actress who played Keesha. "And he refused to do it. He said—and I remember this vividly—'I need a stunt fee.'"

Juice was Harris's first film. Had Dickerson asked, she would have hugged a viper for extra screen time. But, somehow, Tupac knew his rights. A stunt fee is where an actor handling his own stunts receives extra pay. When you see Tom Cruise parachuting and cycle jumping, it's not out of the goodness of his heart. He's making bonus dough. "When you're in-

Perhaps no artist in hip-hop history felt more comfortable with microphone in hand than Tupac Shakur, who used his theatrical background to bring a performance to life. Here he shows out at New York's Palladium on July 23, 1993.

Photo by Al Pereira

As a child, Tupac cut his teeth rapping before friends and neighbors on the steps of 2260 Walton Avenue in the Bronx. His nickname: MC New York.

Photo by Yaasmyn Fula

Young Tupac—circa 1982, with his sister, Set, and lifelong friend Yaki Fula—never fully enjoyed the innocent bliss of boyhood. "There were days where my mother would drop us off at a movie theater," his sister recalled, "because you can sit in a movie theater all day."

Photo by Yaasmyn Fula

Tupac and Yaki Fula enjoy a boyhood spin at Rye Playland, the Westchester County amusement park a stone's throw from the Bronx. *Photo by Yaasmyn Fula*

Though later loath to be identified with New York City, Tupac was a Bronx-created rapper whose stylings were heavily influenced by such Big Apple artists as LL Cool J, Run-DMC, and Kurtis Blow. *Photo by Yaasmyn Fula*

Tupac with Yaasmyn Fula and her son, Yaki. Throughout his life, Tupac was rarely able to trust those around him. Until his death, Yaasmyn proved a steady and loving presence. *Photo courtesy of Yaasmyn Fula*

Tupac's love for his mother, Afeni Shakur, was eternal. But so were his frustrations with a woman who preached empowerment and independence, yet often fell short of the associated attributes. "U taught me 2 be strong," he wrote, "But I'm confused 2 C U so weak." *Photo by Yaasmyn Fula*

SOPHOMORE ENSEMBLE

Yvette Ebb
Tiffany Pringle

Teresa Altoz
Cameron Francis
Elizabeth Rumsey

Seth Bloom
Jennifer Goldberg
Gregory Schmoke

Keesha Diggs
Jeremy Kasten
Tupac Shakur

NOT PICTURED: Andre Powell

Tupac arrived at Baltimore School for the Arts bursting with raw potential and artistry. He also came accompanied by a limited wardrobe that brought ridicule elsewhere but acceptance inside the halls of BSA.

Courtesy of Baltimore School for the Arts

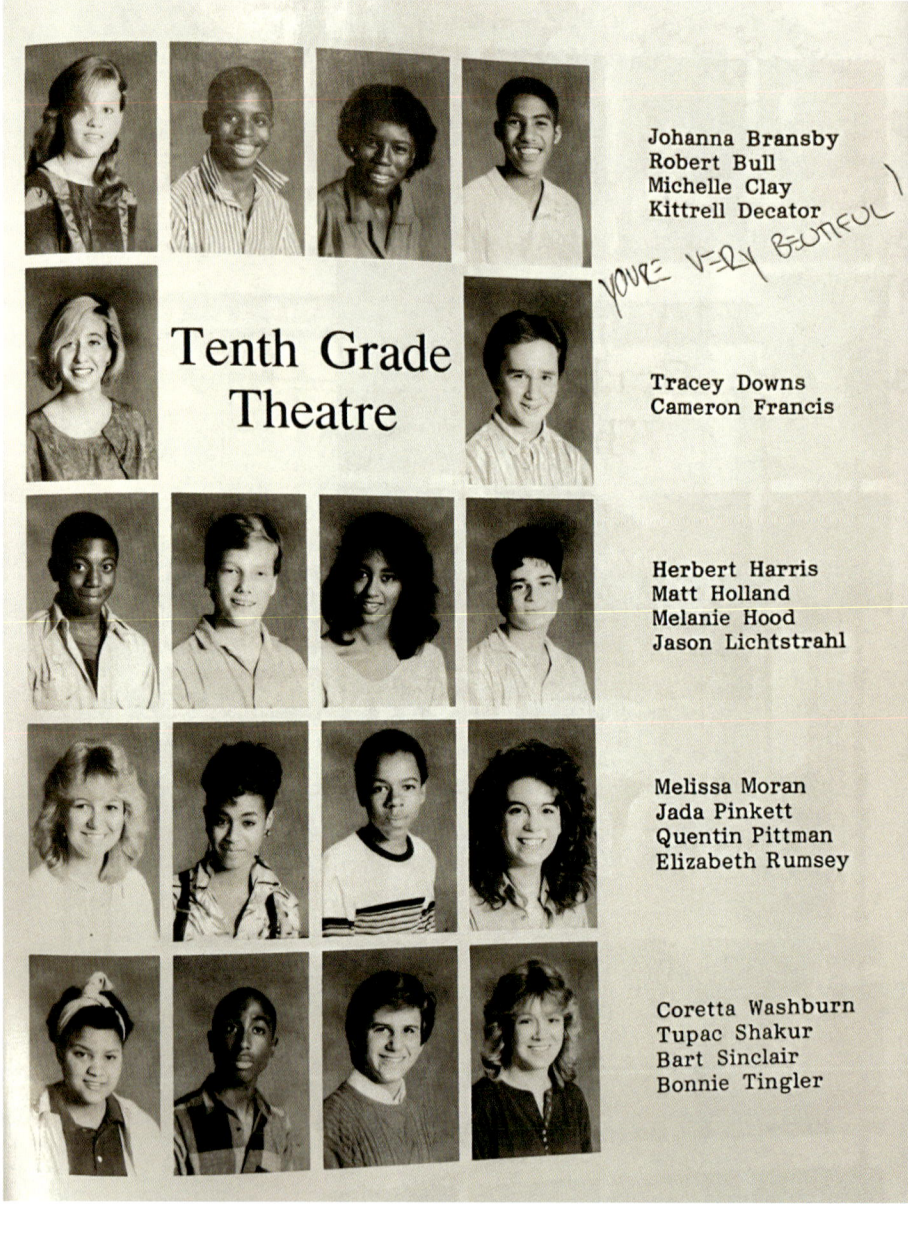

Johanna Bransby
Robert Bull
Michelle Clay
Kittrell Decator

YOU'RE VERY BEUTFUL!

Tracey Downs
Cameron Francis

Tenth Grade Theatre

Herbert Harris
Matt Holland
Melanie Hood
Jason Lichtstrahl

Melissa Moran
Jada Pinkett
Quentin Pittman
Elizabeth Rumsey

Coretta Washburn
Tupac Shakur
Bart Sinclair
Bonnie Tingler

In his second year at Baltimore School for the Arts, Tupac developed a kinship with a fellow student named Jada Pinkett. The two portrayed slaves in a production the school put on at a local museum. "Jada played a housemaid, and Tupac was a slave sneaking over to see her," recalled their classmate Kittrell Decator. "It was poignant." *Courtesy of Baltimore School for the Arts*

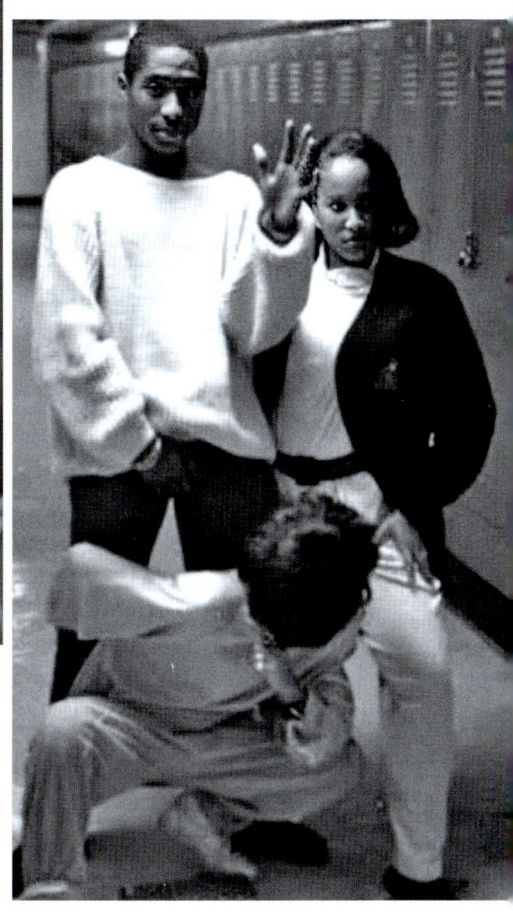

In the hallways of Baltimore School for the Arts, Tupac felt empowered to be himself. Which meant goofy, artistic, funny, and thoughtful. *Photos courtesy of Jojo Perryman*

Tupac (*middle row, first from right*) endured one year at Roland Park Middle School—and hated every moment of it. "Girls laughed about him," a classmate recalled. "He was nice. But the smell, the teeth, no money, so small. Tupac was no catch, I can tell you that."

Photo courtesy of Roland Park Middle School

A young Tupac photographed in Rohnert Park, California, during the early days of his West Coast metamorphosis. Committed to the Afrocentric ideals preached by his mother, Tupac wore jewelry that spoke of a teenager on a mission. *Photo by Kathy Crawford*

Tupac with Leila Steinberg, the jack-of-all-trades social justice warrior who early on grasped the power of his voice. "This kid is special," she noted after meeting him for the first time. She was right.

Photo by Kathy Crawford

Tupac begged and begged and begged for a chance to rap—and was finally granted it by Shock G (*left*) and Digital Underground. Tupac, Shock G observed, rapped "from the pit of his stomach."

Photo courtesy of Pat Johnson/ MediaPunch/IPX via AP

Here with Daddy Rich of 3rd Bass, a young Tupac relished the opportunity to tour with DU and a bevy of other hip-hop artists. "He was all over the map," said Prime Minister Pete Nice, the 3rd Bass MC. "He wasn't making much money . . . so I found myself buying Tupac a bunch of Whoppers, a bunch of Pizza Hut."

Photo courtesy of Pete Nash

Tupac with the Notorious B.I.G. (*left*) and Redman (*right*) backstage at New York City's Club Amazon on July 23, 1993. Before long, the two friends would turn heated rivals. *Photo by Al Pereira*

On Dec. 1, 1994, less than twenty-four hours after being shot at Quad Studios, Tupac appeared in New York Supreme Court to face sexual assault charges. Read the next day's New York *Daily News:* "The jury remained in the courtroom for ten minutes as Shakur, his face twisted in agony, washed down painkillers with a cup of mineral water." *Photo by Eric Miller/Associated Press*

On July 5, 1994, Tupac greeted paparazzi outside the state supreme court in Manhattan with a waterfall of spittle. Recalled one of the victims: "He said, 'I'm not spitting on you, I'm spitting on what you represent.'"

Photo by Bebeto Matthews/Associated Press

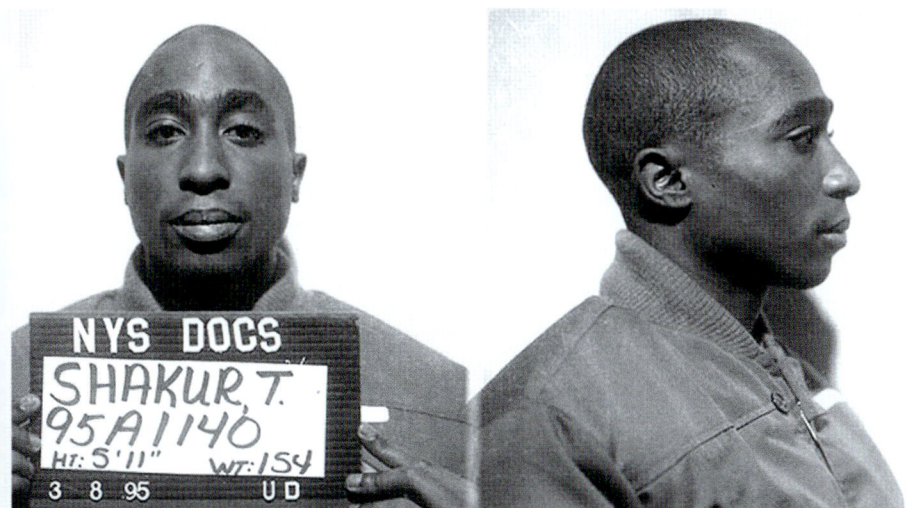

On Feb. 14, 1995, Tupac Shakur entered Clinton Correctional Facility with a new identity—inmate No. 95A1140. With little to do but write and think, behind bars a weed-and-Hennessy-free Tupac created some of his most brilliant material.
Photo by Michael Ochs Archives/Getty Images

On Aug. 15, 1996, Tupac and Death Row CEO Suge Knight attended a voter registration event in South Central Los Angeles. Tupac trusted Knight to guide his career. Others found him terrifying and deceitful. When Knight entered a room, one person recalled, "I could smell the sulfur." *Photo by Frank Wiese/Associated Press*

Tupac backstage at the 1996 Grammy Awards with the reunited KISS lineup. Though loath to admit so in public, Tupac's musical tastes ran the gamut, from Kate Bush and Don McLean to Sinéad O'Connor and the Indigo Girls. Shortly before his death, he had planned on mixing his songs with Frank Sinatra classics.
Photo by Kevin Mazur/WireImage

Tupac on the set of the "California Love" music video with Suge Knight (*left*) and Dr. Dre. Though originally intended to be a Dre solo tune, Knight insisted Tupac be granted lyrics. The result: an all-time hip-hop classic and Golden State anthem.
Photo by Nitro/Getty Images

The myth: Tupac's ashes were set free into the Pacific Ocean. The reality: Some of his ashes were set free into the Pacific Ocean—but the rest of his ashes were buried beneath a headstone on a vacant lot in Lumberton, North Carolina. Dante Powers, a distant cousin, serves as caretaker and visits regularly. Most people know not that Tupac's remains are there.

Photos by Jeff Pearlman

Hat backward, jeans sagging, jewelry blinging, microphone to lips—Tupac Shakur was a dynamic stage presence who, even three decades after his death, serves as a voice for myriad generations.   *Photo by Al Pereira*

experienced, there's no way to know that sort of thing," said Harris. "Tupac did. And he got the stunt fee."

During filming, crowds used to gather by the barriers to watch the action. One day, between shoots, Tupac strolled toward a young woman with long hair, large breasts, a short skirt—and an Adam's apple.

Randy Fletcher, the first assistant director, nodded to Dickerson and said, "He doesn't know."

Dickerson howled. "He *really* doesn't know."

"And you could see he was really working it," said Dickerson. "Talking her up, trying to get in. But she kept shaking her head."

Finally, Fletcher walked toward Tupac, pulled him away from the woman, and whispered into his ear. Tupac spotted the crew laughing at him and burst into a hearty chuckle. "Well," he yelled, "that explains why the bitch didn't wanna give me her number!"

And yet, the laughter was rare. Tupac was constantly getting in arguments. Moritz recalled taking a taxi ride with Tupac to Lower Manhattan. The driver was a Vietnam veteran, and he and Tupac engaged in a heated exchange about America. Tupac was screaming at the man, who pulled the car over and kicked the passengers out. "That intensity," said Moritz, "was unbridled." Another time, Tupac spotted an attractive woman alongside a barrier from the shoot. He approached, hit on her—and then her boyfriend arrived. "Apparently the guy spent quite a bit of time in Rikers Island," Dickerson recalled, "lifting weights." Instead of backing off, Tupac cursed the man out. "Fuck you, motherfucker! I ain't afraid!"

"He got ballistic," Dickerson said. "We had to get Pac in a car and get him out of there before he got his ass beaten down." Less than a week later, Tupac was again whispering sweet nothings to a female onlooker who was accompanied by a boyfriend and the boyfriend's pit bull. "The guy let some slack off the leash, and the dog lunged at Tupac," said Moritz. "Tupac jumped back, but he hated that he showed weakness. So he started talking shit to the guy."

"OK," the man said. "I hear you. And I'll be back in a few minutes with my gun."

"All right, big man," Tupac yelled. "Go get your fucking gun! We'll see how tough you are!"

With the dog owner out of sight, Paramount security whisked Tupac off to a safe location.

"Tupac was a time bomb," said Moritz. "Always ticking."

During the period when *Juice* was being filmed, Avra Warsovsky, Tupac's old flame from the Baltimore School for the Arts (the one whose ex-boyfriend came to beat Tupac up), was living on Manhattan's Lower East Side, finishing up at a conservatory acting program.

One day, Tupac reached out. Was she interested in getting together?

They met at his apartment. She was thrilled to see him—"It had been a long time," she recalled. And they spent the night hanging out, talking old times, laughing, crying, smoking weed. She got, Warsovsky recalled, "higher than I'd ever been before and ever would be after."

The two reconnected a few nights later, this time at her place. The Tupac who arrived was unrecognizable. He walked with swagger and this new to-the-side lean. He talked shit. "I was like, Um, okay . . ." she recalled. "Who are you?" The next evening, they were back at Tupac's place—this time with a bunch of his friends. "I didn't know who they were," she recalled. "He made it clear to the guys that I was not to be fucked with. That I was more like a sister and I was to be left alone and there was no running anything on me."

It was all bizarre. Who was this person? What had he become? Where was the Tupac with the painted fingernails and spray-painted jeans? On their last night together, Avra and Tupac went out for a meal. On the taxi ride home, he curled up against her—"kind of like the Tupac I remembered from high school," she recalled. Before they parted, he offered a confession. "Avra," he said, "I don't know what I'm doing. I don't know what people want from me. I don't know who to trust. I don't know who I am."

She hugged him. "Take care of yourself," she said. "You can always call me if you need someone who loves you."

Tupac walked off, and Avra was left with a pit in her stomach. She was twenty-one and felt as if she was witnessing a friend split apart at the seams. On the one hand, there were glimpses of the old, carefree, fun-loving Tupac. And yet, he wasn't entirely there. This other Tupac Shakur, the darker, more intense one . . . what was that? Who was he?

Answer: Bishop.

It sounds ludicrous in hindsight. And maybe it *is* ludicrous in hindsight. But the longer Tupac devoted himself to embodying Bishop, the more those around him felt that he was sinking into another persona. With each passing day on set, Tupac sort of vanished and Bishop sort of emerged. Not just on film, but in life. His antics. Hand motions. Patterns of speech. Verbal aggressiveness. It's not that Tupac didn't have Bishop-like impulses before *Juice*. He had been preternaturally confident and impulsive dating back to the stoops of New York City. "He always thought he was the best," said Leila Steinberg. "From the first day I knew him." The movie, though, unlocked restraints. He liked the feel of Bishop. The mojo. It fit him like a snug robe.

The most alarming moment took place one afternoon when the crew was preparing to film a scene that took place outside Raheem's house. Dickerson was going through notes when he looked up and saw the three producers huddled in a corner. "Guys," he said, "what's going on?"

"Ernest," replied David Heyman, "you don't wanna know."

"Well," he said, "I sort of need to know, because it'll affect the day's work." Tupac, Heyman informed Dickerson, had recently invited some people to hang out in his trailer. One of them stole his jewelry. Tupac reported the crime to the staff, and was assured he would be reimbursed the value of the goods. But that wasn't good enough. Tupac enlisted Randy "Stretch" Walker, a rapper/producer pal, to track down the potential thief—and he did. "On a nearby street," said Dickerson. "And Tupac and [Stretch] were stomping the shit out of him in the middle of the avenue. And people were yelling from their windows, 'Stop! Stop!' But they kept stomping until the guy broke away, jumped on the back of a car, and took off." Dickerson was equal parts furious and terrified. Furious, because why would the star of his movie think a wise career move might involve boot-crushing a skull? Terrified, because who was to say the victim wouldn't return to the set, this time armed?

"I've thought about this a lot through the years," said Dickerson. "A lot of times when an actor plays a character, it's a combination of people they know and a little bit of themselves. There was a lot of Tupac in Bishop, but there's also a lot of Tupac that's not like Bishop. He had an intense intellectual curiosity about the world. But there was also an un-compromising part of him that was very much Bishop. So did the lines blur? Probably."

Filming wrapped in mid-April, and a few days later Tupac was back in Northern California. One of the first homies he ran into was Ryan Rollins, aka the rapper Ryan D, who was excited to see his old friend and hear about his adventures as a movie star.

The two hugged, and as Tupac sat down he removed two items from his pants: a pistol and the sixteen thousand dollars he earned from *Juice*, rolled up into a wad of cash.

"That wasn't something the earlier Tupac would have done," Ryan D said. "That was the Bishop in him."

Chapter 12

The Scraps

n December 1990, three months before *Juice* commenced filming, Tupac Shakur met his mother inside the historic Greyhound bus station on San Pablo Avenue in Oakland.

He could barely summon the strength to make eye contact.

Here she was, forty-three years old, a decayed mound of skin hanging off bone. Her skin was pallid. Her eyes were sunken. Her teeth were stained from cigarettes. She looked malnourished and battered and a far cry from the Panther 21 icon of two decades earlier. That the station— once an architectural mecca featuring a fifty-six-foot octagonal rotunda— had fallen into graffiti-covered disrepair felt appropriate.

Within the past few weeks, Afeni's sister, Gloria, had wired her the money for a one-way bus ticket to New York City. It was time, the family believed, for Afeni to return to her people and seek recovery. Yet after receiving the dough, Afeni and her boyfriend used it to buy crack cocaine. "I'm an addict," she later explained. "I do as addicts do."

So now she was at the station, looking to her only son for help. Not all that long ago, she had stolen the three hundred dollars he needed to fly to Atlanta. But now Tupac reached into his pocket and pulled out sixty dollars in cash. He handed it to her and hated every moment of the engagement. In a normal world, *she* would be taking care of *him*. She would be feeding him, clothing him, nurturing him. But in this fucked-up space the family occupied, a nineteen-year-old kid was paying for his mother's transportation. As far as he was concerned, this woman before him could go to hell.

Afeni boarded the bus and commenced with a dreadful journey—there were multiple vehicle breakdowns, and one in Denver was made bearable only by the kind Salvation Army volunteers who presented passengers with soup and blankets. When she finally touched down at Manhattan's Port Authority on Christmas Eve, Afeni was broke and despondent. Because the ride went long, nobody was there to pick her up. She slumped against a marble pillar in the building's basement, lit up a Newport, and wondered whether this was a reflection of her remaining days. "I had ceased to be or feel like a human being," she said. "I didn't know who I was anymore, or even who I used to be." When her sister finally arrived, Afeni felt "a signal that I belonged."

But it would be a grueling process. For the next five months, she holed up inside Gloria's apartment at 1370 St. Nicholas Avenue in Washington Heights. She devoted most of her days and nights to plopping down on the toilet, taking hits from her trusty crack pipe, and blowing the smoke out the window.

In New York City for *Juice*, Tupac made some efforts to visit his mother. But instead of hoisting love upon her, he remained disgusted. Although the location had changed, she was the same strung-out fiend from Marin City. "I don't think people understand what that level of dysfunction and instability did to Tupac," said Karen Lee, his longtime publicist. "Tupac loved his mother. Even when he probably hated her. But it was complicated. You can't just walk away from it."

To his credit, Tupac didn't walk away. Instead, he used the pain. The heartache. The sadness. The resentment. It fueled much of the rage that propelled Bishop through *Juice*, and it also thrust Tupac toward his next goal: recording original music.

This was something he had thought about for years, only the gulf between *wanting* a record deal and landing one is wide. Atron Gregory, his manager, had been unsuccessfully shopping a Tupac demo tape for months. Atlantic Records said no. CBS said no. Echo Records said no. Even with the talent displayed on "Same Song," nobody bit. "It was frustrating, because we knew Tupac had ability," said Gregory. "But it was a strange market at the time. The medium was being flooded by new artists, and the people judging them often weren't sure what they were looking for." At one point, Gregory told Tupac that he might just have to release the album on his own, and sell it independently. "I'm not happy about it," Gregory said. "But . . ."

Then one day Gregory's attorney, Ken Guggenheim, called his client to fill him in on an upstart label based out of Santa Monica. It had been started by two veterans of the industry, Ted Field and Jimmy Iovine (the former producer of John Lennon and Bruce Springsteen), and they named it Interscope Records.

"They're looking for fresh music," Guggenheim said.

"What have they done thus far?" Gregory asked.

Well . . .

In its infancy, Interscope's big song was "Rico Suave," a cheeseball rap from an Ecuadorian hip-hop artist named Gerardo. Interscope followed by releasing the debut album from a rock band named Primus, then Marky Mark and the Funky Bunch's *Music for the People* (featuring the hit single, "Good Vibrations"). Though a far cry from Run-DMC and Led Zeppelin, beggars couldn't be choosers. And Tupac Shakur was a musical beggar.

Gregory sent a copy of Tupac's demo to Tom Whalley, Interscope's thirty-nine-year-old A&R head. A meeting was arranged, and Gregory headed to the Interscope office armed with another copy of the demo. This time he sat in a room along with Field and Leslie Gerard, an assistant at the company. The three listened to every track, and when the music ended there was a pained silence.

"It's a little hardcore," said Field, an heir to the Marshall Field estate whose background was in auto racing and film. "Don't you think?"

Gerard wasn't sure what to make of Tupac Shakur. Was he N.W.A? Was he Marky Mark? Was he Gerardo? "I didn't know a ton about rap," Gerard said. "It was all sort of new to me."

Field brought the demo tape home. It wound up in the mitts of his twelve-year-old daughter, Danielle. Unlike her father, the girl was into rap, and she felt the music of this Tupac guy. He was, she said to her father, *really good.*

Gregory told the men that to meet Tupac was to love Tupac. So, along with Whalley and Kevin Hosmann, an Interscope art director, they arranged a lunch with the young rapper at the Daily Grill, a restaurant across from the Burbank airport. Having never seen Tupac before, Gerard had an image in his head—burly guy, probably a bit menacing, maybe a durag. "Well, Tupac walks in," he said. "And I was like, *Fuck*, he's beautiful."

Tupac looked like a model, what with his long eyelashes and high cheekbones. Plus, the accessories. "I've never seen that many rings on one human in my life," Hosmann recalled. "He was so blinged out." When the group sat down to talk, Tupac owned the table. He looked you in the eye. He laughed at jokes. He conveyed every emotion under the sun. "He was articulate, passionate, wise," said Gerard. "He knew who he was, knew what he wanted, was bursting with creativity. I know people overuse the whole 'it factor' thing, but, damn, he had it."

The meeting lasted no longer than an hour. When they returned to the car, Field and Gerard were in agreement: They *needed* Tupac Shakur. The following week, Tupac returned to Los Angeles to sit down for dinner with Field and Whalley at Genghis Cohen on Fairfax. "Look, so that this can be a relaxed dinner, just know we're signing you," Field said. "You don't have to worry. If you want to be with us, this is happening."

On August 13, 1991, Tupac signed a contract with Interscope Records.

He would live the dream and get paid to make music.

"Tupac was an asshole."

The woman talking is Roniece Levias. It is October 18, 2023—thirty-two years since she entered the Starlight Sound studio in Richmond, California, to help a young artist create his debut album. There is a bite to the sentiment. She is not playing.

"By asshole," said the veteran singer, "I mean *asshole*. But with complexities."

For example, Levias said, "Not too many people like carrots in their spaghetti—but Tupac did. That's nasty shit."

And?

"And when he started rapping, he was corny," she said. "He would free-style silly stuff, like, 'I ain't fake / I am real / Just like a bird / On a window sill.' Stupid stuff like that."

And?

"He just had an attitude that ran hot and cold," she said. "A lot of times ice cold. Like an asshole."

Back in the day, Levias was one of Tupac's closest confidantes. Both products of the Bay Area, they met working with Digital Underground and bonded over shared geography and musical tastes and oft-ignored status. "With the Underground, Pac was an underdog and I was an underdog," she said. "Which meant we basically slept on the floor of the studio every night, hoping for our chance on the mic."

Yet when Tupac wrapped working on *Juice*, he was furious with Levias, who, in his absence, had scored microphone time on Digital Underground's latest album, *Sons of the P*. He accused her of stealing his mojo and merging rapping and singing as he had aspired to do. "I honestly thought he was going to hit me—he was *that* mad," she recalled. "People had to back him off of me. He thought I'd done him dirty, and he was relentless in his anger. I was like, 'Pac, you know me. You know I'm not that person.'"

This was the Yin and Yang of Tupac in the late summer/early fall of 1991, when—for the first time—there were musical expectations placed atop his shoulders. With Digital Underground, he was a tiny piece of the machinery. An underwhelming crowd or butchered line were not his burdens to carry. But now, Interscope was asking for *a lot*. He was barely twenty, and emotionally unprepared, and they expected a top-shelf debut album. The goal, he was told, was to have it out before the holiday season. Not done—*out*. "Which," recalled Levias, "is sort of insane."

Tupac's idea for the album—ultimately titled *2Pacalypse Now*—was to get away from the upbeat silliness of Digital Underground and offer a manifesto on what it was to be young, Black, and hunted in modern America. His inspirations weren't LL Cool J or even Chuck D, but Malcolm X and Bobby Seale and the up-and-down saga of his mother. "Rebel songs" is how he described the material. "Just like, you know, back in the sixties you had folk songs. . . . That's what this is. This is soul music. It's like, music for us to carry on with. For us to move on. It's battle songs. It's songs talking about strong Black men fighting back."

Life in the studio with Digital Underground had been a party. People came and went, oftentimes bringing in all manner of food, drink, smoke. Tupac, however, meant business. The Starlight Sound schedule was jam-packed, and artists were booked months in advance. A seven-hour block ended precisely after seven hours—no exceptions. Tupac knew this, and also knew Interscope was paying for the time. So he developed a system—step to the mic, record a song. Step away, take a few minutes, smoke some weed, record another song. Then another. And another. "He always felt like he was running out of time," said Lisa Smith-Putnam, who worked with Tupac at TNT Records. "And he was trying to cram his whole life into as many days as he could." Tupac was a machine, and those involved had never seen anyone so devoted to churning out product. Musically, most knew Tupac as the kid from "Same Song." They didn't know him as 2Pac (his musical alter ego)—the never-take-a-break dynamo. "Tupac could spit out a thought and gather the next thought all in one motion," said Ramon Gooden, a producer on the album. "His brain worked uncommonly fast."

At the time, Starlight was known as a place where 95 percent of the artists and employees were Black. The facility was located off the beaten path, surrounded by warehouses in a quiet corner of Richmond, California. Much of the studio time was funded via drug money, in the form of cash peeled off from a wad of bills.

When Tupac reported for work, he was surprised to be greeted by a recording engineer named Marc Senasac. A thirty-one-year-old white man from nearby San Mateo, Senasac had cut his teeth as a drummer with a local rock band, American Dream. He'd spent enough time inside studios to fall in love with the environment—"Seeing all these buttons and knobs and meters," he recalled, "I knew this was what I wanted to do"—and in the early 1980s a small San Francisco studio, Bear West, paid him a grand total of $0.00 to hang around, repair headphones, soak in the ambiance. One morning, the singer Chris Isaak was scheduled to come in for a session. The head engineer needed an assistant, and looked toward the nerd in the corner. Senasac spent the next decade working with artists ranging from Blue Öyster Cult and Lindsey Buckingham to the Tubes and Exodus. He was a rock and roll engineer who knew a little hip-hop, and when Digital Underground used his talents on its *Sons of the P* album, he was amused and intrigued.

Then the new client arrived.

Senasac knew not what to expect the first time Tupac entered the studio on his own, but he was won over. The rapper was quiet and polite and,

Senasac recalled, "super low-key." The next day Tupac arrived accompanied by an overweight twenty-year-old Black kid with thick glasses held together by a Band-Aid. This was Deon Evans, aka Big D the Impossible, Tupac's producer of choice. Beneath his arm Evans lugged an MPC60, a bulky one-box-does-it-all sequencer-sampler workstation. "I loved both of them," Senasac said. "Big D had all these beats already programmed, and he'd usually show up to the studio first and we'd work together to put the beats down. Tupac was nice, and Big D was even nicer. He was this savant guy who was super geeky—from looking at him, you'd never think he was the one making all this amazing music."

From jump, Tupac had the album's thirteen tracks polished and ready to go. "Brenda's Got a Baby," inspired by the article he had read in the New York *Daily News* while filming *Juice*, was a lock. So was "Trapped," a song written long ago on notebook paper by Ray Luv, his Strictly Dope cohort, but crumpled up and thrown away. "Part of it was sticking out of the garbage can," Ray Luv recalled, "and this nigga came in, pulled the paper out of the trash, started reading it, and said, 'This is dope.' He asked if he could have it. So I gave it to him."

One by one, Tupac, Big D, Senasac, and a slew of contributors and collaborators came to Starlight and put in the work. "It was usually one or two songs every night," Senasac said. "No nonsense. Just hard work."

According to the sound engineer, however, things quickly soured. Songs would be completed, Tupac would celebrate the accomplishment—and then, on multiple occasions, someone from Interscope or Gregory's management company either disapproved or designated the beats for Digital Underground's next album. This happened time after time, Senasac said, to the point where an exasperated Tupac was near tears. "It was very defeating to him," Senasac recalled. "To all of us. He had a vision of what he wanted his first album to sound like, and this wasn't it."

Toward the end of the recording sessions, Tupac acknowledged that *2Pacalypse Now* was not the record he had dreamed of. It was a compilation of scraps and B-sides—"leftovers," Senasac said. "Tupac was so polite and humble and grateful to be there, but it was like watching this young flame get stomped out."

Around this time, Shock G threw a listening party at his Oakland crib.

He invited dozens of music friends, and told Tupac he should play the unfinished *2Pacalypse Now* for the guests. Though underwhelmed by the album, Tupac complied. "So he put the tape in, and it was good," said DJ Daryl, who was at the affair. "Not amazing, but definitely above average. And he felt good about the response." Another attendee was Ice Cube, recently solo after leaving N.W.A. He, too, brought an album—the explicit version of *Kill at Will*, an extended play with seven tracks. "It'd been out, but some of us hadn't heard it," said DJ Daryl. "And oh my God—everyone in the party was in awe. It was so dope. And you could see Tupac was hurt. He probably wasn't used to getting his ass kicked."

The song that mattered most was "Brenda's Got a Baby"—and Tupac would have thrown punches had someone tried removing it from the album. Yes, he initially wrote it on the quick in his *Juice* trailer. But the narrative struck a chord. Brenda wasn't merely a character from a newspaper article. She was his mom. She was his sister. She was so many girls he knew in New York, Baltimore, and Marin. "To me, it was more important than *Juice*," he told the talk-show host Arsenio Hall. "And right now, no Black males talk about Black females like we should. Because if we don't take responsibility for our sisters, who will?"

When it was time to lay down "Brenda's Got a Baby," Tupac requested the presence of Senasac, Big D the Impossible, Money-B (who had a nine-word cameo), the future Blackstreet singer Dave Hollister, and . . . Levias. Starlight was unusually quiet this night, and before work commenced, Levias asked if she could speak with Tupac alone.

"Pac," she said, "I never meant to hurt you. I want to do this song with you and make it right."

He nodded approvingly.

Tupac asked for the five to join him in a circle. He handed out the "Brenda's Got a Baby" lyrics and explained the origin story. "He was very quiet and solemn about it," Levias said. When he was done, Tupac had the crew break up and—in their own corners—write out what they were going to do with their blank spaces. The song was incomplete, and required stuffing. Money-B jotted out his line—"That's not our problem. That's up to Brenda's family"—and submitted it to Tupac. Hollister wrote up what he thought would work as a chorus, as did Levias. "It's the most unique songwriting experience I'd ever had," Levias said. "We came together to produce this piece of beauty."

One by one, the performers recorded their parts. Levias was last to go. She stepped into the booth and gave everything she had—wailing away, stretching out syllables, raising her voice to a new level. "I looked up from the microphone," she said, "and there wasn't a dry eye in the studio. Everybody was crying, including Tupac.

"I knew we were good."

Because his mother was poor and addicted and his father was . . . somewhere out there in the universe, Tupac Shakur rarely got to enjoy the conventional highs of Christmas or his birthday.

Maybe there'd be a present or two. Some cheap supermarket cake and a thrown-together party around the kitchen table. A pathetic Charlie Brown tree alone in the corner. Mostly, the holidays reminded him of all the things others had but he did not.

In the coming months, Tupac would finally experience the career equivalent of Santa Claus sliding down the chimney.

On November 12, *2Pacalypse Now* would be released and on sale in record stores across America.

On January 17, 1992, *Juice* would be released in cinemas across America.

Put differently, within a three-month span, Tupac's life was about to change. "He always wanted to be famous," said Leila Steinberg. "This was his chance."

First, however, Tupac Shakur needed a proper biography.

That's why, as *2Pacalypse Now* was being pressed and packaged, a man named Sal Manna came calling. A thirty-six-year-old freelance journalist who once covered music for the *Los Angeles Times* and *Los Angeles Herald Examiner*, Manna had been hired a decade earlier by Elektra Records to sit down with an unknown heavy metal band and write a biography of its four members. That group, Mötley Crüe, went on to become one of the decade's biggest acts, and (hardly a coincidence) Manna one of the decade's most in-demand music bio writers. Two months pre-Tupac he had interviewed Kurt Cobain and the members of Nirvana in anticipation of their major label debut album, *Nevermind*.

"I had standards," Manna said. "I will write it the way I want to write it, and if I interview somebody there's no one else in the room. No manager, no publicist, no record company hack. It's them and me."

Although he recorded *2Pacalypse Now* in Northern California and maintained his Oakland apartment, Tupac was also renting a detached house in Sherman Oaks, just outside of Los Angeles. So when Manna was assigned Tupac, he drove to 4628 Nagle Avenue. Tupac, Manna was told, lived alone, and the Q&A would be strictly a one-on-one affair.

That's why he was taken aback when the door opened and a woman in her early forties greeted him, holding a plate of freshly baked chocolate chip cookies.

"Hello," he said. "I'm Sal Manna."

"Come on in, Sal," she replied. "I'm Afeni Shakur."

Manna wasn't well-versed in the history of the Black Panthers, but he had done some research on his latest subject, and he knew about Afeni's role with the Panther 21. "But I had no idea she would be there," he recalled.

No one did. During much of his time filming *Juice*, Tupac was furious over his mother's continued allegiance to crack cocaine. But on May 12, 1991, something snapped. While attending a twentieth anniversary reunion party in Connecticut for the Panther 21, a friend's daughter convinced Afeni to accompany her to a weekly Alcoholics Anonymous meeting at the local hospital. Afeni was emaciated from years of personal neglect. Her head was shaved, her nose pierced. She was exhausted. That day, Afeni attended three recovery sessions. By the end of the final one, she sensed a change. "I was an addict," she said. "I felt like all of those people [in the meetings] were in my head and knew my secrets. Every time one of them talked, they talked about me. They described my own very special experiences, my feelings, my thoughts."

Roughly three and a half months into her recovery, Afeni received a letter from her son. It was supportive and pessimistic. He hoped her commitment was real, but remained skeptical. "It was a loving, honest, truthful letter," Afeni said, "but I was devastated." Around this time, Tupac wrote a poem, "When Ure Hero Falls (My Hero My Mother)," that included this crushing sentiment:

U taught me 2 be strong
But I'm confused 2 C U so weak

Yet Afeni slowly regained her son's trust. Enough that—skepticism be damned—he asked her to come to Southern California and stay with him for a spell. He was lonely outside of his regular turf, and she was his mother. Even if he didn't fully believe in her, he *wanted* to believe in her.

Manna followed Afeni into the home, took a cookie, and retreated to a den, where Tupac was waiting. Manna was struck by his youth—though only four years younger than Cobain, Tupac appeared doe-like compared to the "Smells Like Teen Spirit" singer. "He was neither big in stature nor imposing in attitude, but rather small and slight," Manna recalled. "When he talked, he had the focus of a man on a mission, someone who knew what he wanted to say, but actually was rather mild-mannered. I was surprised. I guess I was expecting someone more in-my-face, more angry, more on the edge. Why? Because I am white."

Wrote Manna in an essay titled "On Meeting Tupac":

When he could have easily hitched his wagon to gangster rap, he insisted that was not what his songs were about. "These aren't gangster raps," he said. "Gangsters are a fairy tale. The only reason they've got the confidence of the Young Black Male is because they're the only ones who shoot back. . . . I'm not a gangster, I'm a NIGGA, I'm from the underground." He had turned the "nigger" pejorative into NIGGA, Never Ignorant Getting Goals Accomplished. If any other self-possessed young music artist had done that, he would have been surrounded by the stench of self-promotion. But you knew, you felt, that Tupac had lived the life and meant what he said. It is an overused term but Tupac exuded "real."

For nearly every question, Tupac surprised with his answer. When I expected him to be hard, he showed vulnerability. "I can't front," he said. "To say I'm 'hard' is too fashionable. I'm not hard, I'm soft. Life's made me crazy soft. If you hit me, I'll fall." When I expected him to praise blacks who romanticized life in the ghetto, he riffed on his song "Trapped," saying: "We're trapped in our own ghettos and some people are braggin' about it! White people can go anywhere except the ghetto and we can't go anyplace but the ghetto. Who do you think has the best of that deal? It doesn't make any difference if your hair is permed or braided or in dreads, if you're in the ghetto then you're trapped." In a subsequent interview, he would tell me: "Nobody *wants* to be in the ghetto! We're all trying to get *out* of the ghetto!"

After wrapping his interview, Manna rose and shook Tupac's hand. He bid farewell to Afeni, who walked him to the door.

"He will do great things," she told him, "if he lives long enough."

Back in music's prehistoric era of records, tapes, and CDs, the release of an album was preceded by a single. The goal, for the company putting out new music, was for the first song to catch a wave, grab the attention of consumers, and propel the artist toward riches or—at the very least—steady radio play.

On September 25, 1991, Interscope announced the coming of *2Pacalypse Now* by dropping "Trapped," the Ray Luv–penned song about an antagonized young Black man. Because Tupac was largely unknown, and because hip-hop radio was still in its relative infancy, the song generated the buzz of a hiccup. This was, in large part, emblematic of a period in time: Back in the 1990s, album releases weren't events in the way they would one day become. But that wasn't the lone issue. Ted Field and Jimmy Iovine had worried that the album lacked a grab-listeners-by-the-ears single, and "Trapped" was proving them right. Nobody seemed to care.

In Tupac's life, however, the song proved prophetic. Included in the lyrics is this passage:

Tired of being trapped in this vicious cycle
If one more cop harasses me I just might go psycho

Less than a month after "Trapped" dropped, John Burris, an Oakland-based civil rights attorney, received a call from Atron Gregory. Digital

Underground's manager had a client—a young kid named Tupac Shakur—who was in a bit of a pickle. According to Gregory, on October 17 Tupac was crossing the intersection of Seventeenth and Broadway in downtown Oakland when a pair of police officers stopped him, accused him of jaywalking, and demanded to see his ID.

Tupac told his manager that when he handed over his driver's license, as well as two other forms of identification, the police mockingly referred to him as "Amaru"—his listed middle name. They said he was being angry and hostile, to which Tupac replied, "This is just two white cops who want to stop a nigga."

The policemen, according to Tupac, threw him to the concrete, cuffed his hands behind his back, and choked him until he lost consciousness. "My final words to them was 'Fuck y'all,'" he recalled. "Next thing I know I was in a choke hold passing out with cuffs on, headed for jail for resisting arrest." He was locked away in the Oakland Police Department's booking facility for seven hours.

Burris had heard a million of these stories, and—even though he was Black, and even though he had lived through racism's ugliness, and even though it was uncommon for people to make up tales of abuse—he approached each saga with a spoonful of skepticism. Did the police have just cause? Was the apprehended suspect breaking the law? "I had done a lot of police misconduct cases," Burris said. "I knew the questions that needed to be put out there."

"Do you have the names of the officers?" he asked Gregory.

"Yes," he said.

Alexander Boyovich.

Kevin Rodgers.

"Really?" Burris asked.

"Yeah," Gregory replied. "Why?"

Earlier that year, Boyovich had been sued for allegedly beating Darrell Hampton, a popular Black recreation director, before a group of children. "They were notorious," Burris said. "There was a pattern with those guys of harassing people of color. I'd been determined to get those two guys fired for a long time. So as soon as Atron mentioned the names, I was interested."

Tupac came to Burris's office on the twelfth floor of a building at 1212 Broadway. Tupac's right cheek was bruised, and above his right eye sat a bloody slit. Burris asked him to remove his shirt, and dark marks covered his chest and back. A mere seven months earlier, a twenty-five-year-old motorist named Rodney King had been pulled from his automobile and beaten and tased by four members of the Los Angeles Police Department. The assault was caught on video, and wound up exploding onto the national scene. Tupac, on the other hand, had been battered with no witnesses. "Tupac was very excitable when he told me the story," said Burris. "He had an edge about him. He kept referring to himself as a young Black man, and he had some historical reference to it. He knew the story of police and young Black men. He wasn't afraid to address it. Hell, he *wanted* to address it."

Back at the Interscope offices in Southern California, this was all . . . confusing. On the one hand, it probably wasn't ideal to introduce a new musical artist to the world via mug shot and police report. On the other hand, this was precisely what so much of *2Pacalypse Now* covered. Tupac wanted America to see how Black men were treated. He thought he'd be doing so via his music, but if it had to come via a lawsuit against the Oakland Police Department, so be it.

On November 12, 1991, the same day *2Pacalypse Now* hit stores (with a whimper), Burris arranged a press conference at his office, announcing a ten-million-dollar lawsuit against Boyovich and Rodgers. Standing before a half dozen microphones, Tupac was flanked by members of Digital Underground. He wore a hoodie beneath a jacket, and a backward Starter baseball cap. Burris told those in attendance that his client also suffered a headache and a sore neck, wrists, and arms. Tupac's tone was earnest and agitated. "They said that even though I was a member of a rap group that I still have to 'know my place in Oakland' . . . that I wasn't above the law," he said. "Finally, I told them to give me the ticket. I uttered profanity and told them that I wasn't a slave and they weren't my master. One said, 'Hey, I like the sound of that . . . master.'"

Tupac took some questions, and before the press conference ended he noted that—oh, by the way—his debut album was now available for purchase.*

It bombed.

Tupac feared this would happen, mainly because *2Pacalypse Now* was, in his eyes, the exact type of mid-level hip-hop pulp he hated when made by others. An artist needed to be bold and loud and bombastic. He could deal with poor sales as long as he was proud of the product. This album—*2Pacalypse Now*—did not make him proud. It felt as if he had settled.

Thus far, 1991 had been a hit-or-miss year for the genre. De La Soul's *De La Soul Is Dead* was brilliant. So were Gang Starr's *Step in the Arena* and *The Low End Theory*, by A Tribe Called Quest. But N.W.A's *Niggaz-4Life* was a drop-off, as was MC Lyte's *Act Like You Know*. Queen Latifah, Tupac's old touring comrade, put out *Nature of a Sista'*, an album that peaked at number 117 on the *Billboard* 200 chart and later materialized in America's bargain bins. Tupac talked the talk and walked the walk, but he knew this album would disappoint those who believed in him.

If the letdown of *2Pacalypse Now* burdened Tupac, he failed to let it show—in part because he knew the album was so-so and the muted reaction fair. Also in part because he had a bigger prize to focus upon—*Juice* was slated to open nationwide on January 17, 1992.

Nine days before curtains went up, Tupac was back in New York with his costars, in town for an advance screening at the Loews Astor Plaza. The evening was sponsored by the Black Filmmakers Foundation, and attendees included Diana Ross, Grace Garland (of *All My Children* semi-fame), and Samuel L. Jackson (who had a minor role in the film). It was a 98 percent Black audience, and when the movie ended and the credits rolled, Tupac and his cohorts were saluted with a standing ovation. The joy shot through him. These were his peers—*his Black peers*—showering him with the approval he sought.

This was going to be a *great* few weeks.

---

* Tupac wound up settling for $42,000, and Boyovich and Rodgers ultimately left the force.

And . . . it was a great few weeks.

Mostly.

What Tupac didn't foresee was the gulf between the love *Juice* received in Black America and the shrugs that greeted it elsewhere. For Black audiences, it was an honest, edgy peek at inner-city life and the choices four friends might be forced to confront. Of the fifty top-grossing movies of 1991, only three (*Boyz n the Hood*, *New Jack City*, and *Jungle Fever*) featured Black actors. Was *Juice* as inventive as these other Black-led films? No. But it addressed themes undetectable in mainstream cinema. Not long after the flick came out, Tupac was hanging with the rapper Richie Rich and the producer DJ Daryl, both of the Oakland group 415. They were walking through the Eastmont Mall, and an employee at a hat store recognized Tupac. "Aren't you the guy from *Juice*?" he asked. "Man, you were good in that movie."

Tupac thanked him, and when they entered a shoe store more fans approached—this time three or four. "And you have to remember, at the time Richie Rich was a big deal in Oakland," said DJ Daryl. "But everyone was looking past Rich and right at Pac." Before long, an army of admirers followed the trio through the mall, besieging Tupac for autographs.

"So we get to Richie Rich's car in the parking lot," said DJ Daryl. "We drive a bit, and we get to a stoplight near Skyline Hill where a bus is letting kids off. And all these high school girls are yelling, 'Tupac! Tupac! We love you, Tupac!'"

Richie Rich turned to the young rapper. "This is the last time we'll be able to hang out with you," he said. "It's over."

Chapter 13

A One-Take Motherfucker

O n the evening of April 11, 1992, Linda and Bill Davidson were at their home in Victoria, Texas, eating dinner with their two children. This was far from unusual. Oftentimes, when Bill worked the 3:00 p.m.-to-midnight shift as a Texas highway patrolman, he used his break to dine with the family.

Once her husband returned to the job, Linda went about her domestic household routine, which generally involved the living room television offering background noise. That's why, on this day, her ears picked up a terrifying breaking news report. *A Texas Department of Public Safety patrolman has been shot seventeen miles north of Victoria . . .*

Oh, no.

Linda dialed the highway patrol number, but no one answered. She flipped on the police scanner and heard that Officer 3148—*her* husband—had been shot. "A trooper took me to the hospital," she recalled. "We were going down highway 59 where Bill was hit. And for miles all I could see were red and blue lights flashing." When they arrived at nearby Citizens Medical Center, Linda was overwhelmed by the scene before her. Doctors and nurses and police officers and a blur of colors and sounds and the hazy fog of disbelief. She was taken aside and told that, at 8:20 p.m., Bill had pulled over a Chevrolet Blazer with a broken headlight and what appeared to be a cracked rear window. When he approached the driver's side, a man stuck out a 9 mm handgun and fired a hollow-point bullet into Davidson's neck.

The suspect, an eighteen-year-old unemployed cook named Ronald Ray Howard, was a mid-level drug dealer and lightweight Crips gang member who was en route to Port Lavaca, Texas, to make a cocaine sale. Apprehended within a couple of hours, he was placed inside Jackson County Jail and charged with attempted capital murder. He confessed to the crime.

Three days later, on the night of April 14, Bill Davidson died. He was forty-three.

The local police department conducted a full investigation. They interviewed Ronald Ray Howard, his friends, his family members. They did a background search, tore through his home and his belongings. And, naturally, they deep-dived the Chevrolet Blazer. That meant looking in the seat cracks, beneath the rugs, inside the ashtray, behind the plastic paneling, and—of course—inside the cassette player.

This is where they found *2Pacalypse Now*.

The craziest year of Tupac's life may well have been 1992.

That's saying something, because few *Homo sapiens* have experienced as much raw-level insanity as Shakur did over his 9,220 days on earth. As a man who believed his life would be short, Tupac didn't take baby steps. He stomped. It was all out, all the time.

Although the year kicked off with the inglorious fade of *2Pacalypse Now* and the good-yet-underwhelming reception to *Juice*,* Tupac received a major jolt to the system when—based largely upon the strength of his performance as Bishop—he was asked to star in a movie written and directed by John Singleton, who had recently been nominated for an Academy Award for *Boyz n the Hood*. At age twenty-four, Singleton was both the first Black director and youngest director to be a finalist for the honor. And while he wound up losing to Jonathan Demme for *The Silence of the Lambs*, the bloom was on the rose.

A product of South Central Los Angeles, Singleton stayed out of trouble as a youth by eschewing drugs and partying for the nerdier pursuits of fantastical escapism. "When I was growing up," he once said, "comic books, video games, and movies were my buffer." He graduated from Blair

---

* In its defense, *Juice* wound up becoming a fairly iconic piece of American film, at least in regards to Tupac's performance, which has been referenced in pop culture endless times.

High School in 1986, and after a stint at community college attended USC's School of Cinematic Arts. It was there that Singleton fell in love with the work of Akira Kurosawa, the Japanese filmmaker. Kurosawa was famously dynamic, and known for his collaborations with Toshiro Mifune, the actor who—under Kurosawa's guidance—went from obscurity to superstardom. "Mifune had a face that was so expressive," said Bruce Cannon, a film editor who worked with Singleton. "John was looking for his own Mifune, and he believed he found it in Tupac."

Like most people in the business, Singleton did not consider *Juice* to be brilliant. It was certainly no *Boyz n the Hood*. Tupac as Bishop, however, was perfection. The intensity. The nonverbal communication. Some actors needed decades to develop the range Tupac displayed in his first film. "He had that thing that makes you pay attention," said Robi Reed, Singleton's casting director. "It was organic. Who he was. How he was raised. All his experiences. He put all of that into his acting."

Now on the short list of hot directors, Singleton had a good amount of say on the follow-up to *Boyz n the Hood*. The all-white studio heads at Columbia Pictures (where Singleton had a multi-film deal) assumed it'd be a safe return to the tried and true—a Black director doing what (they presumed) a Black director would do best: gangbanging and violence and street slang.

Only Singleton had a different vision. The role he offered Tupac was for a . . . *love story?* Involving . . . *a postal worker?* And . . . *a hairstylist?* With dialogue overflowing with . . . *Maya Angelou poetry?*

The working title: *Poetic Justice.*

No.

The studio hated it.

"There were a lot of people who were like, 'What in the world . . .'" said Steve Nicolaides, one of the producers. "But John had a vision."

The leading female role was offered to Janet Jackson, the twenty-six-year-old pop star whose primary acting experiences involved cameos and short stints on 1970s and '80s TV shows like *Good Times*, *The Love Boat*, *Fame*, and *Diff'rent Strokes*. Coming off of her wildly successful *Rhythm Nation 1814* album and tour, Jackson was paid two million dollars to headline the film.

Prior to Singleton's focusing on Tupac, his first choice for leading man had been Ice Cube, the former N.W.A rapper who starred as Doughboy in *Boyz n the Hood*. It was a brief pursuit—Cube read the script, liked it, but took issue with some elements of the character that Singleton refused to change. Ice Cube was out.

Before making a formal offer to Tupac, Singleton requested that he and Jackson come to Reed's office for a screen test. It was the first time the rapper and the pop star met, and they seemed to have a nice rapport. They spoke about music, about acting, about the film. Tupac was reserved and warm. "We knew we wanted both, but the chemistry had to work," said Reed. "I felt like it did. I remember him just being willing to do anything and everything he needed to give all of us the confidence he was right for the part. He made you feel like you were the most important person in the room."

Later that night, long after his meeting with Jackson, Tupac kicked back with his Oakland crew and—over joints and drinks—told them she was one of the hottest bitches he had ever seen, and he would most certainly have sex with her.

"Bet on it," he said.

Following two weeks of rehearsal, *Poetic Justice* shot from April 14, 1992, until July 4, 1992. Along with Tupac and Janet Jackson, the film starred another pair of relative silver-screen newcomers—the actress Regina King (coming off a successful half-decade stint on the TV show *227*) and a stand-up comedian, Joe Torry. Initially, Singleton pushed the foursome to become a unit. He wanted them to have dinners and understand the intricacies of one another. "There was definitely a kinship," said Torry. "Regina, Tupac, and I hung. Janet—not as much. And I think, being honest, it was hard for Tupac. Janet was a star. She was the one with her own trailer, her own this, her own that. A little standoffish. And Tupac also knew that Janet was making a lot more than he was, and it definitely rubbed him the wrong way. He thought they should be equals. She didn't share that."

"Tupac definitely did not have warm feelings for Janet," said Dupré Kelly, a friend and rapper from Lords of the Underground. "I remember him talking about her—'I got a car service bringing me to work every day.

This chick has helicopters landing her on set. Every day I'm eating chicken and waffles. She's getting her stuff catered.'"

"He made it clear he was pissed about getting less than Janet," said John Cothran, who played Uncle Earl. "To me, that seemed absurd. Because I didn't even know who the hell he was."

Indeed, while Jackson was pulling in seven figures, Tupac made less than a hundred thousand dollars. For much of shooting, the cast was lodged at the Loews Santa Monica, and Tupac was placed in the smallest available room (Jackson had a suite). "There were about five of us Black employees," recalled Lesa McRoyal-Fouther, a reservation desk manager, "and they'd always send one of us to ask Tupac to turn down his music or lighten it up with the marijuana smoke. Other guests were complaining."

From a talent standpoint, the Janet-Tupac financial gap was unjustified. For all her stage presence, Jackson was a one-note actress. She arrived on time, remembered her lines, but brought little to the table. Tupac was the opposite. He was the best part of the movie—"Every scene he's in, he owns," said Jenifer Lewis, the actress who played the mother of Tupac's character, Lucky. But he was also chronically late and unwilling to memorize his lines. Once, in a unique display of chutzpah, he arrived an hour behind schedule to film a highly anticipated love scene with Jackson. The middle of his chest was covered with a large, gooey piece of gauze. When asked the cause of the injury, Tupac lifted the paper to reveal a new tattoo—one he had had done (impulsively) the previous night. It read 50 NIGGAZ, atop a rifle. Singleton was apoplectic, and told Tupac the tattoo not only violated his contract but made the scene tricky to shoot.

"What am I supposed to do?" asked the director.

"Fuck if I know," Tupac replied, then stormed off to his (tiny) trailer.

According to Torry, as the days passed, Tupac's attention waned. His tardiness increased from a few minutes here and there to a few hours several times per week. He not only failed to memorize the script, but tried ad-libbing far too often. He was high all the time, drunk some of the time—and it showed. As a musician, being impaired can inspire creativity. As an actor, it lends itself to sloppiness. "He was usually ready when he got to set," said Cothran. "*If* he got to set."

Though not in Tupac's class as an actor, Jackson was a pro's pro—a by-product of spending almost two decades in the spotlight, and knowing what it meant to have a crew of people depend on you. Predictably, she was turned off by Tupac, by his approach, by his weird efforts at being sexual, by his need to always steal attention. He was a child in a man's body. It all felt like some sort of act—an insecure kid trying to prove his worth. It was exhausting.

Shit hit the fan late in the process, when it was time to film a kissing scene. In the days beforehand, Tupac talked nonstop about overwhelming Jackson with his lips and tongue. He thought he was being cute. She did not. Three days before the sequence was to be shot, Nicolaides was summoned to Jackson's trailer, where she sat with her fiancé, a dancer named René Elizondo Jr. "You know, Tupac's reputation is that he's a cat about town," Jackson said. "And I don't want to swap saliva with him until I'm really sure that he's healthy and clean."

"OK," Nicolaides replied. "Have you talked to John about it?"

Jackson looked disgusted. "John just walked off when I mentioned it," she said. "So I'm asking you to handle it."

The forty-three-year-old Nicolaides did not relish what was to follow. He had worked on a bevy of high-profile films, including *When Harry Met Sally* and *The Princess Bride*, and knew all too well the wrath of an actor's ego. He took a couple of deep breaths and walked over to Tupac, who was sitting alone in his trailer.

"Sooooo . . . Tupac," he said.

Tupac looked up.

"I'll just spit this out to you, man," he said. "Janet wants you to have an AIDS test before you kiss her."

"You kidding?" Tupac asked.

"No," said Nicolaides.

"Fuck her," Tupac said. "I ain't doing shit for that bitch. Tell her to go fuck herself."

"Um, OK," Nicolaides said. He prepared to leave, and Tupac flashed a big smile.

"So . . . you'll do it?" Nicolaides asked optimistically.

"Hell no," Tupac replied.

"I honestly think he found it amusing," Nicolaides said. "And the truth is, I can't blame Janet for asking. It was the early 1990s, and people were still dying of AIDS. And Tupac, God love him, had a reputation.

"But he never got the test."

There were reasons Tupac acted the fool. His need for attention was rooted in a childhood of being ignored. His brashness came with deep fears of being rendered forgettable. In the case of his two and a half months on *Poetic Justice*, some of his behavior could be chalked up to simple immaturity. Maya Angelou, the poet and civil rights activist, had a small speaking role in the movie (her poetry was featured throughout) and grew so fatigued by Tupac's on-set antics that she took him aside and said, "When was the last time anyone told you how important you are? Did you know our people stood on auction blocks, were sold, bought and sold, did you know, so that you could stay alive today?"

Tupac, to her shock, lowered his guard and wept.

Much of Tupac's poor behavior was likely tied to stress, anxiety, and an intensifying spotlight that didn't always feel warm. At the same time he was making *Poetic Justice*, Tupac was trying to monitor his mother (who was living at his place in Southern California and attending Alcoholics Anonymous meetings), figure out the logistics of his next album, manage his money (Tupac still had yet to open a bank account), and overcome his lingering disappointment over the negative reception to *2Pacalypse Now*.

Midway through filming, the biggest problem arose. Tupac was first made aware of the shooting death of Bill Davidson, the Texas highway patrolman, while on set. He did not understand what it had to do with him, even when someone brought up that the alleged killer had supposedly been listening to the *2Pacalypse Now* cassette right before pulling the trigger.

"So?" Tupac asked. "What does it matter?"

With his client lacking a defense, Howard's attorney argued that rap music predisposed him toward violence. "I didn't know what gangsta rap music was, but here's a young kid from Houston who had had problems with police," said Allen Tanner, Howard's lawyer. "I was kind of fascinated by this music that he was listening to. And that's where I got the idea to use that as a potential defense."

Linda Davidson, the widow of the patrolman, was about to file a civil lawsuit against Tupac.* She hired a Texas-based attorney, Jim Cole, whose plan was to go after Howard (who had nary a dollar to his name), but *really* go after Tupac and Interscope Records. When an actual suit was filed, Cole admitted (quietly) that he was unsure which song Howard had been listening to when he was pulled over, but it certainly could have/might have/ probably had been "Soulja's Story," which featured the lyrics:

Cops on my tail, so I bail till I dodge 'em
They finally pull me over and I laugh
"Remember Rodney King?" and I blast on his punk ass
Now I got a murder case?†

Howard was found guilty on July 14, 1993, locked up at the O. B. Ellis Unit in Huntsville, Texas, and executed twelve years later. "He was a very smart man who had a horrible upbringing," said Jaboria Rosemond, his daughter. "In prison he wrote a lot of poems and short stories. He was an intellectual never given the opportunity." For Tupac—who wound up having a federal district court judge rule that his album was fully protected by the First Amendment—being tied to Davidson's murder felt like pure hell. Combined with the stress of the Oakland jaywalking experience, he was a bundle of nerves, anxiety, fear. On the outside, he tried conveying calm. But, inside, he felt broken. He could not understand the blame game taking place. He didn't order Ronald Ray Howard to shoot Bill Davidson. He didn't even know Bill Davidson. "There isn't a doubt in my mind," Linda Davidson told the press, "that my husband would still be alive if Tupac hadn't written those violent, anti-police songs." Before long, Dan Quayle, the American vice president, jumped into the fray, traveling to Texas to meet with the Davidsons and demanding that Tupac's music be banned.

---

* Toward the end of an interview for this book, Linda Davidson noted, "Tupac was killed on my birthday. So I celebrate the day twice."
† The odds that those defending the Davidsons actually listened to "Soulja's Story" are somewhere between 0 percent and 0 percent. Had they, they would have realized it actually tells the story of "Soledad Brother" George Jackson and the failed 1970 attempt at a San Quentin Prison jailbreak.

"There is absolutely no reason," he told the media, "for a record like this to be published." It was simple chum for Quayle, the self-appointed "family values" champion who—along with President George H. W. Bush—was in the midst of a heated reelection fight. What better foil than the Black gangsta rapper spewing bile? "Dan Quayle couldn't have listened to more than eight seconds of Tupac's music," said Soren Baker, the hip-hop journalist. "But he was an easy target—Black kid with a bandanna."

Tupac complained to Torry about sleepless nights and clumps of hair falling off his skull. "He constantly wore a hat, because his head was all messed up," recalled Torry. "He was biting his nails all the time, just really on edge. He put on a good front, but it was all getting to him. This was the time period when Tupac was becoming Tupac, meaning everyone knew who he was.

"There was no escape."

On June 16, 1992, Tupac Shakur celebrated his twenty-first birthday by buying a new Jeep Cherokee from an Oakland dealership. The vehicle was black, with tinted windows, an automatic transmission, and a tow package. He put $10,000 down against a purchase price of $29,298, and couldn't have been happier.

Having grown up with so little, he viewed the car not merely as a device to take him from here to there, but a symbol of manhood. It was one thing to create music, to appear in films. But to possess something tangible mattered. *A lot.*

Tupac's driving skills were inversely proportionate to his rapping talents. Or, to be blunt: He was terrible. Always distracted, always waving to some hottie, checking himself out in the rearview mirror, looking in the wrong direction. He kept the Jeep at his Oakland apartment on MacArthur Boulevard, and within a few weeks of ownership scraped up the left side when he tried to navigate through a narrow passageway alongside his home. After exiting the car, he examined the multiple dents and giggled.

It mattered not how the vehicle looked.

It mattered that it was his.

That is why, on the afternoon of August 22, Tupac made the decision to drive his new Jeep the twenty-six miles from Oakland to Marin City to attend the community's fiftieth annual Festival on the Green. For those residing nearby, the event—held on the area baseball field—was a late-summer beacon of light. Along with rides and games, it featured food concessions, face painting, and a large stage for a bevy of performers. "It wasn't just a community fair," said Meloni Page, a Marin City denizen whose mother, Connie, was one of the organizers. "It was people getting together to remind themselves life was worth living."

Of late, Tupac had kept his distance from Marin City. Part of it was logistics—he was a busy man. But there was more to the matter. As his sister, Set, would note decades later, Marin City seemed to eat its own. The majority of folks Tupac had hung with were drug dealers going nowhere fast and aspiring musicians lacking his talent and drive. Also, for Tupac, Marin City represented the low of his mother's addiction. It was the place where she fully transitioned into a zombie-like crack fiend. "Why would he want to go back there?" asked Set.

And yet, having now starred in two major motion pictures and preparing to record his second studio album, one could hardly blame twenty-one-year-old Tupac for peacocking before those who knew him way back when. He had made it, dammit. He had survived and thrived and soared above.

Not that everyone in Marin City felt compelled to celebrate. His former apartment-mates (Demetrius Striplin, Ryan D, and August Terry) shared a belief that Tupac relied on them, rose through the ranks—then kicked them to the curb. The same went for many of the neighborhood drug dealers who, once upon a time, slipped him dough for studio time, for trousers and a T-shirt, for a bite to eat. Watching Tupac own the screen as Bishop was an indescribable high ("A brother making it!" said Striplin). But where were the phone calls? The nods of appreciation?

Even worse, rumor spread that Tupac had recently appeared on the popular television show *Yo! MTV Raps*, and spewed shit about Marin City. "He said that all the women down here were pregnant and all the guys were dealing drugs," said Darren Page, the local rapper who went by Klark Gable. "Then he had a party over in Oakland and when people showed up, he told them at the door that no Marin City people were allowed. So people let it be known he was not welcome here anymore."

That Tupac had neither derided Marin City on MTV nor held a no–Marin City–people party was beside the point.* Locals were angry and angling for a fight. "Jealousy," said Marku Reynolds, Tupac's old Marin City friend. "Too often in our communities someone makes it out, and the number-one reaction is jealousy."

When Tupac made clear he would attend the festival, Leila Steinberg, his old manager and friend, as well as a voice of reason throughout his life, urged him to reconsider. "I called him that morning," she remembered. "I said, 'Whatever you do, do *not* come to Marin City!'"

"Nah," he replied. "It'll be good."

"No," Steinberg said. "I'm there all the time, and people are mad at you. They all think you grew a big ego and forgot about everyone. People will assume you're there to get attention. Trust me, don't come."

Tupac was the product of a long line of stubbornness. Afeni was stubborn. His aunt Glo was stubborn. His grandmother, Rosabelle Williams, had been stubborn. You didn't survive as a strong, empowered Black person in America by wilting. Tupac was the king of stubbornness. "How are you gonna tell me not to go?" he barked at Steinberg. "I'm coming home to let everyone know I love them and support them."

Steinberg resigned herself to the inevitable ugliness.

"His ego was too big to hear what I was saying," she said decades later. "He thought he was indestructible."

The Marin City Festival kicked off at noon and ran until sunset. The weather was perfect—sunny, with temperatures in the low seventies. Tupac pulled up in his Jeep Cherokee, parked in the nearby lot, and walked toward the festivities. He came accompanied by a crew of approximately a dozen people—including two bodyguards and Maurice Harding, a twenty-four-year-old hip-hop artist who had appeared on the scene two years earlier via his rap feature on the Tony! Toni! Toné! single "Feels Good." The son of Mutulu Shakur, Harding (who went by both "Mopreme" and the hip-hop moniker "Mocedes") was Tupac's stepbrother. He was born in

---

* Tupac said of Marin City: "All through my time there they used to diss me. I got love but the kind of love you would give a dog or a neighborhood crack fiend. They liked me because I was at the bottom." This, however, was to *Vibe* in 1994—two years after the festival.

Jamaica, Queens, but the two-year age difference (as well as having different mothers) kept them from being particularly close as children. Harding joined the army, and when his commitment wrapped he settled down in Oakland. "I had been a rapper since I was a kid, and now that the service was over I could do my own thing much easier," he told the journalist Jake Brown. "So I started recording my demo." One day, the members of Tony! Toni! Toné! overheard him rapping. They asked whether Harding would appear on their upcoming release. "I was like, 'Yes, yes, yes,'" he recalled. "I had never had nothing out professionally, so that was it."

"Feels Good" spent two weeks at number 1 on the US R&B charts. Yet what felt like a big break did little for Harding. While Tony! Toni! Toné! soared into the American mainstream, Harding's twelve-second cameo came and went.

After not seeing one another for eight years, Tupac and Harding had recently reconnected over music, weed, and family ties. Tupac longed for kinship. Harding was a nice guy with familiar bloodlines and a tie to the past. He wasn't particularly talented, but he was talented enough. He rapped. He breakdanced. He provided emotional support. Tupac craved family. Mopreme was sort of family.

Tupac and co. arrived as 51.50, the Marin City hip-hop group, was performing. "He showed up with all these guys who weren't from our area," said Dameene Dedrick, a Marin City native. "I don't think he meant disrespect with that. But it definitely rubbed some people wrongly." Though casually dressed in a white T-shirt and jeans, Tupac was now recognizable among young Black audiences. Surrounded by autograph seekers, Tupac happily signed away while also posing for photographs. Clearly, Steinberg's warnings had been the exaggerations of a well-meaning yet misinformed white woman. These were Tupac's people, and he felt embraced. "He was fooling himself," Steinberg said.

The 51.50 gig lasted five or six songs, and toward the end of the set a bunch of spectators spotted Tupac. These were Marin City diehards and friends of Striplin who also felt wronged by the rapper.

They began to chant . . .

Fuck Too-pack!

Fuck Too-pack!

Fuck Too-pack!

One of the agitators was Striplin's cousin, Jimmy Hempfield. Tupac stepped forward, surrounded by his crew.

"What the fuck are you saying?" he yelled.

"Fuck you," replied Hempfield.

"Excuse me?" said Tupac.

"You heard me," Hempfield snapped.

Horace White, a forty-four-year-old festival organizer, charged toward the hostilities. A hefty figure who weighed more than three hundred pounds, White stood between Hempfield and Tupac and placed his arms around both men. The temperature dropped. "I had things pretty cooled out," White recalled.

Striplin approached from behind. He had smoked a blunt and was feeling the high. "I was having fun," he said. "But when I saw Tupac arguing with my cousin, the good feelings wore off." Jerome Wade had been hanging with Striplin, and he recalled his friend being desperate for a fight. "He was very much like, 'Let's go fuck with Tupac,'" Wade said. "He wanted to bully him. He was pissed." Striplin tapped Tupac on the shoulder. The two hadn't seen one another in some time. It was uncomfortable. The tension was raw. Not only was Striplin upset over feeling abandoned, he also believed Tupac had stolen one of his beats and used it without providing credit or payment. "It was dishonest bullshit," Striplin said decades later.

Tupac looked his old friend up and down. Perhaps Steinberg's warnings ran through his mind. "I didn't come here for that," he said. "It's not going down that way." Striplin was mad and high and itching for a confrontation. Tupac, he later said, "was looking at me with disrespect." Striplin pulled back his right arm and—SMACK!—slapped Tupac across the mouth with the back of his hand. "Demetrius snapped," said Dedrick. "Punched him for no good reason."

Tupac fell to the ground, and as soon as he landed he reached into his waistband and pulled out a .380 Colt automatic handgun registered in his name. Throughout his life, Tupac had envied people who brandished weapons with dangerous flair. He did not grow up shooting guns, and those who knew him as a teen maintain he would have been the last person you want armed in a tense situation. "Too erratic," said August Terry.

"Too impulsive." Now, Tupac rose to his feet and pointed the weapon at Striplin. His hand was quivering. It felt like an act, like something out of *Juice*. The former friends stood about six feet apart, and an onlooker screamed, "Run!" as attendees sprinted away from the standoff.

Then—POP! James Finesse, Striplin's brother, rushed forward and punched Tupac in the cheek. The rapper fell to the ground yet again, and his gun left his hand and plopped onto the dirt, slightly out of reach.

"Get the motherfucking gat!" Tupac yelled. "Get the gat!"

At that moment, witnesses observed a member of Tupac's entourage reach for the weapon, pick it up, and fire. "I saw the guy cock it," said Striplin. "And I ran." Two shots were fired. "I was on one knee and kept my head down," said Melvin Atkins, a community organizer. "It all happened so fast. I can't see a face. The shooter has no face. I thought he was shooting high, but that may have been because I was down on my knee."

A once peaceful, blissful festival turned crazed. Folks ran left, ran right. Screaming, dashing, seeking the exits.

And then . . .

"*Nooooooooooooooooooooo!*"

The cry came from a playground alongside the North Bay Marin School, adjacent to the baseball field and roughly one hundred yards from the altercation. Qa'id Mansour Walker-Teal, a gap-toothed six-year-old who lived with his mother, Ocita, in the Jungle, had been riding his bicycle when a single bullet pierced the front of his forehead. Thor Thomas, Tupac's former Tamalpais High classmate, was standing inches away and saw the child fall back. Thor knew Qa'id—the child was his girlfriend Shannon's cousin. He rushed toward Qa'id and was immediately horrified. Blood everywhere. A lifeless body.

Decades later, K. C. Graham, another former Tam student, recalled the scene. "I was just back from a family reunion in South Carolina, and I was wearing a Bart Simpson South Carolina State T-shirt," he said. "I saw the bullet hole right between the kid's eyes, and I took my shirt off to stop the bleeding. I mean, the hole was perfectly placed between his eyebrows. He had a little tear coming down his eye, man. I'll never forget that tear. The kid was laid on his bike. It was still under him."

For a second, time stood still. Shots had been fired. A child had been gunned down. In a month, Qa'id had been scheduled to begin kindergarten. Now he was dead.

Then—*anger*. Tupac and his cohorts sprinted for the parking lot. Six or seven of the men jumped into a small Nissan and sped off onto Highway 101. Tupac and Mopreme made it to the Jeep Cherokee, but before they could start the engine the vehicle was surrounded by festival attendees, who pounded on the hood and smashed the windows. "I was one of the people at this car, enraged and looking for blood," said Meloni Page. "Tupac was hiding in the back seat like a baby. The windows were tinted, but we knew he was in there. I'm screaming—'Get out! Get out, you coward! We all know it's you!'"

"I saw Tupac running, and the look on his face was pure fear," said Dameene Dedrick. "People destroyed that car." Hands and arms reached through the shattered glass, grabbing for Tupac, grabbing for Mopreme, hungry for retribution. After a couple of seconds, a pair of sheriff's deputies drew their guns and demanded everyone back away. Mopreme, sitting behind the wheel, hit the gas. Wrote Craig Marine in the *San Francisco Examiner*: "Harding puts the car into gear and speeds from the lot. Their getaway is short-lived, though, when Harding chooses to turn left instead of right and heads not for the freeway but toward a sheriff's substation. The Cherokee is stopped no more than 150 yards from the parking lot and Tupac, Harding and the rest of his group are spread eagled upon the ground in no time."

The .380 Colt automatic handgun used to shoot Qa'id Walker-Teal had been launched from the Jeep and was later found on the ground by police. So was Mopreme's driver's license, which was tossed into some bushes. All the members of Tupac's entourage were taken to Sausalito for questioning, and while no one admitted to the shooting, a witness described the man who fired the gun as outfitted in a Nike baseball-type jersey with JORDAN written across the chest and the number 23 stitched onto the sleeve. They said he wore three-quarter-length shorts and high-tops.

This eliminated Tupac.

Mopreme, however, sported that exact outfit.*

---

* He has long denied firing the gun.

No usable fingerprints were found on the gun. Mopreme took the Fifth, and the other members of Tupac's group repeated the same story of "Gun? What gun?" Nobody wanted to be the rat. Though briefly arrested, Mopreme was released due to insufficient evidence. Detectives searched Tupac's Oakland pad and seized ammunition. He denied having a gun or knowing that any of his friends had a gun—both lies. Years later, a wrongful death suit was filed against Tupac, and he settled for approximately four hundred thousand dollars. The sum was paid by his record label as an advance on his earnings.

Leila Steinberg, who had begged Tupac to steer clear of the Festival on the Green, was there that night. The mother of three children at the time, she and her kids saw Qa'id Walker-Teal as he took his final breaths. "It was all so avoidable," she said. "But Tupac's need to be seen . . ."

Steinberg said that, for the remainder of his life, Tupac was haunted. Qa'id Walker-Teal's name appeared in one of his songs (in "Something 2 Die 4," Tupac raps, *Young Qa'id, rest in peace / Remember that name*"), and permanently stuck in his mind. He knew, deep down, that he was responsible for the child's curtailed existence; that his own stubbornness and ego had proved too large for the moment. The same man whose first album was an ode to Black strength had caused a young Black boy to die. Even worse, he knew the shooter's identity. The weight of it all was unbearable.

"There are certain lines you can never come back from," Steinberg said. "After that, so much changed. That day was a marker, and there was no return for Tupac. He played a role in a child dying. He could never come back to Marin City. He ruined everything."

Chapter 14

The Most Intelligent Stupid Dude

I n 1991, shortly before the release of *2Pacalypse Now*, Tupac Shakur agreed to be interviewed by a new monthly magazine, *SuperFly*.

Founded by a socialite named Gloria Goldwater, the publication sought to boost hip-hop as it continued to transition from fringe to mainstream. So it profiled stars on the rise, ranging from Will Smith to Ice-T to MC Hammer, in an effort to introduce the artists to a wider audience.

Enter Tupac.

Save the brief videotaped session from Tamalpais High, Tupac had rarely been asked to discuss his life for any sort of documented record. So, when he sat down across from a *SuperFly* reporter who went by "Hamza," Tupac was chatty and engaged and fun and flip . . . and largely full of shit.

He told Hamza that he came to the Bay Area "to try to make it [as a rapper]." He told Hamza he was a gangster. He told Hamza he didn't "give a fuck if they don't put out my record" and he told Hamza his real love wasn't music or film, but "the streets." It was performative nonsense, an aspiring superstar selling a hardened image.

In the midst of it all, however, Tupac offered something viscerally real.

When asked about his pathway from the streets to hopeful musical superstardom, he turned his attention toward a performer who made his blood boil.

Tupac Shakur detested Vanilla Ice.

What is Vanilla Ice talking about? I don't appreciate him being on every fucking Black magazine in the city. What the fuck is up with Black Beat and WORD UP! and the others who put this nigga in centerfolds all over their damn magazines? Put Chuck D in there. Forget Vanilla Ice. That nigga ain't doing things for the people. He ain't doing nothing. If he don't like that I'm talking about him he can do something about it. I'm not shutting up.

Ever since the August 22, 1990, release of "Ice Ice Baby," Tupac cursed Vanilla Ice's very existence. It was bad enough that Robert Van Winkle (aka Ice) had lifted the song's sample from "Under Pressure," the iconic Queen and David Bowie jam (and a tune Tupac loved). But "Ice Ice Baby" as cultural phenomenon . . . one that would sell more than 15 million copies and absorb both white *and* Black listeners—well, that was too much to swallow.

So Tupac went after the album and the artist, and when it was time to create a follow-up to *2Pacalypse Now*, he committed himself to creating something that was real, raw, and—unlike his debut release—true to himself.

He knew the perfect collaborator.

In Bay Area hip-hop circles, the name Daryl Anderson wasn't recognizable. But drop "DJ Daryl," and you could feel the sizzle. The lone child of a single mother, Daryl was raised in the West Oakland projects of Cypress Village. His dad, a Vietnam veteran named Larry Earl Anderson, was nowhere to be seen. His mom, Rosie, suffered from debilitating mental illness. He was sixteen and about to drop out of Oakland's McClymonds High School when he met a local disc jockey named Keith Massey. "I used to watch how he was doing things," Daryl recalled. "He had all this equipment—you'd look in his living room and it'd be speakers and turntables and amps. For a kid like me, it was life-changing."

Daryl would save up his spare change and bring it to the Alameda Flea Market, where he'd buy mismatched pieces of used equipment. He was eighteen when he DJed his first gig at a club, Crosswinds, located on the local army base. Nicknamed "Scratchmaster," he was three years too young for admittance. But it mattered not. He became a Crosswinds regular, and before long partygoers swapped his goofball nickname for the straightforward "DJ Daryl."

"What Keith taught me is how to keep people dancing," Daryl said. "He taught me how to blend records without pausing. And people are dancing so hard, and they're sweating, and they're having a great time. They're not fighting. Just dancing."

On the side, Daryl created mixtapes and peddled them around Oakland. In 1988, he was introduced to J.E.D., the executive producer for an up-and-coming Bay Area rapper named Richie Rich. Together, they started the hip-hop group 415.

Although it never blew up nationally, 415 was a local phenomenon that influenced rappers like Snoop Dogg and Warren G. They were early pioneers of the gangsta rap genre, and their 1990 debut album, *41Fivin*, featured such tracks as "Niggas Just Jock Me" and "Groupie Ass Bitch." While critics (predictably) never much appreciated the material, the community gobbled it up.

As did one Tupac Amaru Shakur.

In many ways, the jagged edginess of *41Fivin* was what he had aspired for *2Pacalypse Now*. Haunted by its shortcomings, Tupac reached out to Daryl. The men could not have been more opposite—Daryl was shy and quiet and uninterested in smoking weed. Tupac was high 80 percent of the day. But they shared a passion for music.

On an early Thursday morning, Tupac had Daryl fly to Los Angeles and meet him at Echo Sound Studios. Daryl grabbed his drum machine, rushed to the airport, and, the next morning, found himself alongside Tupac at a sound board. For Daryl, it was the greatest of experiences. Richie Rich was a unique enough bird, but Tupac—*sweet Jesus*. There was only one.

"He did something in the studio that nobody was doing," Daryl recalled. "Back then, rappers just rapped. But Tupac rapped through his track, then he asked the engineer for another track so he could do some ad-libs on it. That was unheard of back then, because we were only working with twenty-four tracks, and sixteen of those were being utilized with just drums and instrumentation. So you basically had eight left for vocals. And Tupac was using up two and three of those tracks. And it was like, 'What are you gonna do with those tracks?' But he had this alter-ego solider come out. He'd have an engineer speed the tape up, and he'd be on yet another track, just laughing and saying stuff on the track. And then when he put it back to regular speed, it sounded like he was talking real slow. As an engineer, I was amazed and confused. What was he doing? And how did he know to do it? It was genius."

Several weeks earlier, Tupac had invited Daryl and Richie Rich to his Oakland pad, and over dinner asked, "What do y'all think will make a million people go out and buy a record?"

"Some street shit," Richie Rich replied. "If you say shit about the streets, people can gravitate to it. Because that's our reality."

Tupac shook his head in disagreement.

"I believe," he countered, "if you make music for women, the streets will follow."

Unbeknownst to Daryl, Tupac had been cobbling together the lyrics for a uniquely sensitive song titled "Keep Ya Head Up." The inspiration was his sister, Set, now sixteen years old. Set had been raped, abandoned, abused, scorned, and ridiculed. As her brother soared, she remained in the shadows. Though back in Marin City Tupac had failed to realize the pain he inflicted upon Set, he was now old enough to know.

Like most of his lyrics, Tupac composed "Keep Ya Head Up" in less than two days. It was groundbreaking for its texture and sensitivity.

Wrote Tupac: *But please don't cry, dry your eyes, never let up / Forgive but don't forget, girl, keep your head up.*

"In hip-hop, most of the stuff we did was about drugs, shooting, money," said Daryl. "And this was *all* heart."

Tupac recorded the vocals in one take, and Daryl slowed the bass line to match the sample of another song, "O-o-h Child," by the Five Stairsteps. "It was so dope," said Daryl. "All told, we recorded twelve songs in one day. Tupac was a force that couldn't be stopped."

The name of the second album would be *Troublesome 21*. Tupac had had this in his head for a good while—the word representing his reputation, the number representing his age.

Much of its inspiration came from the Los Angeles riots, a six-day-long

whirlwind of anger, looting, and arson following the acquittal of the officers who beat down a Black man named Rodney King.

Tupac had been inside Echo Sound with the producer Laylaw when
the riots broke out. The two were watching everything unfold on TV, and
Laylaw—a product of the streets of Los Angeles—felt compelled to jump
in. He and Tupac sped toward Hollywood in Laylaw's truck. "We see this
one motherfucker over to the side," Laylaw recalled. "We jump out, we
dust this motherfucker off real quick. We don't even know what's going
on. We just think it's everybody for themselves. So we beat the hell out of
this one motherfucker. We jump back in the motherfucking car." On the
radio an anchor reported that the heart of the riot was the intersection of
Florence and Normandie Avenues. "So me and Pac go straight to motherfucking Florence and Normandie," Laylaw recalled.

"Our stupid asses went into that liquor store that was still smoking.
We went into that liquor store, got any kind of liquor we could get, we
left. We grabbed whatever we wanted." In an essay for *The Real State*,
Tupac pinpointed this as the moment when he developed a kinship with
Los Angeles. "As I drove through L.A. . . . . thuggin' to the fullest, I fell in
love with L.A.," he wrote. "I met true boss playaz who tried to school me
on the next level. Many niggaz never survive the second level of Thug
Life. They become addicted 2 death. A true bloss playa knowz when 2
advance."

Like the riots, *Troublesome 21* overflowed with rage. It featured tracks
with titles like "The Streetz R Deathrow" and "Don't Call Me Bytch" and
"Still Don't Give a Phuck" and lyrics that screamed retribution. When
Tupac finished up, he submitted the demo to Interscope, the company
that would release the album under the umbrella of Atlantic Records,
which was a division of Warner Bros. music. Tupac could not have been
more proud. This was his masterpiece. "He knew it was tremendous," said
Daryl. "So did I."

Alas, a month earlier, on March 10, 1992, the rapper Ice-T and his
thrash metal band, Body Count, had birthed a self-titled album on Sire
Records (also beneath the Warner Bros. umbrella). One of the songs, "Cop
Killer," expressed the first-person viewpoint of a man who, fed up with

police brutality, goes on a murderous spree. The lyrics were easy enough to interpret.

> *Cop killer, better you than me*
> *Cop killer, fuck police brutality*
> *Cop killer, I know your momma's grieving (fuck her)*
> *Cop killer, but tonight we get even, yeah*

George H. W. Bush, president at the time, denounced the song as "sick." The Combined Law Enforcement Association of Texas called for a boycott of Time Warner (which owned Warner Bros.) and demanded an apology. Ice-T begrudgingly pulled the song from the album, but the corporate suits were shaken.

Mo Ostin, head of Warner Bros. music, held a meeting inside the company's office. Atron Gregory, Tupac's manager, was present, as were several of the rapper's associates. According to Gregory, Ostin said he was ending the distribution of albums that "glorified" violence against police. In addition, according to the author Staci Robinson, "any label or artist under the Time Warner umbrella would have to submit lyrical content for approval before the product was released to market."

When Tupac learned that *Troublesome 21* couldn't exist as is, he flipped. When he learned that the album couldn't exist because a bunch of white corporate suits were against it, he flipped even more. He chewed out Gregory, chewed out Interscope's decision-makers. He called Daryl to share the news—"You're not gonna believe this shit," he said. And Tupac was correct—DJ Daryl couldn't believe this shit. All that time working together. All the craftsmanship and effort. Gone.

Of the twelve songs Tupac and Daryl had recorded, only "Keep Ya Head Up" made the final cut. Tupac changed the name of the album to *Strictly 4 My N.I.G.G.A.Z . . .* , a smackdown of the all-white group of people who had canceled his initial effort. He returned to the studio, this time without a dejected DJ Daryl. "I'm not saying this because my work wasn't used," said Daryl. "But it's not a good album. When we worked together, everything had to be perfect. The lyrics, the production. Everything. He had this incredibly high standard, and the album—I believe—achieved it. But the one he put out was sort of cheesy. It was unfocused. A few songs save it. But it's not good."

By *a few*, DJ Daryl means *two*. One is "Keep Ya Head Up," which remains a Tupac classic. The second is a jam that feels out of place on a compilation that Tupac wanted to be heavy, intense, rugged. It was birthed by Shock G, the Digital Underground mastermind, who developed a beat he had planned on keeping for a future DU album. In the midst of the nightmare of *Troublesome 21* force-transforming into *Strictly 4 My N.I.G.G.A.Z . . .*, Tupac called his old friend to ask whether he had a spare sound lying around. "And Shock had this thing that we'd been riding with for a while," said Money-B, the Digital Underground rapper. "We knew it was a dope beat, we knew we didn't wanna fuck it up. But Pac had a deadline for his album, and he was pretty desperate. So Shock was like, 'Take this one . . .'"

Shock G's work featured a sample from Zapp's "Computer Love" and a bit off Gang Starr's "Step in the Arena." It was fast and upbeat, and Tupac *loved* it. He wrote the lyrics to "I Get Around" in a matter of hours, and insisted both Shock G and Money-B take verses. "I told Pac it's a shame when someone comes along and kills you in your own song," said Money-B. "Pac is great—but I killed it."*

Strictly 4 My N.I.G.G.A.Z . . . dropped on February 16, 1993. Tupac felt as he had when *2Pacalypse Now* was born more than a year earlier. He liked some of it, but hated that his voice and music were being controlled by the Man. Interscope made the decision to release the song "Holler If Ya Hear Me" as a first single, and while Tupac signed off, he knew it wasn't his strongest work. DJ Daryl urged him to go with "Keep Ya Head Up." Shock G *begged him* to go with "I Get Around." Alas, those singles came later.

To help get things going, Interscope hired Stephen Ashley Blake to direct the "Holler If Ya Hear Me" music video, and handed him a forty-thousand-dollar budget. Blake had shot and coproduced the videos for "Brenda's Got a Baby" and "If My Homie Calls" off the first album, and he found Tupac to be . . . OKish to work with. Not great, not awful.

---

* This isn't as controversial a take as one might believe. "That's a legit argument for many people," said Reggie Williams, curator of the hip-hop site Ambrosia for Heads. "Money-B's flow is crazy, but Pac has more quotables."

For this venture, Blake organized a two-day shoot. The first session taped inside a house on Fifty-Third Street between Hoover and Vermont that belonged to Irene White, Blake's bemused yet game grandmother. "Everything went great," Blake said. "Tupac was engaged and fiery. I like trying to evoke electric performances, and he had it." Day 2 was problematic. Blake had rented out a Compton-based shooting range, and Tupac arrived late and high with a collection of obnoxious hangers-on. When it was time to act, Tupac was nowhere to be found—he and his crew had bolted for the nearby Roscoe's Chicken & Waffles. When he finally returned two hours later, Tupac was ornery and agitated. Blake had mapped out the entire video with Tupac's earlier approval. Now the rapper was complaining and telling Blake the story didn't work for him.

Blake shot back, "Pac, we've been over this already . . ."

Tupac wasn't hearing it. He cursed out Blake, cursed out the workers, went off on a hostile tirade about Blake being white and half of his employees being white and how white people fucked everything up. "I mean, I never heard Tupac say anything like that before," Blake said. "I'd never experienced that in him, but I had the sense that he felt he was being exploited or abused or ripped off in some way, or cheated in some way. It was a scary rage because his boys were with him. Some of them were packing. And he just kept going and going—*This is my video* and all that. And it was such a violent outburst. There was such a menace to those words and the people he was with. I just said, 'You know what? I need to walk out and I need to process this and think about this.'"

Ultimately, Blake surrendered to Tupac's demands and finished the video. They forged an uncomfortable truce, and three days later Blake drove to Tupac's home to record a requisite behind-the-scenes interview demanded by the record company. He was greeted warmly by Afeni, then sat across from Tupac, microphone in hand. He warned the artist the questions would be basic and banal, but they served a purpose. *Have you ever known someone who died tragically? Have you ever experienced police brutality?* Once again, Tupac flew into a rage and stormed from the room. "I wound up giving him the mic and letting him rant," Blake said. "When I left the home that day, it was the last time I'd ever see Tupac."

What Blake didn't know—*couldn't have known*—was that the anger directed his way was bigger than a music video. It was the heartbreak of a second-straight album failing to meet his expectations.

Tupac was starting to wonder whether anything ever would.

In the early-to-mid-1970s, a man named Dennis Coelho was living in Odessa, Texas, working in oil sales for the Eckle Power company. It was probably his seventh or eighth job since leaving the army in 1965, and the gig brought little joy. The hours were long, the rejection ceaseless. So when he visited Houston on a business trip in the summer of 1974, Coelho sat down with a friend, Dale Livingston, and complained about the direction of his life.

"Well," said Livingston, "I can teach you how to ink."

Livingston owned the Black Dragon Tattoo Studio in West Houston, and he took Coelho on as a protégé and employee. Two years later, Coehlo—who went by Dago—opened his own shop on Houston's north side. The vast majority of his customers were bikers, and business exploded. One day, a friend who worked as a Denny's waitress told Dago she wanted a tattoo.

"We don't do that," he said.

"Do what?" she asked.

"Tattoo Black people."

Dago didn't think he was being racist. Why, as a boy growing up in Fort Smith, Arkansas, he spent much of his free time tagging along with his grandmother, Ellen Mae Watkins, who was one of the few white employees at a mattress factory. "The Black women there raised me like I was their own," he said. "They loved me." Still, in the 1970s, tattoos weren't really a Black thing. Black athletes didn't sport them. Black singers didn't display them. "You couldn't find a tattoo shop that did Blacks," Coelho said. "And the ones that did Black tattoos raised the prices. And it got me thinking—'Why *not* do Black tattoos?'"

Coelho tattooed his waitress friend, and she told other Blacks about his shop and craftsmanship. Before long, Dago's was overflowing with Black customers—not just waitresses and accountants and farmers, but Houston's celebrity class. Members of the NBA's Rockets and NFL's Oilers frequented his business. Rappers passing through town knew where to get inked up. Dago's morphed into not merely a tattoo parlor, but an after-the-club hot spot. It opened at 5:00 p.m., closed at 5:00 a.m.

In the summer months of 1992, Tupac Shakur was in Houston, visiting a stripper he had met during his Digital Underground days. Her name was Dahlia "Poochie" McCutchen, and she was a Dago's regular who, a year earlier, had first brought Tupac by the shop for a pair of tattoos (one the Egyptian Nefertiti, the other 2-PAC in block letters). Tupac loved Dago's professionalism and craftsmanship, and now was back for something new. He was increasingly toying with the word "Thug." He liked the sound. One syllable with the power of a chain saw. Back in Marin City, Tupac marveled at the real thugs (gangbangers, drug dealers) while knowing he wasn't of their ilk. Real thugs didn't listen to Kate Bush.

So, entering Dago's late one night, blunt in hand, he put in an order: "I want the words THUG LIFE tatted across my stomach."

Hmm.

"Explain that to me," Coehlo replied.

Tupac pulled out the letters as he had designed them on a piece of white paper. The *I* in LIFE was a bullet. He went into a long and rambling riff about the streets and standing up for yourself and being a thug in the name of this and that and that and . . .

"OK," Coehlo said. "I can do that."

Over the next four hours, the artist went to work. Even though Tupac was high, Coehlo marveled how he barely flinched. Each letter was three inches tall. It was hardly a painless process. "That part of the body can have a tender nippy feeling," Coehlo said. "I've had people pass out, pee themselves, poop themselves. Tupac took it."

When the work was done, Tupac hugged Coehlo, dropped a hundred-dollar bill as a tip, and bolted. He flew back to California a couple of days later to meet with Watani Tyehimba—his *new* manager.

Over the previous few months, Tupac had decided he needed a career boost. His longtime manager, Atron Gregory, was a good man who had connected him with Digital Underground and put him on the map. But along with managing Digital Underground, Gregory handled the rapper MC Smooth as well as the group Gold Money. "I'm gonna be the best,"

Tupac told Gregory. "And if you can't work with just me, I have to go with someone who will."

That someone wound up being Tyehimba, the longtime family friend who, back in 1989, had asked an eighteen-year-old Tupac to relocate to Atlanta and head the New Afrikan Panthers. Although his background was in neither music nor artist management (he began working as a legal investigator and paralegal for law firms in 1979, and also did weapons training as part of security consulting), Tyehimba was savvy. Tupac wanted him to serve as both business and personal manager. "I didn't know shit about management," Tyehimba said. "I told Tupac that. But he said, 'You can figure it out. You always figure stuff out.'" Initially, Tyehimba said, he planned on splitting the work with Afeni, who was now (mostly) clean and in Tupac's good graces. However, she wasn't interested. "She said, 'I don't have to work—my son is gonna take care of me,'" Tyehimba recalled. "So it was just me."

One of his first acts as the rapper's manager was incorporating Tupac by forming 2Pacalypse Entertainment and Out Da Gutta Records. "Too many artists are taken advantage of and don't control their own work," said Tyehimba. "This was a way for Tupac to have empowerment."

Tyehimba felt deep empathy for the youngster. Like so many Black men in America, Tupac rarely paused to smell a rose or watch the sun rise or appreciate the richness of a fresh-baked brownie. It wasn't how he was programmed. Tyehimba and his wife, Ahadi, had three children. They lived in a home where family members sat down for dinner and snuggled on the couch for a weekend movie. Tupac enviously referred to them as "The Cosby Family."

Tyehimba developed a game plan that combined music, acting, and public service. He believed that with the right approach, the artist could transcend the normal bounds of others in the business. Many of the rappers Tupac grew up admiring were either on the fade or had vanished (Where have you gone, Count Coolout?). With rare exceptions, hip-hop shelf life was a blink of the eye. Only, it didn't have to be that way for Tupac. He could be special.

But then he showed up . . . *with the* THUG LIFE *tattoo.*

Tyehimba was repulsed. "Tupac," he said, "what the fuck have you done?"

"You don't like it?" Tupac replied.

"*No*, I don't like it," Tyehimba said. "That's the stupidest shit I've ever seen."

Tyehimba knew Tupac could be impulsive. If a thought entered his mind, there was no pause button to consider the ramifications. "He just acted," said Tyehimba. "Often foolishly. He was the most intelligent stupid dude you'll ever know."*

And now, Tupac Shakur had this inane saying sprawled across his stomach. His explanation ("It looks dope") sucked. So, Tyehimba believed, would the inevitable backlash. Tupac was already facing heat for the shooting deaths of Qa'id Walker-Teal and Bill Davidson. His career could survive only so much negativity.

So, in his new role, Tyehimba reached out to Mutulu Shakur, Tupac's stepfather, who was now in his third year behind bars at the Lompoc federal penitentiary. Tupac had very few male role models in his life, but Mutulu was one of them. They exchanged letters and phone calls. When Tupac found himself overwhelmed, Mutulu was oftentimes his go-to. He symbolized Black strength and courage. He never let prison get to him. He was resilient and intelligent. Theirs was very much a Yoda-Luke relationship. When Mutulu opened his mouth, Tupac dared not interrupt.

"Mutulu was as annoyed by the tattoo as I was," said Tyehimba. "And he let Tupac know it. But I think he was smart enough to see it as an opportunity, if played correctly."

Tupac had recently broached the idea of something he referred to as "50 N.I.G.G.A.Z."—"50" for all of America's states, "N.I.G.G.A.Z." an acronym for "Never Ignorant Getting Goals Accomplished." The plan was to recruit one Black man in every state to become a leader in the movement to bring forth equal rights. Only, um, there was no plan beyond Tupac saying he had a plan. For all his communication skills, Tupac didn't know how to galvanize a community or raise funds. Even behind bars, however, Mutulu Shakur did. According to the estate-authorized 2023

---

* According to Kendrick Wells, Tupac's first exposure to the idea of "Thug Life" came during his time in Marin, when a local group, the Crew, had a little-known song titled "That's the Way You Living the Thug Life." Marku Reynolds, an area dealer/rapper, came up with the phrase.

Tupac biography by Staci Robinson, Tupac's "plan was to embrace people whom America labeled as 'thugs' and flip the negative connotation of the word." To fire up the movement, the story goes, Tupac created the acronym THUG LIFE: The Hate U Give Little Infants Fucks Everybody.

It was amazing! Brilliant! Revolutionary!

It also wasn't Tupac's idea. *At all.*

Mutulu came up with it, as well as a corresponding "Code of THUG LIFE"—a series of dos and don'ts for being a righteous thug.

Among the twenty-six rules were:

- The Boys in Blue don't run nothing; we do. Control the Hood, and make it safe for squares.
- No slinging to pregnant Sisters. That's baby killing; that's genocide!
- Know your target, who's the real enemy.
- Civilians are not a target and should be spared.
- Crew Leaders: You are responsible for legal/financial payment commitments to crew members; your word must be your bond.

"I think even gangs can be positive," Tupac said when asked to explain the code. "It just has to be organized. It's a code to put order to the violence on the streets."

The pivot from misguided tattoo to twenty-six-rule code was one of Tyehimba's greatest marketing achievements. According to multiple reports, thanks to Tupac, leaders of the Crips and Bloods came together, sat down, broke bread, hugged it out, and agreed to sign a document that squashed any beefs once and for all. Tupac Shakur wasn't merely a rapper, but a man who could shock the world and make peace.

Had the Crips and Bloods actually sat down?

Was a document signed?

Well, no.

But it made for tremendous PR.

What Watani Tyehimba learned quickly in his new job was that managing Tupac Shakur was similar to herding an army of cats through a maze coated in butter. Even if the Code of THUG LIFE was the offshoot of an impulsive tattoo, Tupac emphasized the ideals of Black unity and togetherness.

Yet as 1992 rolled into 1993, Tupac struggled to meet his own standards.

Or, put differently, he just couldn't help himself.

"Tupac," said Dupré Kelly, a rapper from Lords of the Underground, "was caught up in the stuff he was actually trying to stop."

On February 16, 1993, *Strictly 4 My N.I.G.G.A.Z . . .* hit stores. Interscope sent Tupac on a mini promotional tour. Leslie Gerard, one of the label's employees, organized things. The plan was for Tupac to stop in on underground radio stations, visit high schools, maybe perform a song or two. "You have to remember, he wasn't all that big as a rapper yet," said Gerard. "He did *Juice*, but he was still on the rise and trying to establish himself."*

Everything went smoothly, and on March 13 Tupac was gifted with an enormous career break—he would travel to the Fox Studios in Hollywood and tape a segment for the hit TV show *In Living Color*. This was no small thing. A sketch comedy show inspired by *Saturday Night Live*, *In Living Color* scored big ratings and served as a launching pad for such superstars as Jamie Foxx, Jim Carrey, Tommy Davidson, and Jennifer Lopez.

So late that evening, Fox sent a limousine to Sherman Oaks to pick up Tupac and carry him to the studio. The driver, David Deleon, worked for an independent car service that contracted out to corporations like Fox. When Deleon arrived at the meeting spot, he was greeted by Tupac, the rappers Macadoshis and Rated R, and his friends Charles "Man Man" Fuller and Calvin "Babez" Nunley. "So we're smoking weed in the back of the limo," recalled Babez, a Marin City native and former drug dealer. "The driver was salty from the beginning, and as soon as we got to Fox Studios the dude turns around and says, 'Y'all shouldn't be smoking that weed in another man's car.'"

The men left the vehicle, entered Fox, and rehearsed, and at two o'clock in the morning Tupac and Fuller returned to the limo for a break. They

---

* During musical performances, Tupac was usually introduced to audiences as "Tupac from *Juice*."

plopped down in the front seats and again broke out the weed. Deleon, leaning against the door, was not happy. "You guys can't do that in here," he said. "I already told you. Get out of my car."

It wasn't an unreasonable request.

1. The vehicle was Deleon's responsibility.
2. Weed leaves a stench.
3. He had other passengers to pick up.

Tupac, however, was not having it. "We pay for this limo!" he screamed. "You can't tell us to smoke weed or not!"

Deleon popped the trunk and reached for a bag. Tupac viewed this as an aggressive act ("We didn't know if the guy was getting a gun or what," he later said) and rose from his seat. By now, his entire crew was standing nearby. "The dude started huffing at us," said Babez, "and Pac took a swing. Then we all got on the guy. We beat the dude down *hard*."* Someone from the show called the police, and the actress Rosie Perez—an *In Living Color* cast member who had casually dated Tupac—came running out, crying. When the police arrived, Deleon was bloodied on the ground. Tupac and Fuller were arrested for assault with a deadly weapon, and freed on fifteen thousand dollars' bond. "They apparently got angry," said John Zrofsky, the police sergeant, "and pounced on him and beat and kicked and stomped on him."

To Interscope's dismay, not only was the *In Living Color* gig canceled, but the following day's newspapers ran an Associated Press article headlined POLICE ARREST '2 PAC' RAPPERS. The lede: "Two members of the rap group '2 Pac' were arrested Saturday for allegedly assaulting a driver who complained they were using drugs in his limousine, police said."

That was just the beginning.

Less than a month later, Tupac was in East Lansing, Michigan, as part of

---

* Years later the songwriter Harold Scrap Fretty, a former gang member, recalled this as the moment when he knew Tupac was out of his depth. "The gangster thing to do would have been to shake the man's hand with a hundred-dollar bill and say, 'Hey, is this still off limits?' That's how we move. If you're going to be a real gangster, act like one. Don't be a fool."

the *Strictly 4 My N.I.G.G.A.Z...* promotional tour. Interscope booked him to headline a talent show inside Michigan State University's auditorium, and he arrived to be greeted by the familiar face of Chauncey Wynn, co-owner of Fly Records, an independent label. Wynn and Tupac had met the previous year in Atlanta, at the annual hip-hop festival Jack the Rapper. They shared a friendship with Falcons wide receiver Andre Rison, and one of Wynn's groups, M.A.D., performed on the same day as Tupac. "We were cool," said Wynn. "Tupac and one of my artists did a song together, pictures were taken. All love."

Now, in East Lansing, Tupac spotted Wynn—who was at the show with M.A.D.—and flashed him a smile. "Hey, Chauncey," he said. "What's up?"

While waiting for the gig to begin, Tupac agreed to a videotaped interview with someone named D Phife out of nearby Flint, Michigan. Standing behind Tupac were four men—Serge, Babez, Man Man, and Syke—who doubled as aspiring rappers and posse members.

Syke was holding a baseball bat.

Phife introduced Tupac to viewers, then asked, "What's up? What's coming up for the summertime?" He listened as Tupac rolled a blunt and rambled incoherently: "Thug Life is the only thing up in the nineties. Thug Life! A little bit, then Thug Life like a lot. These are my Thug Life niggas and we fittin' to do this while I'm rolling a blunt. Thug Life. Thug Life niggas is the craziest niggas! If they ask you, you tell them, these my niggas. That's how we ruling this shit. Smoking blunts, pumping funks, and punking chumps. That's how we doing that shit. Fucking niggas up! Fucking niggas up real bad! Two times quick in the nineties. And we drinking and smoking weed all the time. We high till we die, you know what I'm saying? Man, we ain't stopping. Can't nobody fuck with us either."

Phife looked bewildered. *What the hell was Tupac talking about?* Still, the rapper was friendly and engaging enough. He certainly seemed pleased to be in East Lansing. And, really, how many people were pleased to be in East Lansing?

Shortly before the show kicked off, however, something snapped. According to Wynn, it began when Tupac was passed some strange weed and his demeanor shifted from peppy to dark. Tupac demanded event organizers let him perform first (as opposed to last). Why? No one knows. When the request was denied, he lost it. "Do you have any fucking idea how far I traveled to be here?" he said. "Just fucking change the motherfucking schedule!"

The lineup was shuffled, and Tupac opened the show shirtless, with his jeans dangling down past his underwear. He started rapping, only the microphone malfunctioned, and his vocals were overtaken by static. Wynn had recently purchased a six-hundred-dollar wireless mic for his group, and he called Tupac over and handed it to him. Tupac smiled and resumed his performance, but unleashed a flurry of expletives after being told the night had to be curse-free (in his defense, Tupac was not to be confused with Young MC or Kurtis Blow). When the soundman cut him off, Tupac held the microphone—Wynn's *six-hundred-dollar microphone*—aloft and slammed it to the ground.

Wynn picked it up, and Tupac said, "Hey, Chauncey, lemme see the mic again."

"All right," Wynn replied. "Just don't break it."

Tupac snatched the microphone from his hand. "Gimme that fucking thing, motherfucker!" he said. "I don't tell you how to do your job! Don't tell me how to do mine!"

Then he again slammed the microphone to the ground.

Tupac knew Wynn, but he didn't *know* Wynn. He didn't know he had been an all-American college wrestler at Morgan State. Didn't know that James Phillips, his old coach, nicknamed him "The Animal." Wynn was six feet tall and weighed 190 pounds. He was all muscle. Tupac, by comparison, was a pipe cleaner.

"I walked up to Tupac," Wynn recalled, "and I bent down in his face and my exact words were, 'Fuck you, you boneheaded motherfucker.'"

Nobody spoke to Tupac Shakur that way. Which is why—just in case anyone *ever* spoke to Tupac that way—someone with his crew always had the baseball bat nearby. As soon as the phrase "boneheaded motherfucker" entered the universe, Tupac reached for the bat and swung wildly. Wynn caught some Louisville Slugger to the back of his head, but—fueled by anger and adrenaline—barely flinched. He was rushed by the other members of Tupac's posse, who cornered him near the rear of the stage. Wynn assumed the wrestling position he had mastered at Morgan State.

Syke stepped forward, fist cocked.

"Y'all might get me," Wynn barked, "but if you hit me I will chew your ass up! I wrestle! I'm gonna pull you on top of me and I'm gonna chew your fucking face off! Then I will break your neck!"

Somehow, any further violence was avoided. Tupac leapt from the stage into the audience, cursed a bunch of attendees out, and laughed as the show wrapped prematurely. "It was pandemonium," said James Davis, a Michigan State student in the crowd.

The next morning, while waiting for his flight at Lansing's Capital City Airport, Tupac was arrested and charged with one count of felonious assault, which carried a maximum penalty of four years in prison and a two-thousand-dollar fine. "We all went to jail," said Babez. "We weren't there long, but it wasn't great. I guess the lesson is, never bring a baseball bat to a concert."

Chapter 15

Rebound

There was another incident.

There *always* seemed to be another incident.

For some reason, Tupac Shakur just couldn't help himself. Was he trying to live up to Bishop, the character he played in *Juice*? Maybe. Was he attempting to cultivate a hip-hop image that might align with his lyrics? Perhaps. Was he just an impulsive young man lacking the tools to pause, take a deep breath, and move on? Likely.

But, alas—there was another incident.

When *2Pacalypse Now* dropped in 1991, Interscope had hired the nineteen-year-old twin brothers Allen and Albert Hughes to direct the videos for the album's three singles—"Trapped," "Brenda's Got a Baby," and "If My Homie Calls." Allen had first stumbled upon the rapper a year or so earlier, when he was dining at a breakfast joint with the members of Digital Underground. Not only had he never met Tupac Shakur—he didn't know such a human existed. "There were about twelve guys there," Allen recalled, "and at the end of the table was this kid just snapping on everyone, roasting everyone. I was like, Who *is* this person? And how does one dude have this much charisma?" Later, as the two stood side by side at bathroom urinals, Tupac told Allen that he was about to make a record and he knew *just* the brothers to create his videos. "I'm sort of like, 'Yeah, yeah—whatever,'" said Allen. "But I'm obsessed with the kid, because he has this magic. There aren't many people you love from go. He had it all."

For Allen Hughes, the "Trapped" experience was marvelous ("We were on the exact same page as Tupac, and everything was lovey-dovey"), the "Brenda's Got a Baby" experience was life-changing ("That was us doing great stuff"), and the "If My Homie Calls" experience was battery acid ("By then Tupac was starting to get very difficult. He was very volatile from moment to moment and hour to hour and day to day").

Now, in 1993, the siblings were working on their first feature film, *Menace II Society*. Based on the Hugheses' own screenplay and set in Los Angeles, *Menace II Society* was the story of a young man and his friends navigating the plights of urban life. The Hughes brothers hired an unknown actor, Tyrin Turner, as the star, and—mixed experiences aside— they wanted Tupac to have a role. Did he have a great industry-wide reputation for professionalism? Hardly. Hollywood is a small universe, and his hot-and-cold behavior on the sets of both *Juice* and *Poetic Justice* pointed to a talented problem child.

Yet Allen Hughes's pitch was direct and to the point: *You're a great actor and we're trying to make the type of raw, gritty, edgy movie you'd dig.* Tupac was offered the role of Sharif, the low-key Muslim member of the crew. It was not a particularly meaty or deep character, but Tupac expressed satisfaction with both the offer (three hundred thousand dollars for three weeks of work—more than he'd made for either of his first movies) and the limited nature of the gig. "I'll do it," he said. "But me and John Singleton, we're like Scorsese and De Niro. I'm only fuckin' with him from now on as far as my leading roles."

The Hughes brothers had the paperwork sent over, readied themselves for a terrific directorial experience . . .

And watched as *everything* with Tupac went to shit.

After a movie is fully staffed, but just before filming begins, the cast and directors sit down for what's called a table read—where the participants congregate to run a script aloud for the first time. For *Menace II Society*, the table read was held at the film's production office, and when Tupac arrived he was giddy to see Jada Pinkett, his long-ago Baltimore School for the Arts classmate who was currently starring in the NBC sitcom *A Different World*. The Hughes brothers had taken his advice and cast Pinkett in a small role. "When Tupac came in the first day he literally ran over to Jada," said Allen Hughes. "He took her and threw her in the air and caught her on the other side of the room and hugged her."

For the most part, table reads tend to be uneventful. There might be some complaints or suggestions. On occasion a fringe member of the cast is cut loose. But, generally, those involved know what they're in for and come prepared. So as Tupac sat down alongside Pinkett, Turner, Larenz Tate, Samuel L. Jackson, and the other performers, there was no reason to think any sort of drama would flare up.

Well . . .

Tupac behaved like a child. He hated his lines, sighing audibly before reading them. He complained about the writing, complained about the flow. Mostly, he complained about Sharif—the character he had agreed to play knowing full well it was a modest role. Because Sharif is, at best, the film's eighth-most-important figure, the Hughes brothers didn't lay out much of a backstory. Sharif just . . . *is*. Yet Tupac couldn't get past this, and devoted much of the table-read time to making the case there needed to be some space for Sharif to grow. Allen Hughes tried to reassure Tupac that the script was set—"as is"—but Tupac didn't care. He *knew* he was right and that this was bullshit.

The table reading came to a merciful end, but Tupac's attitude failed to improve. He was supposed to sit with the movie's makeup artists, but instead took off in his new Mercedes. One day later, before a second table read, Allen Hughes pleaded with the other cast members to restrain from reacting when Tupac cracked jokes or made snide comments. It was pathetic—an up-and-coming director trying to create a great film while having to double as a preschool teacher.

The second table read was, again, a disaster. Tupac dropped a string of crass gripes. He was a petulant, immature kid.

"Tupac," Allen Hughes finally said, "why are you acting like a little *bitch*?"

That word—"bitch"—wasn't stated casually. It burst from Hughes's tongue like a bullet.

"What the fuck did you just call me?" Tupac said.

Hughes said nothing.

"I said," Tupac repeated, "what the fuck did you just call me?"

Hughes didn't fear Tupac. He insisted they retreat to his office, where they argued before the rapper, once again, stormed off. Tupac was fired and replaced by Vonte Sweet, later saying he learned of the dismissal not via Hughes or Watani Tyehimba (his manager), but a report on *MTV News*.

This was not entirely true—Allen Hughes had phoned him to offer either improved behavior or the end of the job. "We can no longer proceed like this if we're not on the same page," he said.

"Well, call my manager!" Tupac snapped. "I'm not dealing with you!"

"Tupac," Allen said, "if you won't deal with me, I'm gonna have to let you go. Because there's no way we can do this."

Allen contacted Tupac's representatives and told them the same thing. A few days later, executives from the film's studio, New Line Cinema, drafted a termination letter.

"Tupac was let go, and it wasn't a secret," Allen Hughes said. "That was him making stuff up."

A few weeks later, Tupac drove to Los Angeles International Airport to pick up Spice 1, the Bay Area–based rapper in town to record the music video for his new song, "Trigga Gots No Heart." After exchanging hugs and pleasantries and heading to the car, Tupac pulled out an industry newspaper that included details of his *Menace II Society* firing. "He threw the fucking newspaper in my lap and he was like, 'Read this shit! Look at this shit!'" Spice 1 recalled. "I'm still kind of fucked up [from drinking on the plane] and I can barely read the shit. I'm just reading it . . . all I seen was TUPAC COMES TO THE SET OF THE FILM HIGH AND DRUNK AND CAN'T REMEMBER HIS LINES. And I'm like, 'That's bullshit.' I know damn well this nigga . . . he don't get down like that. So I automatically got pissed off." Tupac told Spice 1 that he was gonna "beat their motherfucking ass!"—to which Spice 1 replied, "Nigga, you ain't gonna do shit."

The sentiment was authentic—Spice 1 doubted Tupac had it in him to beat anyone's motherfucking ass. He wasn't even sure the scrawny rapper *could* beat anyone's motherfucking ass. Yet one day later, on some barren hills alongside the 110 Freeway near downtown Los Angeles, Spice 1 was joined by Tupac at the shoot. In the spirit of the American hip-hop video scene of the 1990s, dozens of nonessential people lingered—"We was like thirty, forty deep," Spice 1 said. "Like different sets. We had Oakland dudes down there, dudes from Compton, and some LA cats down there. It was just shooting dice, smoking bud and shit. And everybody was cool."

Because "Trigga Gots No Heart" was slated to appear on the *Menace II Society* soundtrack, the Hughes brothers made an unannounced appearance. Tupac was shooting dice with members of the Rolling 40s Neighborhood Crips, a gang out of the West Side of Los Angeles. He spotted Allen and Albert pull up in their car. The rapper approached the passenger-side window.

"Both of y'all get out," Tupac said. "I'm gonna beat both of y'all asses."

Allen did not take this seriously. Tupac, to him, was all jabber. So as his sibling dashed off (literally, Albert Hughes ran up a hill), Allen exited the vehicle. Harsh words were exchanged. "I don't have any time for this," Allen finally said, and as he turned to walk away Tupac—holding a pipe in his right hand—popped him in the back of the head.

"Tupac started with a sucker punch," Allen recalled. "I couldn't believe that." Allen, who stood about five foot eleven and weighed 210 pounds, turned, grabbed the feathery Tupac, picked him up, and slammed him on the hood of the car. Seeing this, the gang members swarmed. They threw Allen to the ground, kicked him, punched him. Once. Twice. Ten times. Twenty times. Without mercy. Blood poured from his head and mouth. "I just seen Allen getting beat by about ten people," said Tyrin Turner, the film's star. "Tupac [is] one of the people. Allen is there taking a beating. It happened so fast. I felt like it was some sucker shit."

It was, indeed, some sucker shit. When the brawl wrapped and the Rolling 40s cleared out, Tupac stared down at Allen Hughes and barked at his battered body as if he hadn't accomplished the KO with the help of a dozen others.

"I've obviously thought about this a lot," Allen Hughes said decades later. "Why did he do that? What snapped in Tupac? And I just have to believe that, starting from when he was in Afeni's womb, he was gestating and incubating surrounded by the PTSD and instability of one woman's spirit. We talk a lot in Western culture about nature vs. nurture and DNA and what you inherit, but we don't talk about the soul someone is born with. And I think that's the power of Tupac, because he was born with this unique soul that comes from a broken mother. And pieces of him were broken, too."

A few weeks later, Tupac was charged with assault and needed to show up at Los Angeles County Municipal Court. On July 15, while appearing on the television show *Yo! MTV Raps*, Tupac committed one of the dumbest acts of his young life—he looked directly into the camera and said, "I beat up the directors to *Menace II Society*. Lemme tell the whole world, all right. These chump, punk, slump—you know what I'm saying . . . Check this out. They fired me but did it in a roundabout punk snitch way. So I caught 'em on the street and beat they behinds. Do you know what I'm saying? I was a menace to the Hughes brothers, and it ain't over. I still got more for you chumps."

When the Hughes brothers needed evidence in court to prove assault, Exhibit A was the MTV footage. "The boy," said Watani Tyehimba, "never knew when to shut up." Tupac wound up serving fifteen days in jail, but even worse was the uppercut delivered to his acting career. Once word spread of the Hughes brothers affair, lining Tupac up with A-level projects became near impossible. Not only was he difficult to insure, but the industry collectively shuddered. With the fight, Tupac was downgraded from filet mignon to chuck.

"All these white men in this white institution of Hollywood, the film business, are already scared of Black people even when they work with them," said Allen Hughes. "It's not like the music business, which is all about Black culture. It's a white universe. So do you think the Spielbergs of the world, or the James Camerons of the world, want to deal with that? Tupac had as much acting talent as anyone. But the film business doesn't fuck with niggas at all, so they're definitely not gonna fuck with this guy. There's a reason Tupac was never in a great film, and I guess it comes down to trust.

"No one trusted him."

For Watani Tyehimba, it was all a fucking nightmare. How could someone with so much talent, so much compassion, so much empathy, have so little self-control? And yet, while he found himself asking those questions, he also understood the answers. Tupac Shakur knew no better—and couldn't have known any better. He was raised without a male role model, with a female role model who was unavailable and incapable under the fog of addiction. Why didn't Tupac clean up after he pissed all over the floor?

It never occurred to him. Why didn't Tupac check in more often on his sister, Set, now seventeen and pregnant with her first child? It never occurred to him. Why didn't he open a checking account? Invest in the stock market? Get the best auto insurance? Have regular doctor checkups? Seek therapy? Eat healthy doses of fruits and vegetables? Exercise?

Why would he have? Nobody taught him to do a damn thing.

If nothing else, Tupac was determined to convey *his* image. He was . . . Tupac. The rapper. The actor. Bravado and guts and street. But what did it all mean? "Look, he was a guy without nurturing," said Wood Harris, the actor and Tupac's friend. "He was a fatherless child. A motherless and fatherless child. His formulative years weren't spent being formed. He hung out with a lot of the wrong people, even though he was smart enough not to. Users gravitated toward him, but he didn't have the wisdom to recognize what they were after. He was incomplete."

Perhaps the greatest frustration was that Tupac could be gold. Enormous heart. Mounds of compassion. Rarely walked past a homeless person without offering dollars or a meal. *Poetic Justice* was scheduled for its cinematic release on July 23, 1993, and in the lead-up Tupac plopped down inside a Beverly Hills hotel suite to conduct promotional interviews. Just a few weeks past his twenty-second birthday, Tupac actually hadn't done many of these, and there was reason for his camp to worry. Yet over the course of six hours, he sat across from a bevy of reporters and owned it.

Wearing baggy purple jeans, a vest, and a T-shirt, with his white socks stuffed into Timberlands, Tupac kicked back on a couch and smoked a couple of packs of Newports (said MTV's Bill Bellamy, "Pac and Dave Chappelle smoked the most cigarettes in thirty seconds that I've *ever* seen") while laughing, lecturing, debating, joking. He was funny ("I won't play just anything," he told Ken Parish Perkins of *The Dallas Morning News*. "I won't play a butler unless I kill everybody"), he was thoughtful ("Revolutionary doesn't mean AK-toting assassin," he said to Yardena Arar of the *Los Angeles Daily News*. "It doesn't mean terrorist attacks. It could be small things. [My movie character] is a revolutionary by being a committed and dedicated father, by being there for his daughter, by having a job and by every day being there on time"). He was a master code switcher—schmoozing older white women journalists with charm and dated cultural references, bonding with younger Black journalists by acknowledging their rare place in a profession still unkind to minorities. His longest session came with Esther Iverem, a reporter for New York's *Newsday*. He looked the veteran scribe in the eyes and broke down his love of performing in concise terms. "Acting is a way to state your case," he said. "You tell your story. That's what I do. I tell my story and I let go of my pain by telling. I'm just letting them see it. It feels good and then I'm back to fighting."

In her piece, headlined "POETIC JUSTICE" SHOWS A SOFTER SIDE OF SHAKUR, Iverem got to the heart of Tupac: "His [life] experiences have produced a rage, nihilism, fatalism and absence of hope that would be shocking if it didn't capture the sentiment of so many disenfranchised youth for whom he speaks—'all the underdogs, all the niggas with no daddies . . . all the niggas in juvenile hall in jail and everything.'"

"He was great," Iverem recalled. "But he started getting really intense toward the end and talking about how heartless everything was. And his agent or manager stepped in and said, 'OK—you got more from him than most people do. Let's wrap it up.' I liked him. He felt authentic."

He *was* authentic. Tupac might have needed handlers, but he had no *need* for handlers. He didn't want to be packaged. He wanted to be Tupac.

Poetic Justice debuted as the nation's number-one movie, grossing $11,728,455 on its opening weekend. Was it good? Depends on who you ask. Black audiences (as was the case with *Juice*) flocked to see it. White audiences, not nearly as much. The Janet Jackson–Tupac Shakur connection seemed to fascinate people, and Jackson's featured ballad "Again" melted hearts. Those who worked on the movie walked off fairly indifferent to the finished product, exasperated by a tough shoot marred by Tupac's behavior. "It's a B minus, maybe a C," said Rose Weaver, the actress who played Tupac's aunt. "It meanders."

"John Singleton was a talent," said Allen Hughes. "But was *Poetic Justice* corny as fuck? Yes."

Gary Thompson of the *Philadelphia Daily News* didn't mince words when he wrote (beneath the headline "POETIC JUSTICE": BAD TO VERSE): "The payoff for a movie this predictable is in the details. [John]

Singleton's are not vivid." Yet he correctly called Tupac's portrayal of a postal worker "infallible—a natural screen performer who stole his debut picture 'Juice,' Shakur is the only reason to watch 'Poetic Justice.'"

Thompson was right—it is impossible to ignore Tupac. Similar to his portrayal of Bishop in *Juice*, his every motion in *Poetic Justice* carries purpose. His long eyelashes dance. His limbs feel fluid. Few actors (especially of his limited experience) convey vulnerability so profoundly, with so little effort. "I never wanted to cut away from him," said Bruce Cannon, the movie's editor. "He held the screen."

Thanks to *Poetic Justice*, Tupac's public reputation shifted ever so slightly. At the same time headlines told of an artist behaving badly, he was appearing on T-shirts and posters, popping up in magazines like *Teen Beat* and *Tiger Beat*. *Rolling Stone*, the publication that embraced hip-hop as one embraces a canker sore, assigned Danny Clinch, the highly regarded celebrity photographer, to shoot Tupac for an upcoming profile. The rapper-actor came to Clinch's New York City apartment and was—in the photographer's words—"absolutely wonderful. He was smart, he presented himself well, he wanted to be there and he knew the value of *Rolling Stone*. He 100 percent got it."

In short, Tupac was fighting to no longer strictly be Bishop, but also Lucky—a sensitive thug heartthrob. It was peculiar, but not altogether unwelcome. If anyone needed an image softening, it was Tupac. Also, not for nothing, he had recently undergone an impossible-to-miss physical shift. Tupac had dental work to straighten his teeth. He stopped walking like a duck. Though he was loath to pump iron, his physique magically took shape. He went to the salon for a quality trim. Clinch's photograph in the October 28, 1993, issue of *Rolling Stone* shows a shirtless Tupac looking far more Sugar Ray Leonard than Steve Urkel. Tupac was (gasp) ripped. "Sexy," said Lisa Lisa, the singer. "Tupac was big-time sexy."

Wrote Kevin Powell in *Vibe* magazine: "With his razor-sharp cheekbones, long, feminine eyelashes that curve upward at the edges, and busy eyebrows framing his distinctive, wide, and piercingly dark brown eyes, he looks like the black prince he says his mother's friends called him as a boy."

With the recalibration, music fans started taking a second look at his recent material. Eight months after *Strictly 4 My N.I.G.G.A.Z . . .* had been released to stifled yawns, the album debuted on several pop charts. Meanwhile, the third single, "I Get Around," landed on the *Billboard* charts for twenty-five weeks and emerged as Tupac's first-ever go-to party jam. The song, wrote Michael Namikas in his fantastic *Tupac Encyclopedia*, "was instrumental in elevating Tupac from bubbling rap talent into one of his generation's most iconic musicians."

The accompanying video, directed by David Dobkin (who later directed the film *Wedding Crashers*) and featuring a shirtless Tupac strolling through a Burbank mansion with his homies and droves of scantily clad women while drinking and smoking blunts, was even better. And crazier. During breaks in shooting, Tupac would pull aside the actresses, escort them to private spots, and have sex. Lots and lots of sex. "It was his happy place," said Money-B, the Digital Underground rapper who cameoed in the song and video. "Tupac wasn't shy."

A friend who briefly appeared in the video was Brian Times, the drug dealer who had helped the newcomer out when he first arrived in Marin City. Times spent the day in Southern California, and during the shoot he looked at Tupac's stomach and noticed the enormous THUG LIFE tattoo. Having grown up in the projects with few escape routes, Times was thrilled to see his young friend rising above. Times wasn't one who needed Tupac to stay in Marin City to keep it real. No. As far as he was concerned, make your money and get out. Move to Beverly Hills. Have a slew of white neighbors. Join a country club and wear knit sweater-vests. Just get *far* away . . .

"Why did you get that?" Times asked, nodding toward the ink.

"You don't like it?" Tupac replied.

"Nah," he said, "I guess it's cool."

But, really, it wasn't cool. It was ill-advised and impulsive. Times, who was of the streets enough to know Tupac was most certainly *not* of the streets, drove back to Marin City that night wondering where this all was headed. Why would a non-thug want to label himself—in permanent ink—a thug?

"My entire time I was in the dope game, I was a target," he said. "And the minute I got away from it, I was no longer a target. It ended. Tupac—in getting that stupid tattoo—was changing the way he was perceived. He was turning himself into a target."

Although Tupac Shakur was a New York City kid with White Plains ties, Baltimore loyalties, Marin City scars, and Oakland vibes, a place he loved in ways big and small was Georgia.

While his time in the Peach State had been brief, Tupac's connection was profound. Atlanta, through his eyes, was rich and passionate, bountiful and engaging. In a 1988 Associated Press article, a local cabdriver named Ray Herston told a reporter, "Atlanta is a black city. They got Andy Young for mayor, a black city council president, a black chairman of Fulton County and now a black archbishop." Tupac could not have said it better. Atlanta oozed Blackness. Of the city's 3.7 million residents, roughly 1 million were Black. Tupac loved the food. He loved the women. He loved the city's two annual marquee events—Jack the Rapper, a wildly popular hip-hop jamboree, and Freaknik, a Black spring break festival that drew partygoers from around the nation. Washington was the United States capital. But Atlanta was the *Black* capital.

In September 1993, Tupac went so far as to use some of the money he'd earned ($240,000, to be exact) and purchase his first-ever home, a split-level twenty-four-hundred-square-foot pad in Lithonia, Georgia, twenty-six miles east of Atlanta. Afeni had relocated to the state months earlier along with her sister, Glo, and brother-in-law, Tom, and was living in a small apartment in nearby Decatur. By now, Tupac had largely (though not completely) forgiven his mother for past transgressions. He wanted a loving relationship, and chose to look forward instead of harping on the years of neglect. Aside from marijuana (which, like her son, she smoked as most breathe air), Afeni was—at long last—drug-free. She took walks. She drank water. On the day a moving truck arrived in front of her son's new crib, Afeni watched and wept. According to the biographer Staci Robinson, this was the first time a member of the family had purchased a house since Millie Ann Wooten, Afeni and Glo's great-grandmother, did so in Lumberton, North Carolina, four decades earlier. "It was not a U-Haul, and it wasn't the uncles and cousins draggin' mattresses up the stairs," Gloria recalled. "It was a moving van. It was a big day for us."

Technically, Lithonia (population: 2,448) was *a* home for Tupac, not *the* home. He still had his rental in Oakland, as well as the rental in Sherman Oaks. But the purchase felt like a step in the right direction. It was a sign of maturity, and he anointed the house "Thugz Mansion." Though still the age of a college student, Tupac had been through a dozen dizzying lives. This felt comfortable. Cozy, even.

Which is why what ensued was so damn disconcerting.

On the night of October 30, 1993, approximately one month after his relocation to Georgia, Tupac was scheduled to perform at homecoming ceremonies for Clark Atlanta University, an HBCU (historically Black college or university) located in the heart of the city's downtown. From the start, things went awry. Tupac flew in from New York City, picked up his new BMW at the Lithonia home, recorded an in-studio interview with Ryan Cameron of B103 radio . . . and arrived at the campus nearly an hour late. He also arrived slurring his speech. "He was out of it," said Lasherelle Morgan, a Clark student in attendance. "Gone."

Two months earlier, Tupac had played at Chicago's China Club, and during his (equally high and drunk) forty-five-minute set he warned female attendees that, should they come to his hotel room late at night, they would likely be sexually assaulted because, hey, they were asking for it. Wrote Rohan B. Preston in a *Chicago Tribune* review: "When he directly addressed the oft-leveled charge of misogyny in rap music by distinguishing 'good' women from 'bitches,' the wall-to-wall audience fell eerily silent." A few days after that, Tupac stormed off a stage mid-concert at the Des Moines (Iowa) Convention Center when the sound system malfunctioned. He returned ten minutes later, but—according to Tyrone J. Tyler of the *Des Moines Register*—"the audience no longer seemed interested."

Those two gigs were bad. What went down at Clark, however, was a new low.

Tupac was greeted backstage by a half dozen familiar faces, including Billy Lesane, his cousin who was fresh out of prison after serving eighteen months for a parole violation. The attendees let out a roar as Tupac sauntered onto the stage and yelled a half-hearted greeting into the microphone. He performed five or six songs—all lesser tracks from the first two albums. No "Brenda's Got a Baby" or "I Get Around" or "Keep Ya Head Up."

Why? "Honestly," said Lesane, "I'm not sure."

Students stood in stunned disbelief, eventually filing out mid-show—a rarity for an artist who usually held your attention and left you craving more. Frustrated by a muffled speaker, Tupac stopped midway through one of his tunes and screamed, "Everyone yell, 'Fuck the soundman!'"

Everyone yelled, "Fuck the soundman!"

When Tupac tried lighting up a blunt mid-song, the school's security guards stopped him. He reamed the men out, but to no avail. "I don't know who failed to inform him that he was playing at a show for college students," said Morgan, "but he went on and on with the cursing, on and on denigrating women. There were so many cringe moments where we were all standing there in awkward silence. Our sports teams were never good, so the best thing about homecoming was the possibility of a great show. But this was awful."

Cameron, the radio host, was at the performance. He said the wildest moment came when Tupac spotted an attendee flashing gang signs and, from the stage, gripped a bottle of Dom Pérignon and hurled it at his head. "He's knocked out cold in a puddle of blood," Cameron recalled. "They just drag him off the floor." By the time the forty-five-minute performance concluded, Tupac and co. stood before a 70 percent empty auditorium, blunts again ablaze, rushing out the rear exits to elude law enforcement.

Tupac had booked a night at the Sheraton in downtown Atlanta, which was located a mile or so from Clark. He had rented out a suite for a post-show party, and his BMW approached the hotel parking lot trailed by a fleet of vehicles from his entourage. From his window, about ten feet away, Tupac spotted two white men, brothers Mark and Scott Whitwell, slugging a Black man in the head and pounding on him as he fell to the ground. This was not the type of scene he could simply ignore. Would the Black Panthers have watched a brother take a beating at the hands of white men? Would Afeni? No. They would have fought. They would have, in the spirit of Malcolm X, relied upon any means necessary.

Tupac stopped his car and shouted at the perpetrators. According to

Dante Powers, Tupac's cousin, one of the men—Mark Whitwell—pulled out a gun and yelled, "Fuck y'all niggers! I will kill all you motherfuckers!" Then Whitwell directed the firearm toward Tupac.

"Someone give me my gun!" Tupac said to one of the men in his BMW. No one flinched.

"Someone give me my gun!"

At that moment, Mark Whitwell used the butt of his gun to shatter a window on Tupac's car, then took off running with his sibling. "Get those motherfuckers!" Billy Lesane yelled. "Get them!"

Tupac reached for his 9 mm pistol, knelt, warned his friends to watch their heads, aimed, and fired three times.

He hit Mark Whitwell in the abdomen.

He hit Scott Whitwell in the buttocks.

"He shot two white people right in front of me," said Billy. "My mind is blown. Like, this kid—my cousin—is a nut."

Tupac cackled, watched the bloodied white men hobble off into the distance, and invited everyone to the suite to drink and get fucked up and listen to music. Before long, his room was filled with laughter and marijuana smoke. Billy took the gun and hid it behind a hallway fire extinguisher. Tupac, meanwhile, pulled out a demo tape from a bag and asked for everyone to be quiet.

He popped in a song. It was titled "Dear Mama."

For a moment, everything seemed to stop.

"And we're listening to this amazing new piece of music," said Billy. "We're all mesmerized. But then . . ."

BANG! BANG! BANG!

It was the police.

Tupac was arrested, cuffed, and led to a car. He was charged with two counts of aggravated assault, and bond was set at $55,059. It turned out the Whitwells were not mere white bumpkins, but white bumpkin police officers spending a night out on the town with their wives. An internal investigation revealed that the Whitwells' report from that night included the sentence: "Niggers came by and did a drive-by shooting." Ultimately, Tupac was set free and all charges were dropped after it was learned the Whitwells' guns had been stolen from the Henry County police evidence locker and that they'd lied to investigators about the incident.* But that did not satisfy Tupac's record label or management team. Why, oh why, did he do this shit? Why couldn't he just leave a situation alone? Everything had finally been going so well, and now here was a reminder—yet *another* reminder—that Tupac Shakur was sort of toxic. "He had no ability to step back and ask himself, 'Is this wise?'" said Justin Tinsley, author of *It Was All a Dream: Biggie and the World That Made Him.* "It's like, 'Bro, you don't know who these people are. You don't know what this will lead to. Just don't do it, bro. Don't do it.'

"But he did it."

---

* Mark Whitwell was charged with providing false statements to investigators and firing at Tupac's car. The district attorney later dropped the charges against him, but Whitwell resigned six months later.

Chapter 16

All Praise Belongs to Allah

On April 4, 1993, Tupac Shakur performed the infamous show inside Michigan State University's auditorium. This was the one (to refresh your memory) where he slammed down a microphone, engaged in a slew of heated arguments, and swung his Louisville Slugger toward multiple people. Even by mid-nineties hip-hop standards, it was high-level craziness.

When the building finally cleared out, Tupac and co. retreated to the nearby hotel, where dozens of young, sexy female fans awaited. "There were more bitches—um, young women, than you could count," said Kenneth Lesane, his cousin. "I'd never seen anything quite like it."

At the time, Lesane—whom Tupac referred to as "Black"—was fighting to purify his soul. He had spent three years in and out of prison, had battled crack addiction, had worked the corners of New York City's Times Square as a hustler and thief. Now, at twenty-six and fresh out drug rehab in Detroit, he felt revitalized. Lesane had recently turned his life over to the teachings of Allah, with the kufi and the long beard to prove it. He was a man seeking to reach a higher plane—meaning no pork and no pussy. On a camcorder video taken that night, Tupac actually introduced Lesane by saying, "Looking at my hairy-ass cousin. He's a Muslim now."*

Thanks to his nights studying the Qur'an, Lesane felt prepared for the debauchery unfolding before him. Tupac had rented out a dozen side-by-

---

* If you're wondering, Lesane is the subject when Tupac raps, "Oh, you a Muslim now? / No more dope game / Heard you might be comin' home, just got bail / Wanna go to the mosque, don't wanna chase tail" in "I Ain't Mad at Cha."

side rooms for this very moment, and the terrain reeked of weed, Hennessy, and sex. But all of it was off limits for Lesane. The words of reinforcement that he had devoted his life to learning were glued inside his head: "*All Praise belongs to Allah, the Cherisher of all the worlds . . . the Most Compassionate, the Most Merciful . . . Master of the Day of Judgment . . . We worship you alone and from you alone we seek help . . . Guide us to the straight path.*"

Lesane had lost track of his cousin, and when he knocked on one of the doors Tyruss "Big Syke" Himes answered. A Los Angeles native and reformed member of the Imperial Village Crips, he and Tupac met at Echo Sound Studios in 1992, and bonded over music and bud and shared life experiences. Tupac not only wanted to help Syke make music, but found him a reassuring road presence.

So, there Syke was, standing at the door, staring at the bearded, kufi-wearing Kenneth Lesane.

"Hey, man," Syke said. "Pac is looking for your ass. He's in the back of the room."

Lesane entered and tiptoed toward the rear. He knew whatever he was about to behold was something certainly off limits.

"Pac is with two French girls," Lesane said. "The finest twins I've ever seen in my life. They came all the way to this nigga's show in Lansing . . . said they were reporters who needed to interview him. Well, Pac is fucking both of them. And I'm looking at these women and their faces are both red because he's fucking the shit out of them. Now, as Muslims, we're not allowed to look at another man's body part at all. It is forbidden in Islam. But I was already that type of dude. I don't look at another man's dick."

It was one of the most uncomfortable moments of Lesane's life.

"Yo, Black," Tupac said. "Come here, man."

"Nah," Lesane replied, "I'm good."

"Yo!" Tupac yelled. "Come here!"

As he spoke, Tupac was pumping in and out of one of the twins, while the other was grabbing him from behind. "And Big Syke had just finished with that one," Lesane said. "So this was some freak shit."

Lesane came a little closer.

All Praise belongs to Allah . . .

And a little closer.

All Praise belongs to Allah . . .

And a little closer.

"Yo, Black," Tupac said, "pull out your dick."

"No," he replied. "I don't do that. I'm a Muslim."

"Nah, fuck that," Tupac said. "She's gonna suck your dick."

"Pac, no!" Lesane replied. "I can't do that."

All Praise belongs to Allah . . .

A familiar rage crossed Tupac's face. "Yo, you mean to tell me you're gonna bitch out?" he said. "Is that what you are? A bitch?"

All Praise belongs to Allah . . .

Lesane sighed, reached for the button on his pants, and reluctantly began to unsnap. The woman, however, turned toward Tupac, and said, "I don't wanna do him. I just want to do you."

"Nah," Tupac said. "This is family. If you're gonna do me, you have to do him."

Simultaneously unaroused and ashamed, Lesane raised his pants and told his cousin he didn't wish to proceed. "I can't do this, Pac," he said. "I appreciate you, but I'm *not* doing this."

Tupac shrugged.

Tupac Shakur liked sex.

This is neither a secret nor a controversial statement. He liked sex with short women and tall women, heavy women and thin women. He preferred chocolate-hued skin ("the blacker the berry, the sweeter the juice") and large, perky breasts ("See, it all started simple, turned into me lickin' the nipples"), but the man was hardly picky. You could be Black, white, Native American, Asian—if you were down to fuck, Tupac was more than happy to engage. On myriad occasions, Tupac took part in running a train—aka having sex with a woman, then passing her to another man to fuck, then another. "We're not all alike when it comes to appetites," said Spantaneeus Xtasy, the adult film star who had a relationship with Tupac. "Trains were common in music. They're fine if the female is OK. I know many women who liked having it run on them." As he noted in his lyrics, almost none of it was personal. Tupac was rarely on the lookout for love, instead pursuing raw, carnal sex. Sometimes, when the copulation wrapped, he took a few moments to chat. *Oh, where do you go to school? You like it?* "He was a gentleman," said Dahlia McCutchen, one of his many girlfriends. "Very courteous."

Mostly, however, it was flirt, fuck, cum, goodbye. Having failed to grow up under the care of a steady male role model, no one ever sat young Tupac down for "The Talk" about sex. He watched his mother be mistreated, discarded, and disregarded by a long line of men (most of whom were addicts) and surely took notes. Hell, his first sex came at age fourteen with a cousin. Sex wasn't about "making love" or forging a bond or looking deep into another's soul. For Afeni, in particular, it was transactional. Sex got you a meal, got you drugs, got you a few minutes of escape.

Tupac's worldview was little different.

There are few memories of him backing away from a sexual opportunity or rejecting something as too extreme. Kendrick Wells, Tupac's longtime friend beginning with their time in Marin City, recalled attractive women "being saved" for Tupac. "We used to play a game called 'Player's Court,' where we'd make someone a judge, and we'd plead our cases in front of him," Wells recalled. "And a lot of times it'd be over who gets a woman—like, which one of us *gets* to fuck her. Ultimately, because he was Tupac, the women were reserved for him, and delivered to him. I'm not proud of it in hindsight, but we did think of women as possessions."

By 1993, Tupac was spending a good deal of his time on the road with four men he put together to form a hip-hop group that went by the name Thug Life. The members (along with Tupac) were Big Syke; Maurice (Mopreme) Harding, his stepbrother; and Walter "Rated R" Burns and Dave "Macadoshis" Rivers, two young rappers out of Los Angeles. Tupac's goal was to ultimately release a hard, gangsta-personifying Thug Life album that felt raw and street-worthy. But, in all honesty, Thug Life wasn't about the music; it was more about providing Tupac the companionship he craved. "In many ways the project was the unofficial Shakur reunion," said Jake Brown, the fantastic hip-hop journalist. "It was the first time he and Mopreme got to really spend time in a studio together, creating something. And it also was Tupac's emancipation from the Digital Underground sound and movement toward the Thug Life ideal. It was where he first took that gangsta thing and experimented with it. And he was doing it with people he felt tight to." In other words, Thug Life was a family affair. Tupac paid for meals and lodging, had its members accompany him on-stage during performances, shouted them out and sang their praises and lavished them with gifts.

In the Thug Life world, women were to be shared. If one member fucked someone, there'd inevitably be a question of whether you, too, planned on fucking her. It wasn't a competition so much as a collegial game. And if the woman's feelings were ever taken into consideration . . . well, scratch that. The women's feelings were never taken into consideration. This was not about them. As Tupac noted during the concert in Chicago in early 1993, if a woman came to your hotel room, she was asking for it.

Period.

Despite the mixed results of *Juice* and *Poetic Justice*, and despite the ill-advised beatdown of Allen Hughes, Tupac somehow lined up another motion picture job.

This one, titled *Above the Rim*, was the directorial debut of Jeff Pollack, and starred Duane Martin, Bernie Mac, Marlon Wayans, and twenty-three-year-old Wood Harris, appearing in his first-ever film. The plot concerned an on-the-rise New York City prep basketball standout (Martin) and his dealings with a drug dealer named Birdie (played by Tupac). If Tupac had hoped his acting career might start leaning in a Redford/Poitier direction, he couldn't have been thrilled with the relatively low-budget ($6.5 million) New Line Cinema offering, what with its thin script, star-light cast, and Bishop-ish dialogue.

However, there was a bright side: *Above the Rim* returned Tupac to New York City.

West Coast posturing be damned, Tupac still loved the Big Apple. He loved the food, the women, being able to hit up a club at 2:00 a.m. and having a bevy of pizza places still open afterward. He loved that New York remained home to a good number of family members, and that the city seemed to embrace him as one of its own.

So when he learned shooting for *Above the Rim* would take place over a six-week span ranging from October 18, 1993, until the tail end of November, Tupac booked a room at the Le Parker Méridien, a swank hotel located on West Fifty-Sixth Street, near the lip of Central Park, and came with plans to act his ass off and light up the town.

As was the case in his first two films, Tupac did a lot with a little. His portrayal of Birdie—who occupies the screen for a relatively brief span—is menacing, cold, fierce, textured. "He was a tremendous actor," said Harris. "Because he was a tremendous storyteller. That's the crossover in hip-hop and film. You're telling the audience a story and your job is to make them believe it." But as was also the case in his first two films, Tupac was incorrigible. "This sounds cold, but his human self isn't as likable as his artistic self," said Harris, who went on to a lengthy cinematic career. "He was always high. A pain. And Napoleonic. He was a feisty dude who you couldn't tell shit to. And he was always trying so hard to sound like he was from Cali, acting like a gangbanger. Bro, you're no gangbanger. You went to an arts school. And he had twenty thumbs and two left feet when it came to sports. This was a basketball movie. Tupac shooting a basketball—he wouldn't even do that shit twice with us because he just looked too corny."

Harris remembered a day when Tupac filmed a scene that required him to drive a car to Harlem's Rucker Park. "So they say 'Action!'" Harris recalled. "We drive, and Tupac has a difficult time getting out of the car because the knob you pulled to unlatch the door didn't have a head on it, and his fingers kept sliding off. So we did one take—not smooth. We do another take—same thing. And Tupac is getting *angry*." Finally, Tupac stomped out of the vehicle, screamed, "Y'all fix the fucking car!," vanished into his trailer, and emerged more than an hour later, several blunts down and unable to competently recite his lines. "He was useless after that," Harris said. "It wasn't professional."

Tupac filled his evenings with plans. The city was his oyster, and he wasn't one to stay inside his thirty-eighth-floor Le Parker Méridien suite and meditate alongside a cup of herbal tea. That's how, on the night of Sunday, November 14, he found himself on the dance floor of Nell's, the trendy West Village nightclub. Nell's was a place where the famous went to be famous and the anonymous went to feel grand, a high-flying party spot named for Nell Campbell, the co-owner famous for her role as Columbia in the 1975 film *The Rocky Horror Picture Show*. As Bob Colacello noted in a 1987 *Vanity Fair* article about the club, the limousines lined up outside of Nell's—"and out of them steps everyone from the new first couple of cosmetics, Ronald and Claudia Perelman, to John Malkovich, Francesco Clemente, Susan Minot—even the clean mother of the night, ancient Regine." It cost five dollars to enter, and the line usually extended toward the Hudson River.

Inside, the two floors offered disparate experiences. Upstairs, one could feast on casual food in a paneled dining area. Downstairs was a dance floor powered by pulsating music. In the depths, the alcohol flowed. The drugs were smoked and snorted. Dark corners lent themselves to all sorts of sexual experimentation. At its height, Nell's, John Marchese wrote in *The New York Times*, was as hot as a flame: "Its heat came largely from people burning the candles at both ends."

This was Tupac's type of joint.

He entered Nell's that night with a companion he should have avoided. His name was Jacques Agnant, but he was better known as Haitian Jack. Tupac met the thirty-year-old Queens-based "talent manager" (quotes intended) while researching his part in *Above the Rim*. Agnant served as Tupac's model for Birdie. Which is to say, he was the type of person who robbed drug dealers and jacked pimps and slit throats and evoked terror with a simple glare. Wrote Tayannah Lee McQuillar and Fred L. Johnson III in their Tupac biography, "From Tupac's perspective, being in the company of a supposed bona fide gangster was thrilling. It was also dangerous. Word on the street (which Tupac initially did not believe) was that Agnant was also a government snitch. Haitian Jack loved fancy clothes, flashy cars, and dropped names of famous people. He traveled in all of the right circles, went to all of the right parties, and used his showbiz connections to further his business." Put differently, Agnant possessed mojo Tupac envied. He wasn't someone who spoke about crime—he committed it. He wasn't someone who longed for the streets—he *was* the streets. Tupac Shakur was a performer. "Pac shape-shifted," said Money-B, the Digital Underground rapper. Agnant was the real deal.

At one point, Carol Crooks, Afeni's long-ago lover and a veteran New

York hustler, heard that Tupac was rolling with Agnant. The news horrified her. "She knew what type of pussy Jack was, and she tried getting word to Pac to stay far away," said Yaasmyn Fula, the longtime family friend. "She went to the *Above the Rim* set to try and talk to him. She wound up sticking a letter under his trailer, warning him. But she didn't think he read it."

"These Haitian guys were no joke," said Kevin Dalton, a Nell's DJ who went by DJ Strip. "They were dudes. There was another cat, Haitian Jimmy, who literally scooped the eye out of a kid working the door at Nell's because he wouldn't let him in to sell drugs. You don't fuck with Haitians."

During their time together, Agnant took Tupac on shopping sprees, steering him away from hoodies and baggy jeans and introducing him to Prada and Rolex. On November 6, they watched the Evander Holyfield–Riddick Bowe fight in the VIP room of the Manhattan strip club Scores, while drinking a twenty-six-hundred-dollar-a-bottle Louis XIII de Rémy Martin cognac. "Jacques had all this gold and diamond jewelry," said Charles "Man Man" Fuller, Tupac's friend and road manager. "He had money. He had a nice BMW. He could get you in any club. Pac was just starting to be known then, and he couldn't get in all the clubs. Jacques spent about four or five thousand dollars on Tupac in the beginning—he just overwhelmed him." Not all that long before, Tupac had turned up his nose at Black men proving their worth via bling. "He was all about leather medallions in Afrocentric colors," said Pete Nice, the 3rd Bass rapper. Now, under Agnant's guard, Tupac's perspective shifted. He was cultivating a look.

New York was Agnant's kingdom, and he cruised the streets reeking of royalty. So, in his company, did Tupac. That's why they skipped the Nell's line, walked past the bouncers, through the front doors, and down to the basement. A couple of celebrities were present—Ronnie Lott, the New York Jets' Pro Bowl safety, was there. So was Derrick Coleman, star forward for the New Jersey Nets. This is where a friend of Agnant's—identified in court records as "Tim"—pointed Tupac toward the dance floor and a curvaceous Black woman. Her name was Ayanna Jackson. "She had a big chest," Tupac later said. "But she was not attractive; she looked dumpy."

Initially, he kissed Jackson on the cheek. Shortly thereafter, he returned, this time from behind, and slipped his hands into her rear jeans pockets as she was dancing. She was nineteen and holding a glass of champagne.

"I turned around," she recalled. "And he said, 'I'm Tupac.'"

Jackson knew exactly who Tupac Shakur was. Though not a die-hard fan, she was familiar with his music. She also thought he was handsome, with a swaggy sex appeal. Tupac escorted Jackson to the roped-off VIP section of the dance floor, where they started to kiss. The music was playing. The room was warm. Someone handed Tupac a blunt, and as he smoked it, Jackson lowered her head toward his pelvic region, unzipped his pants, and gave him a blow job.

On the dance floor.

In full view of others.

"I was there," said Wood Harris. "That was a wild girl. She was literally in the club blowing Pac."

Later that night, Tupac and Jackson retreated to the suite at the Le Parker Méridien and had sex two or three times. Though he had a 5:00 a.m. *Above the Rim* shoot, he asked Jackson to sleep over, and had a car take her home the next morning.

"He said, 'Leave your number,'" Jackson recalled. "So I left my number."

Four days later, Ayanna Jackson was inside her Brooklyn apartment when she received a phone call from Charles "Man Man" Fuller. People liked to joke that Fuller was Tupac's literal shadow—if you saw the rapper, you saw Man Man. Back in Marin City, when Tupac was broke and occasionally homeless, Fuller had provided a bed for the night. That kindness was never forgotten. Hence, Tupac brought Man Man to New York, put him up in the swank hotel, and had him handle tasks big and small. Dinner reservations. Paid appearances. And placing booty calls.

"Pac," Fuller told Jackson, "wants to see you."

They arranged a time, and Fuller sent a car to drive her back to the Le Parker Méridien. Jackson expected to enter the suite and see Tupac. Maybe he would be fully clothed. Maybe he would be nude. Maybe he would be high. Maybe he wouldn't be. But it would be Tupac, and he would be alone.

When she walked through the door, however, Jackson said she was greeted by the sight of Tupac along with Fuller, Agnant, and someone identified as Ricky Lee. The men were watching television, drinking Absolut. "So [Tupac and I] go into the bedroom, and he's like, 'I'm tired. I'm stressed,'" she recalled. "So we go in there and he's like, 'Yo, can you give me a massage?' And I'm like, 'OK.' So he's lying down, face down on the bed, and I'm massaging his back. And then he turns over and then I'm straddling him, and . . . I'm just like massaging his shoulders and so forth.

"I'm massaging him. He grabs the back of my head. He pulls me down, and we start kissing. We were adjacent to the living room where everyone was. So it was very dark. It was very quiet."

The door opened and, according to Jackson, the other men entered. Here is how Jackson explained what transpired: "I'm looking at him while I'm straddling him, and I'm looking at him face-to-face. And I hear people talking and I hear people saying, 'Look at her' and 'Her ass is fat' and this and that. And I'm looking at him dead in the eye. And I'm like, 'What's going on?' And he's saying to me, he's like, 'Relax, relax, relax, relax, relax, baby. These are my boys. I like you so much, I decided to share you with them.' And when he said this to me, I was trying to lift my head up. And as I was trying to lift my head up, he still had my hair, and he was holding it. And I was like, 'No, no, no, no. I don't want this. I came here for you. I don't want this. This is not what I want.'"

According to Jackson, Tupac raped her, then got up and left. She proceeded to be violated by Agnant and Ricky Lee. "So I was raped by Tupac," she said. "I was raped by Haitian Jack. I was raped by a tall, dark-skinned gentleman."

Tupac later told the journalist Kevin Powell a different story—but not altogether different. According to his recollection, the massage happened, and he was anticipating more oral sex. However, before she could begin, "some niggas came in, and I froze up more than she froze up. If she would have said anything, I would have said, 'Hold on, let me finish.' But I can't say nothing, because she's not saying nothing. How do I look saying, 'Hold on'? That would be like I'm making her my girl. So they came and they started touching her ass. They going, 'Ooh, she's got a nice ass.' [Agnant] isn't touching her, but I can hear his voice leading it, like,

'Put her panties down, put her pantyhose down.' I just got up and walked out the room."

When the assailants ultimately departed, Jackson said she was left alone with Fuller, who, she said, never touched her. She was sobbing and screaming, and Fuller instructed her to go to the bathroom, wash herself off, and calm down. When Jackson insisted she wanted to go home, she said Fuller told her she couldn't leave. He mentioned that Mike Tyson, the imprisoned heavyweight champion, had had his career destroyed by a recent sexual assault allegation. "You know what happened to him," he told her. "Pac doesn't need that."

At long last, Jackson exited the room and told a hotel staffer that she had been raped. Detectives from the New York Police Department quickly arrived.

Around this same time, a green Acura Legend was parked outside the Le Parker Méridien. Its inhabitants were the rap producer Easy Mo Bee and two of his old neighborhood pals, A.B. and J.R. They had been inside Tupac's suite earlier in the day, smoking blunts and talking music. Tupac invited them to return later that evening and accompany him to Sensations, a club in Newark, New Jersey, where he was booked to appear. Now, in the shadow of the hotel, Easy Mo Bee and his friends debated whether to pay the fifty-dollar valet parking fee.

"Yo, park the car," A.B. said. "Let's go up and party."

"Nah," Mo Bee replied. "That shit's way too expensive. Let's just wait for him."

So they waited.

Here is how Easy Mo Bee remembered it: "We found a street spot and we're standing by the car, waiting. Well, a cop car pulls up and the cops go into the hotel. We're looking at each other like, 'What the hell is going on?' About another half hour passes and a couple more cops come. And after a while, the big emergency service truck comes. Now we're looking at each other. 'Yo. What the fuck?' Because Tupac is supposed to come downstairs and meet us, but he's nowhere. After a while, the cops bring Tupac down. And because we were standing outside the hotel, some cops came up to us and asked, 'Hey, what's your business here?' And we told them, 'None. We're actually waiting for Tupac to come downstairs. We're going to a club together.' Well, then they bring this girl to the window—there's a window separating us from inside the hotel, and it's big. These cops were on the other side of the window with the girl. And we're reading the cop's lips through the window. He's pointing at each one of us. 'Was it him?' And she had her face all squished up to get a good look, and she shook her head no. The cop pointed to all three of us and asked, 'Was it him? Was it him? What about him?' She said no to all of us. But can you imagine if she would've said, 'Fuck it, I wanna nail somebody. Gonna say it's that guy right there.' I've always said not parking the car and not going up to Tupac's room wound up being the best decision I ever made."

That night, at 11:15, Tupac, Fuller, and Agnant (who went by a half dozen different aliases, and was identified to police as "Ricardo Brown") were arrested. Tupac was brought to police central booking at One Centre Street and charged with first-degree sodomy and first-degree sexual abuse. There were also weapons charges due to two guns found in his room. Somehow, Agnant's attorney got his client's case severed from Tupac's and Fuller's, because Agnant was not charged with possession of weapons (he pleaded guilty to a lesser charge and never served time). Tupac was set free on $250,000 bail.

In the immediate aftermath, seemingly everyone who knew Tupac insisted he was incapable of raping a woman. Tupac, after all, was hip-hop's greatest booster of women. He was a mama's boy who wrote the song "Keep Ya Head Up" to inspire women to stay strong, stay steadfast, continue to move forward even when the world pushes you down.

"I know for a fact Tupac didn't rape that woman," said Kendrick Wells, his longtime friend. "I literally spoke to him that night, and he told me he would never do that to someone. He had no reason to lie.

"Tupac Shakur *loved* women."

From the moment word of Tupac's arrest hit the news, his supporters insisted their man could not have done such a horrible thing.

And maybe they're right. Maybe Tupac was screwed over. Maybe he was incapable of violating a woman. Maybe, on this confusing planet we call Earth, Tupac was merely guilty of being in the wrong place at the wrong time. Maybe it was a whole lot of nothing.

But, unbeknownst to the public, the Jackson case was not his first alleged sexual assault.

The *other* police report—with RAPE/SODOMY REPORT typed across the top of a page in capital letters—was filed on July 23, 1993, four months *before* the Le Parker Méridien episode. In this case, the woman's name was Lita Rodriguez,* and four days earlier she had been celebrating her twenty-first birthday. Lita, who worked as a model and Miller Genuine Draft girl, spent much of the afternoon and early evening partying with friends in her Los Angeles apartment, and that night she and her three roommates hit up Carlos' n Charlie's, a West Hollywood club. They arrived at approximately eleven thirty, and within an hour she was approached by a Black man. He introduced himself as Blurry,† and told Lita that his friend wanted to speak with her. "Well, his [friend] was Tupac," she recalled decades later. "I obviously recognized him. He was a big deal."

Lita and Tupac chatted and danced ("Nothing unusual," she said), and after a few hours her roommates were ready to leave. "OK," Lita recalled saying. "Let me finish this dance. Just wait for me."

When the song ended, however, Lita walked outside and couldn't find her posse. They had left. "I was really furious," she recalled. "There were no cell phones back then, and there was no pay phone. I had all these emotions like, 'What the hell am I supposed to do?' I didn't have enough money on me to get a taxi. There was no Uber in 1993." Lita had planned on heading toward the University of Southern California campus, where her boyfriend—a Los Angeles native and member of the Trojans football team—resided. "So I'm drunk, I'm abandoned," she said. "I didn't know what I was supposed to do."

Tupac and his entourage emerged from the club. They spotted Lita, inquired as to why she was loitering all alone, and offered a lift.

Lita recalled hesitating. She was not one to receive a late-night intoxicated ride from a gaggle of strange men. However, there was no other option. Plus, she considered Tupac's fame a safeguard. "He's a celebrity,"

---

* The woman's real name is not Lita Rodriguez. She agreed to speak for this book under the protection of a pseudonym.
† The man's nickname was not Blurry. For legal reasons, he is not being identified.

she recalled thinking. "Everybody sees me getting in his car. I don't think he'd take a chance."

The vehicle was Tupac's black four-door Mercedes. Lita didn't recognize the driver, and she slid into the front passenger seat alongside Tupac, who—she recalled—was smoking weed. She offered an address, but the car headed in the opposite direction.

"Where are we going?" she asked.

"I have to stop at the crib and get something real quick," Tupac replied.

The Mercedes pulled up to the two-bedroom, two-bathroom house he was renting in Sherman Oaks. Tupac opened the passenger-side door and exited. Lita did not budge.

"Come on in," Tupac said

"I'll wait here," Lita replied. "You're gonna take me home anyhow."

"Actually," Tupac said. "I'm gonna have Blurry take you."

"Can't he take me now?" Lita said.

"No," Tupac replied. "I need to get something real quick. Just come in the house."

Lita followed the men inside. She said she lingered in the foyer before Tupac insisted she check out his room. She noticed a revolver on a nightstand, surrounded by a smattering of bullets lying on their sides. "So I was like, Oh my God, this is not a good situation. How am I going to get out of this?" she recalled. "I don't know what their temperament is. I don't know where their minds are at. I'm drunk. I'm trying to sober myself up by thinking, like, Okay, think, think, think. How are you going to get out of here?"

The police report broke down Lita's account:

Once inside Shakur closed the door to the bedroom and began kissing her on the mouth and neck. She said that she was standing against the dresser with the door behind her and Shakur was standing in front of her next to the bed. The vict was afraid to run out the door because of the numerous male blacks in the front of the house.

Shakur began undressing the vict and she did not protest citing her fears that he would become violent. She saw a chrome revolver on the night stand next to the bed and said nothing to Shakur about it fearing that he would use it to force the issue further. Shakur placed her on the bed, laid her back and after he removed his clothes he placed a condom on his penis and had vaginal intercourse with her. He turned the vict over on her stomach and attempted to enter her rectum. She began to protest by screaming for him to stop. She said that he was hurting her and she began to scream.

While Shakur was undressing the vict she added that he had to untie her boot-like shoes in the process. She removed her large hoop earrings herself because she did not want them caught and possibly ripped from her lobes. She also had a hat on which she also removed herself. The vict said that the television was on in the bedroom, but was not on very loud. No one came to her assistance when she screamed.

When the vict kept protesting the sodomy Shakur sat up and placed his hand on the back of her head and tried to force her head down towards his erect penis. She refused this activity and Shakur got up and went to the bedroom door, opened it and according to the vict invited the remaining individuals in to have sex with her. One male black came in and began removing his pants when the vict began yelling that she was not going to allow the second male to engage in intercourse with her. Shakur then stated "She's a seven eleven, call her a taxi or somethin'."

According to Lita, Tupac dismissed her as "just a fucking groupie"—to which she replied, "You have the wrong idea about me. I just needed a ride." A detective later told her that choosing not to resist was a wise move. "He's capable of a lot of things," the officer explained. "He's done some heinous stuff. I have police reports on him. You don't know if he would've pistol-whipped you and made you disappear. He had a whole entourage. They could have done anything."

When Tupac was done with Lita, she said he ordered Blurry to drive her to a 7-Eleven on the corner of Moorpark Street and Fulton Avenue and use the pay phone to call her a taxi. Now, at the 7-Eleven, they waited for the yellow car to arrive. When the vehicle pulled up, Lita refused to enter. According to the report, she said the taxi driver looked "scary," and pleaded with Blurry to take her home. They reached a compromise: He would drop her back off at Carlos' n Charlie's, which was six miles away.

The police report details what allegedly happened next:

Susp-2 added that she would have to have sex with him before he would comply with her request. She begged him to reconsider, but after he declined to waiver from his demand she gave in.

Susp-2 took her to a nearby park and had sex with her after purchasing the condoms. After completion of the sex act susp-2 pulled out of the parking lot and asked the vict for a second act. She refused, but submitted again citing the same fears as before.

Susp-2 took her back to the club in West Hollywood and after discovering it was closed took her to the USC campus.

Lita said that when he pulled up to USC, she leapt from the BMW as it was still moving. "I was screaming and yelling and I pounded on the door where my boyfriend lived, because it was all football players that lived there with him," she said. "They opened and they saw that I was hysterical. I was crying so hard. I just was freaking out. I didn't even look behind me to see if [Blurry] was following. I just was trying to hurry up and get in the house. I ran so fast and then my boyfriend was trying to get me to calm down. 'What happened? What happened?' And I couldn't talk. I was just crying, crying, and crying. I just felt disgusted."

According to Lita, she told her boyfriend about the kidnapping and rape. They agreed she should file a police report, but that first he would take her to her apartment and confront her roommates. "When we got there I went to the bathroom," she recalled, "and that's when I realized my rectum was bleeding. We called the police."

Decades later, Lita said her boyfriend wanted to rally his Trojan teammates (several of whom had Los Angeles gang ties), track Tupac down, and pummel him. She encouraged him not to. A detective came to her apartment and took a statement, then she went to the West Hollywood precinct, where she handed over a plastic bag filled with her clothing from the evening. She underwent a rape kit examination and described the THUG LIFE tattoo from Tupac's stomach. Photographs were taken of her shoulders and lower legs, which were bruised. She supplied wads of toilet paper covered in vaginal blood. As terrifying as the entire night had been, she knew she was doing the right thing. She had been kidnapped and raped. There was no ambiguity.

Only . . .

Lauren Weis, head of the Los Angeles County District Attorney's Sex Crimes Unit, reviewed the details and rejected the case. According to the report, "the vict's decision to have sex with susp-2 as opposed to notifying the police via 911 at the first available pay phone or notifying 7-11 clerk of her dilemma, etc were the fatal details that derailed any hopes of a successful filing against either Shakur or susp-2. . . ."

Lita was devastated. When, in 2024, she read the official report for the first time, she felt like punching a wall. She told the officers that she had been intoxicated that night, and—in regards to running away or dialing 911—she was both compromised and terrified. "Obviously, if it was that easy I would have done whatever I needed to do to save myself," she said. "But it wasn't. Also, I had a boyfriend. They met my boyfriend. He wound up my husband. Did they really think I wanted to have sex with two strangers, then go to my boyfriend's house? How does that make any sense?"

To Lita's chagrin, not only were Tupac and Blurry never charged—they would never even know she called the police. "It was just sex to them," she said. "A piece of meat."

She paused. Thirty-one years had passed. Lita was now in her early fifties, the mother of three adult children. She relocated to the South and did her best to keep the night of July 19, 1993, out of her mind. But it was always there, she admitted. Always lingering.

"I'll tell you one thing—I know a lot of people thought that woman in New York was lying," Lita said. "Well, I've been through it. I learned who Tupac Shakur was.

"I have no doubt she was telling the truth."

Chapter 17

Image Award

I n the late months of 1993, members of the NAACP gathered together to decide upon the nominees for the organization's upcoming Image Awards.

An annual celebration of Black achievement, the Image Awards were created twenty-six years earlier to honor outstanding performances in film, television, theater, music, and literature. Past winners ranged from Sammy Davis Jr. and Sidney Poitier to Aretha Franklin and Virginia Capers. The Image Awards weren't merely another forgettable opportunity to worship celebrity. No, the Image Awards were the Black Oscars/Emmys/Grammys.

So maybe, just maybe, Benjamin Chavis, the NAACP's executive director, should have reconsidered when Tupac Shakur was nominated in the Best Actor category for his work in *Poetic Justice*.

That would have been wise.

By the time the award ceremony was held, on January 5, 1994, inside the Pasadena Civic Auditorium, the Image Awards' most notorious nominee had:

- Allegedly beaten up a limousine driver in 1993.
- Allegedly shot two off-duty police officers in 1993.
- Allegedly beaten up Allen Hughes on the set of a music video.
- Allegedly raped Ayanna Jackson in a Manhattan hotel suite.

That last one, the alleged rape, did not go over well. In advance of the event, members of the National Political Congress of Black Women demanded the nomination be revoked. Dionne Warwick called Tupac "out of control." Elmer Smith, associate editor of the *Philadelphia Daily News*' opinion pages, penned a column headlined NAACP SHOULD CROSS GANGSTA RAPPER SHAKUR OFF IMAGE AWARDS LIST. "Tupac Shakur was probably too busy to prepare much of an acceptance speech for the NAACP Image Awards," he wrote. "His fans understand the felony charges he's facing all over America don't leave him a lot of time for speech writing."

The naysayers had a point. For much of 1994, Tupac's image languished in the gutter. He had finally attained the level of fame he sought, yet much of that was caked in negativity. When the New York *Daily News* wrote about Tupac's upcoming January 15 show at Trafalgar Square in Queens, it referenced him as "rapist/rap sensation Tupac Shakur." The *Detroit Free Press* tagged him an "actor, rapper and general miscreant." A high school teacher in western New York named Sean Crowley penned a lengthy letter to *The Buffalo News* that spoke for many by concluding, "As an inner-city teacher, I'd like to say thanks to Tupac Shakur for all the disruptions, suspensions, arguments, and needless educational distractions his T-shirts have caused in classrooms, hallways and cafeterias . . . if he had a clue he might stop promoting guns and drugs and the finger-flipping attitude—in short, all the things that are getting kids murdered in every American city, every single day." John Singleton, the director Tupac considered to be his personal Martin Scorsese, had planned on casting the rapper in his latest project, *Higher Learning*, but pulled back when Columbia Pictures demanded he look elsewhere. "The media is trying to play 'good nigga versus bad nigga' and say I don't want him in the movie," Singleton said. "That ain't true. In their minds, it doesn't matter if he's guilty or not. They don't want nothing to do with him." (Tupac never forgave Singleton's perceived disloyalty.)

On February 10, Tupac was found guilty on assault and battery charges stemming from his beatdown of Allen Hughes. He was sentenced to fifteen days in the Los Angeles County Jail, fifteen days working with a state transportation road crew, thirty days of community service, and a two-thousand-dollar fine.

The national mainstream media gobbled it up. Tupac's legal issues—

coupled with those of fellow rappers Snoop Doggy Dogg and Da Lench Mob's T-Bone and J-Dee (all charged with murder around the same time period)—resulted in article after article heralding RAP'S TROUBLE (*Los Angeles Times*), GANGSTAS ARE FACING THE RAP (New York *Daily News*), SOME RAPPERS NOT 'GANGSTA,' BUT VIOLENCE SELLS (*Baltimore Sun*), and 'GANGSTA' GETS BAD RAP (*Detroit Free Press*). It was a gilded opportunity to run scary mug shots of famous Black men and terrify Mamaw and Papaw reclining before their televisions in Dubuque. Reporters scurried toward predictable arbiters of correct Blackness to condemn the behavior (Jesse Jackson, in particular, never bypassed an opportunity to label Tupac as a nihilist), while shrugging off the troubling actions of white celebrities. "There has always been a double standard," said Cheo Hodari Coker, the longtime journalist and screenwriter. "Some people just fail to see it."

On March 23, Tupac's third movie, *Above the Rim*, was released. And while he was once again brilliant ("violent yet seductive," raved Stephen Wigler of *The Baltimore Sun*), efforts to promote the film were thwarted by Tupac's legal troubles. He wasn't an actor, he was a rapist. He wasn't the next Denzel, he was the next Willie Horton. In anticipation of the premiere, Tupac sat down for a string of (contractually stipulated) interviews, and one white face after another white face after another white face asked predictable questions about life as an outlaw. He wanted to talk *Above the Rim*. They did not.

Tupac found a sympathetic ear in Kevin Powell, the *Vibe* magazine staffer best known for his turn as a cast member on the original season of MTV's *The Real World*. Five years Tupac's senior, Powell seemed to grasp Tupac. He, too, had been raised by a single mother with family roots in the Carolinas. He, too, was abandoned by a father he barely knew. He, too, was drawn to words at a young age. He, too, lived through poverty. He, too, faced police brutality. He also understood that his childhood experiences impacted his adult behavior. "There was no concept of self-love," Powell told the reporter Anna Sale. "You know, those things were actually foreign to my vocabulary at that time. And, you know, what do you do when you get upset, at least when I was growing up? You get angry—you lash out, you know? And it's inevitable that there's going to be a series of explosions 'cause it's like we're walking time bombs." The words could have belonged to Tupac.

In *Vibe*'s February issue, Powell bylined the first truly exceptional Tupac profile. The cover featured the subject photographed in a straitjacket alongside the words: IS TUPAC CRAZY OR JUST MISUNDERSTOOD? The accompanying article was richly reported, and sought to explain the hellscape from which Tupac had emerged.

Wrote Powell:

> Throughout his life, Tupac has been struggling to define himself: First as the son of a radical political activist, then as the son of a gangster, then as an outcast in Marin City, and, finally, as a rapper and movie star living the self-described "Thug Life." Like many young black men, his struggle has been outright rebellion—both internal and external—against a life he sees as stacked against him. I look at Tupac and I see myself, my homeboys, all the brothers I've ever encountered, trying to prove ourselves to the world. But I wonder why Tupac's efforts to validate his existence are so destructive. Over the past several months, as the media reported one violent incident after another, many people asked, "Is Tupac on a self-destructive mission? Does he have a death wish? Is he crazy?" Ultimately, though, those are the easiest questions to ask. The tougher ones—about race and class in America—no one wants to think about.

Shortly after publication, Tupac invited James T. Jones IV, a thirty-four-year-old Black *USA Today* music journalist, to his Georgia home (Tupac bounced back and forth between Georgia and Los Angeles). As was the case with Powell, the scribe was greeted by a man overcome by anxieties and insecurities and pain. "I feel like I'm being crucified," Tupac told Jones. "It was like a train. After I got labeled as a troublemaker, everybody just started on me. It really made me sad at first. I was just not taking care of myself. I was on the edge. I started seeing everybody against me, and that's what made me want to fight. I'm not as deep as Martin Luther King or Gandhi. I only know how to strike back. That's the only thing I've seen that works."

And what followed it all took Tupac by genuine surprise. Despite the NAACP Image Award upheaval, the bashings from the likes of Warwick and Jesse Jackson, the emergence of a decidedly anti-rap culture warrior named C. Delores Tucker, and the unmistakable feeling that the world was crumbling upon him, a large percentage of young Black Americans— "my people," as Tupac liked to say—seemed to have Tupac Shakur's back.

"You have to realize, to us Pac wasn't what was being portrayed," said Ant Banks, the Oakland rapper and producer. "He was a guy who represented realness, who represented the streets. So a lot of Black people looked at Tupac and thought, You know what? He's not perfect. But he's ours."

In the midst of the uproar, on March 23, 1994, Tupac headed out to the Santa Monica College Amphitheater to make an appearance at a concert featuring a pair of African musicians, Kofi and King Arthur. Tupac had agreed to the cameo months earlier but didn't know what to expect when he strolled onto the stage forty minutes into the show to perform "Keep Ya Head Up." There had been so much negativity, so many awful headlines, so many taunts, and . . .

The crowd *loved* it.

Wrote Frank Costelloe for *The Corsair*, the Santa Monica College student newspaper, "Shakur brought the Amphitheater crowd to their feet as they waved and swayed to the catchy rap music." Fifteen minutes later, Tupac returned to join the headliners as they wrapped the evening with a rousing "Afrikan Thing." As he exited, the 99 percent Black crowd offered Tupac a standing ovation. He bathed in its bliss.

And, truly, that was much of Black America's relationship with Tupac. They acknowledged he was a screw-up. But he was *their* screw-up. So as the dark clouds hovered above his every move, Tupac somehow stayed afloat. He was, among other things, arrested (and briefly jailed) when police found an unregistered 9 mm handgun and a half-gram of marijuana in his car, sued for ten million dollars by one of the undercover Atlanta police officers he shot, blamed for the cancellation of a Philadelphia concert over an insurance dispute, forced to go on trial for hitting a concert pro-moter with a baseball bat, the subject of a potential Pennsylvania House bill that would make it a crime to sell explicit rap CDs to people under eighteen, and blamed (for the second time—this one in Minneapolis) by a person who shot and killed a police officer and said he was inspired to do so by Tupac's music.

On July 5, as he left state supreme court in Manhattan following a pre-trial hearing on the sodomy and sexual abuse charges involving Ayanna Jackson, Tupac—wearing a Detroit Red Wings jersey and red bandanna—exited through the revolving door, followed by Afeni and Yaasmyn Fula. A dozen or so newspaper photographers lined the sidewalk, and Fula re-minded Tupac to just stay cool and enter the awaiting car. "Don't say anything," she said. "Keep in control."

Tupac nodded, walked forward—then went photographer to photogra-pher and spit on them.

"No!" Fula yelled. "Pac, no! No!"

"He asked me what paper I was from," recalled Bolivar Arellano of the *New York Post*. "He said, 'I'm not spitting on you, I'm spitting on what you represent.'"

On the surface, it was a nightmare. But it also wasn't. Tupac's resiliency resonated. The way he flashed a middle finger toward law enforcement. The way he told a crowd what was on his mind, whether they liked it or not. The way—in a world that gave a fuck—he simply refused to give a fuck. He was stubbornly unafraid and challenging of authority. He was the son of Afeni.

On September 3 in Milwaukee, Tupac headlined Phat Rap Phest at the city's downtown MECCA center. Two days earlier, in nearby Chi-cago, an eleven-year-old member of the Black Disciples named Robert Sandifer had been killed in a gang-related murder. Now, in front of four thousand spectators, Tupac looked toward the crowd and screamed, "Y'all motherfuckers is killing the kids! Y'all can't be killing the motherfuckin' kids! Fuck that shit!" According to Spice 1, a rapper on the bill, a barrier between stage and audience toppled, and attendees charged. Tupac later recalled the evening in a phone conversation with Sanyika Shakur, aka Monster Kody: "So I'm rapping to the niggas that just killed this little kid.

And they all screaming out, 'Thug Life!' I felt bad, like, 'Wait a minute, they got it twisted.' So I start cursing them niggas out, like, 'Y'all niggas is cowards. Y'all killed that kid. Y'all niggas is punks. Man, I hate all you niggas.' Them niggas start throwing shit. We had a shoot-out in the stadium. I was tough, man. The whole gang tore up the whole neighborhood. Then I started getting letters from that area with all the mothers, the girls, was like, 'Thank you for doing that 'cause everybody scared of these niggas.' See? That's what I want to do. If these gang niggas ain't gonna get straight then I want to take 'em out the game."

Security ferried the performers to the nearby Hyatt Regency, and Tupac was urged to stay in the room he was sharing with the Houston rapper Scarface. From the street below, concertgoers were throwing rocks at windows, demanding their new enemy to come out and get his. The artists sat down on their beds, and Scarface flipped on the TV for a chill night of movies and weed and room service.

"Well, Pac isn't having that," Scarface said. "He was all gung ho about running downstairs and fighting the motherfuckers. And I said, 'Man, you better take this motherfucking remote control and sit your ass down!'"

Tupac begged, pleaded, and threatened Scarface to let him out.

Scarface did not let him out.

"He was just a crazy motherfucker," Scarface said. "But I admired it."

On September 26, the album *Thug Life, Volume I* was co-released by Interscope and Out Da Gutta, a label Tupac said he was in the process of creating/running that, in reality, was a bunch of drug dealers he knew from back in Northern California who were willing to throw some coin behind his talent. It had now been two years since Tupac had the THUG LIFE tattoo inked onto his stomach, and even though it began as a thoughtless lark ridiculed by his manager and friends, he gradually bought in. To Tupac, "Thug Life" could be a rallying cry for Black men to step up and handle business. Before long, he was hollering "Thug Life!" a solid dozen times per day, and while it oftentimes came off as insincere and silly (Tupac was hardly a "thug" in the traditional sense of the word), he believed in the mantra and wanted it to take off. A big piece of that was the formation and development of the hip-hop group Thug Life—Tupac; his stepbrother,

Mopreme; Big Syke; Walter "Rated R" Burns; and Dave "Macadoshis" Rivers.

When Tupac initially broached the idea to Interscope's heads, it was dismissed as the ramblings of a crazy man. Why in God's name would Tupac Shakur—a rapper on the rise with mounting name recognition—fold himself into a group? Why would he want to split profits five ways, split publicity five ways, split . . . *everything* five ways? *With these relative no-names?* What they didn't understand—*couldn't* understand—was that Tupac had a vision, and when Tupac had a vision he was incapable of hearing "No." And he *knew* there was something to this.

First, the members of Thug Life were (more or less) actual thugs. Second, all Interscope had to do was worry about distribution—the album would be financed by Tupac, Charles "Man Man" Fuller, and, last but not least, Calvin "Babez" Nunley, a gangbanger and drug dealer from Richmond, California. Three years earlier, at age nineteen, Babez had been approached about putting some of his dough into *2Pacalypse Now*, but decided against it. "It felt like too big a risk to me," he said. "I worked hard to make my money, and to drop it into music . . . I didn't feel it." Once Tupac started to blow up, however, Babez reconsidered. "He was just really passionate about Thug Life," he recalled. "Interscope was giving him a lot of shit. So I jumped in."

The CD was recorded over a lengthy span (mostly) at Echo Sound, and its arrival was greeted by the gentle chirping of crickets. The first single, "Pour Out a Little Liquor," also appeared on the *Above the Rim* soundtrack, and it never received much radio airplay. The second single, "Cradle to the Grave," came out six weeks later, and it, too, faded. Many who took the time to listen to the album considered it among Tupac's most authentic and intelligent works. "It's not a good album—it's a great album," said the rapper Glasses Malone. "I don't know why more people don't bring it up."*

"Interscope never got it," said Babez. "They refused to promote it. Amazing music. But no support. They wanted to keep him in a certain

---

* The primary criticism of the album is valid—"There's not enough Shakur," wrote Dennis Hunt of the *Los Angeles Times*. "The rest of this new group isn't in his class of rappers."

spot, but Pac wanted to be a revolutionary. They didn't want that album to be the way it was—hard. But Pac didn't give a fuck."

If Tupac found himself down over the mediocre sales figures of *Thug Life, Volume I*, he never let it show. Instead, he, Babez, and Man Man launched a mini eight-city tour featuring Thug Life, the Newark, New Jersey, hip-hop trio Lords of the Underground, the Jamaican singer Patra, and an obscure duo from Atlanta named OutKast.

Decades removed, Dupré Kelly, the Lords of the Underground rapper who went by "DoItAll," laughed at the memories. Tupac had originally met Kelly and his two cohorts (Al'Terik "Mr. Funke" Wardrick and Bruce "DJ Lord Jazz" Colston) three years earlier, when they were undergrads at Shaw University in Raleigh, North Carolina, and Digital Underground stopped on campus for a show. The three students had never heard of this Too-pack character, but they wound up rolling with him after the performance. "We're at a party and Tupac starts dancing with this girl, and her boyfriend didn't like it," Kelly said. "So he addressed Pac, and of course Tupac backed down from nothing, ever. And he starts challenging the dude, and it has to be broken up."

One of the Thug Life tour stops was Orlando, and it will forever go down as the oddest day of Kelly's life. The musicians arrived in town early that afternoon, checked into the motel, then planned on heading over to the club for a sound check. At the designated time, all five Thug Lifers, as well as two of the three Lords of the Underground members, were sitting in the van, motor running. Wardrick was missing. "This is bullshit," Tupac snarled. "This is my tour, and one motherfucker is gonna make us late."

The other Thug Life guys doubled as Tupac groupies, and laughed whenever Tupac joked, complained whenever he moaned. "They needed to stay on his good side," said Kelly. "Well, I felt like we were being disrespected, so I started combating Pac, letting him know I wasn't gonna be walked on."

The tension in the van grew—an uncomfortable silence punctuated by the arrival of Wardrick, who apologized for his tardiness. Sound check went off without issue, and the musicians returned to the motel to rest before the 7:00 p.m. start time. Kelly was lying on his bed, reading, when there was a knock on the door. Kelly peeked out, and spotted Tupac. "He's by himself," Kelly recalled, "and he has an armful of stuff."

Instead of answering, Kelly called Colston on his room phone. "Yo," he said, "Pac is at my door."

"Really?" Colston replied. "You good?"

"Yeah," Kelly said. "I'm just letting you know if anything goes down."

Kelly opened up. He looked at Tupac.

"Hey, Pac," Kelly said.

Tupac stood expressionless. Finally: "You ain't gonna let me in?"

Kelly slid to the side, and Tupac entered, handed over one of the two forties in his grip, sat on one of the twin beds, cracked open *his* forty, took a sip, pulled a Newport out from behind his ear, lit it, and pulled in a long, dramatic drag.

He looked at Kelly, stone faced. "You know you were wrong, right?" he said.

Kelly said nothing.

"But I like that," Tupac said. "You go down with your crew. I respect that."

And then Tupac changed directions. "Man," he said, "you know what we've gotta do as artists? We've gotta sell millions of records. We've gotta grind. Because the more records we sell, the more people we can turn into voters."

"Voters?" Kelly said. "What are you talking about?" Kelly was twenty-three. He had never heard anyone speak this way. Certainly no one this young.

Tupac continued. "You and Redman gotta do it in Newark," he said. "And Treach has gotta do it in East Orange and I gotta do it in Oakland and Ice Cube needs to do it in LA."

"I don't get what you're saying," Kelly interjected.

"We gotta protect our communities," Tupac said. "We gotta protect our women, we gotta create youth initiatives, we gotta start nonprofit organizations. And we have to stay in the communities where we're from. I've moved all around. Don't be like me. Represent Newark. *Be* Newark."

With that, Tupac uttered an idea that drilled itself in Kelly's brain. "Fuck," he said, "we might have to become legislators."

"Legislators?" Kelly said. He barely knew the word.

"Yeah," Tupac replied. "Because if we don't make the laws, they'll be made for us. And those laws always hurt us because they're gonna be against us."

Tupac hugged Kelly, grabbed his forty, and left the room.

Twenty-eight years later, Dupré Kelly was elected to the Newark City Council.

But wait.

The night doesn't end with Tupac leaving the room. Things were rarely tidy in the Thug Life universe.

An hour or so later, the tour acts arrived at the club. They were met by a promoter who didn't have the full payment. "Tupac," Kelly recalled, "threw a fit."

"I got seven rooms at the hotel!" he screamed. "There's gonna be seven broke lamps! It's gonna be seven messed-up rooms! It's gonna be seven broke windows! You do not know who you're fucking with, but it's with the wrong man!"

Tupac was calmed by Hafiz Farid, the Lords of the Underground's manager. The show, they decided, would not happen. The rappers all retreated to a limousine to smoke weed. Because Tupac knew seemingly every human being on earth, he called Dennis Scott, star shooting guard for the NBA's Orlando Magic.

"Yo, D—we're coming over," Tupac said.

"Who's we?" Scott asked.

Before long, Tupac and every rapper and rap groupie within a one-hundred-mile radius of Orlando was at 9832 Laurel Valley Drive in Windermere, where Scott—twenty-six years old and in his fifth professional season—lived a relatively tranquil life in a six-bedroom, ten-bathroom, 11,100-square-foot mansion. "It was crazy," recalled Colston. "Bitches in bras walking around everywhere, just a carnival of flesh."

Tupac was dressed in his Tupac best—no shirt, baggy jeans, no underwear. "His pubic hair was showing, and I'm like, 'Pac, pull your fucking pants up,'" Colston said. "And he was like, 'Fuck that, man.'"

In between the drinking and the smoking and the eating and the dice games, Tupac overheard a young woman complain about "wannabe thug niggas acting like they're hard."

"Bitch," Tupac said. "What did you say?"

Silence.

"Bitch," he repeated, "what the fuck did you just say?"

The woman flashed a snide look, and Tupac unloaded. "Look at you," he said, "in your hoochie outfit and your fat ass!" He pointed to his THUG LIFE tattoo.

"That's right, bitch," he said. "Thug Life."

For the rappers in attendance, it was the greatest party of all time. To Scott, it was a nightmare. Multiple neighbors called to complain about the noise until, finally, two police officers knocked on the front door. Scott answered and offered polite reassurances that the shindig was coming to an end, and . . .

"Fuck them pigs!" Tupac screamed from behind. "Fuck you, you punk-ass coppers!"

Scott spun and begged Tupac to be quiet.

As soon as the door shut, Tupac rushed to the stereo and spun the dial to maximum volume.

"Yeah," he said. "Go fuck yourselves."

For Tupac, rolling with Thug Life was existence at its best. It was *his* guys, *his* tour, *his* record label. He felt the love of Black America seeing him for who he really was—a champion of their plights.

Ultimately, however, reality hit.

On November 7, 1994, Tupac was in Manhattan's state supreme court to begin his trial on sexual assault charges dating back to the alleged rape of Ayanna Jackson (Fuller, his friend and road manager, was also on trial. Jacques Agnant was scheduled to be tried separately). The potential for a legal soap opera had the media abuzz. Nothing moved newspapers like menacing Black faces splashed across a front page. "He was nothing like the press depicted," said Iris Crews, one of his attorneys. "He was so intelligent. He would come to court with two or three newspapers, and read them cover to cover. For God's sake, he was quoting Mark Twain." In the lead-up, Tupac insisted he was innocent and that, while the American justice system rarely did Blacks right, he knew he would somehow prevail. God, he promised, was the only being who could judge him. And God was on his side. "But was he nervous?" asked Yaasmyn Fula. "He had to be. This was no joke."

It was a uniquely disorienting time to be Tupac Shakur, who along with the pending trial was also:

A. In the Big Apple filming his fourth movie, the low-budget *Bullet*, starring Mickey Rourke. Though noted as an odd combination by myriad media outlets, Rourke and Tupac were kindred spirits. "Mickey was forty-two going on twenty-two, and wishing he was Tupac Shakur instead of Mickey Rourke," said John Flock, the film's producer. "Tupac was high all the time, but he had so much talent it didn't matter. I'd literally knock on his trailer door to have him come to set, and it was like Cheech and Chong were in there with him. I also remember he and Mickey went to Johnny Depp's birthday party in a giant pink limousine, just living their crazy lives in mid-nineties New York City."

Tupac and Rourke hit the town nightly, and oftentimes arrived to work without a wink of sleep, smelling of beer and weed. One of their favorite spots was Scores, the famed Manhattan strip club whose publicist, Lonnie Hannover, alerted the *Daily News* whenever the pair arrived. "Once Madonna was there with them," John Roca, the *Daily News* photographer, said. "That was tremendous." Rourke was later described by Debra Feuer, his ex-wife, as "the most thin-skinned, over-sensitive person I have ever met . . . he was like an abused dog."

He was Tupac's type of guy. One early morning, around two thirty, the New York *Daily News* columnist A. J. Benza was asleep when his phone rang. It was Tupac. "You gotta come meet me and Mickey and [*Bullet* actor] John Enos," he said. "Mickey wants to kick [*Daily News* gossip columnist] Richard Johnson's ass and he's out of control." Benza rushed to Frederick's, a bar and restaurant, to be greeted by an inconsolable Rourke, who had torn up the men's bathroom. He demanded Benza escort him to Johnson ASAP—the scribe had apparently mocked Rourke's boxing skills in print. "I knew I couldn't take Mickey to Richard's, so I convinced him to get in my car and we'd drive around and he'd cool down," said Benza. "I'm driving down Fifth Avenue with Pac and Mickey and Enos, and Mickey screams, 'If you don't tell me where Richard Johnson lives, I'm gonna kill myself!'" When the car came to a red light, Rourke jumped out and lay down spread eagle in the middle of the street.

"Well, Tupac loved Mickey," said Benza. "And he got out and said, 'Fuck it!' and lay down, too. Right next to him in the heart of Fifth Avenue."

Cooler heads prevailed, and Rourke and Tupac rose, laughed, and returned to the vehicle.

"Shit with those guys," said Benza, "was always wild."

B. In the throes of an *actual* romantic relationship. Her name was Keisha Morris, and she was a twenty-year-old New Yorker and full-time student at John Jay College of Criminal Justice. The two had first met in June, when they stumbled upon each other inside a Manhattan nightclub, the Capitol. In the brief moment they spoke, Morris said, "I know you're going through a rough time right now, but you do have some people out here who are supporting you. Just be careful of the people you have around you."

One month later, they met again at another cub, the Tunnel, and Tupac was gobsmacked. "You're the girl who had on a black dress and black boots," he said. "I've been going to every club looking for you!"

Thus began what was, for Tupac, something refreshingly unusual: a fairly conventional bond with a nice young woman who wasn't just looking to sleep with him. Their first date was at an Italian restaurant, followed by a stroll to Chelsea Cinemas to see *Forrest Gump*.* Wrote Staci Robinson, "Tupac settled into the normalcy of this new relationship. . . . Time with Keisha may have been a refreshing break from the entertainment industry, moments of

---

* True story: Tupac read for the part of Bubba Blue, but lost out to Mykelti Williamson.

calm in the whirlwind of fame." Keisha found Tupac to be full of surprises. He made a fantastic barbecue chicken. He loved scary roller coasters. He was sensitive and thoughtful. He called often, and liked startling her by popping in unannounced at her apartment. Far from the bombastic Tupac portrayed in the press, he was always reading a book or manuscript.

Was Tupac faithful to his new girlfriend? Hardly. He still chased women on the road, still hit clubs in New York City and engaged in all sorts of deviant sexual behaviors. But at the same time, Tupac longed for a stability he had only known via a childhood parked in front of a thirteen-inch black-and-white television set watching shows like *The Brady Bunch* and *Happy Days*. Tupac wanted Mike and Carol Brady for parents. He wanted to spend Christmas in Milwaukee with Mr. and Mrs. C. and Richie and Joanie and the Fonz. He *dreamed* of it.

When Tupac wasn't having sex with two French chicks in a hotel room, or shooting at off-duty police officers, or complaining about bitches, he liked the idea of a mom and a dad and smiling kids and a pet and a station wagon and vacations to Disney and neighbors coming over to cook out. Normalcy had eluded him for decades. It was something he could see in people like Leila Steinberg and Watani Tyehimba, but never quite touch. He all but begged Morris to bring that to him. So they dined out as a couple, attended the theater as a couple, held hands as a couple.

In September, Tupac bought Morris a pair of presents—a cocker spaniel to keep her company when he was on the road, and a five-carat engagement ring featuring forty-two diamonds. His proposal wasn't really a proposal. He simply said, "We're gonna get married around your birthday."

"We met in June," she recalled. "He bought me the ring in September, and we were getting married in November."

It made no sense. Neither Tupac nor Morris was ready. Less than a month earlier, Tupac had attended Madonna's thirty-sixth birthday party in Miami, and wrapped the night having sex with the pop star, then calling his mother to brag about it (he also brought

Madonna to meet the rapper Snoop Doggy Dogg when he was in New York—surprising him with, "I'm gonna bring some rich bitch I'm fucking to your hotel"). Around this time, Tupac was also fooling around with Arnelle Simpson, the daughter of O. J. Simpson. And the singer Lisa Lisa (aka Lisa Velez). "I'm not the type of person to kiss and tell," Velez said. "But he hit it."

Soooo . . . about the engagement.

"Tupac and Keisha loved each other," said Karen Lee, Tupac's publicist. "But it was a stupid idea. That wasn't who Tupac was. He was looking for love. Always, I think. But I don't know if he really understood what it entailed."

Heading into the trial, a good number of Americans still were not so familiar with Tupac Shakur—who was famous, but somewhat niche famous. That began to change on November 9, when Tupac arrived at the courthouse accompanied by his mother, Afeni Shakur, and Rourke, a man who had experienced his share of brushes with the law. Tupac wanted to dress in his comfort clothes—sagging baggy jeans, T shirt, bandanna— but his attorneys insisted it would be a mistake. "Any time you're in the public eye," Tupac told a reporter, "you are at an automatic disadvantage."

At approximately 10:00 a.m., Judge Daniel Fitzgerald entered, scanned the room, and had everyone sit.

Melissa Mourges, the prosecuting attorney, began her opening remarks. There was no holding back.

"Gang bang," she told the jury.

A long pause.

"That is what they did to her."

Another pause.

"They set her up and she never knew what hit her. She thought she was there to be with him. But as they were kissing, three men burst into the room. They held her down and they stripped her of her underwear. They groped her and they yanked her hair. They sodomized and sexually abused her."

Tupac, wearing a heavy gray turtleneck sweater, tan jeans, and diamond ear studs, listened sans expression. For those who knew him, it was uncomfortable—seeing a man silenced who was accustomed to firing back. When it was his turn, Michael Warren, Tupac's attorney, argued that Ayanna Jackson (whose name was not used) had lied, and that the oral sex she performed on him at Nell's nightclub was proof of her lowly groupie status. "She is a vengeful suitor," Warren said.

One day later, Jackson took the stand. She was twenty years old, and the media identified her solely as "the woman." Her family members filled up two benches in the courthouse, and flashed smiles, nods, waves. Her mother, in particular, stood out—"[Her] posture is erect, countenance impassive and patience like a monument," wrote Murray Kempton for *Newsday*. Over four hours of testimony, Jackson shook visibly, cried repeatedly, looked at Tupac only a handful of times (according to Robert Gearty of the New York *Daily News*, Tupac "glared" at Jackson). She testified that, initially, she was "happy" to be invited to Tupac's hotel room; that "I had been with someone I didn't ever think I'd get the chance to be with." She admitted she went down on him inside Nell's, but that didn't mean she wanted to be passed off to his friends.

It was gripping, heart-wrenching stuff. This woman was broken. Even Afeni, there to support her son, admitted she felt for Jackson and her family. "When I look at [Jackson's mother], I am proud to be a mother," Afeni said. "She says nothing, looks straight ahead at everything, and sits by her child. She is so . . . so . . . so elegant."

The day in court ended with people shuffling zombie-like from the building. But if Tupac was affected, he didn't show it. After three days, court adjourned for the weekend of November 12, and that Saturday night Tupac and Rourke were photographed by paparazzi dining at Nello's, the Upper East Side bistro with a $275 market-price truffle pasta. If there was one thing Warren didn't want his client to do, it was dump on Jackson to the media.

So, of course, when Tupac was approached by a New York *Daily News* reporter, he posed for a photo with Rourke, then teed off.

"People have no idea what the lifestyle is about," he said. "There are girls like [Jackson] everywhere you turn. And the thing is, all she's doing is complimenting me, talking about how the sex was 'very good' and how she wanted to fuck me inside the club. I'm like, 'Keep talkin', girl.'"

Warren couldn't believe it. Tupac had one job at the moment—shut up. Instead, he was providing the press all manner of ammunition. A few days later, another photograph of Tupac appeared in the *Daily News*, this one with the caption TUPAC SHAKUR PARTIES AND LEANS OVER TWO ASPIRING MODELS EARLIER THIS WEEK. Once again, Warren wanted to rip his head off. Would it be so hard for Tupac to just lay low and meditate? To hang with Morris and their dog? Just for a few days? Pretty please?

In an effort to counter a tidal wave of negative public opinion, Yaasmyn Fula issued a press release headlined: 2PAC IS NO RAPIST!!:

> Recent events involving the arrest of 2PAC Shakur on charges of sodomy in New York is an outrage and attempt by the New York Police Department to silence a young man whose brilliant and politically conscious rap style is seen as a threat by the white power structure. The subsequent tirade of vicious lies and prejudicial newspaper coverage that followed his arrest were carefully orchestrated by the New York City Police Department, whose maniacal tendencies to engage in illegal and immoral behavior have been well documented in the recent corruption hearings. In view of the irresponsible news reporting, outright lies and attempt to portray 2Pac as some mad monster on the loose only demonstrates the pathetic collusion of the press with the NYPD to deny him a fair trial. 2PAC IS NO RAPIST!!

On the afternoon of Monday, November 28, Mourges made her final arguments before the jury. "These two defendants and two other men set her up for a gang sexual assault," she said. "She was lured to the room as a reward for Tupac Shakur's friends.

"It is that simple and that clear."

Warren, too, made his last case. This was not rape. It was a skank desperate to have sex with a superstar. She was a willing, eager participant in everything that transpired. Not only did Tupac Shakur do nothing wrong—he was actually far too kind to a woman trying to take advantage of his good name.

When court was dismissed, Tupac passed a reporter who asked, simply, "How you doing, Tupac?"

How was he doing?

Well, I just had to listen to the prosecution's closing argument and it was just so far from the truth that it really just has me drained at the end of the day, but, I'm leaving it in the hands of the jury. I'm learning a lot about people's innermost fears in this trial because it's not even about my trial no more, it's just about loud, rap music, tattoo-having thugs. It's not even about me no more. It's about, you know, some nightmare these people are having. . . . She [the prosecutor] was like, 'He's definitely guilty. Anybody with Thug Life tattooed on their stomach is guilty.' What type of reasoning is that, you know what I'm sayin'? We got different backgrounds. We come from two different places. Just because I look different than her doesn't mean that I'm a sodomizer or a raper. . . . I can't understand why it's this close. They're talking about there's no evidence that I ever sodomized her even though you put that all over the paper. And every time they take a quote out of this courtroom, they take a quote from out of her mouth, which is, you know, the stuff to put me in jail. It's nothing that's been true. I just want . . . print the facts so everybody can sort it out. My life is ruined because nobody has a chance to get the facts. . . . No semen found, no forcible entry, no entry into the anal. No nothing. None of that. . . . No fingerprints on the guns, you know what I'm sayin'? The only time, ever, there was a act of sodomy, she admitted she did it to me. I should be putting charges on this girl who sodomized me on the floor of a dance club. Why am I in court, you know what I'm sayin', getting my life ripped apart? But I'm here, I'mma go through it, just to show that I have faith in the American system, but for me to have faith in the American system these juries and everybody else has to, you know what I'm sayin', play the same role and keep an open mind. I'm already convicted and my whole life has been turned around. I lost every job. I lost everything, every opportunity. I can't buy cars, can't get rent, can't get none of that. But I'm still a survivor, you know, I'm still comin' to court, still smiling, still signing autographs. But soon, I'mma go crazy, you know what I'm sayin'? And it's up to the world, you know, America eats its babies. No matter what y'all think about me, I'm still your child, you know what I'm sayin'? You can't just turn me off like that. . . . I don't know who owns the gun. . . . I have registered guns, you know what I'm sayin'? I'm a legal owner of guns . . . in California. So I came to New York and wanted to be an illegal gun runner now. That's what they want you to believe. I want to start erasin' . . . come on, man. . . . This is all about my image. This has nothing to do with me. This is all about my image. It's like, MTV, all the papers, they building me up, now they destroying me on the same image that they perpetuated. . . . I'm selling records, this is what I do for a living, I'm selling records. Don't get it twisted. This is not my real life. This is not how my real life is supposed to be. I'm not supposed to be really having all these villains in my life . . . I can't do shows . . . I'm guilty even though the only crime I've been convicted of is fighting, hitting somebody in the face with my fist. Ever. Only crime. But I can't even go to Philly, I can't go to Texas. I can't go nowhere, I can't go nowhere.

Moments later, he was surrounded by journalists outside the building. Holding a rose presented to him by a fan, he smiled and leaned into the microphones. "I'm guilty of probably being a male chauvinist pig," he said. "But I'm not guilty of rape."

Chapter 18

They Shot Me in My Balls

ittle Shawn was a fairly forgettable rapper and writer.

This is not a controversial take. It is, instead, the cold, hard truth of an artist who explained his lyrical approach with: "Most of my stuff is about girls, because they're easy to write about."

Born Tyrone Shawn Wilkins on December 21, 1969, in East Flatbush, New York, Little Shawn was drawn to music as a young lad. He began dabbling in rap at age nine, and laid down his first song, a jam called "My Girl's Mother," for Select Records eight years later. The resulting work was well-intended dreck (sample lyric: "I'm caught up in the middle and you will discover / I'm using my girl to get to her mother"). At age twenty-two he released his debut album, *Voice in the Mirror*, and it spawned one modest semi-hit ("Hickeys on Your Chest") and an unspoken commitment from the hip-hop universe to stop punishing people with Little Shawn music. A single newspaper—*The Press of Atlantic City*—took the time to write up a review. David McKenna, an arts scribe, bequeathed Little Shawn's work one and a half stars, noting (correctly), "It's just empty calories."

And save the 1995 single "Dom Perignon," which made a gurgle or two, that was pretty much that for Little Shawn as a rapper.

Not, however, for a lack of trying.

In the fall of 1994, Little Shawn was spending a good amount of time at Superstar Cuts, a Queens barbershop owned by Jacques "Haitian Jack" Agnant, Tupac's friend and *Above the Rim* muse, and an alleged participant in the rape of Ayanna Jackson. Alongside the shop was a bar named Manhattan Proper Café, and most Tuesday nights Agnant liked to flex his might by having celebrity acquaintances by for a drink. Among those making their presences felt were Madonna, the Jamaican dancehall musician Shabba Ranks, the Jamaican singer Buju Banton, and, on at least one occasion, Tupac Shakur.

Ah, Tupac. Little Shawn met him at the bar, and came away unimpressed. "Tupac is still one of my favorite artists because of his delivery and his songwriting capability," he said years later. "[But] I didn't really get into him personally after hanging out with him." To Little Shawn, Tupac felt a bit bipolar. His music was overflowing with bombast and spirit, yet the human being seemed underdeveloped. Agnant spoke to Tupac as if he were a misbehaving child, and the rapper just took it. "I ain't respect that," Little Shawn recalled.

And yet, Tupac was on the verge of superstardom. So when Agnant suggested to Little Shawn that he could arrange for Tupac to appear on his next song, he knew the value.

For his part, Tupac needed dough in the worst possible way. Although he liked to walk and talk as if he were a man of means, Tupac was borderline broke. He spent *a lot* of money. His relatives spent *a lot* of his money. Tupac was the first member of his family to sniff big loot, and cousins and second cousins and aunts and uncles emerged from the mist with their arms extended and palms open. "He had very little sense when it came to finances," said Yaasmyn Fula. "He saw something, and if he liked it he bought it. He didn't think about costs. And he was *way* too generous. He wasn't raised with a bank account, so he didn't get how it worked." Much of the money Tupac had made in music and film was now going toward his mounting-by-the-minute legal fees. He wasn't one to check his savings, but the digits were turning increasingly tiny.

In the late days of November, as the rape trial reached its conclusion, Tupac was presented an offer he couldn't refuse. It came from a man named James Rosemond, a music manager and record executive Tupac had met via Agnant. Rosemond was better known as "Jimmy Henchman," and among his fleet of meh clients was . . . Little Shawn. Rosemond still believed Little Shawn had the talent to pop as a big-time mainstream performer. He just needed a spark. A jolt. A famous feature. That's why, according to multiple sources, Rosemond offered Tupac seven thousand dollars to make an appearance on Little Shawn's upcoming project.

Tupac agreed to Rosemond's deal during the final few days of the rape trial, but told him he was uncertain when, exactly, he would be able to record. Thus began a nonstop string of pages from Rosemond to Tupac. A new page *Ping!* seemed to arrive *Ping!* every other *Ping!* minute or two. *Ping!* At one point, while in court waiting for the day's trial to begin, an exasperated and annoyed Tupac ripped his pager from his belt and tossed it toward Fula. "Doesn't this fucking guy know," he said, "that I'm sort of tied up?"

At long last, when the trial came to an end on November 28, Tupac told Rosemond he was good to go. One night later, Tupac and his friend Randy "Stretch" Walker headed out to the New York City home of Ron G, a DJ pal who had asked the men to rap on one of his mixtapes. They were accompanied by Stretch's friend Freddie "Nickels" Moore and Zayd Malik, who was dating Tupac's sister, Set.

Tupac busted his lyrics for the song "The Heat" (later known as "Representin' 4 Ron G"), and while doing so continued to receive page after page after page. He knew Rosemond, but not well enough to be *this* badgered. Tupac called Rosemond from Ron G's house and reminded him of the promised seven thousand dollars.

"I've got the money," Rosemond said. "Come."

"OK," Tupac replied. "Hold on."

Before departing, Tupac called Rosemond back. He needed directions to the location—Quad Recording Studios. Rosemond supplied the information (723 Seventh Avenue in Manhattan), but added, "Wait, I don't have the money with me."

What the fuck?

"Well," Tupac said, "I'm not coming."

Rosemond shifted his position on the spot. Andre Harrell, the CEO of Uptown Entertainment (the label to which Little Shawn was signed), was a friend. "I'm going to call Andre and make sure you get the money," he said, "but I'm going to give you the money out of my pocket."

"All right," Tupac said, "I'm on my way."

He said they would be there by 11:00 p.m.

Tupac, Stretch, Fred, and Zayd hopped into a car, but had it stop to buy some weed. "He paged me *again*," Tupac recalled. "'Where you at? Why you ain't coming?' I'm like, 'I'm coming, man. Hold on!'"

Though he kept them to himself, Tupac had some reservations. Ever since the night of the Ayanna Jackson incident, his relationship with Jacques Agnant had grown hostile. Tupac was furious that he and Charles Fuller were facing the daily heat in the sexual assault case, yet Agnant's attorney had somehow arranged a separate trial. Also, more and more acquaintances warned Tupac that Agnant was not to be trusted. Mike Tyson, the imprisoned former heavyweight champion and a Tupac pal, put it bluntly: "Fuck that guy. He's a snake." By trial's end, Tupac was fairly convinced that Agnant had set up the entire rape scene, that someone wanted Tupac Shakur to be arrested and found the perfect vehicle (Agnant) to make it happen. When, on November 15, a New York *Daily News* reporter asked Tupac about his "friend" Agnant, he didn't mince words. "He's not my friend," he said. "He's a hanger-on."

And yet . . . seven thousand dollars was seven thousand dollars. "Everybody knew I was short on money," Tupac said. "All my shows were getting canceled. All my money from my records was going to lawyers; all the movie money was going to my family. So I was doing this type of stuff, rapping for guys and getting paid."

After purchasing the marijuana, Tupac, Stretch, Fred, and Zayd continued on to Quad Studios. They arrived around midnight—and nothing felt right to Tupac. Upon exiting the car, the foursome were greeted by a large man in army fatigues with a hat draped to conceal his eyes. He was Black, and Tupac said, "What's up, brother?" There was no reply. Simply silence. "I've never seen a Black man not acknowledge me one way or the other," Tupac later said. "Either with jealousy or respect." Upon pressing the buzzer to be allowed into the building, Tupac said he saw two other men sitting at a table in the lobby. They, too, wore fatigues. "They didn't look up either," he recalled.

It was weird.

But what kept Tupac from trusting his gut and turning around were two things: First, the dough. But second, before entering the building

Tupac was spotted by the rapper Lil' Cease of Junior M.A.F.I.A., who was standing on a balcony a few floors up. "Tupac!" Cease yelled from above.

Tupac heard him, hollered, "Lil' Cease—that you?"

Indeed, it was. "I'm up here with Big," Cease yelled back. "I'll come on down and get you!"

Before heading toward the elevator, Cease entered an adjacent room to find Christopher George Latore Wallace and inform him of the visitor. "What?" Wallace said. "Go get him!"

Better known as Biggie Smalls, aka Biggie, aka the Notorious B.I.G., Wallace was tight with Little Shawn and even referenced him on his 1993 track "Party and Bullshit." To Tupac, the twenty-two-year-old rapper out of Brooklyn was the ultimate kindred spirit. Though their styles and flows were different, they were next-level storytellers who sought to break down street life. The men had met a year earlier, when Biggie was in Los Angeles and a local drug dealer made the introduction. Tupac invited the East Coaster to his home in Sherman Oaks, where a witness recalled them sharing a "big freezer bag of the greenest vegetables I'd ever seen" and getting preposterously high. Then Tupac lugged out a duffel bag overflowing with water guns.

Recalled Dan Smalls, an intern at Biggie's label: "So now, here we are, in this backyard running around with water guns, just playing. Luckily they were unloaded. While we were running around, Pac walks into the kitchen and starts cooking for us. He's in the kitchen cooking some steaks. We were drinking and smoking and all of a sudden Pac was like, 'Yo, come get it.' And we go into the kitchen and he had steaks, and French fries, and bread, and Kool-Aid, and we were just sittin' there eating and drinking and laughing. And you know, that's truly where Big and Pac's friendship started."

Fast-forward to July 23, 1993. A photographer named T. Eric Monroe was in Manhattan to shoot the rap group Onyx for an upcoming issue of *Thrasher* magazine. The session took place inside a small theater, and when Monroe finished he heard a handful of young Black men from a far corner holler, "Hey, take us! Take us!" Monroe directed the eight guys—wearing matching black T-shirts with the words I'M A BAD BOY printed in white block lettering—to bunch together. As he pressed down his finger and released the shutter, Monroe noticed one of the subjects thrust his middle finger forward. "I thought nothing of it," Monroe said. "But years later I'm going through my photos and I realize, Holy shit! The guy with the middle finger is Tupac. And one of the guys next to him—that's Biggie!"

Later that night, they shared the microphone for the first time at the Palladium in New York City. Tupac jumped up onto the stage to perform "Party and Bullshit" with Biggie. "The crowd went bananas," recalled John "DJ Jahbaz" Dawson, who was in attendance. "Tupac had been in *Juice*, and everyone there knew who he was."

Three months later, on October 25, the rappers made their Madison Square Garden debuts at the Budweiser Superfest, a multi-artist show headlined by Big Daddy Kane, Bell Biv DeVoe, and MC Lyte. Compared to the lineup's other artists, the two were relative newcomers, and they spent much of the evening cracking jokes, telling stories, and smoking weed. "Tupac was backstage with this huge box of Newports," said Darryl "Positive K" Gibson, a Bronx-based rapper whose 1992 single "I Got a Man" hit number 14 on the *Billboard* Hot 100 chart. "Pac handed it to me and I was like, 'Nah, man, I don't smoke cigarettes.' He opens it and it's nothing but blunts. Prerolled blunts. I was like, Holy shit. That's enough to get an army high."

Toward the end of the night, a blazed-out-of-their-minds Tupac and Biggie joined Kane, Positive K, and Fat Joe on the stage for a freestyle jam. And while the depth of their friendship would later be very much exaggerated, Tupac and Biggie were more than mere acquaintances. The next time he traveled to Southern California, Biggie slept on Tupac's couch. And although he was managed by an up-and-coming music executive named Sean "Puffy" Combs, Biggie asked Tupac whether he might take over and handle his career. "Biggie looked like he was wearing the same pair of Timberlands for a year," the rapper E.D.I. Mean said, "[while] Pac was staying at the WaldorfAstoria and buying Rolexes and dating Madonna."

Tupac, however, didn't yet view himself as the manager type. Plus, Combs had produced big names like Mary J. Blige and Jodeci. "Nah, stay with Puff," he said. "He will make you a star."

So when Tupac learned of Biggie's presence inside Quad Studios, he set aside any trepidation and proceeded forward. He would hang with his friend, burn out some blunts, record the feature for Little Shawn, make his dough, and bolt.

Piece of cake.

Ron Johnson used to deliver ice.

It was an early Big Apple job for the native Puerto Rican, who came to New York City back in 1982 seeking purpose and meaning and something more exciting than sunny island life.

So he arrived in the metropolis, peddled bags of ice, and didn't much care for it. Another job followed, this one selling popcorn and sodas at Madison Square Garden. Also not really for him.

Finally, with nothing to lose, in 1990 he became an emergency medical technician.

And he *loved* it.

For the first time in his adult life, Johnson was waking up with a sense of curiosity and adventure. What would the day hold? Three burn victims? Four broken feet? A tomato can plummeting from a high-rise and nailing a pedestrian in the skull? Once, on a particularly memorable afternoon, Johnson responded to a call in the East Village when a woman was electrocuted to death after stepping on a metal grate that was touching a live wire.

In short, Johnson—who never wanted to languish behind a desk and loved helping people—was made to be an EMT.

Which is how, in the early morning hours of November 30, he found himself sitting alongside Steve Gerrard, his longtime partner, when they received a radio call to rush out to Times Square and attend to multiple shooting victims. To both men, the assignment was unremarkable. Shootings happened in New York City. So even when they pulled up in front of Quad Recording Studios, entered through the front door, and saw Fred Moore, one of Tupac's companions, on the ground, bleeding from the stomach and surrounded by a couple of kneeling cops, they barely flinched.

"So we're treating this person, and the paramedics show up," Johnson recalled. "And they told us that someone else was shot, and he's upstairs." Johnson grabbed his tech bag, a backboard, and a cervical collar and entered the elevator. Blood was smeared along one of the walls. Johnson pressed the button for the eighth floor.

From the beginning, Tupac should have trusted his instincts, turned around, and left the building. He should have seen the men dressed in their camos and thought, This isn't right.

But he didn't.

According to Tupac, just before he and his crew were to board the elevator, the men in the army fatigues pulled out 9 mm guns and demanded they hit the floor. Around this same time, Cease's elevator door opened in the lobby, and a gunman spun and pointed his weapon toward the young rapper. "As I walked out," Cease recalled, "one of the dudes put the gun back like—get the fuck back in the elevator."

Cease did as he was told.

Tupac did not.

Wrote Ben Westhoff in his outstanding book *Original Gangstas*, "Instead, Tupac reached for his own gun. He was shot, beaten, and robbed of his [forty thousand dollars' worth of] jewelry. He played dead, and the assailants left, at which time he staggered into the elevator and rode it upstairs."

By the time Ron Johnson reached the eighth floor and the doors opened, he expected the worst. That's what the EMT business does to a person. See enough folks bleed out on a slab of concrete, see enough heroin addicts overdose in a pool of vomit—the experiences don't merely shock you. They harden you.

And yet, what greeted Johnson was fairly pedestrian. A young Black man with a shaved head and some piercings was sitting on a couch, shirtless.

"Are you OK?" Johnson asked.

The person smiled.

"Yeah," he said. "But they shot me in my balls."

"*What?*" Johnson replied.

"Yeah," the victim said. "You wanna see?"

Ron Johnson did not want to see. Not at all. But a job is a job, and Johnson nodded. With that, the man stood and pulled his jeans and Karl

Kani boxer shorts down around his ankles. He plopped back down on the couch, and Johnson knelt on the floor to secure a proper viewpoint. "Sure enough, a bullet went basically right through the scrotum skin and into his thigh," Johnson said. "So I'm sitting in front of him and he's looking down and I look up at him and say, 'By any chance do you have a headache?'"

"No," he replied. "Why?"

"Because," Johnson said, "you were shot in the head."

"Really?" he said, reaching toward his scalp.

Johnson grabbed the man's hand and guided it toward a bump protruding from flesh. "You feel that?" Johnson asked.

He did.

"That's a bullet."

Silence.

"He was surprised," Johnson recalled. "Because the bullet actually went through his skin and I could actually see the hump of the bullet, the actual lead. It went just above the forehead line and traveled to the back of his skull. But it never actually *entered* his skull. So it was between the skull and the skin, wedged there. You could see the hole right on top of the head, a little bit toward the back. There was almost no blood, just a little trickle that the wound sealed up. But he was OK. He was aware."

It was at this moment when Johnson, a hip-hop ignoramus, asked the person with the bullet-punctured testicle his name.

"Tupac," he responded. "Tupac Amaru Shakur."

Johnson had never heard of him.

"And can you tell me what happened?" he asked.

Tupac explained that, after entering the building and walking toward the elevator bank, the men in fatigues approached with their guns (two identical 9 mm handguns, Kevin Powell later reported) aimed forward. They ordered the four men to hit the floor. "Everybody dropped to the floor like potatoes," Tupac told Powell. "But I just froze up. It wasn't like I was being brave or nothing. I just could not get on the floor. They started grabbing at me to see if I was strapped. They said, 'Take off your jewels,' and I wouldn't take them off."

According to Tupac, one of the assailants ordered the other one, "Shoot that motherfucker! Fuck it!" Tupac said, in that moment, he envisioned a lifetime of colonoscopy bags (because the man held a gun toward his stomach)—and didn't much care for it. "I drew my arm around him to move the gun to my side," he said. "He shot and the gun twisted and that's when I got hit the first time. I felt it in my leg; I didn't know I got shot in my balls."

Tupac told both Johnson and Powell that he fell to the floor, and the assailants kicked and punched him while swiping his jewelry. His eyes were shut and he was trembling. "Then I felt something on the back of my head, something real strong," he told Powell. "I thought they stomped me or pistol-whipped me and they were stomping my head against the concrete. I saw white, just white. I didn't hear nothing, I didn't feel nothing, and I said, 'I'm unconscious.' But I was conscious. And then I felt it again, and I could hear things now and I could see things and they were bringing me back to consciousness. They did it again, and I couldn't hear nothing. And I couldn't see nothing; it was just all white. And then they hit me again, and I could hear things and I could see things and I knew I was conscious again."

When the gunmen left, Zayd Malik (who, along with Stretch, was unharmed) turned Tupac over and asked whether he was OK. "Yes," he replied. "I'm hit, I'm hit." He rose, and said he looked out the front door and spotted a police car. Having no trust for law enforcement, his instinct was to board the elevator and head upstairs to Quad Studios. Once he reached the eighth floor, he limped toward a couch, sat down, and—he recalled—"looked around, and it scared the shit out of me."

Tupac told Powell that four men were in the room: Biggie, Sean Combs, Andre Harrell, and Rosemond, the man who arranged the session. "All of them had jewels on," he said. "More jewels than me. I saw [Rosemond], and he had this look on his face like he was surprised to see me. I didn't know why. I had just beeped the buzzer and said I was coming upstairs."

According to Tupac's telling of the saga, none of the men would look at him, and a police officer arrived, saw his bleeding testicle, smiled, laughed, and said, "What's up, Tupac? How's it hanging?"

Only—that's not quite what happened.

Tupac Shakur shot himself in the balls.

Well, *ball*.

When he arrived at the building, wedged between the waistband of his jeans and his boxer shorts was a loaded Glock. Tupac did not yet roll with a bodyguard (that practice began a year later), so he considered the weapon a first line of defense.

According to Johnson, Tupac *had to have* discharged the bullet that wound up passing through his testicle. First, there was no entrance or exit wound on his jeans. And second, there were powder burns on his underwear. "He shot himself," Johnson said. "There's no doubt about it. The way he explained it all happening, from the distance he described, there would have been powder burns everywhere. He told me he was shot. He told me how it happened. But the way the bullet wound up in his leg, the way it went through his balls, the angle it took—he was clearly reaching for his piece."

In a *Vibe* interview, Tupac told Powell he had been shot five times. This, too, was incorrect and untrue. Tupac was shot twice by the perpetrator— one bullet hit his left hand, the other was the one that lodged in his skin above the skull. The third bullet, again, was entirely self-inflicted.* "I've never known for sure whether Tupac shot himself in the balls," Watani Tyehimba, his manager, said decades later. "But the thing with the Glock he had—it does have a safety, but it's not a normal safety. And if you have your finger on the trigger, you're gonna shoot yourself." (Tupac had a history of being an unsteady triggerman. When he pointed his gun at Demetrius Striplin at the Marin City Festival, his hand was quivering. And Shock G, the Digital Underground front man, used to tell a story of Tupac accidentally unloading an AK-47 inside his apartment. "He liked showing off his guns," said Kendrick Wells. "But he *never* held them the right way.")

Not long after Johnson reached Tupac, Craig McKernan, a New York City police officer, emerged from the elevator. The NYPD employs ap- proximately thirty-six thousand officers per year, and—by odd/crazy/wild/ conspiracy-theory-lending coincidence—McKernan had been involved in arresting Tupac one year earlier on sexual abuse and gun possession charges. Even stranger, he had recently testified against him in court.

---

* Said Johnson in a 2024 interview: "I don't know where the number five came from."

"Hey, Officer McKernan," Tupac said upon seeing him.

"Hey, Tupac," McKernan replied. "You hang in there."

Johnson and Gerrard, his partner, secured a brace around Tupac's neck, strapped him onto a wooden board, and brought him to the elevator, which was too small for everyone to fit. As a result, Tupac had to be propped upright. Blood dripped from the head wound.

"Just tell me if I'm gonna die," Tupac said.

"No," Johnson replied. "I think you're gonna be all right."

Also on the elevator, McKernan asked Tupac to identify the shooter. "I didn't even see it," he replied.

Shortly after the shooting, Hector Marin—a paramedic who, unlike Johnson, knew Tupac's music—was sitting inside the Cabrini Medical Center at 227 East Nineteenth Street, his base of operations. "We got a call—shots fired, multiple males down," he recalled. "We don't know who it's gonna be, but we had police radios so we can hear the police talking and they're all excited. We get there, I jump out, and it's like, Whoa! That's Tupac! Holy shit!"

The EMTs rolled Tupac through the lobby and out toward the ambulance, which Marin and his crew had positioned alongside the curb. According to Chico Del Vec, a member of Junior M.A.F.I.A., the hip-hop group formed by Biggie, Tupac saw Biggie and his posse standing by and flashed the middle finger on his left hand in their direction. "He was saying, 'Fuck y'all niggas' . . . looking at us against the wall," Del Vec recalled. "That was to us."

Johnson, Gerrard, and Marin loaded Tupac onto the back of the ambulance and strapped him to the bench. In his right hand Tupac gripped a prayer cloth that a cousin, Barbara Jean Powers, had given him years earlier. It was a small piece of beige fabric that she promised him would serve as a protector, and he always kept it in a pocket (Powers recalled that, months earlier, she had also "consecrated" the Rolex Tupac was wearing on his left wrist by rubbing it against her skin. "That's why they couldn't pull it off him," she said. "It was holy"). A pair of detectives boarded the vehicle, and Tupac again flashed his middle finger, this time in their direction. It felt instinctive, like a threatened wolf revealing its fangs. "Hey, Tupac—don't do that," Johnson said. "That's really rude."

Tupac looked toward the EMT and apologized. "It was his tough guy act," Johnson said. "Because the whole ride he couldn't have been more polite and courteous."

As was the case with Johnson, Marin was most surprised by the bullet to the head. "That bullet should have gone through his skull," he said. "Instead, his head almost acted as a helmet and kind of crowned the bullet. That's very unusual."

Although St. Vincent's Medical Center was a hair closer, the EMTs were affiliated with Bellevue Hospital, so that's where the ambulance headed. By the time the vehicle arrived and Tupac was wheeled into the trauma room, everything felt crazed. "It sucks, but celebrities were always treated differently," said Marin. "With Tupac, everyone wanted to be there. It was cops, it was EMTs, it was the entire surgical staff—nurses, doctors. I guess people want stories to tell their kids, but I never liked that. This is someone's life we're talking about."

Dr. Charles Thorne, the forty-four-year-old chief of plastic surgery (and, coincidentally, an Oakland native), descended from his office to the trauma room. It was well out of the norm for Thorne. "This is something you never see," said Marin. "And he's directing people, telling people what to do. Clearly, he's the man in charge."

Tupac, sitting up and wide awake, looked at Thorne and said, "Hey, Doc. Is one nut gonna be enough for me? Because I've gotta at least be able to have one nut."

A nurse giggled and said, "You'll be fine with one nut, Tupac."

Thorne cleared his throat. "This is not a laughing matter," he said.

"Yo, I'm the one lying here with the bloody ball," Tupac replied. "I can make all the jokes I want."

Roughly thirty minutes after Tupac's arrival at Bellevue, two men entered the waiting room. They were young and Black and vaguely recognizable to some of the staff. A nurse asked if she could help them, and one asked whether they might see their friend Tupac.

It was Puffy.

It was Biggie.

A medical staffer came out and told them it'd be best if they return the following morning, that Mr. Shakur needed rest and wasn't ready for visitors.

They left with Tupac never knowing of their presence.

On the late afternoon of November 30, 1994, Tupac Shakur emerged from surgery after having three bullets dislodged from his body. His most troublesome injury was a damaged blood vessel in his right leg. In a sense, Tupac had lucked out. The bullets were low-caliber. "Had it been a high-caliber missile," said Dr. Leon Pachter of the hospital's trauma department, "he'd have been dead."

The first person to visit him inside Bellevue Hospital was Afeni, who was there with her sister, Gloria. "Look what they did to me," Tupac moaned.

In the waiting room, dozens of people congregated, pacing the beige carpet and drowning out the hums of vending machines and water fountains. Family members. Friends. Fans. Media. Curiosity seekers. Glo spotted Biggie, returning yet again and looking notably glum. "He wasn't standing with the rest of the people trying to see Tupac," she said. "He was by himself standing up against the wall."

The one visitor who made no sense was a forty-five-year-old Black man with a shaved head, pronounced cheekbones, and the lips, nose, and fluttery eyelashes of the patient he was there to see.

Billy Garland, Tupac's biological father, was in the waiting room.

It was ridiculous. It was offensive. It was tasteless. Why, of all the days and weeks and years, was *this* the moment he decided to make a return engagement? Garland has said on multiple occasions that he aspired to make good with his son, but—in his telling—there were always obstacles keeping the two apart. He said Afeni spread mistruths about his identity and his intentions. "It was just unfortunate that a person could lie about a boy's father," he said, "knowing he wanted one."

And yet . . . where had he been? According to Set Shakur, Tupac's sister, when her brother turned twenty-one he was told by a mutual acquaintance that Billy wanted to reach out. "Tupac wasn't having it," she said. "He was like, 'If he has twenty-one years' worth of birthday cards, then I'll speak to him.'"

Now, languishing in the waiting room, Billy jotted down a note on a piece of paper ("*I'm your father. I'm Billy Garland.*") and handed it to one of the nurses, who passed it to Tupac.

Groggy, disoriented, fresh out of surgery, Tupac read the note.

"OK," he said. "I'll see him."

Wrote Staci Robinson:

Moments later, an oddly familiar face appeared beside him. "You all right, man?"

Tupac stared up at Billy Garland . . . the man standing over him was just a stranger, his claim of fatherhood adding to the aftershock of everything Tupac had just experienced. But the resemblance was surreal. Glo recalled, "He told us when he looked up, he thought he had died because he was looking at someone who looked just like him. He was thinking, 'Am I in heaven? Did I die?'"

In her terrific 2004 biography of Afeni Shakur, the actress Jasmine Guy wrote, "The first in line to siphon Tupac's money was Billy Garland, also known as 'the sperm donor'—the father Tupac had never known." The wounded, bedridden Tupac was unsure what to make of it all. His mind wasn't entirely there to begin with. But—who was this asshole? Why was he showing up *now*? Where had he been when his son needed him? *Really* needed him? And was he truly his biological father, or just some money-hungry douche look-alike seeking a handout and a book deal? "We didn't talk much in the hospital," Garland later said. "He was suspicious." Earlier in the year Tupac had released a single, "Papa'z Song," that touched upon his heartbreak over being raised fatherless, and the lyrics ("Had to play catch by myself, what a sorry sight / A pitiful plight, so I pray, for a starry night / Please send me a pops before puberty / The things I wouldn't do to see a piece of family unity") were a cattle prod to Garland's head. For years, Tupac had not merely wanted a father. He'd *craved* one.

Again, what was Billy Garland doing here?

With or without Garland's arrival, the hospital was freaking Tupac out.

Never one for institutions, he felt walled in and confined. So, barely three and a half hours post-surgery, a groggy Tupac rose from his bed, disconnected a monitor, and walked into the nearby waiting room. "His head, arm and leg," wrote Robinson, "were wrapped in gauze and he dragged the IV pole behind him."

The hospital staff was horrified. Pachter said he was "shocked" by Tupac's departure, adding he risked losing a testicle, killing a thigh muscle, rupturing a kidney, or suffering major bleeding. Afeni felt similarly. She demanded to know where her son was going, and he snapped, "Get me out of here!" But she understood, too. For all his bluster, Tupac was scared. Though he remained unsure who, exactly, had tried killing him, there was no reason to believe the person wouldn't try again. And what better way to murder someone than to enter his hospital room and snuff him out? So Tupac insisted he leave, and his mother—twenty-three years removed from the Panther 21 trial and all the justified paranoia that accompanied it—wasn't one to argue. She understood what it was to have the walls watching you. Back when Tupac and Set were little, Afeni literally joined her children in smearing peanut butter on doorknobs and sink handles in case law enforcement might arrive to seek out fingerprints. "He was," wrote Justin Tinsley, "a child experiencing a revolution."

Tupac and co. exited Bellevue, and they headed up to Keisha Morris's Harlem apartment. His fiancée had been given the heads-up that Tupac would be coming, but she didn't exactly embrace the idea. He was in pain, woozy, wheelchair-bound, and wrapped in bandages. Later that day, when Morris noted blood oozing from Tupac's leg, she called Afeni and urged her to get her son some medical attention. He was admitted to Metropolitan Hospital in East Harlem under the name "Bob Day."

Within minutes of entering his new room, the phone rang. Tupac answered, anticipating the voice of a family member or friend. After all, literally almost no one knew he was here.

"You ain't dead yet," the person said.

Click.

On the morning of December 1, 1994, Tupac Shakur arrived at the Manhattan supreme court at 100 Centre Street intent on sending an unspoken message. Later that day, the jury of nine women and three men was scheduled to announce their verdict on sodomy and sexual abuse charges, and he wanted them to see him. To feel him. Really, to *empathize* with him.

So, after being helped out of a town car by his mother, Tupac approached the building and was wheeled inside. His head was wrapped in a turban-like bandage beneath a New York Yankees baseball cap. His left hand, too, was cocooned. Standing before the jury, he grimaced and popped painkillers. A Kevlar bulletproof vest peeked out from beneath his jacket. A gold Rolex watch covered one wrist, and a diamond ring adorned a finger. His attorneys had urged Tupac to ask for a continuance, but he refused. He wanted those in the court to grasp what had happened to him. "Several jurors winced and nudged each other as Shakur struggled to stand and then propped himself against the defense table," the New York *Daily News* reported. "The jury remained in the courtroom for 10 minutes as Shakur, his face twisted in agony, washed down painkillers with a cup of mineral water."

Tupac exited as quickly as he had arrived. He rolled to the car without saying much to the press ("I didn't sodomize her, she's the one who sodomized me!" he uttered), and seven Nation of Islam bodyguards—hired by Watani Tyehimba—shoved reporters who dared ask a question. It was hard to blame them. Earlier that day, Gerrie E. Summers of *Newsday* penned a column comparing Tupac to Jeffrey Dahmer, and reacting to his shooting with a single word: "Good!"

That evening, with Tupac eight miles away inside his Metropolitan Hospital room, the jury found him (and Charles Fuller) guilty of holding down Ayanna Jackson and fondling her. However, it also found the men innocent of sodomy and weapons charges. Richard Devitt, one of the jurors, later told the author Sheldon Pearce that he and his cohorts "believed Tupac to be completely innocent." However, one juror (a devoutly Catholic older woman) held out. So, to end a lengthy trial, the jury found him guilty of fourth-degree sexual assault, with an understanding the punishment would be a wrist slap. A prison term was not legally mandatory, and Michael Warren, Tupac's attorney, greeted the news as a victory. "We're ecstatic!" he said. His client would likely wind up with mere probation.

This all took place on a Thursday, four days before Tupac's scheduled sentencing date. Once again, overcome by paranoia and dread, he checked himself out of the hospital, even though the medical staff urged him to reconsider. He reached out to a friend, the actress Jasmine Guy, who had sat alongside Afeni throughout the trial. Guy and Tupac had worked together in 1993 when he appeared in an episode of her NBC sitcom, *A Different World*. She emerged a supportive confidante who recognized Tupac's flaws, yet never doubted his innocence.

So when Tupac needed a spot to lay low and recover, Guy offered up her 7,120-square-foot apartment on Manhattan's Upper West Side. And Warren, his attorney, called on an old friend to take care of him.

Her name was Dr. Barbara Justice, a native New Yorker and the granddaughter of Robert W. Justice, Harlem's first Black assemblyman. Barbara had a distinguished history—not merely as a physician, but as a physician troubled by Black America's shoddy health and wellness care. She earned her medical degree from Howard University's College of Medicine in 1977, and within a decade was one of the world's leading voices on AIDS treatment and research. At one point, she served as Stokely Carmichael's personal physician. "I wanted to make an impact on the world," she said. "And, to the best of my abilities, I think I did."

When Warren called and asked whether she could lend a hand with his star client, Justice was bewildered.

Justice: "Why does Tupac need me?"

Warren: "Barbara, have you followed the news?"

Jordan: "Sure. He's at Bellevue."

Warren: "Well . . ."

He told her that Tupac was now at Jasmine Guy's pad (*"The actress?"* she asked), and someone needed to oversee his care. Within an hour, Justice was standing alongside the bed of America's most notorious musical star. "I examined him, I stabilized him," she recalled. "I dressed his wounds, made sure he wasn't developing an infection or any side effects from the trauma. Made certain his limbs were functioning and that he was progressing."

Day after day, Justice arrived in the mornings and sat by Tupac's side. He was, she recalled, "paranoid and anxious." He kept a sawed-off shotgun at his bedside and always had multiple armed friends nearby. At any moment, Tupac expected someone to burst through the door and fill his body with lead. "I got set up," he later wrote, "by some jealous busta bitch made playa haters." He wasn't sure who, precisely, but it could be Agnant. Or Rosemond. Or Puffy. Or Biggie.* He went on irrational rants about the Quad Studios ambush. Why, he wondered, had neither Stretch nor Zayd been shot? Were they in on it, too? Was *everyone* in on it? "He also thought the police was in on it, the FBI was in on it," said Justice. "There were probably ten people, total, who knew he was at Jasmine's. But that didn't give him any peace." The New York media spread rumors that Tupac was dissatisfied with the care he had received at Bellevue. Not entirely true. "He was fine with the doctors," Justice said. "But he was certain people were trying to kill him."

What bothered Justice most was the number of visitors intent on convincing him the ambush was the by-product of a blooming hip-hop battle between East Coast artists and West Coast artists. Why hadn't Biggie alerted him to the threat? Even if he wasn't the shooter, he surely knew enough to warn Tupac to steer clear. And what of Puffy? Where was he?

Though he was New York born and Baltimore bred, Tupac identified as a California artist. "I would listen to these people, and it was really stupid stuff," Justice recalled. "I was with him a lot, so I said, 'Listen, ignore these people. Take the high road and try to minimize conflicts. The last thing we, as a people, need is more hatred and bitterness.' But he didn't hear me. He was angry and wanted revenge.

"I looked at him, in Jasmine Guy's apartment, and I thought, This young man is going to die a young man.

"Because he just won't listen."

On December 23, 1994, Iris Crews, one of Tupac's attorneys, visited Guy's pad to speak with her client. Having allowed the rapper to spend nearly three weeks recovering in private, Daniel Fitzgerald, the New York City Criminal Court judge, decided enough was enough. He set bail at three

---

* In Cheo Hodari Coker's excellent book *Unbelievable*, Lil' Cease makes a strong case against Biggie's involvement: "Why would Big do something like that? [Tupac] knows where Big's mom lives. He knows where Big stay at. I called you upstairs. You my nigga. Hell no, I didn't know about it. Why would I come downstairs if it was a setup?"

million dollars—a total Tupac did not possess. As a result, he needed to surrender himself to authorities, and Crews aspired to make the process as smooth as possible. "I get there [to Guy's apartment], and his entourage was with him," she recalled. "And I said, 'You guys have to leave now.' Because he's different when his boys are around." Everyone exited the room, and Tupac and Crews stood face-to-face. She told him it'd be best to surrender at night, without the press. He nodded, then proceeded to sob. Crews hugged him, reassuring the young man everything would be all right.

"Not that I could promise that," she said. "But he needed kindness."

Crews escorted her client to Bellevue Hospital to be booked, and he turned himself in to authorities and was taken to the facility's prison ward. For the next sixteen days, America's criminal du jour sat and stewed, wondering of his unfolding fate. Then, on January 8, 1995, he was moved to the North Infirmary Command at Rikers Island, the prison island on the East River in the Bronx. While Fuller was (strangely, surprisingly) freed on $350,000 bail, Tupac's figure remained $3 million. He would languish as inmate no. 7551377M until Judge Fitzgerald decided upon a sentence. "We knew we had an uphill battle with Fitzgerald," recalled Crews. "He was a close associate of the mayor, Rudy Giuliani, and their politics couldn't have been more opposite than they were from my client's."

Although Tupac had certainly been in trouble before, being jailed here was next level. Beginning at its birth as a detention center in the late 1800s, Rikers was disgusting in every sense of the word. "It was . . . a massive garbage dump," Graham Rayman and Reuven Blau wrote in *Rikers: An Oral History*. "Residents of Hunts Point in the Bronx could smell it from their homes a mile away, and Upper East Siders could easily see the flames from the burning of mountains of trash. Enormous clouds of rats populated the dump to the point where they challenged dogs, and humans, for control of the island." Because celebrities made for easy targets, Tupac was placed alone in the medical dorm, isolated from others. He was in cell number 1, which meant he did not mingle with the general population, though he could hear and see them from behind his bars—and vice versa. "[The inmates] would be there all day rapping to him," recalled Tami Lee, a correctional officer. "'Yo, could you listen to this for me?' He would be in his cell all day listening, like, 'Sigh, all right, all right.'"

Tupac expended a great deal of energy to present the image of a gangsta. But, on the inside, he risked being exposed. Tupac was not particularly tough. He wasn't especially street hardened. He wrote a letter of complaint after a fellow inmate, Henry Cenor, threw an orange at him. Truth is, he cried easily. He liked roses and raindrops and walks on the beach. He listened to the music of the Indigo Girls. It's easy to fool CD buyers and concertgoers with barks of "Thug Life!" Inside a jail, that's less simple. Turk Gumusdere, a former Rikers correctional officer who spent *a lot* of time with Tupac, said there was constant risk of others trying to make names for themselves by shanking a high-profile inmate. Had Tupac killed a police officer or federal agent, no one would have dared mess with him. But he was a rapper who allegedly raped a woman. He was ripe for the picking. "If you're the inmate who stabs Tupac the rapist," Gumusdere said, "that's a legacy for life.

"Also, a lot of the female correctional officers were really hard on him. They were calling him a rapist and shit like that. They weren't starstruck. They just really hated him. Rapists—especially for women—are the biggest no-no in jail."

Tupac's first two days were the worst—weed was unavailable, and the withdrawal proved agonizing. "Emotionally, it was like I didn't know myself," he told Kevin Powell. "I was sitting in a room, like there was two people in the room, evil and good. That was the hardest part. After that, the weed was out of me. Then every day I started doing, like, 1,000 pushups for myself."

Tupac was allowed a pen and notepad in his cell ("So many notepads!" said Gumusdere. "Every time I'd walk by his cell he was chilling on his bed, writing"), as well as books. He kept his mind occupied by reading voraciously. His cousin Billy Lesane was also in Rikers, for a parole violation, and a sympathetic Catholic priest, Lawrence E. Lucas, passed notes between the relatives. Tupac looked forward to Tuesdays and Thursdays, when dinner was chicken, mashed potatoes, green beans, salad, and either lemonade, iced tea, or soda. According to Gumusdere, who later became

Rikers' deputy warden, Tupac received regular visits from a woman. When the woman came to Rikers, Gumusdere said Tupac would be escorted to the visitation room—where they would be left alone (in the presence of a single guard). "The visiting room was on the same floor as his cell," Gumusdere said. "Tupac would always be banging [this woman] or getting a blow job from her in there. It wasn't common for people to have sex in that space. But that was Tupac.

"We made an exception."

On February 7, 1995, one month after entering Rikers, Tupac returned to court to stand before Fitzgerald and learn his fate.

There was a maximum potential sentence of seven years, and despite Warren's reassurances, it was a terrifyingly real possibility. Celebrities were ideal candidates to serve as examples to the public. Especially Black celebrities. As he was wont to do, inside the courtroom Tupac greeted several benches of friends and supporters with smiles, laughs, waves. It was all show. It had always been show. He was nervous. When Fitzgerald asked if he had anything to say for himself, Tupac stood.

"I want."

Pause. Long, deep pause.

"I want to apologize to Ayanna."

Pause.

"I'm not apologizing for a crime," he said. "I hope in time you'll come forth and tell the truth—I am innocent."

Addressing Fitzgerald, Tupac refused to hold back. He believed the trial had been a sham. "You know, Your Honor, throughout this entire court case, you haven't looked me or my attorney in the eye once," he said. "It's obvious that you're not here in the search for justice, so therefore, there's no point in me asking for a lighter sentence. I don't care what you do, 'cause you're not respecting us, this is not a court of law; as far as I'm concerned, no justice is being served here, and you still can't look me in the eye. So I say, do what you want to do, give me whatever time you want, because I'm not in your hands, I'm in God's hands."

Tupac later apologized to the youth of America for misrepresenting their interests. He also apologized to Fuller, facing his sentencing as well

(Jacques Agnant's indictment, meanwhile, was dismissed, and he pleaded guilty to two misdemeanors. This led to endless speculation from Tupac and others that Agnant was a government informant). "I took Chuck off the streets of Richmond," he said. "I promised him a way out of the street. Chuck, you've done nothing but be a friend. When all the world was turned back on me, you were there. I was so involved in my career that I didn't see what was coming. I'm sorry I wasn't more focused, and I apologize to you."

Tupac proceeded to cry.

Murray Kempton, the *Newsday* columnist who, two and a half decades earlier, had covered Afeni Shakur and the Panther 21 trial, was now chronicling the son as he had the mother. Only the empathy he had once lathered upon a hero of the Black Power movement was nowhere to be found. "The scene," he wrote, "evoked the assurance of the entire sincerity of the loneliness of a half-man, half-child who had become a star without ever even having been a bit player.

"He got his sentence and went away laughing again. The sight of the careful stitches on his leather vest was a reminder of how expensive a business it is to maintain the street image; the jauntiness of his bearing was a portent of the long watches of the nights ahead when laughter stops and weeping fills all that's left; and that last thought was a prayer that the tears ahead will wash him back to the better self that has until now fought the worse one and lost."

Fitzgerald sentenced Tupac to one and a half to four and a half years in prison.

He would be heading to the Clinton Correctional Facility.

To the worst place imaginable.

Chapter 19

Prison Changes Everybody
[Aka Don't Fumble My Hos]

On the morning of February 14, 1995, Randi Ferst, Brian Hitney, Matt Ryan, and Ed Szalkowki traveled fifteen miles west from the campus of the State University of New York at Plattsburgh to the middle-of-nowhere eastern New York town of Dannemora.

The undergrads were enrolled in a twelve-credit course titled Non-Broadcast Industrial Video, and as a final assignment Professor Deborah DeSilva required her students to produce a segment for a local enterprise. Some worked with bars and restaurants. Others teamed with nearby middle schools. "We got the one I really wanted," recalled Ryan, "creating a ten-to-fifteen-minute video highlighting the sesquicentennial anniversary of the local prison."

The Clinton Correctional Facility was no ordinary local penal facility. Once named the Dannemora State Hospital for the Criminally Insane, Clinton is New York State's largest and oldest maximum security prison, and notable inmates of the past included David Berkowitz (aka Son of Sam), Robert Chambers (aka the Preppy Murderer), and Charles "Lucky" Luciano. It was known as Little Siberia for the brutal winters and grim exterior. In his book, *The Invisible Walls of Dannemora*, Michael H. Blaine, a forrmer prison correctional officer, called his old haunt "a horrific place."

The goal of the four students was to tour Clinton and, via video, tell the story of how inmates were working to help the local community. So they drove up, endured the security checks, and entered. These were sheltered kids—white, middle class, far from familiar with the world of murderers and rapists. "I remember being in the yard, and around lunchtime the inmates all came out," said Hitney. "I'm like, What's to stop them from beating us all up?"

At one point, the four were walking through a hallway toward the dining area when a guard barked out, "Prisoner transfer!" The students were pushed against the wall, and forty or so of the newly incarcerated marched past. They were all male, mostly Black or Hispanic, still dressed in street clothes. "They walk by," recalled Ryan, "and to our complete and utter shock, one of them was Tupac Shakur. We were all just dumbfounded. To see one of the biggest stars on the planet walking past you at certainly one of his lowest moments was such a strange feeling."

And here's what stuck with Ryan.

Most of the inmates appeared to be shell-shocked. Tupac, however, somehow cruised past with a bounce. "He looked like the cocky, self-assured person who we knew from the videos and magazine covers," said Ryan. "I'll never forget that."

It was all a façade.

The Tupac Shakur who entered Clinton was—like most newbies to the institution—paralyzed with fear. He *knew* he didn't belong there; that were it not for a corrupt legal system and the mechanisms of Jacques Agnant and a litigious young woman screaming, "Rape!," he would be back in California, going about his career. He also believed (rightly) that he was now a target. "All it takes is one guy to feel like, Yo, this is Tupac. Let me make a name for myself and cut him, stab him, slice him," said Daniel Vega, a fellow Clinton inmate. "There are plenty of guys who'd wanna be the one to say, 'I fucked up Tupac.'"

On the day Tupac arrived, he marched past the four Plattsburgh students and entered the prison's reception area, where he and his fellow freshmen stayed for no more than twenty minutes. "Listen up!" a guard said. "Keep your eyes straight ahead and keep your mouths shut. You're not in Kansas anymore." Word spreads fast behind bars, and as Tupac waited inmates could be heard screaming (in mocking tones), "West Side!" and "East Side!" Tupac's steely expression never wavered. A prison official broke down the rules and presented him with a green jumpsuit and an identification card all inmates were required to carry. Michael Christopher,* a veteran corrections officer, watched the scene unfold when a colleague asked, "Which one of those mutts is that movie star rapper guy?"

Christopher nodded toward Tupac.

"Looks like another poor, dumb nigger to me," the other guard said.

The Clinton Correctional Facility was split into blocks identified by letters—A Block, B Block, C Block, etc. Tupac was first placed in E Block, a protective custody unit. He was assigned a six-by-nine-foot cell with a stainless steel sink and toilet. For twenty-three hours per day, Tupac (inmate no. 95A1140) remained in the cell. For a social butterfly, it was torturously dull. He had one hour of yard time and, according to a complaint he filed on March 10, insufficient linen. Showers were permitted on Mondays, Wednesdays, and Fridays, and the hot water rarely worked. From the start, the COs were unkind. The employees were (save one Black guard) all white, mostly male, rural, and uneducated. During Tupac's time, one CO was reprimanded for forcing an inmate to provide him with oral sex. "Not Pac," said Vega. Rumor spread that Tupac had shot himself in the testicle during the Quad Studios attack, and in those early days guards ridiculed him as "One Pac."

"When I first got here, they threw me in with the general population with just a bloody mattress on the floor, no sheets, nothing," Tupac said in a prison interview with the writer Jamie Foster Brown. "When the other inmates saw this, they threw me sheets, towels, T-shirts, pillows, underwear, blankets and cigarettes."

Tupac's life had long been all about speaking up for himself and firing back at those who disrespected him. Even when retribution was unwise and/or unjustified, he couldn't help himself. Yet here, in his cell, he felt powerless. What were his options? Curse a CO out and wind up in solitary confinement? Punch a CO and have his sentence extended? There was nothing he could do—so he did nothing. He took it. Absorbed it. Hated every single moment. "They didn't like him," said Joey Fama, a fellow in-

---

* The corrections officer's real name is not Michael Christopher. He spoke for this book, and published his own autobiography, using a pseudonym. "My job and its history requires some protection," he said.

mate. "They kept trying to give him tickets for bullshit things. They didn't like the fact that a young Black man was smart and rich."

Fama was serving twenty-five years to life for the high-profile 1989 shooting death of a sixteen-year-old Black New Yorker named Yusef Hawkins. The murder took place in Bensonhurst, a predominantly Italian American working-class neighborhood in Brooklyn, and sparked protests and deep racial divide. Fama, who has long claimed his innocence, was briefly the face of bigotry in the Big Apple. That he and Tupac became friends spoke to the new inmate's unique adaptability. Or, as Michael Namikas wrote, "Tupac needed human contact to survive."

Years later, Fama explained the world Tupac had entered: "Prison is not what you see on TV. When someone gets punched in the face, stabbed the fuck up, sliced across the face, hit with a dumbbell or pipe, it's all for a reason. Everything happens for a reason. When I came to prison, the old heads told me to stay away from drugs, gambling, gays, and basically hustling altogether. There's rules to this prison life. If you fuck up you gotta pay the consequences. I've known guys going home in a week and got killed in the yard because he owed someone a pack of cigarettes. Just because you have a set date to go home doesn't necessarily mean you're going to make that date. Some guys are doing life and a young, stupid motherfucker might run his mouth and thinking he's funny, saying, 'Oh, I don't care. I'm going home in a couple of months.' Guys doing life might say, 'Oh, yeah? Take this with you,' and they stick an ice pick in your neck. You can't forget where you are because we are surrounded by criminals and real-life killers."

After a relatively short span in E Block, Tupac was relocated to the APPU (Assessment and Preparation Program Unit), a special housing unit for high-profile inmates and inmates at high risk of victimization. "Inmate Shakur is a well known Rap Singer," a prison official wrote in an involuntary-protective-custody review form. "He is a very high profile inmate and in light of such is victim prone. He is being approached for autographs, and has become the focus of undue attention. His fame and background could possibly make him a target." He was assigned to lower H Block, home to people who—according to Fama, an H Block resident—committed "the worst crimes in New York State. Child molesters, rapists, serial killers, baby killers, and [also] inmates who cooperated against their codefendants. All gang members who were out of whatever gang they were in. Ex–correction officers, ex–police officers, ex-judges, ex–DEA agents."

Lower H Block was made up of two floors, each with forty-four cells. Tupac was placed on 1 company 25 cell—which meant he was on the first floor in cell 25. "Each officer is assigned to a floor, and he's responsible for the forty-four convicts," said Fama. "Whatever officer wants to be a tough guy that day will give you a short speech saying, 'This is my fucking block! You don't look at our women . . . if you have a problem, handle it like men in the yard . . . you fuck around and hurt one of our officers, we will throw you down the stairs.'"*

Much of Clinton smelled of mold and rot; the twin-size cots were uncomfortable and marked by disconcerting stains; privacy was nearly impossible to come by. If a corrections officer demanded an anal cavity strip search, you stripped and he hand-navigated your anal cavity. Karen Lee, Tupac's longtime publicist, recalled visiting and being disgusted. "I got there in the morning so I could stay from nine until three," she recalled. "He had to go to the bathroom. When he came back they made him bend over and cough standing in front of the door. They did it to humiliate him."

"Clinton," said Vega, "fucking sucked."

And yet, life inside wasn't all bad. For the first time in years, Tupac was subsisting without a steady diet of weed and Hennessy, and his mind was sharp. "What they call me is obsessive compulsive," he said. "I read book after book." Never previously one to exercise, Tupac began a steady routine of push-ups, transforming from wiry into sculptured and steel-like. APPU denizens had specific breakfast, lunch, and dinner dining hall hours, but many cooked their own meals in prison-permitted hot pots. Inmates needed to wear green prison pants, but were allowed their own shirts. Within lower H confines, inmates had daily access to an outdoor yard, roughly the size of a basketball court. There were weights and a single hoop, home to daily pickup games. "Tupac was a terrible basket-

---

* Fama said he witnessed many inmates being thrown down the steps by corrections officers. "With your hands cuffed behind you."

ball player," said Vega. "Like, you wouldn't even believe he was a Black kid playing ball. He would literally throw the ball at the hoop like he was throwing a big boulder over his head." Despite a heavily cited New York *Daily News* report that Tupac was raped, by "as many as eight inmates," it wasn't true—no matter how many times the New York shock jock Wendy Williams giddily repeated it. "I guarantee you it never happened," said Vega. "It wouldn't even be possible."[*]

Prison can make for unlikely bedfellows, and lower H Block was no exception. The inmate in the cell directly above Tupac was a flamboyantly gay man who cooked up pots of tomato soup he shared with the rapper. Tupac forged bonds with Fama (convicted of second-degree murder) and Vega (incarcerated for rape)—men he certainly would not have hung with on the outside. Another quirky pal was Christopher, the white corrections officer who took an interest in Tupac's writing.[†]

Tupac's tightest Clinton cohort was the oddest kinship of his lifetime. Three years earlier, on the night of June 1, 1991, a college baseball player named Shannon Siegel wound up at a party he had no business attending. It was a kegger at the home of a student at Lawrence (New York) High School, from which Siegel, who was white, had graduated in 1988. While there he spotted Nikki Diamond, a former girlfriend. Only Diamond wasn't alone—she was in the company of Jermaine Ewell, a Black Lawrence High football star. According to witnesses, after Ewell paid Diamond's five-dollar admission to the party, Siegel mocked her for accepting "nigger money." He and his buddies were ordered to leave. They returned later, this time armed with stickball bats.

Siegel—"Reeling not only from a 40-ounce Olde English malt liquor but also from a potent cocktail of rage, immaturity and humiliation," wrote *Sports Illustrated*'s L. Jon Wertheim—sought out Ewell and crushed the bat against the right side of his head. Ewell fell to the ground, and Siegel and his gang kicked the football star's skull "as if it were a piñata," wrote

---

[*] When asked whether he was raped, Tupac told Jamie Foster Brown, "How can I? I'm not in general population."

[†] In 2021, Christopher authored a book, *2Pac Behind Bars*. If one can get past his unfortunate determination that Tupac communicated via third-grade-level Ebonics, it's enlightening.

Wertheim. By the time Ewell was taken to Peninsula General Hospital, he had neither pulse nor heartbeat.

Amazingly, Ewell pulled through. Siegel was sentenced to seven to twenty years at the Clinton Correctional Facility. In print, Siegel was compared to (coincidentally) Fama, and Al Sharpton organized a march against his very existence. Clinton, no doubt, would be unkind—with an inmate population that was 48 percent Black, there was little empathy for a race hater.

Weirdly though, Shannon Siegel was . . . beloved. Athleticism carries weight behind bars, and here was a young man who had mastered all sports. He devoted himself to helping fellow inmates earn their GEDs, and became the first Clinton prisoner to ever receive an advanced degree (an MBA from City University of Seattle) while incarcerated. "He was just cool as fuck," said Vega. "In prison, you spend a lot of time doing nothing. So if someone is interesting, you gravitate toward them."

Tupac and Siegel, said Vega, "did everything together." Their cells were adjacent, so they held lengthy discussions about race, class, sports, politics, religion. Tupac was allowed a small RadioShack cassette player in his cell, and he entertained Siegel with the sounds of Digital Underground and Ant Banks and Too Short and (of course) Tupac Shakur. Siegel, for his part, didn't hide from his crime. "I was drunk, I was young, I was stupid," he later explained. "This eats at my soul every day."

The men hung out in the yard together. They ate meals together. They committed to watching each other's backs. Siegel was a voracious reader, and he urged Tupac to pick up *The Prince*, a sixteenth-century political treatise written by the Florentine philosopher Niccolò Machiavelli. When Tupac wrapped the 164-page opus, he thanked Siegel for helping open his mind.

"That," he raved, "was on a different level."

Over the course of his final year of freedom, Tupac had worked on his third solo studio album, titled *Me Against the World*.* For the first time in his solo recording career, he felt in control of the output. Also, for the

---

* The album was originally going to be titled *Crucified*. Then *America Eats Its Young*.

first time in his solo recording career, he felt genuinely happy with his own work. The folks at Interscope largely left him alone, and (at long last) trusted his judgment. "The result," said Cheo Hodari Coker, the renowned writer, "is what I consider the greatest music of his career."

Me Against the World isn't a good hip-hop album—it's elite. The fifteen tracks are introspective, sincere, precise. Tupac worked out of eleven different studios, utilizing seventeen different producers. Beforehand, Carsten "Soulshock" Schack, who coproduced the title track and "Old School," wondered whether Tupac would collaborate with a white producer. "He called me one day," Soulshock recalled, "and said, 'Get your fucking white ass in here.'" Watching Tupac spit lyrics felt spiritual. He was aware of everything going on in the studio, from a microphone shorting out to a mouse passing gas, and he wrote the entirety of "Old School" in less than a half hour, loaded up on a Texas-sized blunt. "He felt all that stuff his mom felt from back in the day when she was a Black Panther," Schack said. "He was almost vibrating as he rapped."

The producer Moe Z.M.D., who added his touch to three songs, presumed Tupac operated like any other musician. "I was wrong," he said. The two met up in Soundcastle Studio, in the Hollywood Hills, and Tupac was like a ferret hopped up on speed and an IV stream of Mountain Dew. "I'd never seen anything like it," Moe Z.M.D. recalled. "The dude would have three different studios going at the same time, and he would jump from one to the other to the other. He was making six, seven, eight songs in a day, and I was like, 'What *is* this?'"

Another producer, Brian Gallow, initially met Tupac inside Echo Sound Studios while working on an album with the reggae-funk artist Don Jagwarr. Tupac had a cameo on the song "Skank Wit' U," and he liked Gallow's spirit. "He wanted to hear some of my beats in the studio the next day," Gallow recalled. "So I play him a bunch of tracks. I mean, I'm hitting him with my best stuff. And then I come to this one little nothing interlude, and he's like, 'That's it! I like *that!*'" Gallow tried convincing Tupac there was better material. "Nope," Gallow said. "He wanted that."

The following morning Gallow's phone rang. It was Tupac—calling from his car, driving with cell phone in one hand, pen in the other. He had ripped open a paper supermarket bag and was writing lyrics to a song *while simultaneously* steering the vehicle *and* speaking to Gallow *and* smoking a Newport. "Sure enough, that evening he's back in the studio," Gallow said. "He's got two pieces of paper bag with writing all over them, and one piece of notebook paper. And he created fucking gold." The result was the song "Lord Knows."

The crown jewel of the album is "Dear Mama," a haunting ode to Afeni. "Pac used to make references to [the phrase] 'Dear Mama' in a lot of different songs and I'd always be like 'You know that's a song in itself,'" said Tony Pizarro, one of the track's producers. "And one day he was like, 'I got somethin' for that.' And he was like, 'Man, do you have "In My Wildest Dreams" by the Crusaders?' and I was like, 'Yeah.' So I got the track ready. Pac just came through and just dropped it and blessed it with them vocals."

The record dropped on March 14, 1995, making Tupac the first artist in music history to have an album reach number 1 on the *Billboard* 200 chart (it sold 240,000 copies in its opening week) while simultaneously sitting in a cell. Wrote Michael Saunders in *The Boston Globe*: "It's likely the rapper's promotional tour will be confined to a supervised walk between cellblocks." Reviewers mostly raved over the depth and texture of the music, and the *Rochester Democrat and Chronicle* headlined a sterling review with HE HAS LOST HIS FREEDOM, BUT 2PAC HAS FOUND HIS TALENT.

Indeed.

Despite his imprisonment, Tupac had plenty of people to celebrate with. His fiancée, Keisha Morris, relocated from New York City to an apartment near the prison, and on April 29 the two were wed inside Clinton's North Visiting Room in a ceremony officiated by a local justice of the peace named Ruth Snyder. Tupac enjoyed his bride's regular appearances during daily 8:45 a.m.–to–3:00 p.m. visiting hours (she brought him notebooks and cartons of Newports), but he confided in fellow inmates that his motivation was largely carnal (or, in layman's terms, he wanted to get laid on conjugal visits—which, he quickly learned, the prison did not actually allow), and if Morris thought her new husband would be a loyal spouse, she was being naïve.

Beginning with his early days as an inmate, Tupac (who was allowed only one phone call per month) wrote hundreds of letters. He received back even more. A handful were from male fans encouraging him to stay strong and keep his head up. Despite having never met Tupac, the actor Tony Danza penned a heartfelt note, urging him to straighten up ("I told him maybe there's a way to take into consideration the responsibility that comes with the influence you have," recalled Danza. "He wrote me back and told me he was glad I understand him. I was like, Hmm, maybe I need to write another letter"). Chuck D, the Public Enemy front man, also took time to pen his support ("I just wanted him to know people cared," Chuck D recalled. "It's easy in prison to lose humanity"). Tupac replied, writing, "I'm sure U know how highly respected and loved U R by me. So your letter definitely warmed my heart."

Mostly, however, the letters that arrived were from women. Many of the parcels featured either bras or panties (those were confiscated by the guards before Tupac received them). Even more included photographs of the half-naked (and fully naked) letter writers (Tupac kept those). That he was locked up for sexual assault seemed to be a nonissue. If a woman reached out to Tupac, and it was clear that she was hot, odds were high she would receive a handwritten reply from the man himself.

For example, while Tupac was still inside Rikers Island, a twenty-four-year-old Dunwoody, Georgia, woman named Angela Ardis made a bet with a coworker at her marketing job that she could write the rapper a letter and land a response. "Not that I thought I'd win," she recalled. "But it was a fun challenge."

Ardis penned a three-paragraph note that began warmly ("My name is Angela, and I am writing you this letter, not as a groupie, but just as a black female who thinks there is more to you than what the media portrays . . .") and ended with her phone number and an invitation to call. She sprayed the paper with her signature perfume (Perry Ellis 360) and included a photograph.

Less than a week later, Ardis returned home from work to a message on her answering machine. "Hey Angela. This is Tupac. I got your letter today and thought I'd call, but I guess you're not there."

Thus began a relationship via notes. Barely a month before his nuptials to Morris, Tupac wrote Angela a missive that read, in part,

"I miss looking at your picture and smelling your scent. I don't know why but I'm constantly thinking of you, wondering what you're doing and who you're doing it with. I know I have no right 2 be so inquisitive about your whereabouts but what can I say, a nigga miss u!"

At the same time Tupac was flirting with Ardis, he also wrote Simi Cruise, a twenty-two-year-old Canadian who lived in Los Angeles and worked at a clothing store. Like Ardis, Cruise was stunning. She and Tupac had initially made eye contact a year earlier when they were partying at Glam Slam, a downtown LA club owned by Prince. "You could tell he was interested," she recalled. "But I was shy and reserved. I figured he was a good guy, and when he went to prison I wanted to offer encouragement."

Cruise's first note also included a photograph, and Tupac—imprisoned, horny, alone—wrote back in bulk. Sometimes two letters in a day. On occasion, three. "Know that U R in my heart," he penned on August 26, 1995, "and I think of U often."

In another note, he sent Cruise a poem titled "How Can." It included the lines, "How can I hold your hands and kiss U softly / without making you fear me? / If I whispered promises in your ear / Is it possible you would hear me?"

It was intense.

"When he was in prison he said, 'I wanna have a child with you,'" Cruise recalled. "I was like, 'OK,' because I was completely in love with him. But I told him I wanted two children, because one would be lonely. And he was like, 'Yes, you've convinced me. Let's have two.'"

Ardis and Cruise were two of dozens of female Tupac pen pals.* His letters were almost always boyish and sexual, with more than a hint of desperation. He told the women he dreamed of their breasts, their smiles, their butts, their legs, their vaginas. He wanted to hold them, caress them,

---

* He even wrote a profound breakup note to Madonna, the superstar singer who viewed Tupac as little more than a fun fuck buddy. Wrote Tupac: "For you to be seen with a black man wouldn't in any way jeopardize your career if anything it would make you seem that much more open and exciting. But for me at least in my previous perception I felt due to my 'image' I would be letting down half of the people who made me what I thought I was." Madonna shrugged and moved on.

smother them, smell them, fuck them, and marry them. He wanted to know their deepest feelings. To look into their eyes and witness forever. "He was cheesy as hell," said Ardis. "But I loved it."

The marriage to Morris lasted a grand total of ten months before it was annulled, but in the Clinton notes Tupac reassured multiple women he had kicked his wife to the curb long ago ("Don't trip," he wrote Desiree Smith, another one of his girlfriends, post-annulment. "I'm not depressed. I'm happy almost. The jealousy and immaturity was too much").

Tupac's cousin Billy Lesane had actually spent time as a Clinton inmate four years earlier (he was in Clinton Annex, the adjacent minimum security facility), and now—with family in need—he stepped up. Two or three times per month, Lesane made the drive from New York City to a motel near the prison, and he visited Tupac and served as a personal pimp. "You'd have all these female fans writing him, begging to come see him," Lesane recalled. "So I'd arrange the travel, arrange the dates, make it happen."

With the directive "Don't fumble my hos!," Tupac gave Lesane specific instructions. He wanted the women to come at certain times, on certain days, and he wanted them dressed seductively. Though it was impossible to have sex in the visitors' room, he could hug, kiss, and (mildly) fondle. On her visit, Ardis was greeted not just by Lesane, but also by Mopreme Shakur, the stepbrother who was present for the shooting at the Marin City Festival. She knew nothing of his background. "They were very polite," Ardis said. "They knew I was there to see Tupac."

Entering the prison, Ardis recalled, was terrifying. She didn't know what to expect or how she would be treated. Seeing Tupac for the first time was mildly disappointing—his hair had grown in, his face was scruffy. Though his prison mug shot listed him at five foot eleven and 154 pounds, he was shorter (closer to five foot eight) and skinnier. He was sort of a runt. "The smile was there and the eyes were there," she said. "I kissed him, but that was it."

Cruise also visited, flying from Los Angeles to Buffalo and having Lesane pick her up for a weekend with Tupac. His eyes, she recalled, "were sparkling—and he was genuinely curious about me. He wasn't self-centered like people might think." He also had yet to end things with

Morris, and when she asked about it he replied, "I'm getting it annulled. As soon as I saw your picture I told another inmate, 'I'm not gonna be married for long.'"

"I didn't think it was slimy," Cruise recalled. "I thought it was sweet."

Two other people who visited were Afeni Shakur, Tupac's mother, and Yaasmyn Fula, the former Black Panther and longtime family friend. "Dear Mama," the first single off *Me Against the World*, was gaining traction, and the consensus was that Tupac's ode to his mom was perfection. "[It] is," wrote Michael Namikas, "unquestionably one of the most beautiful [songs] in rap music's 50 year history."

And yet, there was more to the tune and the mother-son dynamic. According to Fula, who became one of Tupac's closest confidantes, "Dear Mama" is less reality, more aspirational. Many of the lyrics are borderline fiction—"Even though I sell rocks / It feels good puttin' money in your mailbox" (Tupac never sold crack); "'Cause when I was low you were there for me" (she wasn't—and he was forever haunted by her absences); "You never left me alone, because you cared for me" (she left him alone for months, especially in Marin City); "And I could see you comin' home after work late / You're in the kitchen, tryin' to fix us a hot plate" (this was a rare occurrence—at best). In truth, "Dear Mama" is the story of the mother Tupac wanted to have, not the one he *did* have.*

In prison, the relationship with Afeni—who visited three or four times during her son's eight months behind bars—worsened. At the time, she was living in an apartment in Decatur, Georgia. The rent was being paid for by Tupac, who was also financing the residences and lifestyles of several other relatives. "So many people were dependent on him," Fula said, "when they should have been handling their own bills." Never adept at saving money, Tupac behind bars was broke. He had no income, very little liquidity, and a $3 million bail that felt unattainable. Wrote Jamie Foster Brown in *Sister 2 Sister* magazine, "Watani, Tupac's manager, says there is no money—with all the court cases, lawsuits and such, there is no money." Family members

---

* "That song is Tupac paying homage to how much he loved Afeni," said Kendrick Wells, his friend. "But she was not a good mother. It's just fantasy."

tossed around terms like "royalties" and "net growth" when it came to justifying their reliance on their favorite cash cow—knowing not whereof they spoke. Tupac told Foster Brown he evicted his relatives from the Lithonia, Georgia, home he had bought them: "My family didn't appreciate [it]," he said.

With each passing day, Tupac turned increasingly bitter toward his family. All they did was take. Did they care about him, or did they care about his dough? For all her street smarts, Afeni was clueless when it came to fiduciary issues, and presumed her son to be an ever-flowing fountain of fortunes. Tupac complained to Foster Brown that while he was rotting in a cell, his mother was crisscrossing America, giving speeches, and finalizing a book deal. "So Tupac is at Clinton, and Afeni had a photograph of a home she wanted to buy in Georgia," said Fula. "She knows I'm going to see him, so she asks me to show it to him and see if he will buy it for her. Well, I refuse. I don't wanna be showing him a picture of *your* house that *he'll* be paying for. No fucking way. So I didn't show him—but she told him about it. More than once. And, to be honest, it made me sick. Her son is trying to survive prison—which, Lord knows, isn't easy. And she's worried about him buying her a house. That's why I've always struggled with the 'Black queen' thing. Afeni was a great woman in so many ways. But she also was selfish and disappointing. Her life was damaged. That's not an excuse, but it's true."

Tupac engaged in many long discussions with Michael Christopher, the corrections officer, and he expressed frustration with Afeni. "In a lot of ways it felt like he hated his mother," Christopher recalled. "I guess, really, it was love-hate. He hated her for what she'd done to him and what she put him through. But he loved her because she was his mother."

Fula, on the other hand, was a rock. Shortly after his sentencing, Tupac asked her to handle his business affairs. The rapper valued loyalty, and Fula had known Tupac since he was an infant. Her son, Yafeu Akiyele Fula (aka Yaki Kadafi), was six years Tupac's junior, but a lifelong friend and member of a hip-hop group known as Dramacydal. Fula was as trustworthy as they came, and a Black Panther to the core. She had worked alongside Afeni as a paralegal at Bronx Legal Services, and in 1981 was imprisoned for eighteen months for refusing to testify before a federal grand jury against family and colleagues in a Brink's bank robbery. "She's the real deal," said Set Shakur, Tupac's sister. "She stood with our family for a long time."

Nearly every week of Tupac's incarceration, Fula made the 310-mile drive from her home in Montclair, New Jersey. There was much to discuss: his mental health, his behavior, the status of his bail, the status of his social life. "It was a lot of chaos and a lot of madness," she said. "Like when he ended his marriage, I was the one to get all the papers signed. He had bought her a car, and she was supposed to return all the property, the possessions. All that fell on me. I felt bad for Keisha. She wasn't his only girl. I had to clean that shit up."

One other thing that needed to be cleaned up was an emotional bruise that Tupac struggled to manage. His twenty-fourth birthday fell on Friday, June 16, and Father's Day came two days later. In the lead-up, Billy Garland, his biological father, requested permission to make a special visit. Despite initial reluctance ("Fuck that guy," Tupac told Fula), Tupac warmed to the idea. He wanted a dad in the worst possible way. The men had actually been exchanging letters, and Tupac was open to forging the tie he lacked. "Father's Day was very sensitive to Tupac, because he never had a father around and it coincided with his birthday," said Set Shakur. "So my mom and I went to see him in jail on his birthday, and he and my mother had an argument about Billy Garland. It got heated, and she left, but Tupac asked me to stick around."

Sitting across from her brother, Set was confused.

"What's going on?" she asked.

"My dad is coming to see me tomorrow [Father's Day] for my birthday," he said. "I want you to be there."

The next morning, the visitors' room opened at nine o'clock, and Set was one of the first in. Tupac was ushered out, and they hugged.

"What time is he coming?" she asked.

Tupac was unsure.

They waited. And waited.

"He never showed up," Set said. "Didn't come."

Tupac felt humiliated.

In prison, you learn to wrap your emotions in a bundle and reveal nothing. Tupac returned to his cell and—to the shock of his neighboring inmates—wept.

"It was," Set said, "unforgivable."*

If nothing else, prison gifts an inmate with plenty of time to think.

For Tupac, that meant thinking not only about the assault of Ayanna Jackson, but the shooting at Quad Studios. He could not get it out of his mind. It wasn't so much that he had been attacked, but that he had been attacked by those he considered his own. "My closest friends turned on me," he said. Dating back to boyhood, Tupac assumed the people out to get him were primarily white members of law enforcement. The police. The FBI. The CIA. The paranoia had been drilled home by Afeni and the other Black Panthers whose words he was raised to absorb.

"Up until I got shot, I thought that no Black person would ever shoot me," he said. "I was their representative. I believed that I didn't have to fear my own community. I represent them. I was their ambassador to the world."

In prison, Tupac's mental enemy list grew. First, there was Jacques Agnant. Second, there was James Rosemond. He knew in his gut those two had something to do with the setup. He also started to think differently of Randy "Stretch" Walker, the producer who was in the Quad Studios lobby yet somehow emerged unscathed. "He literally said to me, 'That nigger Stretch, it's his fault,'" recalled Vega. "I asked him what he meant and he was like, 'Stretch, that motherfucker, set it all up. As soon as I get home that nigger is done.'"

The man who earned most of Tupac's wrath, however, was not Stretch, but Christopher (Notorious B.I.G.) Wallace, the New York City rapper who had been in the studio that night.

"Man," said Vega, "Tupac *hated* Biggie."

Maybe it was the isolation. Maybe it was the loneliness. Maybe it was the wrong people whispering the wrong bits of information. Maybe it was drugs, lack of drugs, bad prison food, too many true crime novels. Maybe

---

* In a 2024 interview with the Art of Dialogue, Garland said he later visited Tupac at Clinton.

it was Tupac's lifelong need to find a foil. Whatever the case, Tupac went from initially liking Biggie to loving Biggie to becoming convinced—in every irrational way—that Biggie Smalls was intimately involved in his attempted murder.

It made zero sense.

When Tupac was shot in the Quad Studios lobby, Biggie was up above, smoking weed and helping create music. And even when that point was made to Tupac, it didn't stick. In Tupac's mind, it came down to this: Maybe Biggie didn't pull the trigger, but he certainly knew the men who did. So why didn't he say anything? At least warn him?

During her visit to Clinton, Simi Cruise vividly recalled Tupac steaming over Biggie. "He was *really* mad," she said. "He was basically saying, 'I let this guy with the dirty shoes sleep on my sofa, and this is how he thanks me?'"

Less than two months after Tupac was incarcerated in Clinton, Biggie reached out to Watani Tyehimba about visiting the prison to make good. Not all that long before, Tyehimba and Tupac had actually discussed trying to sign Biggie to a management contract. They knew he was represented by Puff Daddy and Andre Harrell, but Tyehimba believed they had a lot to offer. "Well, Pac had mixed feelings," Tyehimba said. "He wanted us to sign him, but make Biggie a member of the Outlawz [Tupac's subgroup]. My position was, Biggie didn't need to be an Outlaw. Biggie was Biggie. But Pac had a big ego. And he needed to be the only one to shine. He didn't want others shining with him."

Biggie stayed with his management team, but maintained good standing with his suitors. Now, via phone, he told Tyehimba that he would do whatever it took to help Tupac.

The next time Tyehimba spoke with his client, he told him about Biggie's desire to see him.

"I think it's a good idea," Tyehimba said.

"Fuck Biggie," replied Tupac.

"But . . ." Tyehimba said.

"No," said Tupac. "Fuck him."

"Pac and I disagreed about that," Tyehimba said. "Biggie had nothing to do with the shooting. I was literally going to take him to Clinton to sit down with Pac. Biggie felt bad about it. I don't know everything there is to know, but I know—with one hundred percent certainty—he wasn't involved."

On July 3, 1995, Jamie Foster Brown, an editor with the magazine *Sister 2 Sister*, visited Clinton for her Tupac sit-down. She asked, directly, "Why do you blame Biggie for getting you shot?"

He did not hold back: "How come he's the king of New York and I got shot in his studio session? Out on the West Coast, the gangs knew me and respected me. I knew who the gang members were on the West Coast. If something happened out there, I knew who did it and how it went down. A New York rapper had a hit on his life, I went to 60 gang members by myself and explained why they shouldn't kill my homeboy. B.I.G. wanted to get on my label. At the Palladium, I let him rap on my first show. I was buying food for him. B.I.G. had my album (*Me Against the World*) on tape, and I had his."

Decades later, one of Tupac's friends, who requested anonymity, had a different theory.

"He shot himself in the nuts," he said. "That's it. Do you think he could handle that level of embarrassment?

"Could anyone?"

Chapter 20

Out on Bail

Throughout his time languishing within the confines of Clinton Correctional Facility, one thing hung over Tupac: the bail.

The *fucking* bail.

The vast majority of his fellow inmates did not possess such a get-out-of-prison option. They were murderers, thieves, rapists, pedophiles facing locked-in sentences of ten, twenty, thirty, forty years. There was no chance someone with deep pockets would come along, for that was not a legal option. They were locked up. Period.

But Tupac . . . Tupac could, *conceivably*, be released. In May, a state judge knocked his bail down from $3 million to $1.4 million (pending his appeal), which, well, remained an enormous chunk of change. His relatives, he knew, did not have the funds. Neither did his friends. Plus, even though he desperately needed the dough, everyone was *still* begging him for handouts. Most people seemed far more interested in taking Tupac's (largely nonexistent) money than giving him something. "It was disgusting," said Yaasmyn Fula. "He was an ATM machine to them."

Back in California, Atron Gregory, the man who had initially signed Tupac and still served as part of his management team, was working on an appeal of the sentencing. He had filed paperwork shortly after Tupac entered Clinton, and had hoped for a quick resolution. Yet as the author Ryan Holiday correctly noted, "This is the nature of the American legal system. It's slow, adversarial." A three-judge panel would decide Tupac's fate, but in their own time. "Our lawyers finished the appeal and turned it in," Gregory recalled. "But it was summer, and the judges were on vacation at different times taking two and three weeks off."

Gregory did his best to keep Tupac abreast of what was transpiring. But inmate no. 95A1140 didn't want to hear it. He felt as if attorneys and judges and juries and the American legal system as a whole had let him down—so why would he place his faith in any of it now? Also, not for nothing, how much money had Interscope made on *Me Against the World*, the album that would soon clear two million copies sold? Surely, the record executives could afford $1.4 million. Surely, they could show up for him the way he showed up for them.

As his frustrations mounted, Tupac considered the merits of a man he didn't know well, but simultaneously respected and feared. Nearly three thousand miles away, in Los Angeles, Marion "Suge" Knight, the cofounder and CEO of Death Row Records, was in the midst of building what he believed to be a hip-hop empire. His label was home to such artists as Dr. Dre, Snoop Doggy Dogg, Nate Dogg, and the D.O.C., and back in 1994 he handed Tupac $200,000 to record two songs ("Life's So Hard" and "High 'Til I Die") for the *Murder Was the Case* soundtrack. Although the tracks wound up on the cutting-room floor, Knight paid Tupac in full—an act of generosity not forgotten. Also, before Tupac went to prison, Knight gifted him an eye-catching present—a bulletproof vest featuring the Death Row logo. "Tupac began to see Suge as a well-funded, well-armed potential ally," the author Ben Westhoff wrote in his book *Original Gangstas*. "While in prison [Tupac] asked his wife to relay a message to Suge: He was broke and needed help."

Knight sent a goodwill fifteen thousand dollars, with (it seemed) no strings attached. A giddy Tupac wrote Knight a letter, thanking him and requesting a prison visit. What Tupac didn't know was that Knight had already been making a not-so-subtle play for his services. Throughout the incarceration, he was lavishing Afeni and relatives with gifts, ranging from food baskets and bouquets of flowers to wads of money. "He was wooing the family," said Fula. "These were fairly simple people unaccustomed to gifts like that. They took them, but they didn't realize what they were dealing with."

In the late summer of 1995, Knight traveled via private plane to Dannemora to sit with Tupac in the Clinton visitation room. He wasn't there to talk business or contracts or a possible Death Row future.

Nope—he was there because he cared. Or at least seemed to care. Or at least wanted to show he cared. Or at least—eh, maybe he cared, maybe he didn't. But he made the trip. "Suge was what you call a button pusher," said the rapper Smooth B. "He knew which buttons to push." Another visit followed. Then another. At a time when many of Tupac's closest peers had seemed to forget his existence, Suge Knight was there, with a smile and promises of better days. Before long, Knight and Death Row's head attorney, David Kenner, were whispering sweet nothings in Tupac's ear about the very thing he most craved: freedom.

We will get you your freedom.

"Well, here's the thing," said Atron Gregory. "We were working on a bail package, and we finally had it in place. Warner Bros. [which owned Interscope] was part of it, but we also had other people who put money in. It's up to them if they want to say who they are.* But it was in place. Now, did Tupac know all of this? I would think so, because Watani [Tyehimba] and I were always pretty clear giving him information. But did he want to hear it? Did he believe it? I honestly don't know. But anyone who says we weren't working on it has absolutely no idea what they're talking about. I'd been with Tupac for a long time. I loved him. The narrative that we ignored him is nonsense."

On the morning of September 16, Tyehimba and a handful of colleagues traveled to Dannemora to meet with Tupac and explain that his release was imminent; that a few details needed to be worked out, but the bail money was good to go and he would be free within a few weeks. The men made it to the prison as soon as visiting hours commenced at 8:45 a.m., but Charles Ogletree, an attorney assisting in the effort, was late. "So we're there," recalled Tyehimba, "and we're waiting. And Suge Knight and David Kenner arrive to visit Tupac. Now, I don't know anything about those people. I certainly don't know what they're up to. So I say, 'We're waiting for someone. Y'all can go on in first.' And I let them go ahead of us."

It was, Tyehimba later admitted, one of the great mistakes of his life.

---

* According to Watani, among those who contributed to the cause were Madonna and Jasmine Guy.

Michael Christopher, the CO who had a good relationship with Tupac, vividly remembered Knight and Kenner arriving. "I've seen many men bulk up in prison," he recalled. "But, honestly, Suge was the biggest guy I had ever seen. His shoulders were four feet apart at least. He stood six feet plus, bald head, neatly dressed in fresh blue jeans and a bright red shirt, with a neatly groomed beard. He and Kenner walked up to my desk and stood silent before me with a blank expression. Before I could say anything to them, Pac jumped up from his visiting table and met them at the desk. I just looked up at Suge and thought, 'Holy shit.'"

Knight and Kenner entered the visitors' room armed with a four-page handwritten note ("standing in for a contract," wrote Westhoff) that designated Suge Knight Tupac's new manager and lassoed him to Death Row for three albums. According to Westhoff, the document also guaranteed an advance of at least $1 million per album and $500,000 in expenses (including $125,000 for a car and $250,000 for his legal fund). It also would pay for a house for Afeni—something she had discussed with Knight behind her son's back. "Afeni became very enamored with Suge, because he'd been sending her and the family money and material possessions," said Fula. "She very much wanted Tupac to sign with him, and definitely pressured him to do it. Afeni was smart. But she could definitely be manipulated. She was all in on Suge Knight, even though she didn't know what he *really* represented."

Knight and Kenner wrapped their time with Tupac, walked by Tyehimba, Ogletree, and the gang, waved warmly, and exited with an extra pep in their step. Tupac Shakur—*the* Tupac Shakur!—was coming to Death Row. "So we finally sit across from Tupac," said Tyehimba, "and it wasn't great."

TYEHIMBA: "Pac, how's it going?"
TUPAC: "I'm going to sign with Death Row."
   Silence.
TYEHIMBA: "You're doing what?"
TUPAC: "I'm signing with Suge and Death Row."
   More silence.
TYEHIMBA: "You know I can't ride with you on that, right?"

TUPAC: "Come on, man. We're family."

Even more silence.

TYEHIMBA: "I'm sorry, Pac. But you're on your own."

Tupac returned to his cell certain he made the right move. Suge Knight was liberating him. Somehow, some way, he had made it happen when all others failed.

Only . . . it was sort of bullshit.

"Tupac," said Shawn Chapman Holley, an attorney who later represented him, "sold his soul to the devil."

Death Row Records was, technically, owned and managed by Interscope, the outfit that released Tupac's three solo CDs as well as the Thug Life album. But there was little to no oversight. Death Row made Interscope loads of money. That was the bottom line. Plus, ever since Interscope signed Tupac in 1991, he had been far more annoyance than value. Sure, *Me Against the World* was selling well. But the erratic behavior, the crassness, the antics, the shootings, the accusations, the misogyny, the sexual assault allegations, the arrests—what, exactly, was the ultimate gain for a label that didn't need to be bogged down by one irksome presence? Yes, Tupac was a big name. But where was the bang for the buck? "The main problem was, you never knew which Tupac you were going to get," said Lori Earl, a longtime Interscope publicist. "He was a lightning rod for controversy, and I'm not sure the label enjoyed that."

For Interscope, this wasn't a difficult decision: With—as Westhoff noted—"shuffling paperwork," it could turn Tupac over to Death Row, thereby still making money off his music without having his conduct drag down the Interscope name and image. And while Knight took all the credit for Tupac's soon-to-be liberation, it was largely bluster. The $1.4 million bond required for bail was put up by Interscope and Time Warner (the parent company)—not Knight and not Death Row. In fact, the $1.4 million wasn't, as Tupac believed, a gift of generosity and kindness. The dough was an advance on future album royalties. Tupac was paying his own bail with money he had yet to earn.

"Suge took a lot of credit," said Tyehimba. "Because that's what Suge did. But it was absolute bullshit. Tupac was the kind of person who would say, 'Death Row bailed me out!' And I understand why he thought that. He was naïve. Suge played him."

On the early afternoon of October 12, 1995, Tupac Shakur's $1.4 million bail was officially paid, and the following day he finally exited Clinton Correctional Facility. Before leaving he passed Fama, who yelled from behind his bars, "Keep your head up, Pac!"

Save the notepads he stuffed into a black backpack, Tupac left his possessions—toothbrush, shampoo bottles, pens, books—behind in his cell. He turned in his green prison pants and changed into baggy blue jeans, a white sweatshirt, and a Los Angeles Dodgers cap. Out front he was greeted by a white limousine, stocked with bottles of Alizé and paid for by Death Row (well, by Tupac's future earnings). There to greet him were, among others, Fula and Tyruss "Big Syke" Himes, his friend and co-rapper from Thug Life, who was sent on Suge Knight's behalf. The two embraced in an enormous hug, and tears streamed down Tupac's cheeks. His smile was wide, his mood euphoric. There had come a point, during the grayest and coldest of days, when he wondered if he would ever make it back to liberation. Clinton has a way of suffocating hope. Now, he was out. He entered the vehicle and Syke passed him a plantain-sized blunt. Each hit felt like freedom.

Over the course of several decades, it has been relayed that a chartered jet awaited Tupac and Syke at nearby Plattsburgh Airport. This was true, but only to fly them the forty-five minutes to New York City's John F. Kennedy Airport. From there, they boarded a United 747 to Los Angeles, where, at the conclusion of the five-and-a-half-hour trip, they were met by Reggie Wright Jr., Death Row's head of security, and Kevin Hackie, a label bodyguard. Embraces ensued, then a trip to Monty's Steakhouse, the swank SoCal fixture (and home to a fabled twenty-two-ounce steak) atop the Westwood Center building. There was eating and drinking, and after two hours Wright drove the crew to Can-Am Recorders, the studio located at 18730 Oxnard Street in Tarzana that Death Row called its own.

This is where Knight planned a grand welcome.

"Well, Tupac is so high and drunk, he gets there and passes out," Wright recalled. "Like, drops to the floor and he's gone. And Suge just looked at him, the way Suge looks at people. And he says, 'I've been paying all this money. And *this* is what it gets me?'"

Knight laughed it off.

He knew exactly what Death Row would be getting.

Suge Knight's first name is Marion.

In the history of tough guy incongruity, this ranks right up there with Mike Tyson's effeminate lisp and Arnold Schwarzenegger's enjoying pedicures. Men like Knight—six foot two, well over three hundred pounds, with a serial killer scowl and a reputation for dangling unfortunate souls by the ankles off skyscraper balconies—are named Butch and Spike and Mongo.

Not "Marion."

But this was the decision made by his parents, Marion and Maxine Knight, and they were unwavering. On April 19, 1965, Maxine brought into the world a son who would share an identity with both his father and grandfather.

He would be the third Marion.

The name, however, didn't really stick. As an infant the newest Marion Hugh Knight was bequeathed with an *even wimpier* moniker by his father: "Sugar Bear"—in honor of his striking resemblance to the Post Super Sugar Crisp cereal mascot of the same name. Ultimately, "Sugar Bear" was shortened to "Suge."

Though (like Tupac, perhaps not coincidentally) he worked to convince people he came from a hardened background of fisticuffs and drug slinging, Sugar Bear's boyhood in Compton, California, was largely idyllic. His family home, at 1617 South Orange Street, was 1,604 square feet, with three bedrooms, two bathrooms, and a grass-coated front yard. "The neighborhood was beautiful," said Solomon Wilcots, a childhood friend who went on to play six NFL seasons. "We all had bikes, the lawns were manicured. Compton then isn't Compton now." There was always a hot meal on the table come dinnertime. Sugar Bear's family stressed academics, and he was a sound student. He played every sport under the sun (football was a love) as well as multiple instruments. "His family wasn't this stereotypical negative image—like the father's gone, the mother is on drugs, or he was gangbanging," said Vernard Bonner, a childhood friend. "Suge wasn't gangbanging."

"He later built an image as a fake gangbanger," said James "Mob James" McDonald, who grew up around the corner as a member of the Mob Piru gang. "But it was a joke. Suge has never sat on the corner drinking beer. Suge never walked to school with us while some of the homies smoked weed and some of the homies were drinking. Suge has never shot at a moving car. Suge has never gotten on a bicycle to go to different neighborhoods to fight. Fuck, your name isn't even Suge. It's Marion. Can you believe that shit?"

In 1983, after graduating from Lynwood High (where, at halftime of home games, he dashed out of the locker room—dressed in his football gear—to play drums in the marching band), he joined the football team at nearby El Camino Junior College, where over two seasons he emerged as one of America's dominant JUCO defensive linemen. That resulted in a full athletic scholarship to UNLV (University of Nevada, Las Vegas) and—for the first time—a life away from home.

On the field, Knight was everything Harvey Hyde, the Rebels' head coach, had wanted. "Guys from the inner city often have a motor because they need to make it out," recalled Hyde. "That was Suge." Like many of the Rebels, Knight was a steroid user, and the combination of dogged-ness and juice made him a pass-rushing terror. Off the field, he was . . . a mixed bag. Sugar Bear, according to UNLV quarterback Steve Stallworth, was the first to show up for the team's Fellowship of Christian Athletes meetings. "I don't remember him not coming to chapel," Stallworth said. But there was a flip side. One night, midway through Knight's senior year, Stallworth told him somebody had stolen the ring he earned in UNLV's Cal Bowl triumph over Toledo. Stallworth suspected the culprit to be a former teammate. "We're going to his house," Knight told Stallworth. "I'm gonna knock on his door, take him into the kitchen, knock him around a little bit, and let the motherfucker know what's up. When I'm doing that, you find the ring."

"I was a white kid from Yuma, Arizona," Stallworth recalled with a laugh. "This wasn't my comfort zone."

While in Nevada, Sugar Bear picked up gigs as a bouncer along the Strip. "Suge was a go-to guy to put damage in," said Greg Holder, a former football teammate who later worked for Death Row. "So now you have a twenty-year-old kid at UNLV being paid to do certain violent things to people. Not killing, just beating people up. He liked that."

Knight had dreams of winding up in the NFL, but went ignored in all twelve rounds of the 1987 NFL Draft. Following the third week of the season, however, the players went on strike. The league decided to continue with replacements, and Knight's hometown team, the Los Angeles Rams, offered a contract. The scabs played three games, and Knight appeared in two of them, contributing little. One of his teammates was Bernard Quarles, a quarterback who jumped from the Canadian Football League to the replacement Rams. The men shared an agent, and Quarles recalled Sugar Bear to be "a cool guy, a pretty good player. But what I remember most is he was looking for some investors because he had an idea about getting into music and representing artists."

At the time, twenty-seven-year-old replacement quarterbacks weren't rolling in dough.

"I passed," Quarles said.

"In hindsight, that might have been a mistake."

When the strike ended and the NFL regulars returned, Sugar Bear was released. Over the next half year, he devoted himself to building up a rap sheet—among other things, he was charged with domestic violence after grabbing the hair of a girlfriend and chopping her ponytail off and arrested in Las Vegas for shooting a man in the leg and wrist and stealing his Nissan Maxima.

"You have to understand, Suge was not—and I mean *not*—a gangster," said Wilcots, his childhood friend. "But I'm sure he wanted to make more money than his parents had. Some guys do it the right way. Some guys do it by any means necessary. Which was Suge? I'm not sure."

At this point, a Los Angeles native named Wes Crockett came into Knight's life. The head of security for dozens of musical acts, Crockett hired Knight as a bodyguard for Bobby Brown, the former New Edition crooner. Brown had recently been threatened by some drug dealers, and

Crockett told Knight to handle it. "Suge does whatever he does, and the drug dealers actually apologize to Bobby," said Reggie Wright Jr., a Compton police officer who later became the head of Death Row's security. "I don't know what Suge did, but he got the message across."

Big Wes connected Knight with Dick Griffey, a producer and concert promoter whose label, Solar Records, featured acts ranging from the Whispers to Babyface. Twenty-seven years Knight's senior, Griffey found his new protégé to be a sponge. Say something once, the kid picked it up. "Dick Griffey taught Suge everything he knew," said Bonner, Knight's friend. "He learned about contracts, artist relations. Suge was always intimidating. That came naturally. Once he got the business side down—watch out."

Under Griffey's wing, Knight promoted shows in and around Los Angeles. His initial plan was to represent comedians and athletes, but music presented more opportunities. In 1990, he formed his own music publishing company. One of Knight's first clients was Mario "Chocolate" Johnson, a Dallas-based rapper and producer who wrote the lyrics to Vanilla Ice's "Ice Ice Baby," but received little compensation. Knight paid Vanilla Ice a visit and—depending on who you believe—either (a) suspended him from his ankles off a hotel balcony, (b) had his colleagues suspend him from his ankles off a hotel balcony, or (c) merely terrified the hell out of him. Either way, thanks to Knight, Johnson wound up with publishing money. "Suge kept serious guys around him," said Sean "Barney" Thomas, a Death Row producer. "Guys with names like Neck Bone and Heron who did fifteen, twenty years. Murderers, drug dealers. Problems got handled."

Around this time, Dr. Dre, a founding member of N.W.A, sought an escape from his contract with Ruthless Records. According to court documents, Knight drove to the Ruthless office accompanied by four men, four baseball bats, and four lead pipes. "I know you've heard all the stories," Knight told *The New York Times*. "But you have to realize one thing: results."

Dr. Dre was released, and he and Knight teamed to form Death Row Records.

Before long, thanks to the powers of aggressiveness and intimidation and hustle, Knight was a hip-hop kingpin. Death Row's first release was

The Chronic, the 1992 Dr. Dre album that has sold more than 5.3 million copies. Wrote Lynn Hirschberg in *The New York Times*: "Death Row was the first rap label to get its videos in regular rotation on MTV and the first to crossover into pop radio. And that was pure Suge. From the start, he was on top of everything at Death Row—from choosing artwork, promotional materials, singles and the track for the B side, to hiring the video director and the girls to be in the video, to deciding where the party should be and who should be invited, to what Snoop should wear. All of this is about shaping street culture for consumption by the youth of America, which is Suge's real genius."

And now, at long last, Tupac was a member of the Death Row family.

In so many ways, he encompassed all that Knight wanted from his label. He was an artist who oozed authenticity. Who spoke on behalf of the streets. And even if, like Knight himself, Tupac wasn't an actual gangbanger, he played the part well. Hell, he was exiting maximum security prison. What could be more real?

For his part, in public Knight sported an enormous diamond-and-ruby ring that spelled M.O.B.—an acronym for "Money Over Bitches," the LA street gang (representing Compton, where he grew up) better known as Mob Piru. Knight was never an actual member of Mob Piru. Not growing up, not at UNLV, not in adulthood. "He wasn't built to be a street dude," said McDonald, the former Mob Piru member. "Growing up, Suge never carried a pistol, carried a bandanna, wore a hat that said PIRU, wore a shirt that said PIRU CRIP KILLER on it. He was soft as bare pussy." But, with Death Row, Knight hired Pirus to work for the label, thereby giving off a far-too-real edginess. "I always felt it was a role he played," said Darryl "Big D" Harper, a Death Row producer. "He had the money to live out the fantasy. Where others earn street reps, Suge bought his." Knight's office was painted red—Mob Piru color. The Death Row logo was printed on the red carpet, and stepping on it (even inadvertently) brought forth a beatdown. His suits were red. ("Before he started pretending, Suge had one suit," McDonald said. "And it was green.") His shoes were red. He smoked fat cigars in the presence of others, reveling in the power.

OUT ON BAIL   333

"It was a record label," said Harper, "and also the mafia."

There were no light moments in the presence of Suge Knight. He dripped intensity. When employees angered him, he made them stand in the corner. When a songwriter underperformed, he snarled, "Write a hit, or get hit." Answer the phone incorrectly and earn a smack across the forehead. An office closet stocked baseball bats, and they were not for the company picnic. Daz Dillinger, the producer (and member of Tha Dogg Pound), compared working at Death Row to prison. "People got pissed on, they got their ass whupped, they opened their butt cheeks, they did all kinds of shit," said McDonald. "At Death Row, you were there to humiliate people. It's my job to show you that you don't mean shit."

Roy Tesfay, who served as Knight's assistant, recalled the end of his job interview, when he was escorted toward a large window and offered the position with a warning. "We don't fire niggas here," Knight told him. "We throw niggas out windows."

Two months before Tupac's release from Clinton, Knight attended the Source Awards at New York City's Paramount Theater. While accepting the award for Motion Picture Soundtrack of the Year (for *Above the Rim*) on what was supposed to be a light and celebratory night, Knight leaned into the microphone and let loose. "I'd like to tell Tupac, keep his guard," he said. "We ridin' wit 'em. And one other thing I'd like to say. Any artist out there that want to be an artist and want to stay a star, and don't have to worry about the executive producer trying to be all in the videos, all on the record, dancing . . . come to Death Row." It was a shot at Sean "Puffy" Combs, Bad Boy CEO and partner to the Notorious B.I.G. It also was a message to Tupac, who was watching the show from prison—*your enemies are our enemies.*

Later that night, two white men in a taxi rolled down the window at a stoplight and spit on the Death Row limousine. The doors opened. "Everyone got out, pulled those two from their car and just kicked their asses," recalled Harper. "Suge preached to us that whenever anything happened, we were not just Death Row family, but Death Row bodyguards. You were supposed to die for the label."

On the night of his release, after drinking and smoking and stopping at Monty's Steakhouse and passing out at Can-Am, Tupac slept for several hours on a studio couch—then rose up, phoenix-like, itching to work. A black backpack held his notebooks, and they were stuffed with poems, rhymes, ideas for songs, concepts for movies. It was everything he'd written inside his cell, and what inmate no. 95A1140 had created was of a different stratosphere. Much of the material had been thought up sober, and it was piercing, intense, inventive, real. It was storytelling 101, as much Nina Simone and Joni Mitchell as Dr. Dre and Snoop Doggy Dogg.

During an April interview with *Vibe*'s Kevin Powell inside Rikers Island, Tupac had sworn off Thug Life, insisting, "It was just ignorance. My intentions was always in the right place. I never killed anybody, I never raped anybody, I never committed no crimes that weren't honorable—that weren't to defend myself. So that's what I'm going to show them. I'm going to show people my true intentions, and my true heart. I'm going to show them the man that my mother raised. I'm going to make them all proud." But, like many thoughts that raced through Tupac's frontal lobe, the idea of ditching Thug Life came and (poof!) went as soon as Suge showed interest. Death Row wasn't looking for someone to perform the greatest hits of Tommy Sands. The label added Tupac to send a hyper-specific message. He *was* Thug Life.

One of the men inside the Can-Am studio was Harper, a Death Row producer who knew not what to expect. Harper was accustomed to rappers laying down a track or two, then taking off. Tupac started recording seven songs that night. *Seven.* And he wrote many of the lyrics *in real time.* Literally in front of Harper, with a paper and pen. Tupac's process went thus: I have a thought. I will jot it down. It will be a song. "It was insanity," Harper said. "He was, like, finishing a song and saying, 'Put something else up! Let's get another one going!' He was on the engineers like a gangsta—'Man, listen to me. Mix this one that way, not your way! Just listen to me!' He was a ball of fire. A genius. There are a lot of people who have wit and poise, and they're wordsmiths. But he was just a thinker at a different level. He was Bob Dylan, but in hip-hop."

"I thought, How does he do this? So many times," said Mike Mosley, a producer on the album. "Like, Bro, you just wrote that twenty seconds ago. How are you able to make it sound like you've been performing it for years?"

The first two recoded songs were "Ambitionz az a Ridah" and "I Ain't Mad at Cha"—and the dichotomy was striking. Produced by Daz Dillinger, a member of Tha Dogg Pound and one of the label's superstar beat makers, "Ambitionz az a Ridah" took Tupac an hour to write in his jail cell, and for a man who had recently sworn off Thug Life, the lyrics are *something*. The opening lines—"I won't deny it, I'm a straight ridah / You don't wanna fuck with me / Got the police bustin' at me / But they can't do nothin' to a G"—make clear what's coming. It's a manifesto of his life's travails. Or, as Michael Namikas wrote: "'Ambitionz' sounds like a state of the union address, setting the tone for the rest of the album . . . his anger is palpable. He rails at those responsible for the Quad Studios robbery and promises revenge against those who did him harm . . . the 'thug' persona dominating prior albums shares center stage."

Those fortunate enough to be at Can-Am to witness Tupac's Death Row debut were stopped in their tracks. Many in attendance were music lifers. They had seen great artists record great music. But this was different. This was therapy. Angry, disgusted, enraged, volatile therapy. Behind the mic, Tupac was a typhoon of marijuana and Newport smoke and spittle. He could not stand still—a Vaslav Nijinsky diorama of twitching muscles and blurred hands. "You felt like crying," said Harper. "It wasn't music. It was *pain*."

"I Ain't Mad at Cha" was to "Ambitionz" what a meditative circle is to a Molotov cocktail. Twelve years earlier, while showering in her North Hollywood apartment, Bunny DeBarge, lone female member of the five-sibling R&B group DeBarge, was consumed by a beautiful melody that popped into her head. "I'm lathering shampoo," she recalled, "and I'd been working on some lyrics, but I didn't have the music. Then it appeared. The bass, the harmony, everything. I turned the water off, dried myself, and found a tape recorder to sing into."

The resulting tune, "A Dream," is one of DeBarge's staple releases, with an irresistible hook that's been utilized in dozens of hip-hop songs. Entranced by the sound, Dillinger used it as the interpolation, and as soon as Tupac heard the opening three or four beats—in the words of Kurupt, another Death Row producer—"He flipped out."*

But while the music felt heavenly, the writing was James Baldwin-esque. Like many of his offerings, "I Ain't Mad at Cha" touched on death and mortality. Initially thought up inside his Clinton cell, the song references (without naming names) at least a half dozen people from his life—including Baltimore's Dana "Mouse" Smith ("Now we was once two niggas of the same kind") and John Cole ("We used to be like distant cousins . . ."), an old Marin running buddy named Mike Cooley ("Congratulations on the weddin', I hope your wife know / She got a playa for life, and that's no bullshittin'"), his cousin Kenneth Lesane ("Oh, you a Muslim now? No more dope game"), and his ex-wife Keisha Morris ("And even though we separated, you said that you'd wait"). "It's one of the most beautiful, powerful things ever written," said Tracy Robinson, who directed several Tupac music videos. "Every word carries weight."

Tupac recorded "I Ain't Mad at Cha" in the blink of an eye. Nearly three decades later, many consider it not merely his finest work, but one of the greatest hip-hop songs of all time.

Death Row pulled out all the stops for Tupac.

For the first two and a half months of his time out of Clinton, the label paid for his penthouse suite at the Peninsula Beverly Hills. It paid for his meals, his wardrobe, his security detail, his weed, and his cartons of Newports. It paid for strip club lap dances and fancy shindigs and anything Tupac desired. It bought him a Jaguar (OK, it was leased—not that anyone told Tupac), then a Mercedes (also leased—not that anyone told Tupac) and a midnight-blue Rolls-Royce (also leased—not that anyone told Tupac). Suge introduced Tupac to Mark Mahoney, his Los Angeles tattoo guy, and footed the bill for new ink. Knight oftentimes summoned

---

* A dizzying number of songs are sampled on *All Eyez on Me*. The title track, for example, uses "Never Gonna Stop," written by J. P. Pennington of the Kentucky-based country group Exile. "I can't say the lyrical content is something I would write," Pennington said in 2024. "But when I badly needed money, a check for sixty-seven thousand dollars arrived in the mail. If I had known what that song would have done for me, I would have at least sent Tupac some flowers. I really owe him."

Maloney to Can-Am, where he would set up shop and tattoo artists on the spot. "Before Pac, I was tattooing five or six Black people per year," Mahoney said. "Once he showed up, half my clientele became Black musicians."

In return, Suge Knight expected magic.

Adding Tupac to Death Row wasn't the equivalent of an NBA team acquiring a new shooting guard to slide into the rotation. No, Tupac was—in Knight's eyes—gangsta rap's Michael Jordan. Sure, the label already had Dr. Dre and Snoop Doggy Dogg. But both artists, to Knight, lacked what Tupac possessed in droves: *a big motherfucking dick*. He would say anything, do anything, stand up to anyone. "Snoop and Dre went from being the main men at Death Row to almost feeling invisible," said Harper. "Pac came with an energy nobody could match."

Six days into his liberation, Tupac sat down with Chuck Philips of the *Los Angeles Times* for his first post-release interview. They met inside Can-Am, and Tupac—wearing a baggy sweatsuit and red bandanna— told Philips he had already completed fourteen songs for what would ultimately be a double album. "Shakur comes across as a man of many contradictions," Philips wrote. "Someone who has the words *thug life* tattooed across his stomach but complains about being misrepresented by the media as a gangsta rapper."

The Shakur before Philips was introspective and relieved. "It was tough sitting in jail listening to Jay Leno and Rush Limbaugh and everybody making jokes about me getting shot," he confessed. He praised God for sparing his life after the Quad Studios shooting, raved about Don McLean and *Les Misérables* and Shakespeare ("He wrote some of the rawest stories, man"), argued that "not all women are pure and true," and promised, "You're going to feel the entire 11 months of what I went through on this album. I'm venting my anger." Tupac, the piece emphasized, was a man who did not expect to live a long life and planned to maximize his remaining days. "He knew he would die young," said Mike Mosley. "He thought every day might be his last day."

Over the course of a three-month span, Tupac recorded new songs at a breakneck pace. He didn't live in the studio, but it often felt as if he did. Sessions could run fifteen, sixteen, seventeen hours. Can-Am was home to two recording booths, and Tupac infuriated other artists by simultaneously occupying both. With a blunt or Newport in one hand and a bottle of Hennessy in the other, he bounded back and forth—screaming, "Hold it, motherfucker!" to one producer and "Let's get going, motherfucker!" to the other. His diet was packed with Death Row staples: Chinese takeout, macaroni and cheese, candied yams, wings, Sunkist orange soda, supermarket cookies, Doritos, Apple Jacks, cinnamon buns.

"Sometimes it'd be ten, ten thirty at night and Tupac would say, 'Yo, I'm gonna take a break and go to the club,'" recalled Troy Stanton, a Death Row sound engineer. "I'd be like, 'OK, see you tomorrow.' And he'd say, 'No, no. I'm coming back! Don't go nowhere!'" Those who turned to Knight for help reasoning with the artist's erratic nature had no luck—Tupac was priority numbers 1, 2, 3, 5, and 100. What he wanted, he received. The studio was always stocked with his necessities. Drink—check. Cigs—check. Weed—check. Women—check. His mood fluctuated by the minute. So did his behavior. And judgment. He was often surrounded by small armies of groupies and hangers-on—people there to sing his praises, fetch his bud, offer a quick blow job or closet fuck. You never knew who might accompany him. Lisa "Left Eye" Lopes of TLC made appearances. So did Jasmine Guy. Death Row had recently signed MC Hammer off the rap scrap heap, and Tupac enjoyed having him nearby. It was a carnival of the weird and famous. Bodyguards, aspiring rappers, strippers, drug dealers. One day, while taking a break from recording, Tupac spotted Terrance, Harper's eleven-year-old son, in the studio kitchen holding a can of Coca-Cola.

"You thirsty, little man?" Tupac asked.

Terrance explained that a woman in an adjacent room asked him to fetch her a drink.

"Man," Tupac said, "we don't run for the bitches. The bitches run for us. From now on, little man, you can have that bitch go get her own shit."

"I nearly lost my mind when I heard that," Harper recalled. "Who says that to a little kid?"

Another time, Tupac was laying down a track as Terrance Downs, a member of the Death Row group Six Feet Deep, lingered nearby. A Morehouse College graduate with a degree in philosophy, Downs fit Death Row like a mitten on a porcupine. He heard Tupac unfold a lyric and couldn't help himself. "Technically," Downs said, "that line is grammatically incorrect. It should be . . ."

"What'd you say?" Tupac snarled.

The room went silent.

"Fuck that!" Tupac barked. "Keep that shit to yourself!"

Downs shuffled off.

Tupac's producer of choice was Johnny "J," who had broken onto the scene six years earlier by producing *Ain't No Shame in My Game*, the debut album from the South Central rapper Candyman. Tupac and Johnny "J" first joined forces in 1993 for a pair of terrific songs, "Pour Out a Little Liquor" and "Death Around the Corner." Tupac's reaction to producers had been mixed. Some were great, some were trash. He looked back at his debut album, *2Pacalypse Now*, in horror at the shoddiness of the overall sound. But Johnny "J" was different. A Los Angeles native who'd turned down a full scholarship to the Berklee College of Music in Boston to try and make it on his own, he grasped Tupac. He could feel his moods, read beneath his lyrics, understand what he wanted from a song. They shared a connection, not unlike a veteran pitcher and his preferred catcher. "Me and you are gonna be the new L.A. [Reid] and Babyface," Tupac told him. "I'm gonna be the lyrics, you're gonna be the music." Like Tupac, Johnny "J" went through intense highs and lows. He was a musical savant who hated much of his own work. During his time at Can-Am with Tupac, Johnny "J" learned he had been adopted as an infant. He was twenty-six, and the news was a punch to the gut. Tupac embraced him in a tight hug while offering a sincere "We're all damaged—fuck it. Let's make a great album."

They made a great album.

"[Johnny's] music was West Coast," the artist Lil Eazy-E once told the author Jake Brown. "And he would bring in live instruments, which made you feel the tracks. You really felt that guitar as opposed to some producers who just use a fucking keyboard. It was straight real." Tupac insisted to Knight that Johnny "J" carry a heavy influence on his new material. Ultimately, that meant producing a whopping twelve tracks, including three—"All About U," "How Do U Want It," and "Life Goes On"—that would chart. Tupac enjoyed very few genuinely close relationships, but Johnny "J" was akin to a musical twin. On multiple occasions the two logged forty-eight-straight-hour studio sessions. Sleep was rare. Minimal food was digested. It was record, stop, record some more, stop. Argue, agree, argue, agree. Piss, shit, write. One song, two songs, three songs. "Suge saw Death Row as having the potential to replace Motown," said Jake Brown. "And, to him, Tupac was his Stevie Wonder meets Michael Jackson. Because this guy was so prolific, and Johnny could keep up with him."

During this period, Doug Rasheed, an on-the-rise producer who, a few months earlier, had worked on the monster Coolio hit "Gangsta's Paradise," had a brother dating a Death Row employee. She passed some of his music to Tupac, including a raunchy song, "Funking Up the Backseat," that he had written for a recently defunct group, Human Dogg.

"Two days later my phone rings, and it's Tupac," Rasheed said.

He recalled the conversation like this:

TUPAC: "Yo, it's Tupac!"

RASHEED: "Hey. Glad you're out."

TUPAC: "Thanks. Listen, I heard the tape, man, and I wanna turn this shit into a song!"

RASHEED: "Oh, sweet. When?"

TUPAC: "Right now!"

Rasheed was working in a different studio and could not get to Can-Am until the next morning. But he jotted down notes and—in some spare time—recorded some of what Tupac wanted and messengered the tracks to Death Row. When he finally showed up at Can-Am, Rasheed was accompanied by his friend Anthony Forté, better known as the rapper Rappin' 4-Tay.

"Yo, 4-Tay!" Tupac screamed. "You've gotta be on this song!"

Rasheed brought with him all of his own equipment—not just drum machines, but a guitar, a bass, multiple keyboards. "Dude, I've never seen someone just carry all his own shit with him," Tupac said. "That speaks to your game."

Rasheed set up and, after a few minutes, laid down an instrumental version of "Funking Up the Backseat." Tupac watched, taking mental notes.

"So then Pac goes in to record the other verses for the song," Rasheed recalled. "And the vocal booth is dark. Just a little bit of light. And . . . I don't understand how he did what he did. I mean, I've seen guys write music, and they toil over the lyrics. But Tupac—he writes it like it's water. It pours out. And then he just goes in and dumps it all out. He'd literally just written the words, and somehow he had it all memorized, and was rapping without looking at anything.

"And then," Rasheed said, "he recorded the vocals *again*, because Tupac liked to stack his vocals. So if you listen to his songs, a lot of times you'll hear off vocals. Like, he says a word, but he says it two different ways on two different tracks."

Just a few hours earlier, Rasheed had no idea what "Funking Up the Backseat" would become. But then he heard what Tupac had created—a blistering, holy-fucking-fuck song called "Only God Can Judge Me" (with a top-shelf Rappin' 4-Tay feature). The idea had come to Tupac in prison while listening to Eric Clapton's cover of "Knocking on Heaven's Door." The opening verse—*"Perhaps I was blind to the facts, stabbed in the back / I couldn't trust my own homies just a bunch a dirty rats"*—left Rasheed speechless.

"He created a hood classic," he said, "off a song I'd thought I'd left behind."

At his best, Tupac in the studio could be a joy. He was joined by the veteran singer Nanci Fletcher to help on multiple tracks, including "Holla at Me." Fletcher had worked on hundreds of songs (she toured for years with Barry White), but this experience was a first. As she belted out her hooks, Tupac jumped into the booth and screamed, "Come on! Do that shit!" and "Push it out!"

"He was so proud, like a cheerleader," she recalled.

The following morning, Tupac—clear-eyed and sober and chugging from a large black coffee—sought Fletcher out.

"Nancy," he said, "I just wanna let you know how grateful I am. This song is so good. You really made the difference."

Later, when Tupac had moved to an apartment on Wilshire Boulevard, he invited Fletcher over for a barbecue. She found this somewhat surprising—what exactly did a Tupac Shakur barbecue look like? "So I go out there, and it's the afternoon," she recalled. "And Pac was by himself. He had cooked all these ribs and chicken by himself. He had every type of drink, so many things to eat—all made by him."

When Fletcher walked through the door, Tupac engulfed her in a hug.

"I just wanna show my appreciation for you," he said. "You made my album lit."

In the early days of working with Death Row, Tupac had an idea of what was to come. The album would be named *Euthanasia*. It would include twelve to fifteen tracks, meaning he'd need to experience the hell of narrowing down which to use, which to cut.

Having witnessed his productivity and work ethic, however, Knight bumped Tupac's Death Row debut up to a double album. It would contain twenty-seven total tracks, and *Euthanasia* was tossed to the trash heap.

The project's new name: *All Eyez on Me*.

Release date: February 13, 1996.

"Death Row wanted Pac to fucking be greedy and grimy," said Kendrick Wells, Tupac's longtime friend who, by now, was working with him as an assistant. "So that album was him being a boss baller. Diamonds, girls, nice clothes, Mercedes-Benz, fucking. He'd never been that. Not deep down. But he knew what Suge expected. So, as strange as it sounds, he set aside his integrity to make a great album."

Within the Tupac universe, *All Eyez on Me* is a revered collection of music. Talk to anyone who witnessed the birth of the album and you hear words of praise and glory. "There is so much greatness there," said Fletcher. "It's Tupac at his best."

"That shit," said the rapper Glasses Malone, "is next level."

Yet while the record offers up a little bit of everything—the Snoop collaboration "2 of Amerikaz Most Wanted" is back-and-forth magic; "I Ain't Mad at Cha" and "Life Goes On" are deep and contemplative; "Shorty Wanna Be a Thug" is A-plus birth-of-a-young-G storytelling—a singular track raises *All Eyez on Me* from exceptional hip-hop album to all-time classic.

Not that Dr. Dre had any initial interest in sharing "California Love."

It was *his* song, and it was intended to remain that way. The saga dates back to August 3, 1995, when—while standing backstage at the Source Music Awards in New York City—Dre overheard DJ Quik gently sing-humming "West Coast Poplock," the 1982 funk single from Ronnie Hudson and the Street People. Hudson's song begins, "California knows how to party / California knows how to party / In the city of good old Watts / In the city of Compton" . . . and Dre couldn't extract the worm from his cranium. He returned to Los Angeles two days later, stepped into his home studio, closed the door, strapped on his headphones, and—sampling the Joe Cocker tune "Woman to Woman" and Zapp's "Dance Floor"—laid down the outline of a track for his planned (and ultimately doomed) upcoming album, *The Chronic 2: Papa's Got a Brand New Funk*.

The next step came when he called James "J-Flexx" Anderson, a songwriter he had met two years earlier, at a traffic light in Los Angeles. In the summer of 1993, Anderson was fresh out of the United States Army and debating a move from his home in Maryland to California to make a go at music. When he saw Dr. Dre's Ferrari pull up, his jaw dropped. "I was with my buddy," Anderson recalled. "He rolled down his window and started telling Dre about me. Dr. Dre pulled over, took a demo I had. A few days later we were at Dre's house for a July Fourth party. He said he loved my stuff and wanted to work together."

Though Anderson's dream was to be a rapper, Dre hired him as a songwriter. Now, the Marylander had a unique new assignment—pen an anthem for California. "The first thing I came up with was the beginning—'Let me welcome everybody to the wild, wild west,'" Anderson recalled. "And then I did what I always do—I go down the alphabet for a word that works as a rhyme."

Anderson asked himself, "What's dope and rhymes with west?"

Best? Lame.

Crest? Nonsensical.

Dest? Not an actual word.

"I got to the letter *N*—Ness," he said. "Like Eliot Ness of *The Untouchables*. And I think, Hmm . . . Ness, Untouchables. 'A state that's untouchable like Eliot Ness.' Now *that* works!"

Anderson penned three full verses for Dr. Dre, who, he recalled, "always liked my style. He liked that it was clever and straightforward, but also simple." Dre recorded "California Love" as a solo song, with Roger Troutman singing the chorus.

Then, however, Tupac came out of prison. And, depending on who one believes, either Dr. Dre thought it would be a swell idea to split the song, or Suge Knight insisted (threateningly) that Dr. Dre split the song. According to Kurupt, the rapper and producer, the Death Row ethos was all about sharing. And sharing was caring. And Dr. Dre was the type who cared.

But it's also unlikely. Though Dre admired Tupac's talent, he found Suge's transformational all-Tupac, all-the-time approach to Death Row both annoying and counterproductive. "Let's be clear—Suge was like, 'We about to get Pac. You should put Pac on there,'" said Sean "Barney" Thomas, the producer. "And Dre was like, 'OK, I guess.'"

The song as a solo piece was wrapped, and Dr. Dre loved it. So as he watched Tupac pen his own verse, then record it at Can-Am on November 8, he was surely conflicted. "It was Dre's song," said Anderson. "His baby. But if we're being real, Tupac made it so much better."

When asked on MTV to explain Tupac's addition, Dr. Dre—on the set of the "California Love" music video—expressed all the joy of a neutered dog. "I just happened to be in the studio one day," Dr. Dre said, "and it just came about then. All happened in one night. Recorded him on the song. We mixed it."

Now, instead of having three verses, Dr. Dre had one and Tupac had one.

Now, instead of having a killer song to drop on his next album, Dr. Dre had a killer song to drop on someone else's album.

Now, instead of "California Love" being a Dr. Dre joint, it was destined to be known as a Tupac joint—with Dr. Dre.

"The business," said Anderson, "can be a bitch."

"California Love" wound up being the first single off All Eyez on Me, and it propelled the album into the stratosphere while also emerging as an instant classic. Two music videos followed, and in 2025 "California Love" continues to thump in clubs worldwide.

"I wouldn't say it's a Tupac song and I wouldn't say it's a Dre song," said Anderson. "I'd just say it's everyone's song."

Chapter 21

Just Me and You and the Bitches

There is a visual of Tupac Shakur, Death Row firebrand, that you are likely familiar with. It's Tupac walking with swagger, smoking a blunt, a fat Death Row medallion dangling from his neck, shouting out "West Side!" and looking like a man who owns the world.

And this is plenty understandable.

Although *All Eyez on Me*, Tupac's highly anticipated double album, wouldn't drop for two months, on December 3, 1995, Death Row released "California Love," the first single, and accompanied it with a pair of music videos. The reaction was nothing short of a hip-hop earthquake. It wasn't merely the boldness of the song. No, it was the return of Tupac motherfucking Shakur, announcing his comeback with "Out on bail, fresh out of jail, California dreamin' / Soon as I step on the scene, I'm hearin' hoochies screamin' . . ."

If ever a year looked as if it were set to belong to an artist, it was 1996 and Death Row's new headliner. "California Love" was everywhere. His album was dropping. In a nation where short memories erase the ugly pasts of our most famous figures, his Q rating was suddenly soaring. On February 2 he sat courtside at the Bulls–Lakers game at the Forum accompanied by Jack Nicholson, Denzel Washington, Arsenio Hall, MC Hammer, Jeffrey Osborne, and Suge Knight, basking in the glow of liberation and A-list celebrity status. He was *that* guy.

Although Tupac cut loose nearly all the women who wrote letters to and/or visited Clinton Correctional Facility (his oft-repeated behind-bars promises of "Baby, I can't wait to be with you" only went so far), back in SoCal he was having sex on a near-nightly basis with all sorts of females from all walks of life. He fooled around with Lisa "Left Eye" Lopes. He had a thing with the actress Salli Richardson. He once again took up with Simi Cruise, a beautiful twenty-three-year-old and onetime Dannemora day-tripper. Shortly after his return to Los Angeles, Tupac summoned Cruise to his suite at the Peninsula Beverly Hills. Upon entering, she was shocked—"Way more than shocked, to be honest"—to see Faith Evans, the singer and wife of the Notorious B.I.G., Tupac's sworn enemy. "She was kind of throwing me shade," recalled Cruise, who worked as a sales clerk at a department store. "I was very surprised to see her, because I heard Tupac say how much he hated her and how ugly she was, and that she looked like Miss Piggy. So I figured he was doing this to get back at Biggie."

It appeared to be the ultimate revenge play for both people—Tupac detested the Notorious B.I.G., and Evans had recently caught her husband sleeping with another woman. "I sort of rolled with it," said Cruise. "For all the shortcomings, he was special. To explain how different Tupac was, as soon as Faith left, he sat with me and turned on *The Lion King*. He was like, 'Simi, you need to watch this right now. It's the best movie you'll ever see.' He wasn't the crazy guy people imagined. So you made allowances."

On February 17, Tupac fulfilled what had been a secret life ambition— he was the musical guest on *Saturday Night Live*, a show he'd been watching since childhood. Though usually not one to get nervous, Tupac was terrified. "It's no small thing, going on live television in front of millions of people," said Tom Arnold, the comedian who guest-hosted the episode. "You spend the week preparing, but you can't possibly know what's coming." Tupac performed a pair of songs (his verse from "California Love" without Dr. Dre and "I Ain't Mad at Cha") and attended the cast after-party at a Manhattan restaurant in a jovial mood. Once there, he was sitting alongside Arnold when Suge Knight (who had invited himself) sauntered over.

"Yo, Tom Arnold!" Knight said.

"Yo, Suge Knight!" Arnold replied.

"Where's Roseanne at?" Knight asked of the actress Roseanne Arnold, Tom's wife.

"Roseanne?" Arnold replied. "She's in the trunk of my car."

Knight and Tupac broke out into unbridled laughter.

"Tupac told me not many people talk to Suge that way," Arnold recalled. "I was too stupid to know better."

Eleven days later, in a wonderfully bizarre intersection of universes, Tupac found himself at the Shrine Auditorium in Los Angeles to present the Grammy Award for Best Pop Performance by a Duo or Group. Standing alone at the microphone, looking resplendent in a black Versace suit with a silver Death Row medallion dangling from his neck, he leaned in and said: "Y'all down with this? We're gonna try to liven it up. You know how the Grammys used to be all straight-looking folks with suits and everybody looking tired and no surprises. We tired of that. We need something different. Something new. We need to shock the people."

A pause and a smile.

"So let's shock the people."

With that, Gene Simmons, Peter Criss, Paul Stanley, and Ace Frehley— the four original members of the rock band Kiss—walked onto the stage. This was their first time together in fifteen years, and they were made up as their long-ago kabuki characters. Tupac laughed and cracked, "Now, these my homeboys. And I've seen just about everything now."

The members of Kiss said a few words, then the nominees were read one by one before Tupac ripped open the envelope and said, "Oh, my *other* homeboys! Hootie and the Blowfish!"*

For a sliver in time of true serendipitous weirdness, Tupac Shakur, Gene Simmons, Paul Stanley, Ace Frehley, Peter Criss, Darius Rucker, and the three other Hootie members shared the stage.

"I know it was contrived, but it also worked," recalled Jim Sonefeld, Hootie's long-haired drummer. "There were two cool elements. First, we all grew up idolizing Kiss. But second, as a band we were listening to a lot of Tupac. I know that's surprising, but we were into rap. Tribe Called Quest, Poor Righteous Teachers, 3rd Bass. And certainly Pac."

All Eyez on Me dropped on February 13, 1996, and the whirlwind was something to behold. *The New York Times* placed Tupac (holding a wad of money), Snoop Doggy Dogg, and Suge Knight on the cover of its weekly

---

* Hootie & the Blowfish were, unambiguously, not Tupac's homeboys.

magazine, alongside the words THE GODFATHER OF GANGSTA RAP, AND HIS FAMILY VALUES. The reviews were nearly all positive—Sonia Murray of *The Atlanta Journal-Constitution* called the new release "as menacing as it is engaging." In the *Los Angeles Times*, Cheo Hodari Coker wrote, "The only thing jail time did for 2Pac was make his creative fires burn even hotter." Any concerns over the heft of a double album (list price: $26.99) weighing down acceptance proved unfounded: *All Eyez on Me* debuted atop the sales charts, with 566,000 copies moved. It remained number 1 for a second week, with 270,000 more purchases.

Without debate, Tupac Shakur was emerging as one of America's biggest hip-hop stars.

Wait. Scratch that.

Tupac Shakur was one of America's biggest *stars*.

Which leads to something only one of America's biggest stars could have gotten away with . . .

Back when he was locked up, Tupac spent a lot of time thinking about the visualization of music. He more or less knew what he thought his next album should sound like. But he also knew what he aspired much of it to *look* like. He wanted it to be sexy and seductive and filled with erotic splendor. Tupac thought himself a carnal man, and he dreamed of creating something that personified such.

In short, he wanted to mimic a Ron Hightower movie.

Inside the walls of Clinton, Black inmates *loved* Ron Hightower. The first Black actor to emerge as a legitimate pornographic superstar, his VHS tapes were shuffled from cell to cell, with titles like *Anal Kitten* and *Booty Bandit* serving as both a temporary reprieve from the frustrations of forced celibacy and an upbeat way to pass the time. That Hightower was six foot five, Blair Underwood handsome, and blessed with an immeasurable penis wasn't the point. No, it was that, before them, inmates had their own Nubian superstar, free as a bird and fucking his way to the top. "The one thing I heard all the time back then," said Hightower, "was that so many Black men wished they were me."

Tupac, in particular, idolized his work. So when they met one another at a Death Row party thrown inside the Museum of Flying in Santa Monica (to celebrate three million sales of *All Eyez on Me*), the rapper was starstruck. When the shindig concluded, Tupac invited his hero to an after-party inside his suite at the Peninsula. "Ron," he said, "I'd be forever in your debt if you can come. And I'd be even more forever in your debt if you could bring some of your bitches."

"No problem," Hightower said.

Hightower arrived at the hotel with his harem, but he was distressed by the platoons of camped-out paparazzi. He told Tupac that it wasn't his scene, but he was welcome to hang at his home near Runyon Canyon. "I gave him my address, figuring he won't really come," Hightower said. "An hour later I look outside, and there's Tupac, driving a Bentley, with a small Volkswagen Bug carrying four Nation of Islam security guards behind him."

Tupac entered Hightower's abode, and he and his host stepped into an elevator. As the door closed, Tupac literally dropped to his knees.

"Ron," he said, "*please* direct my next video. When I was locked down, all we talked about was Ron Hightower. *Please*, man, do it."

Hightower had received similar requests from other hip-hop artists. Not once did the work materialize. Usually, the rappers simply wanted to meet hotties. Hightower laughed off Tupac and cracked, "Listen, if it's about fucking the girls, they're gonna fuck you regardless."

"Ron," Tupac replied, "it's not about them. It's about me and you. We can take over this industry! We can make history!"

By now it was three in the morning. Hightower told his new friend he'd think it over, but he needed some sleep. "My house is big, and I went into my bedroom," Hightower recalled. "I'm trying to fall asleep, and all I hear is Tupac banging the crap out of the girls in the living room. One after another."

The next morning, Tupac was wide awake and holding a mug of coffee when a groggy Hightower entered his own kitchen. "Ron!" he said. "I was thinking—we should have a barbecue today, and me and you are gonna be the only niggas here. Just me and you and the bitches."

"OK," Hightower muttered, "I guess." Tupac pulled three hundred dollars in cash from a pocket. "Yo," he said, "go to the store—get some steaks, some chicken, some Alizé! I'll do the cooking!"

The party lasted for—by Hightower's estimation—thirty-six hours.

There was lots of food, lots of women, lots and lots and lots of fucking, and a whole lot of Tupac pleading with Hightower to produce his next video. "I want it to be special," Tupac said. "It's not for MTV. Fuck that. It's for underground clubs all over the world to play on their monitors while people are getting down."

"How could I say no?" Hightower said.

The song was called "How Do U Want It." It featured the R&B duo K-Ci & JoJo and sampled a Quincy Jones classic, "Body Heat." It was a celebration of sex. The opening lines ("*Love the way you activate your hips and push your ass out / Got a nigga wantin' it so bad I'm 'bout to pass out / Wanna dig you and I can't even lie about it / Baby, just alleviate your clothes, time to fly up out it*") make that clear. Hightower, however, did not like "How Do U Want It." He thought it sort of pedestrian. To the great Black porn star, sexiness involved subtlety. This was a hammer smashing a vase.

That said, Hightower's budget was $250,000. It would be filmed at a vacant club across the street from the famed Abbey in West Hollywood. Hightower pulled up for day 1 of shooting and couldn't believe his eyes—there were trailers aplenty, craft services, police barricades. He had enlisted fifty or so of the sexiest female models/porn stars he knew, and came armed with an idea inspired by his favorite film, Bob Guccione's *Caligula*. "I wanted it to be erotic but elegant," Hightower said. "It was supposed to be Tupac touring you through a wet dream. This was the first time anyone thought of me as strictly a filmmaker, and I felt like I needed to prove myself with bold concepts."

Tupac wasn't feeling it. He merely desired a porno music video.

"My plan was sort of destroyed once he started spraying the girls with champagne and rubbing whipped cream all over their breasts," Hightower said. "I've never been mad. Just a little disappointed. I wanted to create an all-time great video."

The X-rated "How Do U Want It" is not an all-time great video—just an all-time legendary one.* It features some of the biggest names in nine-

---

* A clean, made-for-MTV version also exists. It's fairly forgettable.

ties erotica (including Nina Hartley, Angel Kelly, and Heather Hunter), an enormous Albino Burmese python, dozens of cans of whipped cream, a mechanical bull, and breasts and ass galore. Over the course of production, Tupac had sex with at least a half dozen of his costars—including Hartley (as her boyfriend watched) and a threesome with Kelly and Hunter. In one scene, K-Ci drinks champagne from a woman's vagina ("No props," said Hightower. "Real vagina").

"The whole thing was sort of crazy," said Hightower. "But that was Tupac. Brilliant, and a little bit crazy."

Most people with access to out-of-prison Tupac didn't realize they were oftentimes staring at a mask.

His public persona was upbeat, intense, creative. Rolling with Suge and Snoop, mugging for the cameras, Death Row and Thug Life and cars and jewelry and bitches. "Doing his Tupac thing," said the rapper Money-B. "Living up to what people wanted."

At night, he often woke up screaming and in cold sweats, unsure whether he was in his Clinton Correctional Facility cell or his rat-infested Baltimore row house or Demetrius Striplin's Marin City pad or his Beverly Hills suite. He spent an inordinate amount of time pacing on his balcony, smoking a Newport down to the stub, flicking it to the ground, rubbing it out with his shoe, lighting the next one. He ultimately relocated to a Death Row–owned apartment on the Wilshire corridor (a swank spot located between Beverly Hills, Century City, and Westwood), and one day Simi Cruise opened a humongous Tupperware container on the kitchen table. "It was all his pot," she recalled. "He was definitely self-medicating."

Tupac had lots of money. At least it *seemed* as if he had lots of money. Look at the hangers in his closet, dangling Dolce & Gabbana and Versace and Louis Vuitton. Look at the cars he was driving. Should he take the Jag to the studio or the Mercedes? Maybe the Rolls. If he wanted filet mignon accompanied by two bottles of Dom Pérignon, he ordered without hesitation and signed the bill to Death Row. His mother, Afeni, enjoyed similar perks. A nice meal. A new ride. A place to hole up in LA. Just send the bill to Suge. Suge will handle everything. Don't worry about your bank account.

Don't even open a checking account. All those legal fees? Don't sweat it. It's too much of a hassle. Your brothers—Death Row—have it all under control.

What a life.

But . . . what was it, really? What was the existence Tupac was living? He appeared happy. He smiled a lot. He hit the clubs with this woman, with that woman. His legal fees were exorbitant. The gifts Death Row bequeathed upon him came out of his earnings. The bank account of the world's biggest hip-hop star held well below two hundred thousand dollars. "Suge was an executive producer on every album, and he was paid a pretty penny just for that," said Jake Brown, the hip-hop journalist. "Tupac's lavish personal lifestyle was a mirage. In reality, a lot of what you saw that was lavish *at* Death Row was financed by Tupac."

What Tupac wanted, but struggled to find, was family. His mother always had her hand out, his sister was in Georgia with her two kids, his cousins in and out of jail. He had thought Atron Gregory was family, but then he failed to bail him out. He had thought Shock G of Digital Underground was family, but after Tupac joined Death Row he went largely AWOL. He had thought Leila Steinberg was family, but where had she gone? He thought Snoop and Dre could be family, but they sometimes seemed more resentful than happy. Suge Knight spoke of Death Row as "a family"—but was it? *Was it really?*

"I truly believe he felt pressure to live up to being Tupac—the image of Tupac," said Sean "Barney" Thomas, a Death Row producer. "If it was just you and him in a studio, he could be chill. But the minute fifteen people showed up, he needed to be popular, he needed to be loud, he needed to be seen. He got on that Bishop shit. Honestly, looking back, it's pretty sad. It must have been so lonely." For a man who appeared to always be surrounded by friends, Tupac had no real friends. Friends for show? Yes. Friends he'd known for a long time? Certainly. But friends he could confide in? There were none.

On March 16, Tupac accompanied Knight to Las Vegas for the Mike Tyson–Frank Bruno fight at the MGM Grand. Afterward they attended a party at Club 662, a nightspot owned by Knight. A handful of Tupac's Northern California pals showed up, and Tupac was thrilled to see them.

They hugged, hopped on the stage. Then Knight whispered into his ear, "Yo, Pac, who are these fools?" Tupac told him—and Knight booted them without reason. Just because he could. "It was like watching an owner discipline his dog," said Bobby Burton, his old Marin friend and one of the banished. "You don't speak that way to a man."

One week later, Dr. Dre announced he was leaving Death Row to start his own company. The tension between him and Knight had been building for some time—a musician interested in creating innovative sounds vs. a label head interested (increasingly, it seemed) in cultivating an image and being seen. "Suge got caught up in the limelight, and it showed," said Thomas. "He'd made fun of Puffy for being all over the place—and now he *was* Puffy. Dre wasn't interested in that." Wrote Connie Bruck in *The New Yorker*, "The precedent of Dr. Dre's departure from Death Row did not seem especially encouraging. A music-business executive who was friendly with Dre says that Dre left because he was uncomfortable with Knight's 'business practices.' Dre abandoned his interest in the company in return for a relatively modest financial settlement, and Interscope facilitated the divorce by giving him a lucrative new contract."

And while Tupac took to bashing Dr. Dre in public as a sellout and traitor (he referred to him as "gay-ass Dre" on the song "To Live and Die in L.A."), he, too, was growing uncomfortable with some of the Death Row stuff. Three months after Tupac aligned with the label, Knight had hosted a Death Row Christmas party, during which he and some cohorts forced Mark Anthony Bell, a record promoter loosely affiliated with Puffy's Bad Boy Entertainment, to drink a jar of urine as he was robbed, stomped, and beaten with champagne bottles. In a similarly creepy move, Suge had recently demanded two colleagues strip before him, kneel, and pledge eternal fealty. Even for Tupac—who considered Puffy an enemy—it felt perverse. On the outside, he laughed and went along with the tactics. On the inside, he bristled. This was some sick shit.

Without letting Knight in on his plan, Tupac began to consider an eventual escape from Death Row. He no longer felt comfortable with the fealty the label demanded. Tupac was nobody's bitch—and he was starting to feel like Knight's bitch. "Deep down, Pac knew what he was dealing with," said Yaasmyn Fula.

In his ongoing search for kinship, Tupac now devoted a large chunk of time to a pair of women he both dated and sheltered. One was a former aspiring rock drummer turned aspiring rapper turned adult film star named Sharon Johnson, who went by the entertainment moniker "Spantaneeus" ("Spantaneeus Xtasty" as a porn star). A twenty-nine-year-old Philadelphian, she first encountered Tupac three years earlier in Atlanta, when he spotted her eating at a restaurant. "He came in and said, 'I wanna meet you,'" Spantaneeus recalled. "I was like, 'You're Tupac! From *Juice*! I wanna meet *you*!'" This was several years before Johnson's breakout in such films as *Tittytown II*, *The Black Butt Sisters Do Miami*, and *Black Orgies Party 34*. In fact, somewhat recently Spantaneeus had served as an opening act for the rappers MC Lyte and Das EFX. She and Tupac wound up dating, but Tupac also played a role in trying to propel her hip-hop career. He transplanted her from Georgia to California and put her up in a spacious Thousand Oaks apartment that he paid for. They went out, had dinners, took long walks. "He was very sweet and romantic," she said. "He wasn't what people might think."

Then he told Spantaneeus about Dahlia "Poochie" McCutchen—another woman he once had romantic feelings for. A Houston-based stripper and sex worker with a volatile family background, McCutchen and Tupac went back three years. She was the one who introduced him to Dago Coehlo, the tattoo artist who inked THUG LIFE across his stomach. She loved Tupac, and said that when she was nineteen he impregnated her. According to McCutchen, she suffered a miscarriage, which—she said—Tupac was fully aware of. "He would have been a wonderful father," she said. "He was a good man."

In 1995, Tupac had learned that McCutchen was in Texas, being raped and beaten by a boyfriend. "Pac told me I needed to come to Los Angeles," McCutchen recalled. "I'd been going through a lot of shit for a long time, shit I kept from Pac because I didn't want to burden him. But him learning I was being abused—that set him off. And he moved me to California. Paid for it. He probably saved my life."

What Tupac did was something no one in the media knew of—in fact, that very few people in his life knew of. The penthouse apartment he rented for Spantaneeus was so spacious that McCutchen lived there, too, along with several other friends and aspiring artists who needed a safe haven. "I know it might *sound* weird, because Spantaneeus and I both had had relationships with Tupac," McCutchen said. "But it wasn't weird at all. Spantaneeus and I became best friends. And the people in the apartment all had dreams and goals. Tupac was the connector. Looking back, it was mind-blowing. He paid for everything. He made sure we were all safe. He checked in on us regularly. The Death Row thing—it wasn't really him. He was loving. And we were his *family*."

Family. If it couldn't be blood relatives, that was fine. He simply aspired to have people to be real with. People who needed him not for money or fame, but for emotional support. People who were good and earnest.

Along with Spantaneeus and McCutchen, Tupac was particularly tight with Fula, the longtime family friend and business manager who had been his rock for the eight months in Clinton. He asked if she would come out to Los Angeles to help with his business affairs, so she hitched her BMW 525 to a U-Haul truck, loaded up her possessions (and her cocker spaniel, Louie), and drove from New Jersey to Atlanta to pick up items from Tupac's Southern home, then headed the three thousand miles west. She moved into a two-bedroom apartment at 7660 Beverly Boulevard—one room was hers to sleep in, the other served as head-quarters for what Tupac wanted to be his new music recording company, which he enthusiastically named Euphanasia ("I fell in love with that word," he told Kevin Powell. "I feel like that's me. I'm gonna die, I just wanna die without pain").

Fula was, in multiple ways, what Afeni was unable to be—reliable, self-less, competent, on top of things. She was good with numbers, direct with people, unwilling to compromise. Her time in prison gave her both cred and Brillo toughness. She knew Tupac from his days in diapers, and felt responsible for his well-being. He was a victim of lifetime trauma—"*Black trauma*," she said. And she realized how difficult it could be to escape. Black men, Fula knew, spent their lifetimes being beaten down, demeaned, diminished, arrested. It was an existence of being told you are nothing, and then receiving the negative reinforcement to believe it. "And it makes you very vulnerable," she said. "To people selling bullshit."

From the beginning, Fula viewed Knight with skepticism—"a type of shady brother I'd seen far too often," she recalled—and was not thrilled by the company Tupac was keeping. Too many Black men were dying young, and he possessed the gifts to avoid such a fate. But he insisted on rolling with hangers-on and grifters. He felt the need to not merely pay for everything, but flaunt the wealth he didn't actually have. Tupac was quick with an American Express card, but ignorant in the ways of how and when to pay it off. Afeni and other Shakur relatives traveled to California and stayed for months at the snazzy Westwood Marquis hotel—never wondering who was paying for the room (Tupac), the room service (Tupac), the car services (Tupac). "It all came out of his Death Row earnings," Fula said. "Nothing was free." Fula called Death Row's offices on a near-weekly basis, demanding copies of financial accounts. "Instead," she said, "they'd send some bullshit present." Tupac exhibited the least Black Panthers behavior imaginable—placing wealth and glory over virtue. But he was easily swayed.

Early in her time in Southern California, Fula showed Tupac the company's new business cards—featuring the logo he designed (a kneeling angel of death gripping an Uzi filled with keyboard-like bullets), his full name (Tupac Amaru Shakur), and both a phone (213-935-9631) and fax (213-935-9632) number. Holding the small cardboard rectangles in his hand, smoothing them over with his fingers—it was as emotional as Fula had seen Tupac. The business cards symbolized something. He had made it. He was an entrepreneur. A real one.

His eyes watered, and Fula thought that—just maybe—this type of thing would lead him on a righteous path.

"He could have been anything he wanted to be," said Fula, "if he just got out of his own way."

When, way back in 1983, Franne Golde sat down to write a song for former Temptations singer Dennis Edwards, she wasn't thinking of bitches, Glocks, murder, revenge, or East Coast vs. West Coast.

At the time, she was merely a thirty-year-old musician trying to pen some hits. So she met up with a collaborator, Duane Hitchings, smoked some top-shelf herb, and came up with the music and lyrics to "Don't Look Any Further."

"It's all kind of funny," she said of what would become one of Edwards's biggest solo hits. "Because the song has a bunch of beautiful African chants, and those were all found by two stoned, white, Jewish songwriters."

Over the course of her lengthy career, Golde created music for artists ranging from Randy Travis to the Commodores to Selena. But a conversation from early 1996 trumps all.

"I went to my publisher's office," Golde recalled, "and someone said, 'We have this record coming out by Tupac Shakur, and we need your approval for a sample.'"

This was a no-brainer. The mother of an infant son, she could certainly use the extra money.

"Sure," Golde said. "He's very popular."

"Well," a rep replied, "you might wanna read the lyrics on this one."

She was presented a piece of paper . . .

First off, fuck your bitch and the clique you claim
Westside when we ride, come equipped with game
You claim to be a player but I fucked your wife
We bust on Bad Boy niggas fucked for life

Oh, my.

"I don't know," Golde said. "This kind of goes against my beliefs."

There was an awkward pause, and a representative from Warner Chappell Music, Golde's publishing company, was summoned. He wore the pained expression of a man with thousand-pound dumbbells strapped to both shoulders.

"So, Franne," he said. "Tupac recorded this song already for Death Row."

"And?" she asked.

"Death Row is owned by Suge Knight," he said.

Golde shrugged. The name meant nothing.

"This is strange to say," he said, "but if you don't want people with guns showing up on your doorstep, I'd let them have it."

Golde gave Tupac the rights. "Not sure I had a choice," she said with a laugh.

With *that* decision, in *that* moment, a seismic shift in music occurred.

Those who knew Tupac best insist he was merely playing a part. Not a gangsta being a gangsta, but *a gangsta rapper* being a gangsta rapper. With "Hit 'Em Up," however, perceptions and realities collided. The song—released on the B-side of the "How Do U Want It" single—was a musical bullet to the skull of the Notorious B.I.G. "You don't start a song like that," said Jill Munroe, a Tupac friend, "and think no one will notice."

The origins date back to Clinton, when Tupac sat in his cell reading Sun Tzu's *The Art of War* and plotting revenge against those he blamed for the Quad Studios shooting. "Let your plans be dark and impenetrable as night," Sun Tzu wrote, "and when you move, fall like a thunderbolt." The words hit Tupac *like* a thunderbolt, and after leaving Dannemora he penned an initial version of the song that included a verse—"Heard they call you Big Poppa, nigga, how you figure? 'Cause to me you'll always be a phony, fat nigga"—with the jaggedness of splintered glass. Tupac made the (wise, in Fula's opinion) decision not to include "Hit 'Em Up" on *All Eyez on Me*, but then circumstances forced a change in plans.

On the night of March 29, Tupac and Knight arrived at the tenth annual Soul Train Music Awards in Los Angeles, accompanied by a fleet of cars holding labelmates and security guards. "That attracted every security guard we had," said Don Cornelius, *Soul Train*'s founder. "Plus the LAPD." Only Tupac and Knight were allowed admittance, and as they walked from their car to the Shrine entrance, Tupac was overheard screaming gang slogans and obscenities. He wore a camouflage jacket and black sideways cap; Knight sported a maroon sweatshirt with THEE ALMIGHTY P-FUNK—COMPTON'S FINEST stitched across the back and a gold Death Row medallion dangling from his neck.

Award shows served as ideal peacocking turf for Tupac, who wasn't one to turn down a look-at-me opportunity when surrounded by fame and wealth. Big Gipp of Goodie Mob said that during a commercial break Tupac and Knight "interrupted the ceremony by kicking in the door and making a grand entrance." He and Knight charged directly toward Biggie, shouting profane threats. Some said Tupac pulled out a gun. Others said he did not. "That was the first time I really looked into his face," Biggie later said. "I looked into his eyes and was like, 'Yo, this nigga is really bugging the fuck out.'" According to Reggie Wright Jr., the label's security chief, Death Row's master plan was to storm the stage during Biggie's Song of the Year acceptance speech and shot-put him into the crowd. However, before that could transpire, Cornelius booted Tupac and Knight from the building. Moments later, the singer CeCe Peniston and the members of the group Solo took the microphone to announce the nominees for Best Rap Album, and Tupac was declared the winner. The crowd cheered until Peniston swiveled her head to look offstage, then said, to boos, "Tupac couldn't be here tonight so we're gonna accept this award on behalf of him."

When the show concluded, Tupac and Knight lingered in the parking lot, waiting for Biggie and the Bad Boy contingent. They never showed. "There could have been a fight," said Sean "Puffy" Combs, "but there wasn't."

The Soul Train Awards ended at 8:00 p.m., and within a couple of hours Tupac was back in Tarzana inside Can-Am Studios. He was joined by the Outlawz, a group of mostly young rappers he had recently reintroduced after their original run, as the questionably named Dramacydal, had fizzled. The members—including Malcolm "E.D.I Mean" Greenidge, Bruce "Hussein Fatal" Washington Jr., Katari "Katsro" Cox, and Yaasmyn Fula's son/Tupac's childhood pal, Yaki "Kadafi" Fula—were all nurtured by Tupac, all housed by Tupac, all financed by Tupac. And, ironically, most were (like Tupac) East Coast natives. "Tupac didn't really care about geography—he just wanted to be surrounded by people who were loyal to him," said Kendrick Wells, a longtime friend. "Pac would order those Outlawz guys to fight each other—'Yo, beat the fuck out of each other!'—and they would. Punches. Kicking. Violent shit. Just to prove themselves to their daddy." Despite their East Coast roots, the Outlawz eagerly jumped on what Tupac considered to be his new calling—a ferocious rerecording of "Hit 'Em Up." Everyone in attendance was given forty or so minutes to write their lyrics, then step to the mic and spit. If the song's aim was at all ambiguous, Tupac cleared that up with his opening KO of Biggie—"*That's why I fucked yo' bitch, you fat motherfucker.*"

Damn.

"He was angry," said Napoleon (aka Mutah Beale), an Outlaw who rapped on the track. "And I remember sitting there and thinking, Wow, this guy is not faking. He's upset and he wants to get a message across."

Along with the rappers, attendees at the session included Knight, Lisa Lopes (the TLC singer/rapper who—in one friend's recollection—"just refused to leave Tupac alone"), the producer Mike Mosley, the four members of the Atlanta-based hip-hop group Goodie Mob, and their manager, Bernard Parks. "This might sound weird, but I was laughing for a lot of it," said Mosley. "Pac was talking crazy, murdering guys on wax, bringing the anger. But it also felt funny. To me. Also to Pac. He liked what he was doing, and took joy in it."

Though hip-hop remained a fairly young medium, diss tracks dated back. Roxanne Shante's "Roxanne's Revenge" kicked things off in 1984. Eazy-E's "Real Muthaphuckkin G's" and Ice Cube's "No Vaseline" brought serious heat. "Hit 'Em Up," however, was next level. No matter how many times Biggie insisted he had nothing to do with the Quad Studios shooting, Tupac refused to believe it. No matter how many intermediaries told Tupac that Biggie wanted to speak with him—it made no impact. Why, when Biggie released a song called "Who Shot Ya" in early 1995, Tupac *immediately* insisted it was a direct reference to Quad Studios. Wrote Cheo Hodari Coker, "It didn't even matter to Shakur that the song was recorded in September of 1994, months before the shooting—he thought it was disrespectful that the song would even be released for people to speculate that it *might* be about him."

Now, in the studio, Tupac held *nothing* back. He fucked Biggie's wife.* He will shoot Biggie. He went at Puffy; at Prodigy of Mobb Deep ("Don't one of you niggas got sickle cell or something? You fucking with me, nigga you fuck around and get a seizure or a heart attack"); at Lil' Kim and Chino XL. At the offspring of his enemies ("All of y'all motherfuckers, fuck you, die slow, motherfucker / My .44 make sure all y'all kids don't grow"). "He had a lot of anger in his soul," said Kevin Swain, who later produced a video for the song.

---

* In a 2005 interview with *Vibe*, Evans refuted any reports of romantic involvement with Tupac. "I can clarify it," she said. "The nigga lied on me."

When "Hit 'Em Up" came out on June 4, the reaction was disbelief mixed with excitement mixed with condemnation. In New York, Biggie was dumbfounded. Puffy initially played it for him at a video shoot for Total's "Kissin' You (Remix)," and after digesting the lyrics he asked, "Are you fucking serious right now?" He was less angry, more hurt. The song's intent sliced deep. Tupac had been his friend—and now he was not only allegedly fucking his wife, but bragging about it to millions?

Around this time, Tupac agreed to sit down with Angie Martinez, the twenty-five-year-old radio personality from New York City's Hot 97 who flew to California for the interview. Martinez landed at LAX, headed to Tupac's apartment, and launched a two-hour discussion that, decades later, Tupac fans consider the holy grail of explaining his feelings toward the East Coast.

When asked why he was so mad, Tupac didn't bite his tongue. "Niggas that represent New York, some of these rappers—there's a lot of cool niggas out there," he said. "But as far as Bad Boy, Puffy is the head of Bad Boy. He's a cream puff. He's being extorted. So the niggas that's extorting him don't pump no fear in my heart. They pump fear in *his* heart. I rode against the niggas extorting him. They tried to kill me. Biggie and them watched it and acted like they didn't know what happened. So now I'm gonna end his business. I'm gonna end it so the extorting niggas don't get no money. Biggie don't get no money. Puffy don't get no money. I get all the money, and they be out the rap game. That's what poppin'."

"And how," Martinez asked, "do you intend to do that?"

"I'm doing it," Tupac replied. "Then niggas ain't doin' no tours. They ain't livin' good. They sleepin' with extra security. They got guns out. They was out here panicky like a motherfucka. It's a military move."

Within hip-hop's tight universe, "Hit 'Em Up" served as both a declaration of war and bonanza for entertainment media. On the cover of its September 1996 issue, *Vibe* magazine celebrated its third anniversary with a photograph of Biggie and Puffy alongside EAST VS. WEST: BIGGY & PUFF BREAK THEIR SILENCE and atop the words JUICE: WHO'S GOT THE POWER. What the magazine failed to mention was that, when he posed for photographer Dana Lixenberg, Biggie assumed it would be a straight profile of his blossoming career. "[Biggie] didn't take that picture thinking 'East vs. West,'" Method Man of Wu-Tang Clan told the writer Soren Baker. "He took a picture thinking 'I'm going to be on the cover of *Vibe*.' What came after is what solidified [the] East-West beef for all the dumb motherfuckers around that don't know how to think for themselves."

For the entirety of 1996, outlets from *The New York Times Magazine* to *The Source* to *Rolling Stone* to *Rap Pages* to the *East Bay Express* titillated the public with stories about the animosity between rap coasts. With hip-hop media populated by a high percentage of inexperienced journalists, writers assigned to chronicle the story found themselves out of their depths. When scribes dared opine negatively on an artist, pledges of physical violence often followed. (Displeased over an article, Tupac once left a threatening answering machine message for Sheena Lester, the editor of *Rap Pages* magazine. Said Lester, "My reaction was, What a lightweight. How big of a fucking loser do you have to be?") Across the industry, there were too few calls to verify information. Mediocre follow-up questions. Acceptance without confirmation. Backstage access exchanged for fawning coverage. Both *Vibe* and *The Source*—archrival magazines itching to land the juiciest material—lived for rappers making threatening proclamations and baseless accusations, but weren't nearly as concerned with fact-checking. So if an artist wanted to take shots at another artist, reporters spread the word.

"Hip-hop magazines did not help," said Michael Saunders, a Black arts writer for *The Boston Globe*. "There were probably some people at those magazines calling the whole East-West thing out as stupid, but very few. Why? First, if you're Black you don't want to kill your credibility in the streets. Second, you don't want to nip this rising genre of music that's paying your salary. And third, people were making big money off the feud."

"You have to understand that at the time a lot of what was done was really advocacy journalism, because you spent so much time defending the art and the culture that you didn't put time in critiquing it," said Rob Marriott, the fantastic former *Source* and *Vibe* writer. "A lot of people were learning on the job, and that meant it was hit or miss with every article." Marriott, one of the best in the field, had once worked at The Village Voice, learning beneath the wing of Peter Noel, an all-time great investigative journalist. That level of training was rare.

"It's easy to say we fanned the flames," said Alan Light, a former editor of *Vibe*. "But at the time, we were reporting what was happening and what our readers were talking about. We weren't creating it. We were chronicling it the best we could.

"But could we have done better? Sure."

As all this was transpiring, Tupac stayed true to who he was at heart: a creative.

Even though *All Eyez on Me* was still producing hits, and even though Death Row was continuing to promote it via new music videos, by the summer of 1996 Tupac was back in Can-Am, working on tracks for a follow-up album.

He was also making movies.

This, Tupac told a handful of people, was what he actually aspired to do. Yes, he loved hip-hop, but he *lived* for acting. It dated back to the thirteen-year-old boy standing before an audience inside Harlem's Apollo Theater to play Travis Younger in *A Raisin in the Sun*. You could lose yourself in a character. You could be poor and depressed in real life but find true escapism on a stage. In many ways, the Tupac people witnessed in public was performance art. The shouting, the screaming, the threatening, the posturing—it was partially real, but was it *fully* authentic? Did he *really* hate Biggie? Did he *really* think of himself as a gangbanger? Did he consider himself a *true* thug? No. It was show business. "Especially after he got shot, he walked the fence of remaining loyal to revolutionary principles, but the revolutionary soldiers were not there for him," said Fula. "They were all dead. So all he had was the streets who were trying to both annihilate and save him. He trusted no one, so the world became a stage."

Though his most recent film, *Bullet*, with Mickey Rourke, was a direct-to-video flop, Tupac's post-prison reemergence as a cultural force resulted in a pair of golden cinematic opportunities. One was to costar in a flick called *Gridlock'd* with the British actor Tim Roth. The other was to costar in a flick called *Gang Related* with the American actor and comedian Jim Belushi.

Both experiences were telling.

Tupac loved the *Gridlock'd* script and was excited to work with Roth, the star of one of his favorite movies, *Reservoir Dogs*. However, before Tupac could sign on, Knight demanded a one-on-one meeting with the producer. That's how Damian Jones—short, white, thirty-one years old, and more than a hair nervous—found himself across from the Death Row kingpin at the bar of the Beverly Hills Four Seasons. "I waved to him, he sat down," Jones recalled. "The meeting lasted seconds. I gave the quick sales pitch and he asked me what was in it for Tupac."

Jones gulped a bit. "Whatever Tim Roth gets, Tupac gets," he replied.

"And Death Row gets the soundtrack?" Knight asked.

"Absolutely," Jones replied.

Knight rose and walked off.

Gridlock'd was filmed over thirty days, almost entirely at Lacey Studios in the Lincoln Heights section of Los Angeles. Playing a recovering drug addict named Spoon, Tupac was phenomenal. It is, many critics agree, his best performance, in one of his better movies, and to watch Tupac—in one particularly gripping scene—take drags from a cigarette and recall his first heroin hit ("*For me . . . that shit was like going back to the womb. I never felt such peace*") is top-shelf thespianism. "He had a stillness you can't teach," said Bill Pope, the movie's cinematographer. "The great ones are the ones who hold something back from the audience. Those are the ones we stare at. Tupac had it."

Before long, the producers figured something out about Tupac: All close-ups had to be shot in the morning, because during lunch break he retreated to his trailer to get high. "Red eyes," said Jones. "He dug him some weed. It was fine. We worked with it."

Knight liked to stop by the set. Not always. But often enough to remind Tupac he was always watching. Knight usually just stood to the side, observing with a menacing glare. When he arrived, Pope recalled, "it was like I could smell the sulfur."

John Bertolli, a Hollywood newbie coming off work on the comedy *Kingpin*, was hired to serve as the *Gang Related* producer. He was instructed to head up to Can-Am, meet with Tupac (the second choice, after LL Cool J turned down the role of a corrupt detective named Rodriguez), and make certain he was genuinely interested. Bertolli arrived at 11:30 a.m., walked through a metal detector, and was offered a Hennessy and Coca-Cola. "I'm like, 'Why not?'" he recalled with a laugh.

Tupac was polite and engaged. He had read the script and craved the job. When Bertolli reassured him he was their guy, Tupac exhaled a sigh of relief. Then he requested something Bertolli remembered three decades later: "Let's make sure the business is right," Tupac said, "and let's also make sure the checks come straight to me."

It was the first time an artist had asked such a thing of Bertolli (said Fula, "Yes, he was demanding those checks came to him and *not* Death Row. I was able to open up his own personal account—it meant so much to be financially independent"), and as *Gang Related* began filming around Los Angeles, the cast and crew came to understand why. Tupac was, for the most part, a beloved presence. The actress Lela Rochon was cast as the leading female character, and she was happy to work with him. "I was a big fan of his music," she said. Unfortunately, the first day of rehearsal coincided with a doctor's appointment, and Rochon arrived late. When she entered the building, Tupac and Belushi were waiting for her. "Tupac had every gold chain on that he owned," she recalled. "And he had white Gucci shoes and a white linen fit. And I just stopped in my tracks and I looked at him, and I thought, Well, aren't you something."

Tupac introduced himself with a trademark crooked grin.

"I'm just glad you were the late one," he said. "Everybody expected it to be me."

This was Belushi's thirty-ninth film, and he was staggered by Tupac's acting chops. "He was fucking beautiful to work with," said Belushi, who also played a corrupt police officer. "We never talked about what we were gonna do in a scene. When they said, 'Action!,' I went into my rhythm and Tupac would slip naturally into his. The next scene I might come in a little lower, and he just instinctively went a little higher. We always had this sense of balance. He was a doll, man. He knew his shit. I've always thought he was one or two movies away from Academy Award talk. He was *that* good."

But, on set, Tupac was also *that* paranoid. He had a security guard follow him everywhere, and if the large man were, say, on a cigarette break, Tupac broke out in mini panic attacks. Oftentimes a movie set can be overrun by extras and crew members, and Tupac hated it. Strangers made him twitch. "I remember him being uncomfortable with the number of bodies around," said Belushi. "It was a lot for him."

The thing that most struck those involved in *Gang Related* was the source of Tupac's anxiety. When filming began, most assumed Tupac was a hardened tough guy who rolled with Suge Knight and hated all things East Coast and Biggie Smalls and, well, white. They half expected him to flash gang signs and scream, "Black power!" Tupac, to their shock, was gentle and even a little effeminate. He viewed acting as a golden escape-the-bullshit ticket. He confided in folks on set with a comfort he didn't show Knight. "We spoke a lot about some of the stuff he was going through," said Jim Kouf, the white *Gang Related* writer and director. "He was a very normal guy who really wanted to get away from Death Row. He felt like he needed to find freedom. He knew he was stuck in a very bad place."

"He was sweet and nice," said the actor Gregory Scott Cummins, who had a small role. "All that badass rapper stuff—I saw none of it."

Actors were due to set at 10:00 a.m. And Tupac arrived accompanied by Knight. *Every. Single. Morning.* It was creepy. "Suge was babysitting him in a way," said Rochon, who was born in Compton and witnessed gang violence as a youth. "I had a hairdresser who I was very close with, and I told her when Suge was around, 'Don't say anything. That guy is trouble.' It felt dangerous to me. Dangerous, scary, and unsafe."

One day, when shooting was delayed for three hours, Tupac asked Rochon if she wanted to pass the time by going to a movie.

"Oh, hell no," she said. "I'm not going to see a movie with you."

"Why not?" Tupac asked.

"Because," she replied, "I don't feel like getting shot."

In Knight's presence, Tupac changed. His body language. His mannerisms. His speech patterns. He spoke less to white crew members. He seemed to be playacting. As soon as Knight departed—back to normal. At the time Tupac was going through a major Frank Sinatra phase, to the point that Bertolli gifted him a portable CD player and a stack of discs featuring

Ol' Blue Eyes. One could lean up against Tupac's trailer between takes and hear him singing "My Way" and "Fly Me to the Moon" and even "New York, New York." He had the words down. He had the pacing down. Tupac told Bertolli he wanted to take full control of the *Gang Related* soundtrack and create a full mash-up of Sinatra and hip-hop. He was dead serious. "I couldn't wait to hear it," Bertolli said. "Tupac plus Sinatra? That's amazing. But I'm not sure how it would've gone over with Death Row."

Tupac found a kindred spirit in Lynn Kouf, Jim's wife and a producer on the movie. Tupac gravitated toward motherly figures, and Lynn (in her late thirties) fit the bill. At the time, Lynn's fourth child, a son named Dylan, was a couple of months old, and Tupac was endearingly playful with the infant. Lynn and Tupac spoke at length on multiple subjects, and Tupac complained how trapped he felt with Knight and Death Row. "It was a classic mafia situation," she said, "where he wanted to move on, but couldn't."

One night, shooting on *Gang Related* ran late. At around nine o'clock, a loud honking interrupted work. "I was in the trailer," Lynn Kouf recalled, "and it started shaking from the bass of the car's stereo." When she stepped out, Lynn was taken aback by the sight of a black Humvee pulling up to set, blasting a Tupac song, driven by Knight. The Death Row CEO hopped out of the vehicle, consumed his client in a hug, and handed over the keys in a deliberately public display. "Fam!" he bellowed. "This is for you!"

Tupac smiled, thanked him, then waited for Knight to depart. As soon as he did, Tupac's expression changed.

"This shit ain't mine," he said. "My house isn't mine, the cars aren't mine. None of the fucking shit is mine. It's all for show.*

"I've got nothing."

---

* Tupac had one car, a Jaguar, that was in his name. It was auctioned off in 2008 with full paperwork.

Chapter 22

Vegas

On June 29, 1996, Tupac Shakur found himself in Milan, floating atop the cloud of an existence he would have never thought possible.

He had been invited to Men's Fashion Week by *Vibe* magazine's Karla Radford, then asked to attend the lineup of spring-summer 1997 shows. For a kid who grew up with holes in his thrift-store-purchased socks, who wore the same ratty outfits day after day to the Baltimore School for the Arts, this was not a dream come true—for it was beyond his wildest dreams.

Shortly after his Alitalia flight touched down, Tupac headed to the mansion of the fifty-year-old Gianni Versace for a chat. He later donned a head-to-toe leather outfit, a gift from Versace, and performed his verse of "California Love" at the Versace event.

Over the course of the next few days, Tupac was seated front row at a series of shows—Gianfranco Ferré, Byblos, and Valentino. He was praised and photographed and deemed one of the royal princes of the city. He ate the finest osso buco and gamberi alla busara, set aside Hennessy for bottles of Barolo Pira Riserva, traveled to Florence and lodged at the luxurious Hotel Stazione Leopolda. Where Tupac went, buzz followed.

Then, on July 2, the moment he had been waiting for: Tupac Shakur, less than one year removed from prison-issued green pants, walked the runway of the Romeo Gigli spring-summer gala sporting a shiny golden suit and a smile as wide as his shoulders. He radiated confidence and success, and on his arm was a striking young woman in a red dress.

She was not a model by profession.

Along with a pair of security guards, Tupac was accompanied to Italy by

Kidada Jones, the twenty-two-year-old daughter of the legendary Quincy Jones, runway superstar for a few glorious minutes . . . and Tupac's girlfriend.

And not "girlfriend" in the traditional Tupac sense, meaning one of six or seven or eight or nine women who orbited him simultaneously, thinking they were special while receiving a sliver of attention in exchange for sexual pleasure. Tupac had lived much of his adult life as a dog, and while he wasn't 100 percent past the canine ways, with Kidada Jones something had changed.

The two first met in 1994 at a Manhattan nightclub, and the initial impression was not a good one. Tupac thought he was speaking with Rashida Jones, Kidada's younger sister—literally referring to Kidada as "Rashida" as he rambled on. (Rashida was seventeen at the time.) At one point, he apologized for an earlier interview he had done with *The Source*, when he took Quincy Jones to task for being in a mixed marriage (his wife was the actress Peggy Lipton) and insisting in print, "All he does is stick his dick in white bitches and make fucked-up kids."*

Kidada was a forgiving soul. Also, Tupac's mea culpa felt genuine. "I want to apologize to you," he said. "I didn't mean that about your dad or you. I didn't see you as real human beings."

They started dating, and Kidada kept it secret from her family. Then, in the summer of 1996, she and her new boyfriend were eating at Jerry's Deli in Los Angeles when a man's hands reached from behind and grabbed Tupac's shoulders. It was Quincy Jones, and he said, sternly, "I need to kick it with you for a minute."

The men retreated to an adjacent booth, spoke for nearly an hour, and hugged it out. "Tupac," Kidada later said, "was the love of my life."

Tupac's friends didn't fully understand what he saw in Kidada. She was pretty, but he'd been with prettier. She was sexy, but he'd been with

---

* Rashida penned a blistering letter to *The Source*, writing: "I do think that anyone who reads this article would be shocked by his ignorance and lack of respect for his people. To demean a man like Quincy Jones, a man who came from the ghetto of Chicago and through his talent and perseverance became a living music legend, demeans the whole progress of African Americans. Where the hell would you be if Black people like him hadn't paved the way for you to even have the opportunity to express yourself? I don't see you fighting for your race. In my opinion, you're destroying it and shitting all over your people."

sexier. She was nearly three years his junior, and wasn't overly warm to people. Yet many of Tupac's hangers-on were, for lack of a better word, simplistic. He surrounded himself with folks who viewed young women as objects, and only objects. They couldn't possibly be deep thinkers, or riveting conversationalists, or future American leaders. No, they were reduced entirely to breasts and ass. Frank Alexander, a bodyguard who accompanied the couple to Milan, later tore into Kidada in his autobiography, questioning her worthiness in Tupac's orbit. Alexander, however, envied the attention she received. "[Frank] was especially unprofessional," said Yaasmyn Fula, "and all Tupac's ghetto friends were trying to hit on her behind his dumb-ass back." Truth be told, Tupac's history didn't suggest any special kindness toward women. His need for companionship, however, was forever looming. He could be two people. Three people. Hot and cold. Polite and rude. Kidada saw through it all.

"She sniffed out the phonies and gave them no time," Fula recalled. "She didn't have to go around grinning and kissing Tupac's ass like he was all that. She was straight with him. She was special and he knew it."

When later asked by the journalist Christopher John Farley to explain their relationship, Kidada reflected on two souls from different universes. Tupac was the impoverished, trauma-plagued product of a Black Panther mother fighting for survival. Kidada was the product of wealth and prep schools. "He would say it's the most romantic story," she said, "because it's the poor prince that comes to the king's daughter and becomes the king and then they make a kingdom of their own."

A few weeks before their trip to Milan, Tupac told Kidada he wanted to buy her a ring. He had recently tattooed DADA on his left inner forearm, but that was ink, not jewelry. "It was funny," she recalled. "I'm not a gaudy person. I don't like big rings. But he told me he wanted me to go in the store and pick a gaudy, huge diamond. This is what he wanted. He was like, 'I'm just [going to give] you this ring so you can show your friends that you've got a man who no one ever thought would settle down.'"

On the night of July 2, after the runway show, Tupac and Kidada were sitting on their bed at the Hotel Stazione Leopolda when he reached into his pocket and brought out the ring she had picked. He placed it on her finger and asked for her hand in marriage.

As she said yes, tears filled Tupac's eyes.

It was one of the happiest moments of his life.

The contradictions of Tupac Shakur can fill a book. Maybe an encyclopedia.

How is one both a misogynistic accused rapist *and* a sensitive future spouse? How is one both comfortable calling women bitches *and* writing the lyrics to "Keep Ya Head Up"? How is one a bibliophile *and* naïve? How does one read multiple newspapers per day *and* oftentimes seem ignorant? How can one be a by-product of the Black Panthers *and* appear to stand for nothing the organization believed in? Even as a man engaged to a woman he referred to as "my everything," Tupac continued to play the field and seek out sex.

Tupac walked with a confidence that suggested he had mastered his own universe, yet he was insecure and uncertain. There were always plans. Big plans. A new record label. A clothing line. A charter school. Death Row was about to embark on Death Row East—a Tupac-led effort to spread the brand nationwide. On and on and on. Ideas and opinions were expressed loudly, as if volume equaled certainty of action. But Tupac spoke far faster than he acted.

On September 4, 1996, he returned to New York to attend the MTV Video Music Awards at Radio City Music Hall. For years, he had loved visiting the Big Apple, his home for the first half of his life. Listen closely, and one could still hear the city in Tupac's speech patterns. The sharp syllables. The speedy pacing. Holler "West Side!" all he wanted, Tupac Shakur remained a New Yorker.

Yet on this night, he was off. More jittery. Looking over his shoulder. One year earlier there had been a shooting in Red Hook, Brooklyn, while Tha Dogg Pound and Snoop Doggy Dogg filmed a video for the song "New York, New York." It had shaken people. Ever since he left Clinton, Tupac had been fielding death threats, and though he could laugh them off, being back triggered something internal. He and Snoop were slated to present the award for Best Hard Rock Video, and they walked onto the stage accompanied by a smattering of boos. Why, seven months earlier he was yukking it up with Kiss and Hootie. Now, he felt targeted. Death Row brought a dozen security guards to Manhattan, but Tupac knew it took but a single bullet. "It was bad," said Josh Tyrangiel, a reporter who covered the show for *Vibe*. "You could tell Pac was super scared. He was playacting gangsta rapper, and it was catching up with him."

When the presentation ended (Tupac shaking hands with Metallica lead singer James Hetfield was odd, though not quite Kiss odd), Tupac and Snoop retreated backstage for an interview with MTV. Tupac was in rare— and weird—form. Less than six months after recording "Hit 'Em Up," he was blaming the press (and MTV specifically) for the coastal beef. "The East Coast vs. West Coast thing is something the journalists and people are making up just to get paid off so it can drag out," he said. "So they're perpetuating it so there can be drama. Which, I still love MTV, but when it all goes down, don't look at me and Biggie and be like, why is there a big East Coast–West Coast war when shooting this to three hundred countries telling them about an East Coast–West Coast war that they would never know exists. So that's where information becomes a problem."

Snoop, normally quiet, added: "If it did exist, Pac, we wouldn't be here. That lets you know it's not existent."

Tupac nodded. "We'll try to be better role models and y'all try to stop putting that drama out there," he said. "You got a lot of power, a lot of responsibility. We both do. We both need to exercise greater restraint."

The rare moment of public introspection suggested that perhaps Tupac was cognizant of the trouble he had wrought. He had quietly begun planning a new project, titled "One Nation," where he aspired to team up with a slew of East Coast artists (*not* Biggie or Puffy) and form a unifying collaboration. Several performers, including Nice & Smooth's Greg Nice, Luniz's Numskull, and New Jersey natives Asu and Capital LS from the group Rumpletilskinz, had visited Los Angeles to help with planning. "I can tell you, Pac had dreams of uniting everyone," said Smooth B of Nice & Smooth. "He wanted to be that guy."

And yet, when the Video Music Awards ended, a more familiar Tupac reemerged. He and his Death Row crew attended the official after-party in Bryant Park on Forty-Second Street, and granted an interview to Tony "Master T" Young from an outfit called MuchMusic. Gripping a microphone, staring at his cameraman, Young asked two of the nation's most famous men to introduce themselves to his viewers . . .

Knight: "I'm Suge Knight."

Tupac: "Tupac Shakur."

Knight briefly delved into his label's upcoming projects, followed by Tupac going into a nearly two-minute-long uninterrupted monologue that started with, "Do you believe in God? Believe in Death Row East," and wrapped with multiple shots at the East Coast and, specifically, Nasir "Nas" Jones, the twenty-two-year-old Queens-born rapper who had emerged as one of the genre's top artists. Tupac first took offense in July, when he interpreted Nas's song "The Message" as a direct-hit diss track (in particular, he was irked by one line—"Fake thugs, no love, you get the slug"). As was the case with Biggie when Tupac accused him of being behind the Quad Studios shooting, Nas was befuddled. "The Message" had nothing to do with Tupac. Ironically, it actually concerned Biggie.

Regardless, there was heightened tension at the after-party. Along with Knight, Tupac attended with several members of the Outlawz, as well as Mob Pirus working security. Nas, too, was surrounded by his people. The two crews approached one another. "We mean mugging they homies," Napoleon of the Outlawz recalled. "They mean mugging us." Tupac and Nas stood face-to-face, unable to be heard by others over the loud music from a nearby DJ stand. Then—to the shock of those standing nearby—they hugged.

Nas told Tupac the truth about "The Message."

Tupac told Nas it was all good.

"We had a great convo, man," Nas later said. "He explained he thought I was dissing him on the song 'The Message.' He thought I was dissing him and I heard he was dissing me at clubs. He was like, 'Yo Nas, we brothers, man. We not supposed to go through this' and I was like, 'That's what I'm saying.'

"We had a plan," Nas said, "to squash it in Vegas."

Vegas.

Tupac *loved* Vegas.

Everything about it. The lights. The sounds. The action. The pussy. Vegas wasn't his home, but it felt like his sanctuary. In the hip-hop world, dozens of artists considered Las Vegas their go-to retreat—fly in with the crew, gamble, eat, maybe catch a fight, chase ass, smoke, drink, eat some more, chase some extra ass, fly out.

Since his release from Clinton, Tupac had spent a good number of nights along the Strip. Las Vegas served as a Death Row satellite campus. Knight had played his college football there, fell in love with the city, and in 1994 opened a nightspot, Club 662, at 1700 East Flamingo Road. Why, in May he purchased the Vegas mansion where Robert De Niro lived during the filming of *Casino*.

So when it was announced that Mike Tyson, the WBC heavyweight champion, would fight Bruce Seldon, the WBA heavyweight champion, at the MGM Grand on September 7, 1996, Knight ponied up for dozens of tickets and invited the Death Row fam to be his guests.

And Tupac initially declined the invitation. A few weeks earlier Tanya Hart, a TV host for BET, had invited him to attend Sunday services at the West Angeles Church of God in Christ in Los Angeles. It was a Black congregation packed with celebrity attendees, ranging from Denzel Washington to Magic Johnson to Samuel L. Jackson. "He promised me he was coming," Hart recalled. "But then he didn't show."

Tupac *loved* Vegas.

It wasn't just the slots and the women. It was Iron Mike Tyson, a man whose life mirrored Tupac's. "Mike Tyson," wrote Rob Marriott in *Vibe*, "is a thug's champion." Five years Tupac's senior, Tyson was (like Tupac) a product of New York City whose childhood was unstable (like Tupac) and filled with trauma (like Tupac). He never had much of a relationship with his biological father (like Tupac) and his primary male role model (like Tupac's) was a street hustler. From an early age, Tyson (like Tupac) recognized he needed to fight to survive. And even though young Mike did so with his fists and young Tupac did so with his words, they mirrored one another. Tyson and Tupac first met in 1991 at a party thrown at the Hollywood Palladium by Magic Johnson, and both lived fast, spoke boastfully, and allowed the trappings of fame to gobble them up. Tupac had even written a song ("Road 2 Glory") to be played during Tyson's ring entrance against Frank Bruno in March.

In 1992, Tyson was convicted of raping an eighteen-year-old beauty pageant contestant named Desiree Washington, and sentenced to six years in prison. In 1995, Tupac was convicted of sexually abusing a nineteen-year-old aspiring model named Ayanna Jackson, and sentenced to one and a half to four and a half years in prison. They wrote letters to one another from behind bars. In fact, before he was locked up, Tupac paid a visit to Plainfield, Indiana, where Tyson was serving his time inside the Indiana Youth Center. The trip was arranged by Watani Tyehimba, who wanted his charge to understand where those who behaved as he did oftentimes wound up. Tupac didn't initially care to go, but when he sat across from Tyson, he felt brotherhood. Tyson shared some hard truths: *Stop hanging around with riffraff. Look after your money. Rise above the drama.* "Afterward Tupac accused me of telling Mike what to say," Tyehimba recalled. "I assured him that wasn't the case . . . that Mike was just being real and honest with him. I wish Tupac had listened a little harder."

Tyson exited prison on March 25, 1995, and while his return to the ring had a watch-a-midget-fight-a-bear level of sadness to it (he was fed a diet of tin cans to batter), Tupac was all in on the spectacle. Why, he even recorded another entrance theme—"Let'z Get It On"—that Tyson promised to use for his Seldon brawl. So on the morning of September 7, two days after returning from New York, Tupac stepped into a black SUV outside his Woodland Hills home for the four-and-a-half-hour journey to Vegas. The fight was slated for nine o'clock that evening, which allowed plenty of time to travel the 270 miles. Under normal circumstances, Tupac would have been accompanied by Death Row bodyguards. However, because of state laws, Reggie Wright Jr., the label's chief of security, had headed to Nevada early with the other protectors to apply for temporary Nevada gun permits. As a result, Tupac was part of a three-SUV caravan that included Knight *and* a half dozen or so members of the Mob Pirus, the Compton street gang affiliated with the Bloods.

Not one to patiently sit and watch the world pass, Tupac grew fidgety as the trip progressed. After 114 miles, the fleet of SUVs pulled off the Lenwood Road exit along Interstate 15 in sleepy Barstow, California, home to one of California's largest In-N-Out Burgers.

From a young age, Tupac could not get enough fast food. It had comprised much of his diet. When you're poor, and living in the projects, there are no organic markets. So it's fatty cheeseburgers, salty fries, sugary sodas. And while many in the West Coast hip-hop scene raved over Fat-burger, to Tupac In-N-Out was equally dope. The meat was seasoned just right. The buns were spongy. The fries, though a bit soggy, filled him. Tupac listed chicken wings and macaroni and cheese as his favorite foods and Sunkist orange soda as his (non-Hennessy) drink of choice. Fast food was his jam.

When the cars reached the parking lot, Knight exited, walked through the restaurant's front doors, and waited on line. Meanwhile, Tupac and the gangbangers hung in the parking lot, smoking cigarettes and stretching out stiff limbs. Around this same time, two buses carrying the football team from Long Beach Polytechnic High School also arrived at the In-N-Out. They had lost a road game to Las Vegas's Green Valley High the previous night, and now—mid-return—were pausing for grub.

The first to spot Tupac was Robert Hollie, a backup quarterback for the Jackrabbits. He looked out the window and said, "Yo, it's Pac!"

"What?" a teammate asked.

"It's Tupac!" he yelled. "It's Tupac!"

A slew of players rushed toward the windows, then were herded off the buses by a coach and into the restaurant. Two players, Hollie and a nose tackle named Gary Barnes, led a dozen or so teammates toward the SUVs. Tupac and the Pirus were facing the opposite direction, and were caught off guard. A pair of gangsters spun and pulled out their Glocks. "Bloods," Tupac said, "you can't be walking up on me like that!"

He cursed the boys out, but took stock of their collective youth. These were high school kids. Zits and peach fuzz.

"Where are all y'all little niggas from?" he asked.

"Long Beach," Hollie replied.

"Oh, so y'all know my homie Snoop?" Tupac said.

With the temperature lowered, Tupac chatted for a few minutes, then dismissed the athletes with a nod. As the buses pulled out of the lot, a few Cal Poly players yelled toward Tupac, who was well out of shouting distance.

"Go fuck yourself, Pac!" one said.

"Fuck you, Pac!" said another.

"There was one guy coming on our bus, and I won't give up his name," said Larry Croom, a running back who went on to play in the NFL. "But he screamed, 'That's why you got shot! And the next time I hope you die!'

"That stuck with me," Croom said. "It really stuck with me."

Bruce Seldon and Mike Tyson were originally scheduled to meet in the ring on July 13, 1996.

That was the date the camps for both fighters agreed upon, and in the lead-up, Seldon—aka "The Atlantic City Express"—worked his ass off. An elite athlete who, at six foot one and 229 pounds, could walk across a basketball court on his hands, Seldon's greatest flaw was flagging motivation. That's why a pugilist with George Foreman–esque talent was a boxing afterthought. "We went out to Vegas eight months before the fight, and Bruce was all in and in peak condition," said Rocco DePersia, his manager. "He was ready, and I'm pretty certain he would have given Tyson all he could handle."

On July 3, however, Don King, the fight's promoter, announced that Tyson had come down with bronchitis, and the event would be pushed back to September 7. Seldon was crestfallen. DePersia, for his part, was skeptical. "It seemed kind of fishy," he said—and when Seldon publicly questioned the postponement, an angry Tyson said he would deliver his opponent "the worst beating of his life."

Whatever the case, the delay changed everything. Without it, Bruce Seldon and Mike Tyson would have fought on July 13. Without it, Tupac Shakur—in the midst of filming *Gridlock'd* that summer—wouldn't have attended.

Once he arrived in Las Vegas, Tupac met up with Kidada, who drove out on her own and checked into their room at the Luxor hotel. This was around 1:00 p.m.—five hours before the undercard bouts were slated to start, eight hours before the main event. Although he wasn't anticipating any type of violence, Tupac was aware that the fight scene—especially when Death Row was involved—could turn unsightly. In addition, this wasn't really a plus-one affair. Knight wanted his guys there. His *guys*. Kidada hung back.

Before the fight, Tupac, who loved to gamble, headed down to the Luxor's casino and found his way to the twenty-five-dollar craps table.

He was wearing a rust-colored silk shirt and a thirty-thousand-dollar diamond-studded Euphanasia pendant around his neck. After an hour or so, he and a bunch of Death Row guys walked the 1.1 miles to the MGM, where—according to Frank Alexander, one of his bodyguards—his fortunes changed for the better. "He began winning big," Alexander recalled. "He was covering all the odds and was coming away with $1,400 to $2,000 a roll. Winners always attract a crowd, but as soon as people started figuring out who he was, the crowd got more serious. Tupac loved the attention. What better place for a high-roller gangsta to be seen rolling high than in Vegas at a craps table?"

Tupac gambled, roamed Vegas, gambled some more, returned to his room, changed into a baggy gold shirt and even baggier jeans. He and Alexander were supposed to meet Knight inside the MGM Grand roughly an hour before Seldon–Tyson, but the Death Row CEO was, as was the norm, late. Ever fidgety, ever agitated, Tupac paced back and forth. "I'm gonna get my own goddamn tickets!" he snapped. This was mere talk. The best seats ran a thousand dollars. When Knight finally arrived, it was 7:30 p.m. and someone named Desi ("*Please welcome the talented Horn Records recording artist...*") was brutalizing the national anthem.

Knight and Tupac entered and walked toward their Row E near-ringside seats. Standing nearby was Butch Lewis, the veteran boxing promoter. Tupac tapped him on the shoulder and asked, "Mr. Lewis?"

Butch Lewis nodded.

"You don't know me, but I'm Tupac Shakur," Tupac said.

"Of course I know you, Negro," Lewis replied. "How are you?"

"Your daughter—her name is Sita, right?" Tupac asked.

Lewis nodded reluctantly. Sita Lewis was, indeed, his daughter, as well as a BET producer who had briefly met Tupac years earlier. Devoutly Christian, Sita felt compelled by the Lord to send a note to Tupac while he was inside Clinton, accompanied by several religious books.

"She wrote me a letter when I was locked up," Tupac said. "I just want you to know that letter held me down. Please tell her."

Overcome by the moment, Lewis hugged Tupac.

"Thank you, brother," he said. "Thank you."

By the time Seldon and Tyson met at center ring to hear referee Richard Steele's instructions, Tupac—one of approximately nine thousand in attendance—stood ready. He was a bit high, a bit drunk, buzzing off his casino triumphs, and amped for an entertaining battle.

Alas, Seldon–Tyson lasted one minute and forty-nine seconds—one of the shortest title bouts in heavyweight history. Tyson first dropped Seldon with a left hook seventy-two seconds into the fight, then nailed him again with a phantom left hook moments later, knocking him back to the ground. "I swear he never hit him," said Tim Neverett, a Los Angeles Dodgers announcer who attended the fight. "Watch the replay from every angle. He didn't connect." Seldon rose, but wobbled, and Steele ended the fight. Boos rained down, with chants of "Fake! Fake! Fake!" filling the arena. "It was as one-sided as a shipwreck," wrote Jim Murray in the *Los Angeles Times.* "The *Titanic* put up a better fight against the iceberg."

People anticipating a classic battle left angry. Tupac, however, left giddy. He and Knight exited into a corridor, and Tupac was ecstatic. "Did y'all see that?" he bellowed toward a BET news cameraman positioned backstage. "Fifty punches! I counted 'em! Tyson did it to him. We bad like that. Come out of prison and we runnin' shit!"

Then he entered the MGM casino.

Let's pause for a moment to consider something important: Tupac Shakur was not going to be in Las Vegas.

Yes, he dug the city and he dug the fights. But he had another matter to handle, and it was pissing him off. On September 6, one day before the fight, a relative had called to say that his cousin Kenny Lesane was causing all sorts of trouble at the family home down in Georgia.

"What type of trouble?" Tupac asked.

"He's using crack again," the relative said. "And he pawned off your MAC-11."

Tupac was incredulous. All his relatives did was milk him dry, then ask for more. Did any of these people work? Have a sense of self-sufficiency? Plus, Kenneth Lesane was a Muslim! He talked it up nonstop. *All praise to Allah* and all that jazz . . .

"He did the fuck *what*?" Tupac said.

The MAC-11 was a beloved possession—a military-grade submachine gun that fired twelve hundred rounds per minute and emptied its full thirty-two-round magazine in less than two seconds. To Tupac, the MAC-11 was the Halle Berry of firearms.

And, indeed, Lesane had pawned the MAC-11—which Tupac stored in a closet in the house—in order to score some dough to buy crack. "I begged everyone not to tell him," Lesane said. "I begged my mom, I begged Feni. I told them, 'If he finds out, he's gonna come down here and actually kill me.'"

When the phone rang inside the Georgia home, Lesane's wife, Jacqueline, answered.

Tupac: "Where's your crackhead husband at?"

Jacqueline: "He's out."

Tupac, by far the most well-read member of the family, knew the Qur'an well. In this case, verse 5:38 came to mind: "As for male and female thieves, cut off their hands for what they have done—a deterrent from Allah."

Tupac: "Tell that crackhead fake Muslim I'm coming to Atlanta tomorrow, and I'm gonna cut his right hand off."

Tupac prepared to fly to Atlanta. He called Delta and booked a ticket. He was *that* furious, and also tired of the family drama. He even sat down in the moment and wrote a song, "High Speed," that included the line, "Put your family in danger / just to get high." But . . . for whatever reason, he didn't follow through on the trip. Maybe it was the treasured time with Kidada. Maybe it was the chance to watch Mike Tyson work. Whatever the case, he never made the trek down South.

"I wish he had come, I wish he had chopped off my hands," Lesane said. "Because then he wouldn't have been in Vegas."*

When Tupac and Knight walked into the casino of the MGM, they were accompanied by an entourage that included two members of Comp-

---

* Set Shakur, Tupac's sister, said she blames Kenny Lesane, in part, for her brother's demise. "You're supposed to be his big cousin. You're supposed to be looking out for him. And what are you doing? Getting high and stealing his stuff. That's unforgivable."

ton's Mob Piru Bloods. One was Alton "Buntry" McDonald, a gregarious thirty-year-old who served as Death Row's production manager and was also one of Knight's closest boyhood friends. "He was my brother and I loved him," said James McDonald, a fellow Mob Piru and Alton's sibling. "But he wasn't no saint."

The other was Trevon "Tre" Lane.

Both were—unlike Tupac and Knight—real Gs. They had come up as gangbangers in South Central Los Angeles and knew their way around guns, around drugs, around fighting. Death was not something they feared so much as something they imposed. Trevon, in particular, was no softie. Also Knight's boyhood friend, the twenty-four-year-old was employed by the label as—according to a police report—"one of Suge's thugs," and wouldn't hesitate to throw down. Life was about earning respect and combating disrespect. You did not pull shit on members of Mob Piru.

As the men cruised through the MGM's packed lobby, Trevon stopped in his tracks and pushed his chin forward. He could not believe this. He would not believe this. It couldn't be. *Could it?*

Standing there, mere feet away, appeared to be Orlando Anderson, a twenty-two-year-old South Side Compton Crip better known as Lando or Baby Lane. He was a scrawny, narrow-shouldered Black man with a thin mustache, droopy eyes, and thick eyebrows. Back in South Central, Orlando—raised by his great-great-grandmother Utah in a house on South Burris Road—was known as a feisty kid with lightning-quick fists and the necessary smarts to make something of himself. He peddled bags of weed from a corner, but only to make enough to stay afloat. He was fast with a laugh ("A jokester," recalled a cousin. "Just cracking on people") and—as a boy—spent summers with relatives in Arkansas, leaping into swimming holes and rolling down grassy hills and (for brief spells) feeling unencumbered. He and one of his closest friends, a fellow Crip named Ian "Lil Spank" Salavaria, attended Dominiquez High School together. They shared passions for chasing girls and fighting. "I'd seen him beat the shit out of plenty of guys," said Salavaria. "There were two or three occasions when he was gonna jump a dude in high school, and I wanted to help him but he made me stay out of it." Like Mel Gibson's character in *Lethal Weapon*, Orlando had a loose right shoulder that he popped in and out of the socket. "He'd knock [his shoulder] back in like a warrior," Salavaria said. "But he was not a killer. He fought with his hands, he'd beat your ass good. But you live to see another day when you fight with your hands."

In contrast to many of his gangbanging brethren, Anderson graduated high school. His 1992 class ring was his prized possession. Four years later, he lived with his girlfriend Rasheena in her apartment near Compton. They were parents to two daughters, and another girlfriend had recently given birth to a third. Anderson's dream was to start his own record label. He also loved sports, which is why he and Rasheena and several fellow Crips drove to Vegas for Seldon–Tyson.

Perhaps Trevon would not have noticed Orlando inside the MGM casino but for the one thing that made him stand out: the white, orange, and blue XXL No. 13 Dan Marino Miami Dolphins jersey that covered his body.

Just three weeks earlier, a man named Duane "Keefe D" Davis—a self-anointed "five-star general" of Compton's South Side Crips—had handed four thousand dollars in cash to a local high school football player and his gang member friends. He told them to head to the nearby Lakewood Mall and shop for new clothing. While perusing the Foot Locker, the youngsters ran into members of the rival Mob Piru Bloods. According to Trevon, some of the Crips went on the attack—punching him and tearing the gold Death Row medallion from his neck. The jewelry had been a gift from Knight, and taking it, wrote William Shaw of *The Guardian*, was "like taking a war trophy." Trevon didn't get a clear look at all of the assailants, but he sure as hell recognized motherfucking Orlando Anderson.

Now, with Dan Marino's doppelgänger standing nearby, Trevon turned toward Tupac and whispered into his ear. And, in the moments that followed, Tupac committed an act that would later be rightly described as:

"So stupid." —Yaasmyn Fula

"Totally unnecessary." —Leila Steinberg

"Ridiculously dumb." —Money-B

"Without a second of wisdom." —Prime Minister Pete Nice

"Fucking insane." —Chopmaster J

"Out of his element." —James Anderson

"Insane." —Rob Marriott

"Heartbreaking." —Kenny Lesane

"The most moronic thing ever." —Kendrick Wells

"So, so, so stupid." —Avra Warsovsky

"No judgment to speak of." —Barbara Jean Powers

"Unwise to the extreme." —Wood Harris

"Dumber than dumb." —Lela Rochon

"The worst move ever." —Ernest Dickerson

"Staggeringly idiotic." —Ryan D

"Uncalled for." —Brian Times

Without hesitation, a man lacking the athleticism to competently shoot a basketball, a man who came up dancing through the hallways of his performing arts school, a man who cried listening to the music of Don McLean and Sinéad O'Connor, a man who never joined a gang or even came close to joining a gang, a man who was taught to care for his Black brothers and sisters, a man who had sworn off Thug Life as a thing of the past, a man who mimicked his way through much of existence . . .

That man stepped to Orlando Anderson (who happened to be an enormous fan of Tupac's music), asked, "You from the South?," then punched him in the face with a right hook. Anderson dropped to the ground, and Tupac, Knight, and five others proceeded to kick and stomp him as he covered up. "They made a huge mistake allowing Tupac to play the role of a gangbanger," said James McDonald, aka "Mob James." "It wasn't him. He was acting." Frank Alexander, the Death Row security guard, tried to pull Tupac away and failed, but the jerking motion loosened the Euphanasia medallion from his neck and onto the marble floor. As Tupac reached for it, Alexander begged him to stop. "God damn it, Pac!" he screamed. "You know you can't be doing this!"

Seconds later, with casino security guards approaching, Tupac, Knight, and the Death Row crew bolted—leaving Orlando Anderson on the ground, bloodied, bruised, and humiliated.

And it's simply . . . *unfathomable.* Why was Death Row's biggest artist throwing down in a casino fight? One whose origins had *literally nothing* to do with him? Would Mercury Records have stood by and watched

Lionel Richie punch some antagonists? Would RCA have encouraged Daryl Hall and John Oates to kick ass? Death Row employed hardened gangbangers so—in theory at least—the artists *didn't* have to mess around. Yet here was Tupac Shakur, diving headfirst into waters far too deep. "You don't kick a gangbanger in the face," said Kendrick Wells, Tupac's longtime friend. "It's a pretty basic rule. But Tupac manifested everything about himself. If you're afraid of death, which he was, you make death inevitable."

Because most everything on the Vegas Strip is within walking distance, Tupac and Alexander strolled from the MGM back to the Luxor. Folks gathered around to bask in his glow, and if Tupac was having any moments of regret or reflection, he hardly showed it. "I knocked him out faster than Tyson!" he boasted to onlookers while throwing sad little hooks into the air.

When they reached the Luxor, Tupac and Alexander went back to the room, where Kidada was sitting with Jamala Lesane, Tupac's cousin and the daughter of his aunt Gloria. He changed into a green Nike basketball jersey and sweatpants, and told his fiancée it would not be a good idea for her to attend the Seldon–Tyson after-party at Knight's Club 662 (the numeric name was telephone code for "MOB"). "I don't want y'all around that crowd," he said. Tupac offered Kidada the blow-by-blow of his beatdown of Orlando Anderson. He was twenty-five, and could count on one hand the number of actual fistfights he had even engaged in. This victory—over a Crip, no less—felt great.

According to Alexander, Tupac was encouraged to don a bulletproof vest for the remainder of the evening. However, that would have been impossible—Tupac failed to bring his to Las Vegas. "I had picked him up from New York at the airport a couple of days before," Kidada later told the journalist Christopher John Farley. "He had his vest on, because he usually does always wear his vest. But when we were getting ready to go [to Vegas] I asked him if he wanted to pack his vest and he said, 'It's too hot.' So we just didn't pack the vest." There was some logic to the thinking—on the day of the fight, temperatures had skyrocketed to ninety-four degrees. "Those vests are uncomfortable, especially when it's really hot," said Reggie Wright Jr., Death Row's head of security. "It would've been more sur-prising had Tupac worn the vest than decide not to."

Members of the Outlawz, Tupac's hip-hop group, were also in Vegas, and the plan was for everyone to catch a ride with Knight in his black BMW 750iL and head to Club 662. Yet as Michael Namikas noted in his *Tupac Encyclopedia*, "Frank [Alexander] reached to open the BMW's rear passenger door, but Tupac stopped him before he could get in. Tupac handed Frank the keys to Kidada's Lexus and explained that he would be the Outlawz' designated driver that night. Suge put the BMW's trans-mission in drive and sped off toward his gated mansion on Monte Rosa Avenue, southeast of the Luxor."

The vehicles rode to Knight's home, then, at approximately 10:30 p.m. redirected toward Club 662, on East Flamingo Road. There were three cars in the procession: The lead vehicle was a BMW wagon driven by Kevyn "K-Dubb" Woods, Knight's friend. The third car was Alexander chauf-feuring the Outlawz in the Lexus. The car sandwiched in the middle was Tupac and Knight in the BMW—windows down, the sounds of Tupac's upcoming (and yet unreleased) album, *Killuminati: The 7 Day Theory*, thumping through the dry air.

After a brief police stop (Knight was pulled over by two bicycle cops for playing the music too loudly and for failing to have a license plate. The plates were found in the trunk, and the vehicle was released mo-ments later without citation), the cars made their way to Club 662. At precisely 11:00 p.m., Leonard Jefferson, a boxing fan driving from the MGM, spotted the BMW with Tupac's head peering from the rolled-down window.

"What's up, Pac?" he yelled. "Where you guys headed?"

"We 'bout to go to the club!" he shouted back. "You can follow behind us! Come with us!"

Jefferson reached for his camera and asked permission to take a photo. Tupac turned his way and Jefferson pressed the button. Even though his expression projected gloominess, Tupac was gleeful. *Vegas, baby! Vegas!* He rose and popped his head through the sunroof, hollering toward walkers as Knight navigated the car.

At 11:17 p.m., the BMW ran into a red light at the intersection of Flamingo and Koval Lane, less than two miles from the final destination. The vehicle driven by K-Dubb was in front of Knight and Tupac; the one piloted by Alexander was behind them. When a car occupied by two women rolled up, Tupac—flirty as ever—invited them to Club 662.

Because Las Vegas is a city of perpetual motion, where lights and sound blur into an ever-evolving tableau, it is easy to miss details. People come, people go. Celebrities are here and there and everywhere. There are drunk folks, sober folks, mopeds, motorcycles, scooters, old cars, new cars, fast cars, slow cars.

At this moment, an otherwise nondescript white, four-door, late-model Cadillac pulled forward in a right lane and stopped alongside Knight's BMW, inches away from Tupac's open window. A half hour earlier, the same Cadillac had been waiting outside Club 662, anticipating an encounter that never occurred. The occupants had driven off, but then—by pure luck—spotted Tupac hanging out the window, barking at women strolling the Strip.

Again, it was just a car.

An ordinary car.

A no-reason-to-look-at car.

The driver, a Compton Crip named Terrence "Bubble Up" Brown, would have meant nothing to Tupac.

The man in the front passenger seat, another Compton Crip named Duane "Keefe D" Davis (Anderson's uncle, and the man who gave the young gang members mall shopping dough), also would have meant nothing to Tupac.

The man sitting in the left back seat, *another* Compton Crip named DeAndre "Freaky" Smith, would have meant nothing to Tupac.

But the passenger in the back right seat, the kid in the Miami Dolphins jersey from the MGM lobby . . . had Tupac gazed super closely, he might have looked familiar.

It was Orlando Anderson.

And he had been humiliated in public.

By a *fucking rapper.*

"Did Tupac think Orlando would just take that beatdown?" said Ian "Lil Spank" Salavaria. "Did the motherfucker think he'd just walk away like a bitch?"

Anderson rapidly fired a series of shots through Tupac's open window, all via a .40-caliber Glock 22.

"It sounded like somebody knocking with their knuckles on the top of a roof," said Mike Finnell, who was sitting a few vehicles back while returning from a Doobie Brothers concert at the Riviera. "You wouldn't necessarily think it was gunfire. *Knock, knock, knock.*" The first bullet hit Tupac in his thigh and right hand, mangling his index finger. The second bullet hit Tupac in his right hip, and he twisted awkwardly at the torso. The third bullet hit his chest, and the fourth bullet traveled through his chest and beneath his right arm, puncturing his lung. The Cadillac, driven by Terrence Brown, sped off.

"Get down!" Knight screamed, and he yanked Tupac to the BMW mat. All told, thirteen shots were fired, and eight tore through the vehicle. Bullet fragmentation grazed Knight across the back of his head, not altogether unlike the shot Tupac took at Quad Studios.

In the heat of the moment, Suge Knight didn't know what to do. He was plenty good at flexing his muscles and scowling toward his enemies and making vulnerable foes drink urine. But this was next level. His meal ticket was spewing blood and fading in and out of consciousness. The nearest hospital, the University Medical Center of Southern Nevada, was but four and a half miles away, and, well, this was all uncharted turf. Was he supposed to dial 911 and wait? Would law enforcement even help? Could they be trusted to assist them? What about an ambulance? Knight wasn't a gangbanger, per se, but he played the role with enough integrity that he thought like one. Would a gangbanger call law enforcement for help? No chance.

Knight made a sharp U-turn over a traffic median and directed his BMW back toward Las Vegas Boulevard. The other Death Row cars followed. Around this same time Chris Carroll, a sergeant with the Las Vegas Police Department's bicycle unit, was positioned a stone's throw away. Through his eight years on the job in Sin City, Carroll had learned to dread fight nights. Especially Mike Tyson fight nights. "No other fighter drew the type of crowd that he did," Carroll said. "It was a pimp-and-ho-and-gangster extravaganza. All the pimps would come to showcase their women, and you'd have hundreds of thousands of people here. I hated it." There had been more than thirty calls involving varied sexual harassments and robberies. A couple of gangbangers had looted a liquor store, and several cops had called in sick, leaving their peers overmatched.

Carroll was the lone sergeant on that night, meaning he was solo and in charge of the force's twenty bicycle officers. "So I heard the guys that work for me come on the radio with excitement in their voices," he said. "They said a shooting had just occurred at Koval and Flamingo, and vehicles were fleeing the scene. They were eastbound on the Strip, but headed westbound. So I start riding that way, and I'm heading in their direction. And I have no idea how I'm gonna stop anyone on my bicycle. Especially with people apparently shooting guns. So we're heading right toward one another, but they hang a left on Harmon and they spin out and the car loses control."

Knight's BMW was damaged and a pair of tires were torn up. It finally conked out feet in front of the Aladdin Hotel, at the intersection of Las Vegas Boulevard and Harmon Avenue. Within minutes, four other Death Row–affiliated vehicles arrived.

Sitting on the side of the road, suspended in inanimate bewilderment, Knight was lost. He popped open his door, and Carroll—noticing all the cars—anticipated a shoot-out. "You can tell a lot of these guys are hardcore gangsters," he said. "I knew I was dealing with some rough guys." Carroll pointed his gun at the suspects and walked closer. Harmon Avenue is about fifty feet wide. It took a while for the drama to unfold.

At the same time Carroll was closing in, Malcolm Greenidge, better known as E.D.I. Mean from the Outlawz, bolted from the car Alexander had been driving and scurried toward Tupac. "Get on the ground!" Tupac told him. "They're gonna shoot you!"

Carroll closed in, and the chaos before him was confusing. Some of the people appeared to be hurt. Others were fine. Five vehicles, all with California plates. Engines running. "I scan the cars," he said, "and one guy is sitting there and I can't see his hands. So I approach with my gun pointed and I'm yelling at him to put his hands in the air, which he's not doing. And when I got close enough, I could see he was all shot up."

Carroll wedged open the damaged passenger door, and Tupac's body rolled out. The officer grabbed him with his left arm. "He had blood coming out of his mouth and nose," Carroll said. "He's squirming and he's trying to yell, but he can't do it. So I take him down to the pavement."

Knight approached from behind, yelling, "Pac! Pac!" Carroll turned and pointed his gun in that direction. "He was like six foot seven and four hundred pounds," he recalled. "And if he jumped on my back, I'd be in trouble." Knight backed up.

By now a second police officer had arrived, and he helped Carroll relocate Tupac to the asphalt. Tupac was fading. His energy was low. His skin was going from brown to pasty gray. "I was like, 'He's going to die,'" Carroll said. "So I looked at him and said, 'Who shot you? What happened? Who did it?'"

Tupac turned his eyes toward Knight. Once again, Carroll asked, "Sir, who shot you?"

Nothing.

"Sir, who did this to you?"

Nothing.

"Sir, who did this to you?"

Nothing.

"It reminded me of somebody running a marathon," Carroll said. "They're going, they're trying, they're screaming and getting everything out—and all of a sudden they realize they have nothing left and they just stop. He was lying there on the ground, calm. I've got my arm on the back of his head and shoulders, looking at him."

Out of diligence, Carroll gave it one last attempt.

"Sir," he said, "who shot you?"

As if touched by a live wire, Tupac Shakur's brown eyes widened, then met the blue eyes of Chris Carroll. He opened his mouth, pursed his lips.

"Fuck you," he said.

With that, Tupac Shakur lost consciousness.

Chapter 23

Thug Angel

Tupac Shakur and Suge Knight were rushed via ambulance to University Medical Center on West Charleston Boulevard. Word spread quickly in Death Row circles, and the one thing everyone knew was that Tupac would be fine.

Why? Because Tupac was always fine. Punch him, shoot him, accuse him of sexual assault, imprison him—it never mattered. He was forged of Teflon and tungsten. Forget nine lives. Tupac Shakur was touched by the gods of indestructability.

But . . . upon closer inspection, this situation appeared to be different. While Knight's stay in the ER would be brief, Tupac was suffering from a massive hemothorax (an accumulation of blood inside the gap between his lungs), and within minutes of his arrival at the hospital was wheeled into an operating room for an hour. An exploratory surgery was performed, during which two liters of blood were suctioned from his chest. His right lung was removed, and his blood pressure plummeted. His pulse, a report later said, was "very thready and initially he had a minimal blood pressure, which rapidly declined." An endotracheal tube ran down his windpipe. His head was swollen. His right index finger was gone.

He was on life support.

One day later, Tupac underwent a second operation—this one lasting two and a half hours—to repair internal injuries and remove a bullet from his pelvic area. By now, his mother, Afeni Shakur, his sister, Set, and his aunt Glo had arrived from Georgia, as had Yaasmyn Fula from Los Angeles. Kidada Jones, his fiancée, would come to the hospital every morning and stay deep into the night (she signed the next-of-kin papers and was handed a bundle containing his jewelry and bloodied clothing). According to a *Los Angeles Times* report, "Friends said they were told at first that Shakur had only a 50-50 chance of survival, but hospital officials later said he was likely to live." Whoever supplied this information was either lying or uninformed. Among doctors and nurses, hope was at a nadir.

Sitting inside her home in Lumberton, North Carolina, Barbara Jean Powers was glued to the news when her phone rang. It was Glo, her cousin, and she was screaming. "You've got to get to Vegas!" she said. "We're sending for you right now! Get here! Please!" Two years earlier, when Tupac had been shot at Quad Studios, he was gripping a prayer cloth that Barbara Jean—a seasoned faith healer—had promised would keep him safe. Now Barbara Jean headed to Raleigh International Airport, flew straight to Las Vegas, and was rushed to the hospital. Glo ushered her into Tupac's room. "He was all hooked up and plugged up and everything," Powers recalled. "And when I went there, I said, 'Tupac, this is Barbara Jean.' He jumped. Literally jumped. And Glo said, 'God, it's the first time he's moved.' It's because he knew my presence was there."

According to Powers, that same day she ran into Suge Knight, who was visiting the family. "He walked out the room," Powers said. "And I told Glo and Afeni that that man was the enemy. I said, 'Y'all trusting the devil.' But they didn't listen to me."

The hospital became a circus. TV cameras everywhere. Reporters everywhere. Tupac fans everywhere. Celebrity visitors ranging from MC Hammer and Snoop Doggy Dogg to Jasmine Guy and the rapper Yo-Yo. Tupac's father, Billy Garland, came by. "He was genuinely hurting," Fula said. "It wasn't gross. He was very low-key." There were parking lot prayer vigils and parking lot fistfights. Rumors firing off at the speed of light. Tupac was done in by East vs. West violence. It had to be Biggie. It had to be Puffy. It was karma. Several journalists tried sneaking into Tupac's room. Photographers, too. Tupac's family rented a U-Haul truck and parked it outside his first-floor window—both to block the view of interlopers and as a temporary headquarters to remain vigilant ("The Vegas policemen would always come and harass us," said Fula. "They put my son, Yaki, in cuffs one time because they had a report he had a gun. Of course people had guns. We were scared").

Friends from Marin and Oakland and Los Angeles drove through the night to come and visit, hoping to lift Tupac's spirits but being denied entry. Wrote Cathy Scott of the *Las Vegas Sun*, "A nurse said evening shift employees at the hospital were calling in sick because they didn't want to walk through the crowd." The *Philadelphia Daily News*' Tonya Pendleton penned a jarringly tasteless piece (headline: WHO SHOT TUPAC?) that speculated on the various celebrities who might have (but certainly had not) fired the gun. The Associated Press ran a headline, RIVAL RAPPER MAY BE SUSPECT IN TUPAC SHAKUR SHOOTING—and it was garbage (the rival rapper, the Notorious B.I.G., was twenty-five hundred miles away the night of the incident). Rumors ran the gamut—Tupac was already dead. Tupac was alive and well. According to Liz Smith, the famed gossip columnist, within days of the shooting two different scripts about Tupac (one made for TV, one a feature film) had been put together and shopped. With little new information to share with readers, newspapers grasped at straws. The *Los Angeles Times* interviewed a UCLA lung specialist. *The Atlanta Journal-Constitution* ran a piece speculating how the shooting would impact Tupac's career.

One of the dignitaries gracing the scene with his esteemed presence was the Rev. Jesse Jackson, the civil rights leader who had flown on a private jet from Chicago. For the past several years Jackson had devoted his energies toward damning Tupac and gangsta rap as musical excrement. Now—with flashes clicking—he was in full sad-face mode. He hugged Afeni and asked for the honor to pray alongside her blessed child (whom he certainly didn't remember from 1984, when Tupac performed in *A Raisin in the Sun* during a Jackson presidential campaign appearance at the Apollo Theater). "I begged Feni not to let Jackson in," said Fula. "It was just an opportunist being an opportunist. One of many crows. But she argued with me, and I had to back off."

In her excellent book, *Spirit of an Outlaw*, Fula recalled the hellscape she and Tupac's family endured:

Throughout this ordeal, Vegas police treated us like criminals, never once giving the impression they were conducting an investigation into the shooting. We were getting death threats daily, the callers threatening to "come and finish the job." I was getting phone calls from everywhere, some with information about conversations overheard, suspects, family, friends—potentially important information. There was nobody in the police department to pass on information to. Nobody to trust. It was chaos. Of all the places to be—Las Vegas. We did not know who to trust so we had to protect Tupac ourselves.

Relatives filled the waiting room. Fula hired members of the Nation of Islam security force to stand guard outside Tupac's door, but Afeni objected and sent them home. The members of the Outlawz—each one carrying a firearm—took shifts watching over the hospital hallway. Tupac had known his protégés for years, and considered their successes to be his, too. "We didn't get any sleep, no change of clothes," said Rufus "Noble" Cooper. "We was out there ready to go out with a blaze if somebody was gonna come to the hospital on some bullshit." Afeni and Yaasmyn shuttled between Tupac's bedside and the hospital chapel, hoping for a miracle. On Monday, September 9, a medical center spokesperson called Tupac's injuries "very severe, very traumatic." Two days later, Dr. John Fildes, the chairman of the UMC trauma program, said that by surviving past twenty-four hours, Tupac had greater than one-in-five odds of making it. Then he added, "Statistically, it carries a very high mortality rate. A patient may die from a lack of oxygen or may bleed to death in the chest." Tupac wasn't responding to light or smell or sound. Outside his window, fans were blasting his songs, hoping to provide a jolt. It was singing to a wall.

"He was ravaged," said Fula. "I knew he wouldn't make it."

To the frustration of Tupac's family, Suge Knight—back at his Las Vegas home—was unwilling to help with the local police department's investigation of the shooting. Twice, Knight agreed to come to the headquarters and talk. Twice, he failed to show up. Reputation meant everything, and to chat with the cops would be a slug to Death Row's street cred. His employees also clammed up. A directive from the top was clear: We will not cooperate. Only one person—Yaki Kadafi, the Outlawz rapper, Yaasmyn's son, and an occupant of the car that trailed Tupac and Suge Knight—provided a description of the shooter. "I was so proud of

Yaki for stepping up that night," Fula said. "My boy was the only one. Tupac was surrounded by traitors."

On the afternoon of Friday, September 13, 1996, at approximately 4:03, Tupac Amaru Shakur stopped breathing. His body went lifeless, his extremities turned cold, his heart ceased pumping blood to his tissues and organs. He had suffered a series of heart attacks, and multiple efforts to resuscitate him had failed. After being told hope was gone, Afeni pleaded for her son to be removed from life support. He was pronounced dead by Dr. James Lovett inside the intensive care unit.

"My brother died feeling alone," said Set Shakur. "He died with the world on his shoulders, unable to ever take a break. He couldn't rest because there were no saviors for him. There was no protection for him. There was no big cousin to guide him. There were no best friends. There were no safe harbors. He was so popular, but so alone."

Afeni stood over the bed, both crestfallen and relieved. The official cause of death was respiratory failure and cardiopulmonary arrest, and as Afeni gazed down at a lifeless body that, for twenty-five years, had been powered by weed and Hennessy and Newports and love and hate and music and poetry and passion and anger and sex and touch and feel and sound and smell and a high-voltage current . . . it felt inconceivable.

How could Tupac be dead?

Sitting in the nearby private visitor room was one Marion "Suge" Knight, who—forever a master manipulator of Tupac's mother—convinced Afeni he should be by the family's side. He arrived at the hospital after learning the end was near. Kevin Powell, the veteran journalist, was standing in the UMC lobby when the Death Row kingpin entered. "We all move out of the way, and he gets out with a cigar he's smoking," Powell recalled. "And there's such a nonchalance about the whole situation. It was surreal, like there was no emotional connection there." With Tupac gone, Knight hugged Afeni. It was Showmanship 101.

"That man," said Fula, "was a fraud and a snake."

At 5:10 p.m., after family members said their goodbyes and collected themselves, the lifeless body was placed atop a gurney, rolled through a couple of hallways, transferred into a nondescript white van operated by

Davis Mortuary, and driven three blocks to the office of the Clark County Coroner. This is where Ron Flud, the county coroner, was waiting in a charmless and cold one-story cement building. A forty-four-year-old Texas native who, in his spare time, enjoyed saddle making and leatherwork, Flud had never before heard of Tupac Shakur. However, he was made aware that this was a high-profile case, and that the media pressure was intense. "One of my medical examiners came in and asked if I wanted him to stay overtime and we could get it done and have the body processed before anyone knew," Flud recalled. "I said, 'Absolutely.'"

Because Tupac was a celebrity, Flud limited access to the autopsy to a medical examiner, two forensic technicians, and the homicide detectives. Six thirty-five-millimeter photographs were taken during and after the session—one of which, to Flud's furor, was leaked to the public. It showed Tupac's corpse atop a white table, his chest sliced open via various incisions, the rear of his skull ajar, coconut-like. The four-page report confirmed that Tupac's remains were identified by his mother, and that (for one of the rare times in his adult life) he had no illegal drugs in his system. "I interviewed the decedent's mother, Afeni Shakur, and she stated that the decedent was not married and he had no children," Ed Brown, the coroner investigator, wrote in his report. "She stated that Tupac A. Shakur was his name. She was not able to give any more information than this."

When word spread of Tupac's death, the response was seismic. Family and friends remained inside the hospital until approximately 6:00 p.m., wallowing and crying and hugging. Outside, those holding vigil broke out into a collective sob. It did not make sense. Tupac was too young and too strong to die.

In Albany, California, Leila Steinberg was picking her three daughters up from school when her pager went off. It was Tracy Robinson, the music video producer. The news she had feared was real. "I was in shock," Steinberg said. "I just didn't think he would die."

In Houston, Texas, Dahlia McCutchen, Tupac's former girlfriend who had once been pregnant with his child, was working the pole as a stripper at Fantasy West. A colleague named Red signaled from offstage that McCutchen's phone wouldn't stop ringing. "It distracted me, and I stopped dancing to look up at one of the club's televisions," she recalled. "And

Tupac dying was the breaking news. I just crashed. It was the saddest day of my life."

In Manhattan, Lela Rochon, Tupac's *Gang Related* costar, was inside a concert hall listening to the R&B singer D'Angelo perform. In attendance were a mini who's who of young, Black, and famous—Regina King and Vivica Fox and Mike Tyson and a slew of other stars. A man stepped to the microphone and interrupted the show. "Ladies and gentlemen," he said. "I have the misfortune of informing you that Tupac Shakur has just passed . . ."

Silence.

D'Angelo tiptoed back to the mic and launched into an a cappella version of the Ohio Players' "Heaven Must Be Like This."

"It was," Rochon said, "a moment."

In the Bronx, the rapper Smooth B was on Webster Avenue in Tremont with his musical collaborator, Greg Nice. They had just pulled up to a corner grocery to purchase some beers, and news of Tupac's death was delivered via the car radio. Shocked, Smooth B entered the store, where he was greeted by a familiar employee.

"Yo, Smooth—you hear the news about Pac?" the man asked.

Smooth B nodded.

A young customer overheard the exchange.

"You knew Tupac Shakur?" he said.

The rapper said, "Yeah, little man. I did."

"He lifted up his sweater," Smooth B said, "and he had THUG LIFE tattooed across his stomach."

In Dannemora, New York, Michael Christopher was sitting in his bedroom with the television on in the background. The Clinton Correctional Facility CO had been following Tupac's career since his departure eleven months earlier, and hoped—against logic—that the Death Row relationship was working out.

Then, the voice of MTV's Tabitha Soren . . .

"Tupac Shakur has died from complications from several bullet wounds . . ."

Tears flowed down his cheeks. "I'm a huge John Lennon fan," Christopher said. "The day Lennon died and the day Tupac died felt exactly the same."

In Los Angeles, Carsten "Soulshock" Schack—Tupac's former producer—was sitting at home when the phone rang. It was Afeni. "He's gone," she said, sobbing. "I can't believe Tupac is gone . . ."

In Las Vegas, James "Mob James" McDonald was sick of this shit. Just fucking sick of it. The longtime Suge Knight pal and Death Row intimidator was beaten down by the violence, the fighting, the guns, the barking, the inanity. "You wanna know why Tupac died?" he asked, years later. "He died because he wanted to be like the shit he saw. The shit that was told to him. And Suge sold him a dream, and he allowed Tupac to start participating in some of the bullshit we were doing to people.

"He died because he thought he was a thug. Well, Tupac was no fucking thug. He died a wannabe thug. A damn wannabe.

"How fucking pathetic is that?"

The morning after his final breath, Tupac's body was cremated, and Afeni returned to Los Angeles. She was, according to Jasmine Guy, "broken like a one-winged bird."

The Shakur family had long been a stew of addiction and dysfunction, and Tupac's passing only intensified the messiness. The relatives from Georgia descended upon Southern California, and they were, as a whole, numb, devastated, crushed, confused, hollowed. Not only had they lost a cherished member of their crew, they had also lost their provider. Nearly everything in their lives had been bought and paid for by Tupac Shakur and/or Death Row. The house. The cars. The toys. The food. The travel. Until the day he died, Tupac knew that, without him, loved ones would go without. The burden was unspeakably heavy.

In death, that weight shifted to Afeni, Glo, and the family. When Tupac was imprisoned, and the money dried up, they collectively fell beneath the sway of Suge Knight and his promises and his gifts. They encouraged Tupac to join Death Row. To follow the leader.

Now, having done so, Tupac was dead.

A memorial service was held inside Guy's Los Angeles home, and earlier in the day Kenny Lesane led a squad of cousins and friends to a tattoo parlor on Ventura Boulevard, where they all had the word OUTLAW inked onto their left forearms, just as Tupac had it inked on his left forearm. For Lesane, the pain of needle into skin felt cathartic. He needed something. Anything. "It was all too much," he said.

Somehow, Knight learned of the family collective, arrived at the store, and footed the tattoo bill. "He wouldn't look us in the eye," Kenny Lesane recalled. "That's what I remember most."

Later that night, someone knocked on the door of Tupac's condo on Wilshire Boulevard, and when Fula answered her jaw dropped. A FedEx messenger was holding a rectangular cardboard box, inside of which were Tupac's ashes.

Afeni had asked Knight to handle the final passage of her beloved son—and this was how he handled it. With FedEx next-day service.

"It was," Fula said, "so cold."

And then . . . the outpouring.

Family members and friends knew Tupac was beloved, but in the immediate aftermath of his death the emotion had been obscured by the ocean of raw devastation. In Compton, a ten-day gang war broke out between the Bloods and Crips, resulting in a multitude of murders and the accidental shooting of a ten-year-old girl. Robert Ladd, a former Compton police detective, termed it "the 10 days of hell."

Yet as the weeks passed, and the tributes began pouring in, the world was reminded that, in Tupac Shakur, what we lost was not, first and foremost, a shit talker, a criminal, a buffoon.

What we lost was one of the great artists of our time.

Vigils appeared in cities across the world. Murals on the sides of buildings with spray-painted imagery and phrases ranging from THUG LIFE to ONLY GOD CAN JUDGE ME to KEEP YA HEAD UP. Radio stations spent days playing Tupac music, taking calls from bereaved listeners. Fans placed mounds of flowers outside his residences. One of Tupac's favorite LA spots had been Tattoo Mania on Sunset Boulevard. It's where he had the OUTLAW ink added to his left forearm, as well as MAKAVELI onto the rear of his neck. After he died, hundreds of mourners entered the front door, one after another, asking Mark Mahoney to add a Tupac visage to their bodies. "I started doing millions of Tupac portraits," Mahoney said. "It never ended."

Daily newspapers and magazines like *Time* and *Newsweek* analyzed his life, but mostly swung and missed. Tupac, to the mainstream white writer, was a gangbanger whose actions resulted in his own death. To the Black fan, however, Tupac was a street poet, reflecting what his people went through on a day-to-day basis.

Tupac spoke for a generation of minority men and women who felt pummeled by society. He was their mouthpiece—warts and all. His songs told stories of struggle and heartbreak, of upheaval and violence. He was thought of as a thug poet—strange, because he was no thug. "I think people sometimes misunderstand it all," said Michael Johnson, the legendary Olympic champion who listened to Tupac as psych-up music before winning the gold in the two hundred meters at the 1996 Atlanta Games. "He's very self-empowering, but he's also about trying to be victorious and positive as he navigates this world of racism and police brutality. It's powerful stuff."

When a celebrity dies, we tend to mimic swarms of mosquitoes, following one another toward the brightest lights. With Tupac's death, that meant controversy, chaos, conspiracy. Suge and Death Row and the MGM Grand. Yet, in a weird way, we would have been best served heading to 2115 Main Street in Santa Monica, where a white criminologist and court consultant named Sheila Balkan sat behind her office desk, overcome by sadness.

A mere six months before the events of Las Vegas, Balkan had been hired by Tupac's attorneys to help in a drug possession case that had the potential to land the rapper back in prison. The idea was that Balkan could meet with Tupac, grasp his goodness, then explain to the court that he was not what mainstream society envisioned.

The first time she went to his house, he refused to open the door.

The second time she went to his house, he refused to open the door.

"He didn't trust anybody," Balkan said. "He had no faith that anybody could help."

The third time she went to his house, he relented and opened the door.

"You expect something, because he's Tupac. He's famous for being loud and brash," she recalled. "But that wasn't the person before me. He was overrun with anxiety. He didn't know how to communicate with others except through his writing. He'd never had any type of therapy, and I don't think he ever felt safe enough to explore his feelings."

Multiple sessions ensued, and Balkan—who was not a rap fan and knew zero Tupac songs—came to admire her client while developing tremendous sympathy for him. He was a giver surrounded by takers. He was an artist surrounded by commercialists. He simultaneously liked and loathed himself. He smoked weed and drank to excess because he perpetually hurt. He drove with a gun in his glove compartment because he lived in fear. "He was sweet and kind," she said. "But very much depressed. He wanted to be a light to people, but I'm not sure he always knew how."

Balkan introduced Tupac to A Place Called Home, a Los Angeles–based nonprofit designed to help young people in South Central find positivity in otherwise rough circumstances. It operated out of a church, and from the moment he first visited, and saw little kids running around, Tupac was smitten. Balkan suggested to the court that, instead of doing time, Tupac perform a concert where all proceeds were donated to A Place Called Home.

"The judge went for it," Balkan said. "And Tupac—Tupac was legitimately excited. He saw this as a chance to give back through music, and I think in those children he saw himself. He wanted them to have bright futures. He felt as if he could help spearhead that. But then he died, and it never happened."

Balkan paused.

"He wanted to be the change they needed."

Another pause.

"I think he saw that as his legacy."

Epilogue: Aftermath

Give me a paper and pen, so I can write about my life of sin
A couple bottles of gin, in case I don't get in.

—Tupac Shakur, "Life Goes On"

He is here.

Beneath you.

For nearly three decades, the world has been led to believe his ashes were spread to the wind, a kindred spirit let loose to soar among the angels. That is what we have been told. Time after time. He was cremated. His remains were set free. He is one with the universe.*

But, no.

He is here.

Beneath you.

Beneath *me*.

Perhaps this is a discovery best left undiscovered. Famous resting places are rarely resting places. Think of Jim Morrison, his tombstone in Paris's Père Lachaise Cemetery coated in spray paint and graffiti. Think of Marilyn Monroe, her crypt inside the Westwood Village Memorial Park Cemetery a tacky spot for selfie seekers and shameless gawkers.

But . . . reality is reality and truth is truth.

He is here.

So as I stand above the buried ashen remains of Tupac Amaru Shakur on a warm March day in 2024, I can't help but feel heartbroken by the scene's lack of dignity. For I am not in a beautiful cemetery, surrounded

---

* Some members of the Outlawz later claimed they smoked Tupac's ashes after his death. The Shakur family denied this, um, gross and weird confession.

by perfectly manicured greens and floral arrangements. I am also not beneath a glorious oak tree, or alongside a spectacular waterfall, or in a field of coreopsis and Shasta daisies.

No. I am in Lumberton, North Carolina, at 2630 Seventh Street Road, in the yard of a long-abandoned house surrounded by rusted fencing and overgrown weeds, watching scores of thick black ants scurry in and out of their hills and across a faded headstone that reads:

TUPAC AMARU SHAKUR
JUNE 16, 1971–SEPT. 13, 1996
BELOVED SON, BROTHER, NEPHEW, UNCLE,
COUSIN AND FRIEND
ALWAYS IN OUR HEARTS.

Shortly after Tupac died in 1996, word spread that he was cremated, and his remains were set free into a breeze soaring above the Pacific Ocean.

It was a bit of an exaggeration.

There was, indeed, a release off the coast in Malibu, but only a tiny portion of his ashes were gifted to the water. During a ceremony attended by a gaggle of friends and loved ones, a large, seemingly out-of-nowhere wave crashed into Afeni and sent her sprawling—a message from her son, some of those present thought. Truth be told, Afeni Shakur kept the majority of Tupac's ashes. When she relocated somewhere new, so went her child's cremated remains.

In 2002, Afeni Shakur shocked friends and family members by returning to her native turf of Lumberton, where she had a large home built on fifty-six acres of land. Upon moving in, Afeni decided, at long last, she wanted her son to have a permanent resting place. So she had his ashes buried and placed beneath the headstone.

Alas, her time in Lumberton was far from idyllic. The once-prosperous metropolis had been overtaken by addiction and disrepair, and a downtown she loved as a girl was now a land of broken glass and vacant storefronts. In 2004 she ignored the advice of nearly everyone she knew and married a local preacher named Gust Davis. The union was rocky and weird from the start (Davis referred to himself as "Profit"), and ended in litigation and divorce after twelve years.

Afeni ultimately returned to California, where she resided on a houseboat in Sausalito until her 2016 death. The Lumberton home has remained empty for years. Its hallways are barren. Sealed boxes filled with books and utensils and knickknacks pile in the corners. Dante Powers, a distant cousin who lives locally, is paid by the Shakur estate for basic upkeep of the house and property, but he is one man, and the grave of an icon sits in isolation, alone and overlooked.

"It's crazy," Dante says to me. "Most famous rapper in history. Just here in little ol' Lumberton.

"Resting."

On November 5, 1996, less than two months after his death, Death Row issued Tupac's fifth and final studio album, *The Don Killuminati: The 7 Day Theory*.*

Tupac's plan was to release it using the artist name "Makaveli" (not Tupac or 2Pac), and Death Row agreed. He explained the idea to Rob Marriott in an interview shortly before he passed. "The Italians I speak about were truly great men," he said. "And I find any great man, Black or white, I'm going to study them, learn them, so he can't be great to me no more. Like, Machiavelli. My name is not Machiavelli. My name is Makaveli. I took it, that's mine. He gave me that. And I don't feel no guilt. All these motherfuckers stole from us forever. I'm taking back what's mine. It's just that they recorded it when he said it. It's probably something he took from us that they didn't let us record."

The breakdown made little sense, and was lost in the blizzard of tragedy. But when the record dropped, the conspiracy theorists perked up their ears. Hadn't Niccolò Machiavelli, the Italian diplomat and author of

---

* According to *The Tupac Encyclopedia*, Death Row actually screwed up Tupac's plan, which was to name it *Killuminati: The 7 Day Theory*. He explained the word "Killuminati" in an interview: "That's why I put the 'K' to [Illuminati]. Niggas was telling me about this Illuminati shit while I was in jail. . . . That's another way to keep your self-esteem down. . . . I'm putting the 'K' cause I'm killin' that Illuminati shit."

The Prince, once faked his own death at twenty-five, only to return eighteen years later? Answer: *Cough*—no, he hadn't. But with Machiavelli 469 years off the planet, no one with firsthand knowledge could refute the rumor, and it caught fire. Before long people were legitimately arguing that Tupac Shakur—a man who loved attention as a dog loves sticks—had staged his own death. Seemingly thousands upon thousands of music fans began insisting Tupac was in Cuba planning the revolution, or perhaps in Afeni's house, or maybe, just maybe, in New York, plotting revenge against Biggie. It hardly helped that one of his last-ever music videos, for the song "I Ain't Mad at Cha," depicted Tupac being gunned down in a drive-by, then rising to heaven.

Lost in the inanity was that *The Don Killuminati: The 7 Day Theory* was a masterpiece. Despite the bizarre title, the album sizzles from track 1 to track 12. "Hail Mary" wound up one of the most iconic songs in hip-hop history. "To Live & Die in L.A." is rap's answer to Randy Newman's "I Love L.A." (only with more gang shout-outs). "Me and My Girlfriend" is such a high-level ode-to-my-gun song it was later picked up and reconfigured by Jay-Z and Beyoncé. The album sold 664,000 copies in its first week, making Tupac the first rapper with two chart-topping releases in a single calendar year.

For three years, while working on this book, I have tried to fully understand Tupac Shakur the man—how he was formed, what he became, what impact remains. I trekked to New York City and Baltimore and Marin City and Oakland and Los Angeles, retracing his steps, speaking with his people. The teachers, the classmates, the crack dealers, the music creators, the friends, the enemies, the relatives. The fans. The detractors. Everyone I could find. Tupac wore former Duke guard Jeff Capel's No. 5 Blue Devils jersey to an event—I called Jeff ("I was blown away! Pac is wearing my jersey!"). Tupac spent time with MTV's Bill Bellamy—I hit up Bill ("He's the first person I ever hugged that had a bulletproof vest on. In the daytime!"). In Newark, New Jersey, a professional Tupac impersonator named Richard Garcia bounds from weddings to Bar Mitzvahs to birthday parties, bringing his hero back to life. "I performed 'Dear Mama' at a funeral," he said. "Not a dry eye in the building."

In December 1998, former Virginia governor Chuck Robb was holding his family's annual Christmas party at an estate in McLean. One of the invited guests was Bruce Hornsby, the singer-songwriter whose biggest hit, "The Way It Is," was transformed and reimagined by Tupac into one of *his* best-known posthumous jams, "Changes." En route to the shindig, Bruce and his wife, Kathy, popped Tupac's *Greatest Hits* into the car CD player. "So 'Changes' is on there, which was cool, but so are all these songs we don't know and have never heard before," Hornsby recalled. "Well, we pull up to the party, and it's like a scene straight out of a movie. All the valets are young Black men, all the guests are old white people—and the CD is still playing, and as the door opens you hear, 'That's why I fucked yo' bitch, you fat motherfucker!' just as loud as can be. And it was just a fucking hilarious moment. The parking attendants started laughing their asses off, and so did we. It was an amazing contrast of worlds. But also a commentary on Tupac's profound impact."

Like Tupac's life itself, this journey has been equal parts joyful and exasperating. Never has such a famous figure cast a blurrier shadow. The mystique isn't part of the story. It *is* the story. And as I stand here on Afeni's old property, at the foot of the grave, as physically close to Tupac as possible, I think back to those days after his death, when so many remained convinced he was alive and well and plotting a comeback.

I consider the years that have passed, and all the Tupac-related highs and lows. Movies and plays and a Broadway musical and books chronicling his impact. A star on the Hollywood Walk of Fame. A street naming in Oakland. "California Love" becoming a hip-hop anthem. A terrific six-part Hulu documentary. More than seventy-five million albums sold. "He remains the most prolific hip-hop artist we've ever seen," said Chuck Creekmur, founder of AllHipHop.com. "And it's not even close."

Tupac released four studio records during his life, but dozens of posthumous offerings exist. There are bootlegs atop bootlegs atop bootlegs. "He wanted to be heard," said Leila Steinberg. "More than anything, that's what he wanted." Thanks to Target and Walmart and the Asian sweatshops he would have abhorred, millions *still* sport Tupac Shakur shirts. "I was in Amsterdam and I saw people wearing Tupac Ts," said Theon Hill, who teaches a course, the Rhetoric of Rap Music, at Wheaton College. "I see them in South America. When I'm in Indonesia and I mention Tupac Shakur, they know exactly who I'm talking about because his message—while squarely located in Black America—transcends one group of people."

Tupac was not here for the shooting of Christopher Wallace (aka the Notorious B.I.G.) in 1997, or the death of Orlando Anderson in a gang altercation one year later. He wasn't around on September 29, 2023, for Duane "Keefe D" Davis's arrest after being indicted by a grand jury for first-degree murder (Davis experienced the most modern of downfalls—a faded gangbanger can't resist the siren call of attention, so he goes on the internet and gleefully blabs about his involvement in Tupac's death) or the baby-oil-fueled public flogging and imprisonment of Sean "Puffy" Combs. He has no clue that Suge Knight sits inside cell 127 at San Diego's Richard J. Donovan State Prison, the result of being convicted of voluntary manslaughter in a 2019 hit-and-run accident.

And yet, here's the thing.

The thing I continue to ponder.

Although Tupac's ashes are allegedly buried here in Lumberton, I cannot—with 100 percent certainty—confirm their placement beneath my feet. Perhaps it is merely dirt. Perhaps the stone is a hoax. Perhaps he is alive and well and living his best life.

So maybe, just maybe, he calls Havana home, and is busy planning a revolution. Or he's on a beach in the Bahamas, sipping a pineapple mojito and smiling knowingly as the women stroll by. He could be working the grill at the Freight House Café in Mahopac, New York. Driving a taxi up and down La Rambla in Barcelona. Learning to speak Mikeyir in Ethiopia. Starring as Courfeyrac in a Canadian touring production of *Les Mis*.

We have been told Tupac Shakur died twenty-nine years ago, the victim of a drive-by shooting. We have been told he is gone.

But when Niccolò Machiavelli famously said, "It is double pleasure to deceive the deceiver," maybe he wasn't telling us about himself.

He was telling us about Tupac Shakur.

And an empty plot in Lumberton.

Acknowledgments

On December 20, 2023, my father died from pancreatic cancer.

His name was Stanley Pearlman, and although he knew very little about Tupac or hip-hop or most anything pop culture, he would have read this book, because he read all of my books.

And losing my dad impacted this project in multiple ways. So much of Tupac Shakur's life was layered in grief, and feeling the rawness of that emotion as I tried to understand its significance in another man's journey was no joke. So if you happen to notice any tearstains on these pages, please understand.

I wrote hurt.

Even without loss, this book would have been a beast. It is my eleventh work of nonfiction, and by far the most daunting. I was actually warned by a multitude of people that delving into the hip-hop universe would be all layers of challenging and weird. This was no lie. For a guy who has spent the vast majority of his career covering the relatively predictable (and heavily scheduled) world of sports, chronicling Tupac's journey often felt akin to skateboarding atop a puddle of diluted applesauce while trying to grasp the horns of a six-hundred-pound bull fueled by Skittles and meth. It was a circus of the cool, the odd, the outlandish, the trendsetting, the earnest, the dishonest, the manipulative, the excessive, the earth-shattering.

And I loved it.

First and foremost, big chunks of thanks to Yaasmyn Fula, Set Shakur, and Leila Steinberg—three women who cherished Tupac and were beyond gracious with their time and insights. There is something jarring in being approached by a stranger to discuss a lost loved one, but Yaasmyn, Set, and Leila introduced me to worlds largely uncharted. In particular, I hope people walk away from this book understanding the trauma Set—Tupac's sister and closest living relative—has endured. To sit across from her (as I did) is to feel pain in its rawest measure. She is a woman who should be celebrated, not shunned.

And Yaasmyn—well, Yaasmyn is one of the strongest fighters I have ever had the honor of meeting. Like Set, she is forever scarred by the depths of first-degree loss. Yet she keeps moving forward.

Researching a book like this results in one thousand sleepless nights, and I am fortunate to have Michele Soulli as a dear friend and colleague. It's funny—Michele and I graduated from Mahopac High School together way back when, and probably exchanged no more than five words over four years. Little did I know, the girl with the long black hair concealing her eyes would wind up America's greatest genealogist/researcher. Funny how life works.

Elizabeth Newman, my longtime chum and former *Sports Illustrated* sibling, fact-checked this book—and her efforts are gold. Is she misguided in believing Johnny Gill has a better voice than Daryl Hall? Yes. Has she never scored a photograph in *Jet*? Also yes. But is she one of the best people I know? Without question.

Meanwhile, Michael J. Lewis (not the "Moneyball" Michael Lewis) combed through this manuscript with smarts, precision, and the hip-hop IQ of Bruce Coslet, and Andrew Martin transcribed audio with the ferocity of a young Robert Van Winkle. It took this hellish project for Oliver Cronk—my up-and-coming British cousin/nephew/homie—to learn the hard way that, when an author calls to ask "Can you do me a favor?," *always* say no.

There have been a ton of Tupac-related books written over the decades, and the best, for my money, is Michael Namikas's self-published *The Tupac Encyclopedia: Volume 1*. Michael is one of those rare birds who doesn't merely write on a subject, but takes ownership. That explains the quality of his work, as well as why his insights were so valuable. Equal respect for the brilliant (and warm) Santi Elijah Holley and his *An Amerikan Family*.

Big ups to the folks at HarperCollins for taking a shot on the John Rocker guy to pen a Tupac biography (hey, *why not?*). Matt Harper, my editor, is a kind and gracious soul with a high-level pen, and Peter Hubbard is, sincerely, one of the best I've ever worked with. Thanks to all the other folks at Mariner who helped make this book what it is: Rachel Weinick, Joseph Jasko, Greg Villepique, Megan Wilson, and Kasey Feather.

My agent and friend, David Black, is a man who represents many but somehow makes every client feel special, and Lucy Stille (my print-to-screen rep) is the glorious agent personification of Thug Life. Both David and Lucy have enriched my life in ways far beyond dough.

So many folks from the rap universe assisted in this project. Ronald (Money-B) Brooks of Digital Underground is a hip-hop mensch, as are Jimi (Chopmaster J) Dright and Atron Gregory. Lunches with Chuck D, Christopher (Kid) Reid, and Prime Minister Pete Nice (Pete Nash) felt like free trips to music fantasy camp. Reggie Williams (of Ambrosia for Heads) and Chuck Creekmur (of AllHipHop) were patient and ever-available road maps of an unfamiliar landscape, and Cheo Hodari Coker is one of the best to ever do it. Rob Marriott let me call, then (cough) call *again*. Jake Paine served as a wealth of information, as did Thomas Golianopoulos, Christopher John Farley, Justin Tinsley, Matt Brannagan, Ross Alvord, Will Watson, Jonathan Eig, Mirin Fader, Noah Fleischman, Abby Sharpe, Julie Burt, Tony Danza, Larry Prine-Newman, Laura Cole, Milo Mora, Karin Unger, Quinn Newhouse, Mikey DiLullo, Joe Friezo, Jake Brown, Abraham Zepeda, Mary Seward, Alison Berwitz, Corey Laury, Robyn Deutsch, Kevin Monty, Ramon Maclin, Kyran Cassidy, Kim Bondy, Morgan O'Brien, Greg Villepique, Paul Oren, Alan Barcoff, Matt Webb, Greg Kading, Karen Lee, Lori Earl, Tim Ghianni, Valencia Exum, Robert Lesch, Anna Norris, Scott Bigelow, Marion Thompson, Daks Armstrong, and Jonathan Coleman. A special nod to Natalie Reyes, Rabbi Robert Tellez, Olivia Atkins of the Gearhart (Oregon) Hospitality Association, Christian Francis Duer, president of the Roger Peckinpaugh Fan Club and Pizza Pavillion, and Davonn Hodge—simply the realest of dudes.

There was a night when—broken and battered and feeling helpless—I checked in for a stay at the Best Western Edgewater Inn, and a young woman named Britina Bloomfield greeted me with a smile as warm as fresh buttermilk biscuits. Dave Sheinin of *The Washington Post* did me one of the great all-time journalistic favors, and I am eternally thankful. Vonyeh Clanton of Dunbar High—you're a difference maker. Oh, and Braxton Bender—thanks for living each day as Tupac would.

I interviewed nearly seven hundred people for this book, and roamed from New York to Baltimore to Lumberton to New Orleans to Marin City to Oakland to Richmond to Los Angeles and all points in between. In other words, naming every contributor who kindly gave me time would off far too many trees. But I would be remiss not to cite the assistance of Kendrick Wells, Tupac's longtime friend who passed during the process. Sitting with Kendrick in his home was an honor, and I hope Liza Monjauze, his partner and copilot, can take comfort in knowing this book solidifies not merely Tupac's legacy, but his, too.

Elayne Miller and Jim McNern made my visit to the Novato History Museum a joy, and Jennifer Randall, librarian at the Mary Livermore Library at UNC Pembroke, was phenomenal. Katelon Floyd Hunt and Vicki Locklear of the Lumberton Register of Deeds—gracias for the guiding lights. Huge respect to Debra Elfenbein and Lisa Greenhouse of the Enoch Pratt Free Library. Ramona Rey and Philip Rhodes of the Mill Valley Public Library were lifesavers, as were Kenny and Billy Lesane. Thank you for opening up on some tough topics.

My family has now watched me endure the slaughterhouse of eleven books, and they still continue to invite me to dinner. My mother, Joan Pearlman, has always been more Team Biggie, but despite that offers love and guidance. Jessica and Chris Berman and Jordan Williams served as my weed/bud encyclopedias. Leah Guggenheimer, Isaiah Williams, Amelia Berman, Reese Berman, and Maddie Guggenheimer-Pearlman were marvelous hosts. David Pearlman agreed to start a Tupac-themed cruise to Guam. My daughter, Casey, puts the Thug in Thug Life and the Teeth in Dr. Teeth, and my son, Emmett, has risen from All Mizzoula Fly to hip-hop OG. Catherine, my wife, thinks the Tupac–Elton John "Ghetto Gospel" monstrosity is pretty catchy, and for that (and eight thousand other reasons) I love her to pieces. You can't fully dive into this level of obsessiveness without your copilot screaming, "Go for it, motherfucker!" I, fortunately, am married to a one-kidneyed farm girl supernova who believes jeans can be sweatpants and stories should be told.

Lastly, a moment of silence for Curtis Dorsey, my friend, Tupac guru, and hoops ambassador, who left us during the completion of this project.

Bishop, I hope Thugz Mansion is all you dreamed it to be.

Please save a sip of Henny for Uncle Marty.

And both Normas.

Bibliography

Abrams, Jonathan. *The Come Up: An Oral History of the Rise of Hip-Hop*. New York: Crown, 2022.

Acampora, Andrew. *Tupac: The Modern Day Messiah*. New York: Page Publishing, 2018.

Alexander, Frank, with Heidi Siegmund Cuda. *Got Your Back: Protecting Tupac in the World of Gangsta Rap*. New York: St. Martin's Griffin, 1998.

Ardis, Angela. *Inside a Thug's Heart*. New York: Kensington Publishing, 2004.

Baker, Soren. *The History of Gangster Rap*. New York: Abrams Image, 2018.

Bastfield, Darrin Keith. *Back in the Day: My Life and Times with Tupac Shakur*. New York: Da Capo Press, 2002.

Bellamy, Bill. *Top Billin': Stories of Laughter, Lessons, and Triumph*. New York: Amistad, 2023.

Bhadreshwar, Nina. *Finding CC*. London: WJ Scrivener Books, 2018.

Blaine, Michael H. *The Invisible Walls of Dannemora*. Las Vegas: Gaudium, 2020.

Bloom, Joshua, and Waldo E. Martin Jr. *Black Against Empire: The History and Politics of the Black Panther Party*. Los Angeles: University of California Press, 2013.

Blu, Karen I. *The Lumbee Problem*. New York: Cambridge University Press, 1980.

Bond, Richard, and Michael Douglas Carlin. *Tupac 187: The Red Knight*. Corona, CA: Martin Productions, 2015.

Bowden, Mark. *Life Sentence: The Brief and Tragic Career of Baltimore's Deadliest Gang Leader*. New York: Atlantic Monthly Press, 2023.

Brennon, Timothy M., and Robert Ladd, with Lolita Files. *Once Upon a Time in Compton*. Los Angeles: Comptonpolicegangs, 2017.

Brent, Ronald. *Art Is My Life: The Streets, Tupac, Death Row Records, and Now*. Compton, CA: Riskie Forever, 2022.

Brent, Ronald. *Tupac: The Coloring Book*. Compton, CA: Riskie Forever, 2023.

Brian, John. *Govas Villages and Suburb: A Picture History of a North Baltimore Community*. Baltimore: John Brain, 1986.

Brown, Bobby. *Every Little Step: My Story*. New York: HarperCollins, 2016.

Brown, Claude. *Manchild in the Promised Land*. New York: Simon & Schuster, 1965.

Brown, Ethan. *Queens Reigns Supreme*. New York: Anchor Books, 2015.

Brown, Jake. *Dr. Dre in the Studio*. Phoenix: Colossus Books, 2006.

Brown, Jake. *Ready to Die: The Story of Biggie Smalls*. Phoenix: Colossus Books, 2004.

Brown, Jake. *Tupac Shakur: (2-Pac) in the Studio*. Phoenix: Colossus Books, 2005.

Burris, John L. *Blue vs. Black: Let's End the Conflict Between Cops and Minorities.* New York: St. Martin's Press, 1999.

Chang, Jeff. *Can't Stop Won't Stop: A History of the Hip-Hop Generation.* New York: St. Martin's Press, 2005.

Charnas, Dan. *The Big Payback: The History of the Business of Hip-Hop.* New York: New American Library, 2010.

Charnas, Dan. *Dilla Time: The Life and Afterlife of J Dilla, the Hip-Hop Producer Who Reinvented Rhythm.* New York: MCD Picador, 2022.

Chopmaster J. *Static: My Tupac Shakur Story.* San Francisco: OffPlanet Entertainment, 1999.

Christopher, Michael. *2Pac Behind Bars.* Las Vegas: Prende Publishing, 2021.

Cleaver, Eldridge. *Soul on Ice.* New York: Dell Publishing, 1968.

Coker, Cheo Hodari. *Unbelievable: The Life, Death, and Afterlife of the Notorious B.I.G.* New York: Vibe, 2013.

Cole, Harry, with Martha M. Jablow. *One in a Million.* Boston: Little, Brown and Company, 1990.

Coscarelli, Joe. *Rap Capital: An Atlanta Story.* New York: Simon & Schuster, 2022.

Danielle, Tracy. *Trust Is Amazing: Many Faces Many Moods.* Laguna Beach, CA: Lyfe Expressions Media, 2023.

Danois, Alejandro. *The Boys of Dunbar.* New York: Simon & Schuster, 2016.

Daughtry, Rev. Dr. Herbert. *Remembering Afeni Shakur.* Atlanta: CSJ Media, 2016.

Davis, Allison, Burleigh B. Gardner, and Mary R. Gardiner. *Deep South: A Social Anthropological Study of Caste and Class.* Chicago: University of Chicago, 1941.

Deal, Gene. *My World of Bodyguarding a Hip Hop Star.* Los Angeles, 2022.

Dyson, Michael Eric. *Holler If You Hear Me: Searching for Tupac Shakur.* New York: Basic Books, 2003.

Editors of *Vibe*, The. *Tupac Amaru Shakur: 1971–1996.* New York: Three Rivers Press, 1997.

Evans, Faith, with Aliya S. King. *Keep the Faith: A Memoir.* New York: Grand Central Publishing, 2008.

Farber, David. *Crack: Rock Cocaine, Street Capitalism, and the Decade of Greed.* New York: Cambridge University Press, 2019.

Farr, Joey. *Moguls and Madmen: The Pursuit of Power in Popular Music.* New York: Simon & Schuster, 1994.

Fat Joe. *The Book of Jose.* New York: Roc Lit, 2022.

Frank, Ida. *Vera Greenfield: A Journey from Gadyach to Berkeley.* Berkeley, CA: Judah L. Magnes Museum, 1988.

Fula, Yaasmyn. *The Homicide of Yafeu "Yaki Kadafi" Fula.* Los Angeles: Bearded Dragon Productions, 2022.

Fula, Yaasmyn. *Spirit of an Outlaw: The Untold Story of Tupac Amaru Shakur and Yaki "Kadafi" Fula.* Los Angeles: Bearded Dragon Books, 2020.

Geraldine, Amanda. *Tupac Shakur: The Rise and Fall of a Legend.* Las Vegas, 2023.

Gifford, Justin. *Revolution or Death: The Life of Eldridge Cleaver.* Chicago: Lawrence Hill Books, 2020.

Gobi, *Thru My Eyes: Thoughts on Tupac Shakur in Pictures and Words.* New York: Atria Books, 2005.

Golus, Carrie. *Tupac Shakur: Hip-Hop Idol.* Minneapolis: Twenty-First Century Books, 2011.

Goodman, Fred. *Fortune's Fool: Edgar Bronfman, Jr., Warner Music, and an Industry in Crisis*. New York: Simon & Schuster, 2010.

Goodson, Cindy. *Ladies Stop Thinking Start Shrinking*. New York: Cindy L. Goodson Ventures, 2015.

Green, Simone, with Tara Coyt. *Time Served: My Days and Nights on Death Row Records*. Atlanta: Golden Girls Publishing, 2011.

Greenburg, Zach O'Malley. *3 Kings: Diddy, Dr. Dre, Jay-Z, and Hip-Hop's Multibillion-Dollar Rise*. New York: Little, Brown and Company, 2018.

Guy, Jasmine. *Afeni Shakur: Evolution of a Revolutionary*. New York: Atria Books, 2004.

Healy, Joseph P. *Report of the Governor's Commission on Problems Affecting the Negro Population*. Baltimore: Subcommittee on Problems Affecting the Police, 1943.

Herz, Stanley. *Conquering the Corporate Career*. New York: Kimberly Press, 1986.

Hill, Robert B. *Pen Lucy: A Community Profile*. Baltimore: Morgan State University Institute for Urban Research, 1993.

Holcomb, Eric L. *The City as Suburb: A History of Northeast Baltimore Since 1660*. Santa Fe, NM: Center for American Places, 2005.

Holley, Santi Elijah. *An Amerikan Family: The Shakurs and the Nation They Created*. New York: Mariner Books, 2023.

Isaac, Dexter. *From Friends to Enemies*. Brooklyn, NY: Funnel Vision Publishing, 2018.

Jackson, George L. *Blood in My Eye*. Baltimore: Black Classics Press, 1972.

Jenkins, Sulaiman. *Life Is Raw: The Story of a Reformed Outlaw*. New York: Dio Press, 2010.

Jones, Quincy. *Q: The Autobiography of Quincy Jones*. New York: Doubleday, 2001.

Joseph, Jamal. *Panther Baby: A Life of Rebellion & Reinvention*. Chapel Hill, NC: Algonquin Books of Chapel Hill, 2012.

Kading, Greg, *Murder Rap: The Untold Story of the Biggie Smalls & Tupac Shakur Murder Investigations*. New York: One-Time Publishing, 2011.

Keffe D with Yusuf Jah. *Compton Street Legend: Notorious Keffe D's Street-Level Accounts of Tupac and Biggie Murders, Death Row Origins, Suge Knight, Puffy Combs, and Crooked Cops*. Santa Monica, CA: KingDoMedia, 2019.

Kempton, Murray. *The Briar Patch*. New York: Dutton, 1973.

Kioni-Sadiki, Déqui, and Matt Meyer, eds. *Look for Me in the Whirlwind: From the Panther 21 to 21st-Century Revolutions*. Oakland, CA: PM Press, 2017.

Lawrence, Robert C. *The State of Robeson*. New York: J. J. Little and Ives Company, 1939.

Lewis, Jenifer. *The Mother of Black Hollywood: A Memoir*. New York: HarperCollins, 2017.

Mac Mall. *My Opinion*. Published by the author, 2015.

Machiavelli, Niccolò. *The Prince*. New York: Penguin Classics, 1532.

Martinez, Angie. *My Voice: A Memoir*. New York: New American Library, 2016.

McCall, Nathan. *Makes Me Wanna Holler: A Young Black Man in America*. New York: Vintage Books, 1994.

McConnell, Roland C. *Three Hundred and Fifty Years: A Chronology of the Afro-American in Maryland, 1634–1984*. Baltimore: Maryland Commission on Afro-American History and Culture, 1985.

McCutchen, Dahlia. *I Testify*. Houston, 2017.

McDougall, Harold A. *Black Baltimore: A New Theory of Community*. Philadelphia: Temple University Press, 1993.

McQuillar, Tayannah Lee, and Fred L. Johnson III. *Tupac Shakur: The Life and Times of an American Icon*. New York: Da Capo Press, 2010.

Merritt, Tyler. *I Take My Coffee Black*. New York: Worthy Productions, 2021.

Mills, Clifford W. *Hip-Hop Stars: Tupac Shakur*. New York: Checkmark Books, 2008.

Modu, Chi. *Uncategorized*. Pori, Finland: Pori Art Museum Publications, 2015.

Monjauzie, Molly, with Gloria Cox and Staci Robinson. *Tupac Remembered: Bearing Witness to a Life and Legacy*. San Francisco: Chronicle Books, 2008.

Namikas, Michael. *The Tupac Encyclopedia*. Vol. 1. Published by the author, 2022.

Nielson, Erik, and Andrea L. Dennis. *Rap on Trial: Race, Lyrics, and Guilt in America*. New York: New Press, 2019.

Obafemi, Aiyisha T. *A Light on a Hill*. Chicago: 13th & Joan, 2021.

Ogbar, Jeffrey O. G. *Hip-Hop Revolution: The Culture and Politics of Rap*. Lawrence: University Press of Kansas, 2007.

Parker, Derrick, with Matt Diehl. *Notorious C.O.P.* New York: St. Martin's Press, 2006.

Pearce, Sheldon. *Changes: An Oral History of Tupac Shakur*. New York: Simon & Schuster, 2021.

Pietila, Antero. *Not in My Neighborhood: How Bigotry Shaped a Great American City*. Chicago: Ivan R. Dee, 2010.

Pinkett Smith, Jada. *Worthy*. New York: Dey Street, 2023.

Potash, John. *The FBI War on Tupac Shakur*. Portland, OR: Microcosm Publishing, 2007.

Powell, Kevin. *The Education of Kevin Powell*. New York: Atria, 2015.

Ramsey, Donovan X. *When Crack Was King*. New York: One World, 2023.

Rayman, Graham, and Reuven Blau. *Rikers: An Oral History*. New York: Random House, 2023.

Ro, Ronin. *Have Gun Will Travel: The Spectacular Rise and Violent Fall of Death Row Records*. New York: Doubleday, 1998.

Robinson, Staci. *Tupac Shakur: The Authorized Biography*. New York: Crown, 2023.

Ryan, Hugh. *The Women's House of Detention*. New York: Bold Type Books, 2022.

Samuels, Allison. *Off the Record: A Reporter Unveils the Celebrity World of Hollywood, Hip-Hop & Sports*. New York: HarperCollins, 2007.

Sandy, Candace, and Dawn Marie Daniels. *How Long Will They Mourn Me?: The Life and Legacy of Tupac Shakur*. New York: Ballantine Books, 2006.

Savidge, S. Leigh, with Steve Housden and Jeff Scheftel. *Welcome to Death Row*. Hawthorne, CA: Xenon Press, 2015.

Scott, Cathy. *The Killing of Tupac Shakur*. London: Plexus, 2009.

Shakur, Asata. *Asata: An Autobiography*. Chicago: Lawrence Hill Books, 1987.

Shakur, Sanyika. *Monster: The Autobiography of an L.A. Gang Member*. New York: Grove Press, 1993.

Shakur, Tupac. *The Rose That Grew from Concrete*. New York: Pocket Boots, 1999.

Sider, Gerald M. *Lumbee Indian Histories: Race, Ethnicity, and Indian Identity in the Southern United States*. New York: Cambridge University Press, 1993.

Sleuth, N. J. *Hop-Hop Tales 2.0: From Humpty Dance to Blonde Locks*. Oakland: Sleuth Pro Books, 2017.

Snoop Dogg with Davin Seay. *The Doggfather: The Times, Trials, and Hardcore Truths of Snoop Dogg*. New York: William Morrow, 1999.

Sonefeld, Jim. *Swimming with the Blowfish: Hootie, Healing, and One Hell of a Rise*. New York: Diversion Books, 2022.

Stavig, Ward, and Ella Schmidt. *The Tupac Amaru and Catarista Rebellions*. Indianapolis: Hackett Publishing, 2008.

Steward, Danny Boy. *Stranded on Death Row*. Atlanta: Trumbull Publishing, 2017.

Sullivan, Randall. *LAbyrinth: A Detective Investigates the Murders of Tupac Shakur and Notorious B.I.G., the Implication of Death Row Records, and the Origins of the Los Angeles Police Scandal.* New York: Atlantic Monthly Press, 2002.

Sweeney, Megan. *The Story Within Us: Women Prisoners Reflect on Reading.* Champaign: University of Illinois Press, 2012.

Tinsley, Justin. *It Was All a Dream: Biggie and the World that Made Him.* New York: Abrams Press, 2022.

Tyner, K. Blake. *Images of America: Lumberton.* Charleston, SC: Arcadia Publishing, 2014.

Van Nguyen, Dean. *Words for My Comrades.* New York: Doubleday, 2025.

Wallace, Voletta, with Tremell McKenzie. *Biggie.* New York: Atria Books, 2005.

Weiss, Jeff, and Evan McGarvey. *2Pac vs. Biggie: An Illustrated History of Rap's Greatest Battle.* Minneapolis: Voyageur Press, 2013.

West, Sam. *Our History: Robeson County, North Carolina: 1748–2002.* Waynesville, NC: The Robeson County Heritage Book Committee, 2003.

Westhoff, Ben. *Original Gangstas: The Untold Story of Dr. Dre, Eazy-E, Ice Cube, Tupac Shakur, and the Birth of West Coast Rap.* New York: Hachette Books, 2016.

White, Armond. *Rebel for the Hell of It: The Life of Tupac Shakur.* New York: Thunder's Mouth Press, 1997.

Whitfield, Charles L. *Healing the Child Within.* Deerfield Beach, FL: Health Communications, 1987.

Zoran, Joseph. *Tupac Shakur: Collection of Declassified FBI Files and Court Records,* 2017.

Notes

Introduction

xii   *The piece, penned by:* "Cries in the Night," *Daily News* (New York), Mar. 24, 1991.

xiv   *Via a lightly viewed Epps YouTube interview:* "Omar Epps Recalls Day Tupac Shakur Wrote Famous Track 'Brenda's Got A Baby,'" HipHollywood, Apr. 20, 2018, https://www.youtube.com/watch?v=UZm-UfnIJVQ.

Chapter 1: Panther

1   *"I wanted a baby so bad":* Amy Pagnozzi, "Loyal Mother Passes the Toughest Test of Time," *Daily News* (New York), Dec. 2, 1994.

2   *"My mother almost died":* Kuwasi Balagoon, *Look for Me in the Whirlwind* (New York: Random House, 2008), 182.

3   *And when, in 1958, the Ku Klux Klan:* Stephen L. Carter, "Hey, NFL: How About Lumbee?," *Greensboro (NC) News and Record*, Aug. 31, 2014.

3   *"Resistance is what I felt":* Jasmine Guy, *Afeni Shakur: Evolution of a Revolutionary* (New York: Atria Books, 2004), 13–14.

3   *"[Mom] tried to warn us":* Guy, *Afeni Shakur*, 31.

3   *"I couldn't see the stars":* Balagoon, *Look for Me in the Whirlwind*, 231.

4   *"I kicked his ass":* Guy, *Afeni Shakur*, 32–33.

4   *With the exception of journalism class:* Rudy Johnson, "Joan Bird and Afeni Shakur, Self-Styled Soldiers in the Panther 'Class Struggle,'" *New York Times*, July 19, 1970.

4   *Her mother made about forty dollars per week:* Balagoon, *Look for Me in the Whirlwind*, 231.

4   *"I'd get high off Thunderbird wine":* Guy, *Afeni Shakur*, 44–45.

5   *"When somebody hit me":* Balagoon, *Look for Me in the Whirlwind*, 271.

5   *"The water was blue":* Guy, *Afeni Shakur*, 33.

5   *"The people listening":* Guy, *Afeni Shakur*, 59–61.

6   *"They scared a lot":* "Black Panthers: A Taut, Violent Drama," *Tampa Bay Times*, July 21, 1968.

6   *"And then Bobby Seale says":* Guy, *Afeni Shakur*, 60–61.

7   *Less than twenty-four hours later:* Santi Elijah Holley, *An Amerikan Family: The Shakurs and the Nation They Created* (New York: Mariner Books, 2023), 52.

7   *She found herself under the tutelage:* Guy, *Afeni Shakur*, 62.

8   *Around this time:* Guy, *Afeni Shakur*, 57–58.

8   *"My entire view of men and family":* Guy, *Afeni Shakur*, 70.

8   *Yet two months after his wedding:* "Innocent Pleas Entered in Case," *Hartford Courant*, Dec. 24, 1968.

9   *"Throughout the late 1960s and 1970s":* Holley, *An Amerikan Family*, 11–12.

10 *He turned the stainless steel:* Holley, *An Amerikan Family*, 9.

10 *Inside the apartment:* "Ruse Used in Arrest of Panther," *New York Post*, April 28, 1970.

10 *"When I was arrested":* *Wake Me When I'm Free* Tupac Shakur exhibit, The Canvas @ L.A. Live, 2023.

10 *An Associated Press piece noted:* "21 Panthers Accused in N.Y. Bombing Plot," Associated Press, Apr. 2, 1969.

11 *Sometimes, if she misbehaved:* Hugh Ryan, *The Women's House of Detention* (New York: Bold Type Books, 2022), 77.

11 *Then, on January 30, 1970:* Holley, *An Amerikan Family*, 13.

12 *"Bill Garland, an agile basketball player":* Jim Sermons, "Somerville Tops Franklin as Garland Nets 30 Points," *Daily Home News* (New Brunswick, NJ), Jan. 31, 1968.

12 *Yet one year after graduating:* Stephen Alligood, "No More Colored, Just Black People," *Central New Jersey Home News*, Mar. 14, 1969.

12 *"It relieved tension":* Billy Garland interview with the Art of Dialogue, July 8, 2023, https://www.youtube.com/watch?v=cTnbcEYkujs&t=4s.

12 *"Lumumba called me a slut":* Guy, *Afeni Shakur*, 111.

12 *Two were men:* Guy, *Afeni Shakur*, 97.

13 *Lumumba mocked her:* Guy, *Afeni Shakur*, 97–99.

13 *The Panther 21 had been whittled down to thirteen:* Phyllis Furman, "Judge in Panther Trial Refuses to Step Down," *The Record* (Bergen County, NJ), Feb. 6, 1970.

13 *The presiding judge, John M. Murtagh:* Anthony Burton, "Judge Plays It Cool; He's Hardy Type," *Daily News* (New York), Feb. 4, 1970; Patrick Owens, "Panthers Cannot Avoid Murtagh," *Newsday*, Sept. 16, 1970.

13 *"I was young," Afeni later recalled:* Guy, *Afeni Shakur*, 98.

13 *The prosecution, led by Assistant District Attorney Joseph Phillips:* Donald Flynn, "Panthers on Trial Today in Slay Plot," *Daily News* (New York), Feb. 1, 1970.

13 *Even less credible was Ralph White:* Donald Flynn, "Panther Case Cop Tells of Undercover Activity," *Daily News* (New York), Feb. 1, 1971.

13 *"Had White ever seen her with a gun":* Edward Hershey, "Panther Trial Peaks with Self-Defense," *Newsday*, Apr. 28, 1971.

14 *She pleaded with the court to consider:* Holley, *An Amerikan Family*, 15.

14 *"Afeni Shakur lugged two transcript volumes":* Edward Hershey, "Panther Defendant Makes Her Case," *Newsday*, Apr. 29, 1971.

15 *Five days later, in the midst of closing arguments:* Donald Flynn, "Panther Wife Freed as Birth Time Nears," *Daily News* (New York), May 4, 1971.

15 *"Will you give me your word":* John Cummings, "Pregnant Panther Defendant Released," *Newsday*, May 4, 1971.

15 *He declared "Not guilty" 156 times:* Donald Flynn, "12 Panthers Innocent on All Charges," *Daily News* (New York), May 14, 1971.

Chapter 2: Lesane

16   *Raised in public housing by a single mother:* Hugh Ryan, *The Women's House of Detention* (New York: Bold Type Books, 2022), 280.

18   *"As a fetus, he felt":* Yaasmyn Fula, *Spirit of an Outlaw: The Untold Story of Tupac Amaru Shakur and Yaki "Kadafi" Fula* (Los Angeles: Bearded Dragon Books, 2020), 3.

19   *"Okay, darling dear—there you are":* Staci Robinson, *Tupac Shakur: The Authorized Biography* (New York: Crown, 2023), 23.

19   *"Don't pass him to me":* Ryan, *The Women's House of Detention*, 281.

19   *Space was tight:* Fula, *Spirit of an Outlaw*, 7.

20   *"He was always in my mind a soldier":* Dean Van Nguyen, *Words for My Comrades* (New York: Doubleday, 2025), 104.

20   *"Horses tugged at the end of each rope":* Miguel La Serna, "'I Will Return and I Will Be Millions!' The Many Lives of Tupac Amaru," *Age of Revolutions*, Nov. 10, 2020, ageofrevolutions.com/2020/11/02/i-will-return-and-i-will-be-millions-the-many-lives-of-tupac-amaru/.

21   *"hero who refused to die":* La Serna, "'I Will Return and I Will Be Millions!'"

24   *"When Black radicalism stopped being chic":* Tayannah Lee McQuillar and Fred L. Johnson III, *Tupac Shakur: The Life and Times of an American Icon* (New York: Da Capo Press, 2010), 33.

25   *The author Santi Elijah Holley:* Santi Elijah Holley, *An Amerikan Family: The Shakurs and the Nation They Created* (New York: Mariner Books, 2023), 123.

26   *nearly twenty thousand Black students:* "Rioting Still Raging in Soweto, S. Africa," Associated Press, June 17, 1976.

28   *"We were the no-hot-water":* Molly Monjauzie with Gloria Cox and Staci Robinson, *Tupac Remembered: Bearing Witness to a Life and Legacy* (San Francisco: Chronicle Books, 2008), 13.

29   *Then, on October 20, 1981:* Steve Lieberman, "Brinks Murder Mastermind Mutulu Shakur, Tupac's Stepfather, Released from Federal Prison," *The Journal News* (Rockland/Westchester, NY), Dec. 19, 2022, lohud.com/story/news/local/rockland/2022/12/16/mutulu-shakur-tupac-stepfather-brinks-robbery-released-prison/69735811007/.

30   *"The drug," wrote Parren J. Mitchell:* Parren J. Mitchell, "Crack—What It Is," *Baltimore Afro-American*, July 19, 1986.

30   *"Crack poisoned bodies":* David Farber, *Crack: Rock Cocaine, Street Capitalism, and the Decade of Greed* (New York: Cambridge University Press, 2019), 3–4.

31   *What she wanted:* Staci Robinson, *Tupac Shakur: The Authorized Biography* (New York: Crown, 2023), 31.

31   *"Education is what my son is here for":* Don Weinbrenner, "Little Red School Caught in Rent Bind," *Daily News* (New York), Jan. 3, 1982.

31   *Hailed by* The New York Times: Spencer Clover, "On Lower East Side, an Innovative School," *New York Times*, Nov. 9, 1986.

Chapter 3: Rapture

36   *When Tupac was ten:* Staci Robinson, *Tupac Shakur: The Authorized Biography* (New York: Crown, 2023), 52.

37   *Years later, the rapper Shock G: Thug Angel: The Life of an Outlaw*, 2002.

38   *On November 4, 1983:* Robert A. Jordan, "Jackson Launches '84 Candidacy," *Boston Globe*, Nov. 4, 1983.

39   *"Afeni was going through her problems":* Sheldon Pearce, *Changes: An Oral History of Tupac Shakur* (New York: Simon & Schuster, 2021), 11–12.

39   *"Whatever that 'it factor' is":* Pearce, *Changes*, 11–12.

39   *"I woke up and I was the only person":* Molly Monjauzie with Gloria Cox and Staci Robinson, *Tupac Remembered: Bearing Witness to a Life and Legacy* (San Francisco: Chronicle Books, 2008), 13.

39   *"When the curtain went up":* Paul Papa, "At the Corner of Flamingo and Forever," *Medium*, Oct. 25, 2023, medium.com/@paul_28578.

40   *"That was us trying to expose":* Robinson, *Tupac Shakur*, 60.

41   *After a month or so in town:* Robinson, *Tupac Shakur*, 61.

Chapter 4: Coming to Baltimore

45   *"There has [sic] always been two Baltimores":* R. B. Jones, "Two Baltimores," *Baltimore Afro-American*, July 19, 1986.

45   *To his credit, Tupac made:* Staci Robinson, *Tupac Shakur: The Authorized Biography* (New York: Crown, 2023), 74–75.

46   *Tupac owned two pairs:* Robinson, *Tupac Shakur*, 77.

48   *Decades later:* Robinson, *Tupac Shakur*, 77–78.

49   *When it was his turn:* Robinson, *Tupac Shakur*, 79.

49   *"It smelled like piss":* Robinson, *Tupac Shakur*, 79.

49   *"[Tupac's] offerings were always met":* Darrin Keith Bastfield, *Back in the Day: My Life and Times with Tupac Shakur* (New York: Da Capo Press, 2002), 21.

50   *At one juncture:* Robinson, *Tupac Shakur*, 86.

51   *They played five songs:* Bastfield, *Back in the Day*, 31.

51   *"Tupac," Mouse recalled:* Robinson, *Tupac Shakur*, 82.

54   *"Tupac," he recalled:* Robinson, *Tupac Shakur*, 85.

57   *Less than a year earlier:* Bastfield, *Back in the Day*, 36–37.

Chapter 5: School for the Arts

62   *There was a basement swimming pool:* Jacques Kelly, "Alcazar Ballroom Has Led a Charmed (and Charming) Life," *Baltimore Sun*, Oct. 13, 2017.

62   *By the mid-1970s:* Kelly, "Alcazar Ballroom Has Led a Charmed (and Charming) Life."

62   *In 1977, the building was sold:* Tracie Rozhon, "Board of Estimates Votes to Buy K. of C. Home for Arts High School," *Baltimore Sun*, Aug. 4, 1977.

62   *On April 10, 1979, the new entity:* M. William Salganik, "Arts School Begins Recruitment," *Baltimore Sun*, Apr. 10, 1979.

63   *The dean, David Simon:* Michael J. Himowitz, "N.Y. Music Dean Picked to Head School for Arts," *Baltimore Sun*, July 13, 1979.

68   *Nava Zuckerman, the Tmu-na founder:* Winifred Walsh, "Israeli Play Symbolizes Personal and National Struggle," *Baltimore Sun*, May 2, 1988.

69   *Other times he arrived at BSA:* Darrin Keith Bastfield, *Back in the Day: My Life and Times with Tupac Shakur* (New York: Da Capo Press, 2002), 87.

Chapter 6: Mary, Mary

82   *Similar to Tupac, Pinkett:* Jada Pinkett Smith, *Worthy* (New York: Dey Street, 2023), 35.

83   *"There were no airs":* Pinkett Smith, *Worthy*, 84.

83   *"When you have somebody that has":* Staci Robinson, *Tupac Shakur: The Authorized Biography* (New York: Crown, 2023), 97.

84   *"Having come up":* Darrin Keith Bastfield, *Back in the Day: My Life and Times with Tupac Shakur* (New York: Da Capo Press, 2002), 73.

84   *"She was not living":* Harry Cole with Martha M. Jablow, *One in a Million* (Boston: Little, Brown, 1990), 256.

84   *"I believe God":* Cole with Jablow, *One in a Million*, 261.

89   *"I never seen anything":* Robinson, *Tupac Shakur*, 93.

93   "Tupac has very good potential": Robinson, *Tupac Shakur*, 106.

Chapter 7: The Transition Happened in Marin City

97   *"I didn't kill that woman":* "Panther Geronimo Convicted," *Daily Herald* (Everett, WA), July 29, 1972.

99   *Is this what Tupac Shakur:* Staci Robinson, *Tupac Shakur: The Authorized Biography* (New York: Crown, 2023), 123.

99   *"Everyone was to be in the house by eight o'clock":* Robinson, *Tupac Shakur*, 123.

100   *"Money grew on trees":* "Marin City: Past, Present, Future," Tamalpais Union High School District.

100   *In the years that followed:* Mark Anthony Wilson, "Marin City and Its Buildigs: A Historical and Architecturally Significant Landmark," *Marin Magazine*, Nov. 20, 2015.

Chapter 8: Tam

121   *During this period, Afeni visited:* Dean Van Nguyen, *Words for My Comrades* (New York: Doubleday, 2025), 182.

123   Police are looking for: "Man Assaulted," *Novato Advance*, Feb. 1, 1989.

124   *"Okay. My name is Tupac Shakur":* "Tupac Shakur 1988 High School Interview," June 12, 2017, https://www.youtube.com/watch?v=v_XT9-C5Qu8.

Chapter 9: A Chicken Named Red

141   *In 1987 the musicians had teamed:* Jonathan Abrams, *The Come Up: An Oral History of the Rise of Hip-Hop* (New York: Crown, 2022), 310.

143   *Leila drove Tupac to the studio:* Christopher R. Weingarten, "I Get Around: The Oral History of 2Pac's Digital Underground Years," *Rolling Stone*, Apr. 6, 2017.

144   *"It was street":* Staci Robinson, *Tupac Shakur: The Authorized Biography* (New York: Crown, 2023), 155.

144   *Dright recalled Tupac looking:* Chopmaster J, *Static: My Tupac Shakur Story* (San Francisco: OffPlanet Entertainment, 1999), 1.

Chapter 10: Digital

147 *The song received extensive airplay:* Barry Walters, "Funk from the Rings of Neptune," *San Francisco Examiner*, Sept. 1, 1989.

147 *"Tupac saw me and the DU crew constantly":* Chopmaster J, *Static: My Tupac Shakur Story* (San Francisco: OffPlanet Entertainment, 1999), 8.

147 *And when the seven members of the group jetted off:* Michael Snyder, "Reunited Doobies Romp Through the White House," *San Francisco Examiner*, Aug. 27, 1989.

147 *In London, the* Evening Standard *labeled:* Sorrel Downer, "Crazy Rhythm," *Evening Standard*, Nov. 7, 1989.

152 *"I literally got that demo":* Christopher R. Weingarten, "I Get Around: The Oral History of 2Pac's Digital Underground Years," *Rolling Stone*, Apr. 6, 2017.

152 *"Digital Underground looks like":* John Leland, "The Sounds to Watch in the '90s," *Newsday*, Jan. 7, 1990.

152 *"Digital Underground is the new sound":* Jonathan Gold, "Digital Underground Keeps Hip-Hop on Top," *Los Angeles Times*, Apr. 28, 1990.

153 *Tupac officially joined Digital Underground:* Joel Selvin, "13th Annual Bammies Counting on Star Power," *San Francisco Examiner*, Mar. 11, 1990.

155 *One of Tupac's tasks:* Weingarten, "I Get Around."

155 *"One thing Tupac hated":* Weingarten, "I Get Around."

156 *"I was starting to choose to chill":* "SHOCK G Shares Stories About Tupac Shakur," Mar. 20, 2021, https://www.youtube.com/watch?v=QOg6pTq7qwY.

157 *"It became obvious really quickly":* Chopmaster J, *Static*, 14.

157 *"We were getting the friends":* Weingarten, "I Get Around."

157 *"Pac would choose five":* Chopmaster J, *Static*, 15.

157 *"That shit," recalled Dright:* Chopmaster J, *Static*, 17.

157 *"It was a nasty jar":* Weingarten, "I Get Around."

159 *"Deep down he had that same gap":* Benjamin Meadows-Ingram, "My Brother," *XXL*, Oct. 2002.

159 *"When we found out Public Enemy":* "SHOCK G Shares Stories About Tupac Shakur."

159 *Less than one year earlier:* Staci Robinson, *Tupac Shakur: The Authorized Biography* (New York: Crown, 2023), 134.

160 *Now, they were all on:* John D'Agostino, "Rap Concert Fails to Sizzle in San Diego," *Los Angeles Times*, Aug. 28, 1990.

160 *Public Enemy had recently found itself in hot water:* Susan McNamara, "Public Enemy Tries to Put Trouble Aside," *Rochester Democrat and Chronicle*, June 14, 1990.

160 *"That most dreadful of":* Larry Nager, "Beating Bad Image, Rap Crowd Has Good Time," *Cincinnati Post*, July 12, 1990.

160 *In a review of the Richmond show:* Tracy Wimmer, "Power Men of Rap," *Roanoke Times*, June 29, 1990.

160 *In Macon, Georgia:* James Palmer, "'Taste' Considerations Have Stations Scratching Rappers from Playlists," *Macon Telegraph and News*, July 15, 1990.

161 *"It's a common rock":* Kathy Haight, "Rap Groups' Showmanship Runs Gamut," *Charlotte Observer*, Aug. 4, 1990.

161 *When, a few nights later:* Kevin Q. Murphy, "Man Is Slain After Concert at Kemper Arena," *Kansas City Star*, Aug. 19, 1990.

161 *"Pac had this dude"*: People's Party interview between Chuck D and Talib Kweli, Apr. 4, 2020, https://www.youtube.com/watch?v=C3pBJsVN5s4.

162 *"Every city we went in"*: DJ Vlad interview with Treach, July 5, 2017, https://www.youtube.com/watch?v=LzoMVLXXxE8.

162 *"I was the first one on the floor"*: Gordon C. Williams, "Rappin' All the Way to the Bank," *Reporter Dispatch*, June 14, 1987.

163 *On this night, as the show was wrapping*: James L. Patterson, "Rap Artist Hurt Critically in Fall from Arena Ramp," *Indianapolis Star*, July 16, 1990.

164 *Midway through Brother Elmo*: David Nitkin, "'He Was a Happy, Jolly Guy,'" *Reporter Dispatch*, July 20, 1990.

Chapter 11: Juiced

165 *During a show at the Shoreline*: Barry Walters, "Rappin' the Night Away," *San Francisco Examiner*, Aug. 27, 1990.

165 *The show itself was flat*: John D'Agostino, "Rap Concert Fails to Sizzle in San Diego," *Los Angeles Times*, Aug. 28, 1990.

165 *"The music wasn't for the faint of heart"*: Kevan Goff, "Public Enemy Plays Politics to 2,400," *Daily Oklahoman*, Aug. 20, 1990.

166 *The tune was a little ditty*: "SHOCK G Shares Stories About Tupac Shakur," Mar. 20, 2021, https://www.youtube.com/watch?v=QOg6pTq7qwY&t=289s.

167 *"Where the other rappers"*: Staci Robinson, *Tupac Shakur: The Authorized Biography* (New York: Crown, 2023), 175.

168 *"Tupac pestered Aykroyd every chance he got"*: Chopmaster J, *Static: My Tupac Shakur Story* (San Francisco: OffPlanet Entertainment, 1999), 46.

168 *"At first, Dan Aykroyd"*: Chopmaster J, *Static*, 47–48.

169 *When Candice Russell*: Candice Russell, "Comedy Isn't Worth the Trouble of Buying a Ticket," *South Florida Sun-Sentinel*, Feb. 19, 1991.

170 *"He didn't bitch about it"*: Christopher R. Weingarten, "I Get Around: The Oral History of 2Pac's Digital Underground Years," *Rolling Stone*, Apr. 6, 2017.

Chapter 12: The Scraps

179 *That the station*: Jose Fermoso, "Now an Underground Rave Venue, Oakland's Abandoned Greyhound Station Was Once 'Magnificent,'" The Oaklandside, Mar. 9, 2023.

179 *"I'm an addict"*: Jasmine Guy, *Afeni Shakur: Evolution of a Revolutionary* (New York: Atria Books, 2004), 166.

179 *Afeni boarded the bus*: Dean Van Nguyen, *Words for My Comrades* (New York: Doubleday, 2025), 193.

180 *"I had ceased to be"*: Guy, *Afeni Shakur*, 168.

182 *"I've never seen that many rings"*: Sheldon Pearce, *Changes: An Oral History of Tupac Shakur* (New York: Simon & Schuster, 2021), 84.

183 *"Rebel songs"*: 2Pac, "2Pacalypse Now (Behind the Scenes)," Nov. 22, 2016, https://www.youtube.com/watch?v=JetHaJPzAA4.

186 *"To me, it was more important"*: "The Arsenio Hall Show," March 24, 1994.

188 *"I was an addict"*: Guy, *Afeni Shakur*, 172–73.

189   *"When he could have easily hitched his wagon"*: "On Meeting Tupac" from Sal Manna's personal collection.

191   *Earlier that year:* Will Jones, "Rapper Filed Brutality Suit over Jaywalking Ticket Dispute," *Oakland Tribune*, Nov. 13, 1991.

192   *Burris told those:* Jones, "Rapper Filed Brutality Suit over Jaywalking Ticket Dispute."

192   *"They said that even though"*: Don Martinez, "Oakland Rapper Files Claim Against 2 Cops," *San Francisco Examiner*, Nov. 13, 1991.

Chapter 13: A One-Take Motherfucker

195   *The suspect, an eighteen-year-old unemployed cook:* Joel Anderson, "The Moment Tupac Became America's Most Dangerous Rapper," *Slate*, Nov. 6, 2019, https://slate.com/culture/2019/11/slow-burn-tupac-biggie-ronald-ray-howard.html.

201   *Maya Angelou, the poet:* "Maya Angelou's Conversation with Tupac Shakur," Canadian Broadcasting Corporation, Dec. 23, 2013, https://www.cbc.ca/strombo/videos/maya-angelou-tupac-shakur.

201   *"I didn't know what gangsta rap"*: Anderson, "The Moment Tupac Became America's Most Dangerous Rapper."

202   *When an actual suit was filed:* Jason Sean Garber, "Rap Lyrics Led to Trooper's Death, Wife Says," *Fort Worth Star-Telegram*, Aug. 14, 1992.

202   *"There isn't a doubt in my mind"*: Chuck Phillips, "Testing the Limits," *Los Angeles Times*, Oct. 13, 1992.

203   *"There is absolutely no reason"*: Barbara Ross, "Dan Spins over Rap," *Daily News* (New York), Sept. 23, 1992.

203   *On June 16, 1992, Tupac Shakur:* "1992-06-16 / Tupac Bought a Black Jeep Cherokee," 2PacLegacy.net, Oct. 9, 2016, 2paclegacy.net/tupac-bought-a-black-jeep-cherokee/.

204   *"He said that all the women down here were pregnant"*: Craig Marine, "When a Prodigal Rap Star's Homecoming Took a Tragic Turn, an Angry Community Was Left to Wonder—Where Is Justice?," *San Francisco Examiner*, Mar. 14, 1993.

206   *"I had been a rapper since I was a kid"*: Jake Brown's interview archives.

207   *"I had things pretty cooled out"*: Marine, "When a Prodigal Rap Star's Homecoming Took a Tragic Turn, an Angry Community Was Left to Wonder—Where Is Justice?"

207   *Tupac, he later said:* Marine, "When a Prodigal Rap Star's Homecoming Took a Tragic Turn, an Angry Community Was Left to Wonder—Where Is Justice?"

208   *"I was on one knee and kept my head down"*: Marine, "When a Prodigal Rap Star's Homecoming Took a Tragic Turn, an Angry Community Was Left to Wonder—Where Is Justice?"

209   *"Harding puts the car into gear"*: Marine, "When a Prodigal Rap Star's Homecoming Took a Tragic Turn, an Angry Community Was Left to Wonder—Where Is Justice?"

209   *So was Mopreme's driver's license:* Eric Brazil, "Rap Star Settles Suit Out of Court," *San Francisco Examiner*, Nov. 8, 1995.

Chapter 14: The Most Intelligent Stupid Dude

211   *Founded by a socialite named Gloria Goldwater:* Gloria Goldwater, "'SuperFly: A Personal Journey Behind Hip Hop in the 90s' by Brentwood's Gloria Goldwater," *Brentwood News*, Oct. 17, 2014.

211 *"What is Vanilla Ice talking about?":* Hamza, "2Pac of Digital Underground: A Real NIGGA!," *SuperFly*, 1991.

215 *"We see this one motherfucker over to the side":* "Laylaw Talks About Making of Strictly 4 My N***** with 2Pac and Then Joining L.A. Riots," Money-B interview with Laylaw, Dec. 10, 2023, https://www.youtube.com/watch?v=HPXWr NSGK_I.

215 *"As I drove through L.A. . . . ":* Nina Bhadreshwar, *Finding CC* (London: WJ Scrivener Books, 2018), 293.

216 *George H. W. Bush, president:* J. D. Considine, "It's Easier to Attack 'Cop-Killer' Rap than to Deal with Gun Lobby," *Baltimore Sun*, July 3, 1992.

216 *The Combined Law Enforcement Association:* Davin Lucas, "Rapper Ice-T Pulls Cop Killer," *Rochester Press Democrat*, July 29, 1992.

216 *In addition, according to the author Staci Robinson:* Staci Robinson, *Tupac Shakur: The Authorized Biography* (New York: Crown, 2023), 220.

220 *But along with managing Digital Underground:* Robinson, *Tupac Shakur*, 227.

222 *According to the estate-authorized 2023 Tupac biography:* Robinson, *Tupac Shakur*, 224.

223 *"I think even gangs can be positive":* "Code of Thug Life," Tupac.be., https://tupac .be/en/his-world/code-of-thug-life/.

225 *"We didn't know if the guy was getting a gun":* "1993-03-13 / Tupac Arrested for Limo Driver Assaulting," 2PacLegacy.net, Feb. 13, 2016, 2paclegacy.net/1993-03 -13-tupac-arrested-for-limo-driver-assaulting/.

225 *"They apparently got angry":* "Police Arrest '2 Pac' Rappers," *Victoria Advocate* (Victoria, TX), Mar. 14, 1993.

226 *Interscope booked him to headline:* Natalie Barna, "Rapper Arrested After Concert Clash," *Lansing State Journal* (Lansing, MI), Apr. 5, 1993.

226 *Phife introduced Tupac to viewers:* "D Phife & 2Pac Interview," Feb. 11, 2014, https://www.youtube.com/watch?v=amA-cA2BhG0.

227 *He didn't know he had been:* Anne Goldstein, "Morgan's Wynn Finishes Career as All-American," *Black College Sports Review*, May 1990.

228 *"It was pandemonium":* 2PacLegacy.net, Feb. 13, 2016, https://2paclegacy.net /tupac-was-arrested-to-hit-chauncey-wynn-m-a-d-with-a-baseball-bat/#google _vignette.

Chapter 15: Rebound

230 *"I'll do it," he said:* Staci Robinson, *Tupac Shakur: The Authorized Biography* (New York: Crown, 2023), 231.

232 *"He threw the fucking newspaper":* DJVlad YouTube interview with Spice 1, Nov. 28, 2018, https://www.youtube.com/watch?v=F7_Uz8bGum4.

233 *"I just seen Allen":* DJVlad YouTube interview with Tyrin Turner, Dec. 18, 2021, https://www.youtube.com/watch?v=nVwSsg8rPKs.

234 *"I beat up the directors":* "2Pac a. k. a. Tupac Addresses Hughes Brothers on Yo MTV Raps 1993 Interview," Apr. 5, 2024, https://www.youtube.com/watch?v=WDiqE HFb10I.

235 *"I won't play just anything":* Ken Parish Perkins, "Shakur a Film Rebel," *Mansfield News-Journal* (Mansfield, OH), July 25, 1993.

235   *"Revolutionary doesn't mean AK-toting assassin"*: Yardena Arar, "Singleton's Latest Rapper-Turned-Actor in 'Justice,'" *Plain Dealer* (Cleveland), Aug. 13, 1993.

236   *"Acting is a way"*: Esther Iverem, "'Poetic Justice' Shows a Softer Side of Shakur," *Newsday*, July 20, 1993.

236   *"The payoff for a movie"*: Gary Thompson, "'Poetic Justice': Bad to Verse," *Philadelphia Daily News*, July 23, 1993.

237   *"With his razor-sharp cheekbones"*: Kevin Powell, "This Thug's Life," *Vibe*, Feb. 1994.

238   *The song, wrote Michael Namikas*: Michael Namikas, *The Tupac Encyclopedia*, vol. 1 (Los Angeles: Michael A. Namikas, 2022), 480–81.

239   *"Atlanta is a black city"*: Hugh A. Mulligan, "New Black Archbishop Faces Challenges," Associated Press, May 21, 1988.

239   *"It was not a U-Haul"*: Robinson, *Tupac Shakur*, 248.

240   *"When he directly addressed the oft-leveled charge"*: Rohan B. Preston, "Tupac Offends," *Chicago Tribune*, Aug. 30, 1993.

240   *A few days after that, Tupac stormed*: Tyrone J. Tyler, "Rappers Fail to Spark Crowd's Energy," *Des Moines Register*, Sept. 3, 1993.

241   *According to Dante Powers*: Robinson, *Tupac Shakur*, 258.

242   *He was charged with two counts of aggravated*: Macon Morehouse, "Rapper Accused of Shooting Two Off-Duty Officers," *Atlanta Constitution*, Nov. 1, 1993.

242   *An internal investigation revealed*: Powell, "This Thug's Life."

Chapter 16: All Praise Belongs to Allah

245   *A Los Angeles native and reformed member*: Michael Namikas, *The Tupac Encyclopedia*, vol. 1 (Los Angeles: Michael A. Namikas, 2022), 28.

249   *That's how, on the night of Sunday, November 14*: Bob Colacello, "Nell's Cabaret," *Vanity Fair*, Feb. 1987.

250   *It cost five dollars to enter*: John Marchese, "The Mighty Nell's," *New York Times*, Feb. 27, 1994.

250   *At its height*: Marchese, "The Mighty Nell's."

250   *"From Tupac's perspective"*: Tayannah Lee McQuillar and Fred L. Johnson III, *Tupac Shakur: The Life and Times of an American Icon* (New York: Da Capo Press, 2010), 132.

251   *On November 6, they watched the Evander Holyfield–Riddick Bowe fight*: "Who Is Jacques 'Haitian Jack' Agnant?," 2PacLegacy.net, Dec. 3, 2017, https://2paclegacy.net/who-is-jacques-haitian-jack-agnant/.

251   *"Jacques had all this gold and diamond jewelry"*: Staff ID19, "The Alleged Rape," thuglifearmy.com, Sept. 23, 2004, https://www.youtube.com/watch?v=0CVBOv9O1GA

251   *"She had a big chest"*: Kevin Powell, "Ready to Live," *Vibe*, Apr. 1995.

252   *"I turned around"*: Vlad TV interview with Ayanna Jackson, Feb. 13, 2018, https://www.youtube.com/watch?v=0CVBOv9O1GA.

252   *"He said, 'Leave your number'"*: Vlad TV interview with Ayanna Jackson.

253   *"So [Tupac and I] go into the bedroom"*: Vlad TV interview with Ayanna Jackson.

253   *"I'm looking at him while I'm straddling him"*: Vlad TV interview with Ayanna Jackson.

253 *Tupac later told the journalist:* Powell, "Ready to Live."

255 *Somehow, Agnant's attorney:* Michael Eric Dyson, *Holler If You Hear Me* (New York: Basic Books, 2003), 193.

Chapter 17: Image Award

261 *By the time the award ceremony was held:* Shirlee Smith, "Trouble Brings Out Michael's Sense of Togetherness," *Pasadena Star-News*, Jan. 9, 1994.

262 *Dionne Warwick called:* Sonya Ross, "Tupac's Nomination Angers Black Women," *Kalamazoo Gazette*, Jan. 6, 1994.

262 *"Tupac Shakur was probably too busy":* Elmer Smith, "NAACP Should Cross Gangsta Rapper Shakur Off Image Awards List," *Dayton Daily News*, Jan. 11, 1994.

262 *When the New York* Daily News: "Sound Bites," *Daily News* (New York), Jan. 14, 1994.

262 *The* Detroit Free Press *tagged him:* Neal Rubin, "Roseanne Shows Oprah a Sensitive Side," *Detroit Free Press*, Feb. 11, 1994.

262 *"As an inner-city teacher":* Sean Crowley, "Shakur's Image, Message Send Wrong Signals to High Schoolers," *Buffalo News*, Jan. 16, 1994.

262 *"The media is trying to play":* Kevin Powell, "This Thug's Life," *Vibe*, Feb. 1994.

262 *On February 10, Tupac was found guilty:* "Rapper Tupac Shakur Convicted of Assault," *Newsday*, Feb. 11, 1994.

263 *Jesse Jackson, in particular:* Leigh Jackson, "Jesse Crusades for Political Action," *Philadelphia Daily News*, Mar. 21, 1994.

263 *"violent yet seductive":* Stephen Wigler, "'Above the Rim' Revisits a Grim Inner-City Nightmare and the Dream of Getting Out," *Baltimore Sun*, Mar. 23, 1994.

263 *"There was no concept of self-love":* Anna Sale interview with Kevin Powell, Feb. 8, 2024, https://slate.com/podcasts/death-sex-money/2015/11/kevin-powell -doesnt-fight-anymore.

264 *"Throughout his life, Tupac has been":* Powell, "This Thug's Life."

264 *"I feel like I'm being crucified":* James T. Jones IV, "Actor-Rapper Claims He's 'Being Crucified,'" Gannett News Service, Apr. 7, 1994.

265 *"Shakur brought the Amphitheater crowd":* Frank Costelloe, "Creating Togetherness," *The Corsair*, Mar. 30, 1994.

266 *On September 3 in Milwaukee:* "Rapper Dropped from Tour," Associated Press, Sept. 7, 1994.

266 *"So I'm rapping to the niggas":* "UNHEARD Tupac Phone Conversation with Sanyika Shakur, 1995," June 3, 2014, https://www.youtube.com/watch?v=BO0mI5AbTc4.

273 *Rourke was later described by:* Debra Feuer, "Mickey Rourke: 'He Was a Shy Mummy's Boy. Fame Drove Him to Drink, Drugs & Too Much Plastic Surgery. But Now He's Back on Top,'" *Mirror* (London), Jan. 18, 2009.

274 *"I know you're going through a rough time right now":* Staci Robinson, *Tupac Shakur: The Authorized Biography* (New York: Crown, 2023), 258.

274 *Their first date was at an Italian restaurant:* Tayannah Lee McQuillar and Fred L. Johnson III, *Tupac Shakur: The Life and Times of an American Icon* (New York: Da Capo Press, 2010), 143.

274 *"Tupac settled into the normalcy":* Robinson, *Tupac Shakur*, 258.

275   *Less than a month earlier:* A. J. Benza, "Inside Madonna's Wild Birthday Bash," *Daily News* (New York), Nov. 13, 1994.

276   *Heading into the trial:* "2 Jurors Dismissed," *South Florida Sun-Sentinel*, Nov. 8, 1994.

276   *"Gang bang," she told the jury:* "Accused Rapper Set Victim Up?," *Philadelphia Daily News*, Nov. 10, 1994.

277   *"She is a vengeful suitor":* Samuel Maull, "Shakur's Sex Assault Trial Begins," *York Dispatch*, Nov. 10, 1994.

277   *"[Her] posture is erect":* Murray Kempton, "History's Forgotten Lessons," *Newsday*, Nov. 11, 1994.

277   *Robert Gearty of the New York* Daily News: Robert Gearty, "Rapper Eyes Accuser in Sex Trial," *Daily News* (New York), Nov. 11, 1994.

277   *She testified that, initially, she was "happy":* David Kocieniewski, "Accuser's Testimony," *Newsday*, Nov. 11, 1994.

277   *"When I look at [Jackson's mother]":* Kempton, "History's Forgotten Lessons."

277   *After three days, court adjourned:* Melissa McCart, "Uptown's Pricey Pasta Spot for Jay-Z, Sarah Jessica Parker, and Trump Has Closed," Eater NY, Mar. 8, 2024, https://ny.eater.com/2024/3/8/24094344/nellos-closing-celebrities-upper-east-side-madison-avenue-pasta.

277   *"People have no idea what the lifestyle is about":* "A Tupac Dinner," *Daily News* (New York), Nov. 16, 1994.

278   *"Recent events involving the arrest of 2PAC Shakur":* Yaasmyn Fula, *Spirit of an Outlaw: The Untold Story of Tupac Amaru Shakur and Yaki "Kadafi" Fula* (Los Angeles: Bearded Dragon Books, 2020), 103.

279   *"Well, I just had to listen":* McQuillar and Johnson, *Tupac Shakur*, 146.

280   *"I'm guilty of probably being a male chauvinist pig":* "Jury Weighs Shakur's Fate," *Newsday*, Nov. 30, 1994.

Chapter 18: They Shot Me in My Balls

281   *"Most of my stuff is about girls":* Russ DeVault, "Brenner Keeps on Joking, Looking for TV Exposure," *Atlanta Constitution*, Apr. 3, 1992.

281   *He began dabbling in rap at age nine:* Todd Davis, "Lil' Shawn: Back for the First Time," Jan. 2, 2008, https://thehiphopcosign.wordpress.com/2008/01/02/lil%E2%80%99-shawn-back-for-the-first-time/.

281   *"It's just empty calories":* David McKenna, "Shocked Shines; Little Shawn's Shaky," *Press of Atlantic City*, Apr. 24, 1992.

281   *In the fall of 1994, Little Shawn:* Paul Arnold, "Shawn Pen Speaks About the Quad Studios Attack on Tupac, His History with Bad Boy and Roc-A-Fella Records," HipHopDX, Dec. 9, 2011, https://hiphopdx.com/interviews/id.1816/title.shawn-pen-speaks-about-the-quad-studios-attack-on-tupac-his-history-with-bad-boy-and-roc-a-fella-records.

284   *"He paged me again":* Kevin Powell, "Ready to Live," *Vibe*, Apr. 1995.

284   *"He's not my friend":* "A Tupac Dinner," *Daily News* (New York), Nov. 16, 1994.

284   *"Everybody knew I was short":* Powell, "Ready to Live."

285   *"What?" Wallace said:* 2PacLegacy Staff, "Lil Cease Talks on '94 Quad Studios Shooting: 'Big Would Never Do That,'" 2PacLegacy.net, June 10, 2019, https://

2paclegacy.net/lil-cease-talks-on-94-quad-studios-shooting-big-would-never-do-that.

286 *Three months later, on October 25:* Frank Owen, "Fantasy, Desire, Tumult," *Newsday*, Oct. 26, 1993.

286 *"Biggie looked like he was wearing":* Ben Westhoff, "How Tupac and Biggie Went from Friends to Deadly Rivals," *Vice*, Sept. 12, 2016, https://www.vice.com/en/article/tupac-biggie-friends-to-foes/.

286 *"Nah, stay with Puff":* "The Complete History of Tupac and Biggie's Complicated Relationship," Capital XTRA, Dec. 4, 2020, https://www.capitalxtra.com/features/lists/complete-history-of-tupac-and-biggie-relationship/where-first-meet/.

288 *Blood was smeared along:* Michael Daly, "It's Victim Tupac This Time," *Daily News* (New York), Dec. 1, 1994.

288 *"As I walked out":* "Lil Cease Talks on '94 Quad Studios Shooting."

288 *"Instead, Tupac reached for his own gun":* Ben Westhoff, *Original Gangstas* (New York: Hachette Books, 2016), 303.

289 *two identical 9 mm handguns:* Powell, "Ready to Live."

289 *"Everybody dropped to the floor like potatoes":* Powell, "Ready to Live."

290 *"All of them had jewels on":* Powell, "Ready to Live."

292 *"Hey, Officer McKernan":* Daly, "It's Victim Tupac This Time."

292 *"He was saying, 'Fuck y'all niggas'":* Molly Pike, "Iconic Photo of Tupac After He Was Shot Captured the Moment He Fell Out with Biggie," *Mirror* (London), Oct. 30, 2019.

293 *It felt instinctive:* Devon Bowker, "Can Porcupines Shoot Their Quills?," *The Wild Life* (blog), June 15, 2023, https://thewildlife.blog/2023/06/15/can-porcupines-shoot-their-quills/.

294 *His most troublesome injury:* Dean Van Nguyen, *Words for My Comrades* (New York: Doubleday, 2025), 265.

294 *"Look what they did to me":* Staci Robinson, *Tupac Shakur: The Authorized Biography* (New York: Crown, 2023), 276.

294 *"He wasn't standing with the rest":* Robinson, *Tupac Shakur*, 276.

294 *"It was just unfortunate":* "Tupac's Father William Garland: Here's the Truth in Case I Die," https://hiphopxxiv.com/.

295 *Moments later, an oddly familiar face appeared:* Robinson, *Tupac Shakur*, 276–77.

295 *"The first in line to siphon Tupac's money":* Jasmine Guy, *Afeni Shakur: Evolution of a Revolutionary* (New York: Atria Books, 2004), 189.

295 *"We didn't talk much in the hospital":* Billy Garland interview with the Art of Dialogue, July 8, 2023, https://www.youtube.com/watch?v=cTnbcEYkujs.

296 *"His head, arm and leg":* Robinson, *Tupac Shakur*, 277.

296 *Pachter said he was:* Mark Mooney and Rob Speyer, "Shakur's Hosp Exit a 'Grave' Risk: Doc," *Daily News* (New York), Dec. 2, 1994.

296 *Back when Tupac and Set were little:* Justin Tinsley, "New Tupac Shakur Exhibit, 'Wake Me When I'm Free,' Looks at the Revolution That Created the Revolutionary," Andscape, Jan. 21, 2022, https://andscape.com/features/new-tupac-shakur-exhibit-wake-me-when-im-free-looks-at-the-revolution-that-created-the-revolutionary/.

297 *"Several jurors winced and nudged":* Robert Gearty et al., "Rapper Guilty of Sex Abuse," *Daily News* (New York), Dec. 2, 1994.

297 *"I didn't sodomize her":* David Kocieniewski, "'Raped Again,'" *Newsday*, Dec. 3, 1994.

297   *It was hard to blame them:* Gerry E. Summers, "Poetic Justice," *Newsday*, Dec. 5, 1994.

297   *Richard Devitt, one of the jurors:* Sheldon Pearce, *Changes: An Oral History of Tupac Shakur* (New York: Simon & Schuster, 2021), 144.

299   *"I got set up":* Nina Bhadreshwar, *Finding CC* (London: WJ Scrivener Books, 2018), 293.

300   *"It was . . . a massive garbage dump":* Graham Rayman and Reuven Blau, *Rikers: An Oral History* (New York: Random House, 2023), 5.

300   *"[The inmates] would be there all day":* Rayman and Blau, *Rikers: An Oral History*, 252–53.

301   *"Emotionally, it was like I didn't know myself":* Powell, "Ready to Live."

303   *"I took Chuck off the streets of Richmond":* Murray Kempton, "Time to Face Reality for Tupac Shakur," *Newsday*, Feb. 8, 1995.

303   *"The scene":* Kempton, "Time to Face Reality for Tupac Shakur."

Chapter 19: Prison Changes Everybody [Aka Don't Fumble My Hos]

304   *"a horrific place":* Michael H. Blaine, *The Invisible Walls of Dannemora* (Las Vegas: Gaudium, 2020), inside jacket.

305   *"Listen up!" a guard said:* Michael Christopher, *2Pac Behind Bars* (Las Vegas: Prende Publishing, 2021), 18.

306   *"When I first got here":* Jamie Foster Brown, "The 1995 Tupac Interview from Jail," *Sister 2 Sister*, June 2001.

307   *"Inmate Shakur is a well known Rap Singer":* Paul Grondahl, "When Inmate Tupac Shakur Caused a Stir at Dannemora," *Times Union* (Albany), Jan. 15, 2019.

308   *"What they call me is obsessive compulsive":* Foster Brown, "The 1995 Tupac Interview from Jail."

309   *Despite a heavily cited:* "Shakur Shakeup," *Daily News* (New York), Apr. 19, 1995.

309   *Three years earlier:* Liza Willen and Shirley E. Perlman, "The Suspects, in Profile," *Newsday*, Aug. 5, 1991.

309   *Siegel—"Reeling not only":* L. Jon Wertheim, "Saved by Sports," *Sports Illustrated*, June 27, 2005.

310   *"I was drunk":* Wertheim, "Saved by Sports."

312   *"Pac used to make references":* Jake Brown, *Tupac Shakur: (2-Pac) in the Studio* (Phoenix: Colossus Books, 2005), 44.

312   *"It's likely the rapper's promotional tour":* Michael Saunders, "From Tupac Shakur, a Contradictory 'World,'" *Boston Globe*, Mar. 14, 1995.

312   *Beginning with his early days:* Foster Brown, "The 1995 Tupac Interview from Jail."

313   *"My name is Angela":* Angela Ardis, *Inside a Thug's Heart* (New York: Kensington Publishing, 2004), 7–8.

313   *"Hey Angela. This is Tupac":* Ardis, *Inside a Thug's Heart*, 11.

314   *"I miss looking at your picture":* Ardis, *Inside a Thug's Heart*, 48.

314   *Like Ardis, Cruise was stunning:* Julia Wick, "Prince's Nightclub Was the Coolest Place to Be in Early '90s L.A.," LAist, Apr. 22, 2016, https://laist.com/news/entertainment/glam-slam.

315   *"Don't trip," he wrote:* 2Pac Unofficial, Facebook, Dec. 19, 2016.

316   *"[It] is," wrote Michael:* Michael Namikas, *The Tupac Encyclopedia*, vol. 1 (Los Angeles: Michael A. Namikas, 2022), 246.

316   *"Watani, Tupac's manager":* Foster Brown, "The 1995 Tupac Interview from Jail."

317   *Fula had known Tupac since he was an infant:* Santi Elijah Holley, *An Amerikan Family: The Shakurs and the Nation They Created* (New York: Mariner Books, 2023), 99.

319   *"My closest friends turned on me":* Foster Brown, "The 1995 Tupac Interview from Jail."

319   *"Up until I got shot":* Jake Paine, "How Prison Transformed Tupac but Could Not Save Him from Death Row," Ambrosia for Heads, June 10, 2017, https:// ambrosiaforheads.com/2017/06/how-prison-transformed-tupac-but-could-not -save-him-from-death-row/.

321   *"How come he's the king":* Foster Brown, "The 1995 Tupac Interview from Jail."

Chapter 20: Out on Bail

322   *In May, a state judge:* "Tupac Shakur Out on $1.4 Million Bail," Associated Press, Oct. 14, 1995.

322   *"This is the nature of the American legal system":* Ryan Holiday, "Conspiracy: Peter Thiel, Hulk Hogan, Gawker, and the Anatomy of Intrigue," *Portfolio*, June 1, 2018.

323   *"Tupac began to see Suge":* Ben Westhoff, *Original Gangstas* (New York: Hachette Books, 2016), 307–8.

325   *"I've seen many men bulk up in prison":* Michael Christopher, *2Pac Behind Bars* (Las Vegas: Prende Publishing, 2021), 85.

325   *According to Westhoff:* Westhoff, *Original Gangstas*, 308–9.

326   *For Interscope, this wasn't:* Westhoff, *Original Gangstas*, 308–9.

327   *Out front he was greeted:* Angela Pettera, "Monty's Signs Off at Westwood Penthouse," *Los Angeles Times*, July 8, 1999.

328   *He would be the third Marion:* Hal Boyle, "Old Post Files," *Vicksburg Post*, Nov. 12, 1962.

330   *The scabs played three games:* Justin Tinsley, "Life Before Death Row: The Brief Football Career of Suge Knight," Andscape, Sept. 12, 2017, https://andscape.com /features/life-before-death-row-brief-football-career-suge-knight-espn-30-for -30-year-of-the-scab/.

331   *Around this time, Dr. Dre:* Michael Namikas, *The Tupac Encyclopedia*, vol. 1 (Los Angeles: Michael A. Namikas, 2022), 246.

331   *"I know you've heard all the stories":* Lynn Hirschberg, "Does a Sugar Bear Bite?," *New York Times*, Jan. 14, 1996.

333   *Daz Dillinger, the producer:* Nina Bhadreshwar, *Finding CC* (London: WJ Scrivener Books, 2018), 270.

333   *Two months before Tupac's release:* Eric Deggans, "Rough Start for First TV Rap Awards," *Asbury Park Press* (Asbury Park, NJ), Aug. 5, 1995.

334   *"It was just ignorance":* Kevin Powell, "Ready to Live," *Vibe*, Apr. 1995.

335   *"'Ambitionz' sounds like a state of the union address":* Namikas, *The Tupac Encyclopedia*, vol. 1, 77.

337   *"Shakur comes across as a man of many contradictions":* Chuck Philips, "'I Am Not a Gangster,'" *Los Angeles Times*, Oct. 25, 1995.

338   *His diet was packed with Death Row staples:* Bhadreshwar, *Finding CC*, 276–77.

339   *"Me and you are gonna be":* Staci Robinson, *Tupac Shakur: The Authorized Biography* (New York: Crown, 2023), 308.

339   *"[Johnny's] music was":* Jake Brown's interview archives.

343   *It was his song:* Namikas, *The Tupac Encyclopedia*, vol. 1, 180.

344   *According to Kurupt:* Kurupt interview with the Art of Dialogue, Mar. 24, 2023, https://www.youtube.com/watch?v=Yt8whCBkIhI.

344   *"I just happened to be in the studio":* MTV Vault, "On the Set of 'California Love' w/ Tupac, Dr. Dre & Chris Tucker," 1995, https://www.youtube.com/watch?v =YB3XXXcO9pg.

Chapter 21: Just Me and You and the Bitches

345   *On February 2 he sat courtside:* Kelly Carter, "Magic Matchup Fizzles as Bulls Pound Lakers," Gannett News Service, Feb. 3, 1996.

348   *The reviews were nearly all positive:* Sonia Murray, "Tupac Shakur Locks Up Wickedly Good Hip-Hop," *Atlanta Constitution*, Feb. 22, 1996.

348   *"The only thing jail time did for 2Pac":* Cheo Hodari Coker, "2Pac: Bitter, Remorseless, Brilliant," *Los Angeles Times*, Feb. 16, 1996.

348   *Any concerns over the heft of a double album:* Jeffrey Jolson-Colburn, "Columbia Records Hits Big Time," *Tampa Bay Times*, Mar. 2, 1996.

351   *Over the course of production:* HHL JT, "2Pac Slept with Multiple Porn Stars on 'How Do You Want It' Set," Hip-Hop Lately, 2020, https://www.hiphoplately .com/2pac-slept-with-multiple-porn-stars-on-how-do-you-want-it-set/.

353   *"The precedent of Dr. Dre's departure":* Connie Bruck, "The Takedown of Tupac," *The New Yorker*, June 29, 1997.

353   *Three months after Tupac aligned with the label:* Chuck Philips and Alan Abrahamson, "Rap Mogul Probed in '95 Case," *Los Angeles Times*, Jan. 21, 1997.

355   *"I fell in love with that word":* Michael Namikas, *The Tupac Encyclopedia*, vol. 1 (Los Angeles: Michael A. Namikas, 2022), 337.

358   *"Let your plans be dark":* Rachel Marsden, "It's Time for Canada to Get Behind Airstrikes Campaign," *Morning Call*, Oct. 12, 2014.

358   *"That attracted every security guard we had":* Jeffrey Jolson-Colburn, "'Triple Security' Held Rap Star Confrontation to Yelling, Not Shooting," *Memphis Commercial Appeal*, Apr. 4, 1996.

358   *Big Gipp of Goodie Mob said:* Erika Marie, "Tupac Confronted Biggie at Soul Train Awards, Recalls Big Gipp," HotNewHipHop, Jan. 26, 2023, https://www.hot newhiphop.com/625393-tupac-confronted-biggie-at-soul-train-awards-recalls -big-gipp.

358   *"That was the first time I really looked into his face":* Jake Brown, *Ready to Die: The Story of Biggie Smalls* (Phoenix: Colossus Books, 2004), 114.

359   *"There could have been a fight":* Jolson-Colburn, "'Triple Security' Held Rap Star Confrontation to Yelling, Not Shooting."

360   *"It didn't even matter to Shakur":* Cheo Hodari Coker, *Unbelievable: The Life, Death, and Afterlife of the Notorious B.I.G.* (New York: Vibe, 2013), 151.

360   *In New York, Biggie:* "Jadakiss Opens Up About Special Relationship With Biggie & Representing His Legacy," *ALL THE SMOKE* podcast, Aug. 4, 2021.

361   *"[Biggie] didn't take that picture thinking 'East vs. West'"*: Music Library Thematic Displays: East vs. West Coast Rap, University of Tennessee at Knoxville.

Chapter 22: Vegas

369   *"I want to apologize to you"*: Quincy Jones, *Q: The Autobiography of Quincy Jones* (New York: Doubleday, 2001), 249.

369   *"Tupac," Kidada later said:* From the interview collections of Christopher John Farley.

370   *Frank Alexander, a bodyguard:* Frank Alexander with Heidi Siegmund Cuda, *Got Your Back: Protecting Tupac in the World of Gangsta Rap* (New York: St. Martin's Griffin, 1998), 101.

370   *"He would say it's the most romantic story"*: From the interview collections of Christopher John Farley.

370   *"It was funny"*: From the interview collections of Christopher John Farley.

372   *"The East Coast vs. West Coast thing"*: "2Pac and Snoop Dogg 1996 MTV Interview," Feb. 22, 2018, https://www.youtube.com/watch?v=87NrO3dm5C0.

373   *"We mean mugging they homies"*: "Nas," 2pac.fandom.com/wiki/Nas.

373   *"We had a great convo, man"*: Kyle Eustice, "Naz Reflects on 2pac Beef That Led to Death Row East," HipHopDX, Aug. 12, 2021, https://hiphopdx.com/news /id.63864/title.nas-reflects-on-2pac-beef-that-led-to-death-row-east.

374   *"Mike Tyson," wrote Rob Marriott:* Rob Marriott, "Ready to Die," *Vibe*, Nov. 1996.

374   *Tyson and Tupac first met:* Michael Namikas, *The Tupac Encyclopedia*, vol. 1 (Los Angeles: Michael A. Namikas, 2022), 593.

377   *Bruce Seldon and Mike Tyson:* Michael Katz, "Bowe-Zolkin Bout No Belt Winner," *Daily News* (New York), Apr. 17, 1996.

378   *"He began winning big"*: Alexander with Cuda, *Got Your Back*, 152.

379   *"It was as one-sided as a shipwreck"*: Jim Murray, "This One Was Over Before It Even Began," *Los Angeles Times*, Sept. 8, 1996.

379   *"Did y'all see that?"*: Namikas, *The Tupac Encyclopedia*, vol. 1, 594.

381   *Back in South Central:* William Shaw, "Life and Death in South Central LA," *London Observer*, Jan. 8, 2000.

382   *The jewelry had been a gift:* Shaw, "Life and Death in South Central LA."

384   *"I don't want y'all around that crowd"*: Namikas, *The Tupac Encyclopedia*, vol. 1, 595.

384   *"I had picked him up from New York"*: From the interview collections of Christopher John Farley.

385   *"Frank [Alexander] reached"*: Namikas, *The Tupac Encyclopedia*, vol. 1, 596–97.

385   *At precisely 11:00 p.m.:* "Tupac's Last Photograph," Sept. 13, 2023, https://pma magazine.org/tupacs-last-photograph.

386   *Because Las Vegas is a city of perpetual motion:* Namikas, *The Tupac Encyclopedia*, vol. 1, 595.

388   *"Get on the ground!"*: Joe Coscarelli et al., "How a Chain-Snatching and a Vegas Beatdown Led to Tupac's Murder," *New York Times*, Oct. 5, 2023.

Chapter 23: Thug Angel

390 *While Knight's stay in the ER:* Robert Macy, "'Gangsta Rap' Star Shot in Drive-By," *Santa Maria (California) Times,* Sept. 9, 1996.

390 *she signed the next-of-kin papers:* Dean Van Nguyen, *Words for My Comrades* (New York: Doubleday, 2025), 315.

391 *"Friends said they were told":* Frank B. Williams and Shawn Hubler, "Star Rapper Tupac Shakur Badly Wounded," *Los Angeles Times,* Sept. 9, 1996.

392 *"A nurse said evening shift":* Cathy Scott, "Tupac Shakur Dies of Wounds," *Las Vegas Sun,* Sept. 14, 1996.

392 *The* Philadelphia Daily News': Tonya Pendleton, "Who Shot Tupac?," *Philadelphia Daily News,* Sept. 10, 1996.

392 *According to Liz Smith:* Liz Smith, "A Tupac Bio-Epic?," *Newsday,* Sept. 13, 1996.

392 *"Throughout this ordeal, Vegas police":* Yaasmyn Fula, *Spirit of an Outlaw: The Untold Story of Tupac Amaru Shakur and Yaki "Kadafi" Fula* (Los Angeles: Bearded Dragon Books, 2020), 139.

393 *Relatives filled the waiting room:* Michelle Caruso et al., "Doctors Remove Shakur's Lung," *Philadelphia Daily News,* Sept. 10, 1996.

393 *"We didn't get any sleep":* Staci Robinson, *Tupac Shakur: The Authorized Biography* (New York: Crown, 2023), 342.

393 *On Monday, September 9:* Robert Macy, "Rapper's Condition Still Critical," Associated Press, Sept. 10, 1996.

393 *Two days later, Dr. John Fildes:* "Rapper Tupac Shakur Survives First Critical Phase," Associated Press, Sept. 12, 1996.

394 *He had suffered a series of heart attacks:* Robinson, *Tupac Shakur,* 343.

394 *The official cause of death:* "Tupac's Death Report," angelfire.com/hiphop2/lifeanddeathof2pac/report.html.

394 *"We all move out of the way":* S. Leigh Savidge with Steve Housden and Jeff Scheftel, *Welcome to Death Row* (Hawthorne, CA: Xenon Press, 2015), 316.

397 *The morning after his final breath:* Jasmine Guy, *Afeni Shakur: Evolution of a Revolutionary* (New York: Atria Books, 2004), 187.

398 *In Compton, a ten-day gang war:* Matthew Ormseth and Richard Winton, "Tupac Shakur's Killing Brought '10 Days of Hell' to Compton. The Bloodshed Helped Crack the Case," *Los Angeles Times,* Oct. 6, 2023.

Epilogue: Aftermath

403 *"The Italians I speak about were truly great men":* Rob Marriott, Tupac Shakur interview, bonus CD with the *Thug Immortal* VHS, 1997.

Index